Living Groups:

Group Psychotherapy and
General System Theory

Living Groups:

Group Psychotherapy and General System Theory

Edited by

James E. Durkin Ph.D.

Professor of Psychology
Lincoln University,
Lincoln University, PA.

Brunner/Mazel, Publishers • New York

Library of Congress Cataloging in Publication Data
Main entry under title:

Living groups.

  Bibliography: p.
  Includes index.
  1. Group psychotherapy. 2. Social systems.
I. Durkin, James E. [DNLM: 1. Psychotherapy,
Group. 2. Systems theory. WM 430 L785]
RC488.L58   616.89'152   81-4365
ISBN O-87630-253-3   AACR2

Copyright © 1981 by James E. Durkin

Published by
BRUNNER/MAZEL, INC.
19 Union Square
New York, New York 10003

MANUFACTURED IN THE UNITED STATES OF AMERICA

Foreword

Jim Durkin has blended his own and his 13 colleagues' contributions into a difficult, powerful and challenging work. We are asked to accompany Jim and his colleagues on a journey of discovery and required to set aside our old shoes for an experimental walk in a totally new concept of footwear. It promotes anxiety and requires courage. It is at once confusing and enlightening. My facial expressions ranged from furrowed brow, and painful puzzlement, to a big broad smile and the reflection of excitement in discovery of a new truth or rediscovery of an old one. It is demonstrated that the process of theory building is isomorphic with the process of engaging in group psychotherapy. The person of the theory maker is as much a part of the theory as is the person of the therapist a part of the therapy.

General system theory presents a model consistent with a newly developing paradigm of scientific thought. Four basic departures from the traditional paradigm of objective science are noted: a focus on holism rather than reductionism; an ecological rather than a technological perspective; acceptance of uncertainty rather than determinism; searching for deeper structure, rather than depending only on direct observation. The implications of these shifts require a very different look at the phenomena we work "in" rather than "with." We are asked to focus on the "organized complexity" of our groups, rather than attempt to reduce the data to ever simpler units. The conservation of Piaget's children is used to illustrate what is required of us in order for us to grow in our work: the capacity to shift from our sensing to a higher level of abstraction, as we focus our attention on the variety of systems involved in our work with our groups.

Living groups, our therapeutic groups as one illustration, are conceived of as autonomous. They are capable of changing themselves. Understanding the operation of the group requires an understanding of the structure of the group and the principles underlying transformation at all system levels, from the larger system in which the group operates to the systems of the individual personalities of the member units composing the group.

v

Exchanges in energy and information are made between systems. "Summing" is the term applied to exchanges in information. "Systeming" is the term applied to exchanges in energy. Exchange of cognitions is involved in 'summing.' Exchange of emotions is involved in systeming. Emotional exchanges occur when boundaries are open and permeable. Cognitive exchanges occur when boundaries are closed, either for purposes of restructuring and consolidation or in the service of defensive or resistant positions. Transformations, the goal of psychotherapy, occur only when boundaries are broken and permeable. The autonomous person, the ideal end product of psychotherapy, may be defined in structural terms, as the person who has the ability to engage in summing or systeming when appropriate. Put another way, "when any given target system (the individual patient), achieves an optimal, though continually changing proportion of open and closed boundaries, the member will be ready to regulate his or her own transactions."

The greatest difficulty I have had in teaching my students has been in sensitizing myself and them to process, in contrast to content or meaning issues. I have a new reference work for myself and them in *Living Groups*. The metatheory offered in GST will help me approach students who come to my classes with a variety of psychological theory preferences, which has made it difficult to shape each class into a learning system.

I have slowly and timidly tried to use my new footwear with my groups in the last several weeks. I feel very shaky, and my feeling assessment of my group experiences is much more intense. I am leaving my "psychoanalytic meaning attributions" temporarily on the shelf, and watching the energy flow—I am astonished by how much I have not seen in 30 years of practice! Try it—I promise you a "rollercoaster" ride. You may want the support of the "boundary breakers" in *Living Groups*. I am going to re-read the book—very carefully.

Morris Goodman, Ph.D.

Contents

MEMORIAL FOR WALTER GRUEN (1920-1980)

Walter Gruen was a loyal and dedicated member of the GST Committee of AGPA since its inception in 1971 until his death in November of 1980. Walter's chapter (Chapter 4) on nurtenergy represents an attempt to integrate the palpable phenomena of the material world such as energy with the core characteristics of the spiritual world of humanity such as loving concern. In this sense "nurturant energy" deals with the physics of caring, an idea which reflects the creative synthesis of empirical science and humanism that epitomizes the goal of the von Bertalanffian tradition of GST.

But the nurtenergy chapter in *Living Groups* is only one timebound facet of Walter's contribution to our group and to our field. Within our committee Walter was a living manifestation of the complementarity of scientific discipline and human concern. He regulated our work by insisting on rigorous formulations and connections with established scientific facts. He catalyzed our work by keeping us from losing sight of our ultimate goal of helping people recognize and act upon their own capacity for achieving autonomy when we got lost in intellectual fascinations with new conceptual toys.

Walter was always modest and self-effacing about his contributions. This was a manifestation of his own personal autonomy. We all wish that we had been open enough to take in and digest more thoroughly the material in the book *Foundations of Human Autonomy* which took up his last few years. We will miss him sorely. Without him who will steer us as he did so nobly on our dual course of science and humanism?

Contributors

ARIADNE P. BECK, Ph.D.
Staff Psychologist, Cook County Hospital, Chicago, IL.

DONALD T. BROWN, M.D.
Director of Training in Community Psychiatry, California State Department of Education, Berkely, CA.

HELEN E. DURKIN. Ph.D.
Senior Supervisor, Postgraduate Center for Mental Health, New York, N.Y.

JAMES E. DURKIN, Ph.D.
Professor of Psychology, Lincoln University, PA.

WILLIAM GRAY, M.D.
Court Psychiatrist, Malden Court Clinic, Malden, MA.

WALTER GRUEN, Ph.D.
Staff Psychologist, Rhode Island State Hospital, Providence, R.I.

IRVIN A. KRAFT, M.D.
Clinical Professor of Mental Health, University of Texas School of Public Health; Clinical Professor of Psychiatry, Baylor College of Medicine; Senior Consultant, Texas Institute of Family Psychiatry, Houston, TX.

K. ROY MACKENZIE, M.D.
Associate Professor of Psychiatry, University of Calgary, Calgary, Alberta, Canada

DAVID MENDELL, M.D.
Professor of Psychiatry, University of Texas at Houston

HARRIS PECK, M.D.
Professor of Psychiatry, Albert Einstein Medical School, Bronx, N.Y.

GUSTAV RATH, PH.D.
Assistant Professor of Psychology, Northwestern University, Evanston, IL.

GLENN SWOGGER, JR., M.D.
Staff Psychiatrist, Menninger Foundation, Topeka, KA.

FRANCIS ULSCHAK, PH.D.
Private Practice, Center, N.D.

GEORGE VASSILIOU, M.D.
Institute Anthropos, Athens, Greece

VASSO VASSILIOU, PH.D.
Institute Anthropos, Athens Greece

Introduction

The authors of *Living Groups* are members of the General System Theory (GST) Committee of the American Group Psychotherapy Association. The mission of our book is the same as the mission of our Committee, namely, to explore the ways in which GST can clarify the theory and improve the practice of group psychotherapy. We have been meeting together as a committee since 1971 under the able chairmanship of Helen Durkin. Without her skills of helping us keep open to each other much of the time, it is unlikely that we would have been able to complete this book.

As we have worked together and shared in each other's intellectual and emotional growth, a true systemic relationship has developed among the authors. A dynamic process of self-organization has helped our committee generate a life of its own. This living structure is reflected in our book. We have formed ourselves into a living group and in the process we have given birth to a living book. Our title reflects both the product of our working together and the process by means of which our product has been achieved. Thus, *Living Groups* must be understood in at least two ways. First, it signifies our product by designating the kind of groups we have been studying, groups endowed with the property of life. Second, it signifies our process by designating the lived action experience we went through, both together in our committee work and separately with each of our therapy groups. We hope that you, the reader, can also engage in both our product and our process. Live our book with us and go out and live your groups in the light of what we have to say. This is the way to glean full measure from what we have to say about living groups.

What is general system theory (GST)? How does it relate to living groups? How can GST be used as a basis for clarifying the theory and improving the practice of group psychotherapy? The book is devoted to answering these questions and this introduction sets the stage for the answers. It would be a simple task to answer the question "What is GST?" if GST were a simple monolithic theory such as the mathematical theory of, say, complex functions. But GST means many different things to many different people, as the members of our committee discovered when they began to dig into the GST literature. Thus, even the initial task of defining GST is not a simple one. Some writers define GST as a rigorously defined algorithm designed to provide quantitative solutions to a highly specific set of input data. Other writers present GST as a misty mystical insight that everything in the world is connected to everything else. We came to espouse neither of these extremes. Some writers define GST strictly as a methodology with minimal ontological commitment to the existence of any particular phenomena out there in the world. Others see GST as an empirical model of the way the world actually exists. We came to espouse neither of these extremes. Some writers include a large proportion of the new methodologies of science that have developed over the last half century within the boundaries of GST. Others restrict the boundaries of GST to a very narrow range of ideas that must be carefully distinguished from other conceptual doctrines and methodologies. We came to espouse neither of these extremes.

It became clear to us that GST was a complex structure full of paradoxes. It also became clear that those who drew oversimplified descriptions of GST injected as much confusion into the efforts of the scientific community to understand GST as those who drew undersimplified descriptions. Another complication is that the variation in description of GST extends not only "horizontally" over a range of different phenomena, but also "vertically" up and down the range of abstraction. To some writers it is a first level theory about a phenomenon. To others it is a metatheory, that is, a theory about theories or even theory-making. To still others it is a methodology or even a way of life that is open with respect to the particular phenomena it deals with. Finally, some consider GST to be involved in a fundamental new paradigm of science where some of the basic assumptions about what we know and how we know it have to be radically revised.

Faced with this flood of information about GST, our committee spent its first few years trying to figure out exactly what GST was. One of the most alluring features of GST was that it offered us a whole new vocabulary with which to describe group process. Some of the terms like "negentropy" and "equifinality" were totally new, while others like "feedback," "matter/energy" and "information'' were relatively familiar terms used in a much more general way. We went through a wholesale relabeling process. The idea of ''system'' was most attractive of all. Groups became systems, group members became subsystems, and the community from which our members came became the supersystems. But as the novelty wore off, we began to ask ourselves just what was added in the way of understanding by adopting these new labels. We began to see the trap of calling everything systems and systems everything.

Despite the seductiveness of the new terminology, we slowly began to gain depth and sophistication in the use of the GST framework. We began to delineate conceptual boundaries. We began to see what systems were by discriminating them from what they were not. We began to pay attention to the processes by means of which systems were formed and transformed. We slowly grew from a magical unquestioned faith in ''systems'' to a place where we could realistically discriminate the weaknesses as well as the strengths of these conceptual tools.

Our growing sophistication also enabled us to make peace with the once disturbing finding that GST means many different things to many different people. It began to dawn upon us that GST itself was a living structure which reflected the conceptual activity of many different individuals and communities of investigators. They were each grappling from different perspectives for an expression of the complex of systems within which they saw themselves residing. We didn't quite understand at first how a theory could include the theory-maker within its boundaries, but we lived with the problem and went on with our explorations.

All this development process took a number of years during the decade of the seventies. Our committee had settled upon a format of having a long weekend meeting during the summer and another briefer meeting during the AGPA convention in February. This face-to-face activity was, of course, supplemented with ongoing exchange of manuscripts and correspondence. In the light of the difficult material, this relatively slow pace of exploration and sharing was probably better for us than a program of crash investigation would have been. Our process moved dialectically. We had ideological differences. For example, Helen Durkin held the integrationist position that GST could best opearte as a conceptual umbrella under which the fragmented state of theory and practice in the group therapy field would be restored to unity. Bill Gray and I, on the other hand, saw GST as an almost completely new baseline from which to develop new views of group therapy. At another level, Bill and I debated with loving vigor the issue of whether emotions organized cognitions or whether cognitions organized emotions. This was all an exciting part of the process of learning how to use GST.

After several years of investigation about what GST writers were saying and a good deal of conversation between committee members about what GST was supposed to be, we seemed to arrive at a point of closure about what we wanted GST to be for us. We can call what we developed GST Model I. We didn't hit upon Model I in a sudden flash of insight. Nor was it proclaimed by our committee *en masse* in a bold manifesto. We settled in upon Model I gradually and almost unconsciously. In fact, some of us were already passing through Model I before others of us had fully integrated it into their thinking. Despite the diffuse relationship between this model and our committee, it is important to set forth the basic propositions of Model I because it contributed a great deal to our mission of relating GST to group psychotherapy. Here is a summary:

MODEL I

The world is made up of a population of objects called systems. Subpopulations of individual systems can be observed at all levels of organization from cell to society and, perhaps, from atom to galaxy. Each of these systems has the following four properties:

1) Systems are hierarchically arrayed. Every system except the lowest is made up of interrelated parts called subsystems. Every system except the highest functions as a part of another whole called a suprasystem.
2) Though each system displays a wide diversity of form and behavior, there is an identity of underlying structure or isomorphy common to all systems, as well as common organizing processes.
3) Each system is made up of structures that perform the three functions of (a) maintaining wholeness, (b) achieving self-regulation in the face of environmental disturbances, and (c) achieving progressive self-transformation to higher levels of adaptation.
4) Systems achieve these functions through the operations of opening and closing their boundaries and in doing so engaging in exchanges of matter/energy and information with their environments.

Under the perspective of GST Model I, groups, individual group members, and even group members' internal personality structures are considered members of the population of systems. As such, each is hierarchically related to the other, isomorphic to the others in underlying structure, self-regulating and transforming, and capable of selectively opening and closing its own boundaries. Seeing these components of the group psychotherapy enterprise as members of the population of systems endowed with these properties enabled us to clarify many issues and open up new methods in the field. The perennial controversy as to whether the locus of therapy resides in groups, group members, or members' internal representations is resolved by the postulation of their being hierarchically and isomorphically related. The GST insight that systems have isomorphic structures beneath a diversity of contents opens up a structural path to intervention which can bypass sticky content issues by focusing on the process of opening and closing boundaries. The existence of internally organized and self-sufficient mechanisms for both persistence and change in systems forces a recognition on group therapists that they are dealing with active creative structures rather than passive structures in need of repair. Finally, the assertion in Model I of the central role of boundary control provides the therapist with a pair of key events, opening and closing, which operate as punctuation points in the therapeutic process.

Even as Model I was making its way through the consciousness of our committee, an alternative model of GST seemed to be materializing in the minds of some of us. Model I focused on systems as objects, but it had little to say about the processes which brought these system-objects to life. As clinicians who often dealt with the paradoxes of group life and the strong influence of emotional vibes that were capable of turning the whole mood of the group around in an amazingly brief time, the idea that groups could be just as alive as their individual members seemed intuitively appealing. We were comfortable with the metaphorical expression that groups were living systems. We felt that Model I focused on the noun "system" more than it focused on the verb "living." It focused more on the entities that stood there out in the world of objects than on the living processes than animated them and gave them their own autonomous direction.

GST began as a theory of life. Ludwig von Bertalanffy, or LvB as we shall affectionately call him from here on in this book, was a theoretical biologist who resolved the controversy raging in the 1920s about what life was. On the one hand, the mechanists asserted that living forms were essentially complicated machines whose operating manuals would soon be discovered. On the other hand, the vitalists claimed that life was the product of some unknown, and possibly unknowable, entelechy. LvB resolved the conflict by discovering the open system model as a vital mechanism that could account for the basic facts of the life process. LvB called his model an "open system" to contrast it with the closed system models that were simply assumed at that time, but, actually, the critical operations of his model involved the selective opening *and* closing of boundaries. Thus the term "boundarying" model might be more appropriate.

As LvB and his colleagues went about elaborating and validating the open system model of biological life, they began to realize that the scope of application of the model extended far beyond the domain of biological organisms. The prospect opened up that persons, groups, families, corporations, communities and even society itself could be asserted to be alive in a scientific sense. The open system model provided pathways for the investigation of biological life forms. The general system model did the same for the investigation of the whole range of living structures from cell to society. The discovery of the crucial role of boundarying applied to person structures, group structures and higher level structures alike. A new approach to life across the board was opened up, an approach which focused on its dynamic structures and organizing processes.

Until this point the phenomenon of life was either a given of the scientific situation, an intrinsically unfathomable mystery or, at best, a subject for unverified and unverifiable scientific speculation. In the field of psychotherapy we have a functional concept that, in a way, is a theory of what life is. A functional description is a description in terms of external effects, as opposed to a structural description which focuses on internal configurations. The central concept of this functional theory of life is *autonomy*. Few psychotherapists would disagree with the assertion that the general aim of psychotherapy is to restore or enhance the autonomy of the client and few group psychotherapists would disagree about the therapeutic value of promoting the autonomy of the group. But if they were asked to give a precise operational definition of the state of autonomy they value so highly, they would be hard put to come up with anything in the way of a consistent definition, except to affirm that autonomy is good. Some would say that autonomy means that a person is able to be independent of external influences, but others would claim that autonomy means being open to new experiences and learning. Thus paradoxes abound in autonomy's definition.

The trouble with attempts to define autonomy in content terms is that they inevitably beg the question. One can point to examples of autonomous individuals or actions, but assertions boil down to the circular proposition that what is autonomous is good and what is good is autonomous. A definition of autonomy that can be scientifically useful is a structural definition, that is, one that spells out the configuration of parts and processes that generate observable autonomous events. GST offers a conceptual framework which fulfills this need because it describes the structure of autonomy. Based on the fundamental assertion, first encountered in the restricted domain of biology, that living structure has the capability of boundarying, that is, opening and closing its own boundaries, the operations necessary for all manifestations of life from cell to society are specified in a way that lends itself to experimental observation, testing and verification.

The second GST model, let us call it Model II, is a process-centered model rather than an object-centered one like Model I. It offers a model which defines life from cell to society in terms of autonomy and defines the structure of autonomy in terms of the boundarying operation in a way that evolves directly from LvB's original idea. GST Model II is based on a much stronger and more radical assumption than Model I. Model I was built on the fundamental assumption that there was a set of entities out there in the objective world, entities called systems. Model II is based on the assumption that certain processes autonomously cause themselves. Such an assertion directly violates the fundamental assumption of the paradigm of objectivity that every observable effect has an external cause. Thus, the assumption of Model II requires the assumption of a new paradigm which, because of this central tenet, might be called the paradigm of autonomy. A paradigm, as we shall discuss in more detail in Chapter 2, is a commitment on the part of a community of scientists which delineates a certain reality to be admitted as the subject of scientific investigation. A paradigm shift is essentially a revolution in science.

There is a distinct parallel between Model I and Model II because the population of system-objects and the dynamic process of autonomous living structure upon which Model II focuses have the same set of four properties. The difference, a difference which makes these four properties different, is in the assumption that autonomy causes itself. It must be emphasized here that this basic assumption of the paradigm of autonomy does not need to be proven any more than the assumption of external cause and effect that is so central to the paradigm of objectivity requires proof. The difficult process of changing paradigms will be discussed at length in the epilogue of this volume.

MODEL II

All of life, from cell to society, is based on a dynamic self-organizing process we shall call autonomous living structure. Living structure generates, maintains, evolves and, finally, dissolves its own autonomy. Living structure causes itself through the exercise of the following self-referential processes:

1) Living structure describes its own structure by closing informational boundaries around itself, thus distinguishing itself from its environment and other living structures within it.
2) Living structure transforms its own structure by opening its boundaries to the flow of matter/energy between itself and the environment, as well as between itself and other living structures who open to it.
3) Living structure generates operational configurations based on the basic opening and closing operations working in complementarity which achieve the functions of wholeness, self-regulation, and progressive self-transformation.
4) Living structure utilizes boundarying operations to create hierarchical divisions within itself. A group of living parts open to each other and transform themselves into a whole. A whole cleaves boundaries within itself to transform itself into a set of parts. Living wholes and parts freely redefine themselves through the autonomous boundarying operation.

Just as groups, group members, and members' internal personality structures are considered "systems" in Model I, they are considered autonomous manifestations of living structure in Model II. The paradigmatic assumption that living structure is self-referential and therefore causes its own autonomy has a number of consequences for the theory and practice of group psychotherapy. It puts the therapist in an animated living world of autonomous structures. It calls the therapist to act in terms of his or her own living structure as a co-equal member of the group. It transforms thinking and feeling content into boundarying acts of closing and opening, respectively. It makes the therapist a catalyzer of autonomous change in personal structure rather than an initiator of change in passive systems.

It must be made clear that Model II is no more official and codified within our group than Model I. Because it represented a newer set of ideas than Model

I, fewer of our members got as deeply into it. Because it requires a paradigm shift, it is both more difficult to articulate and requires more courage and daring to champion. But as our work goes on into the 1980s, we are beginning to talk more and more of autonomy and boundarying. It represents one pole of our thinking as the system-object model represents the other. We haven't made a choice of which model is preferred. We probably don't even think that a choice is necessary. We can only report on the progress of our ideas as we report on our long living process of exploration. Model I and Model II represent two reports on our living process of exploring the ways in which GST can clarify the theory and improve the practice of group psychotherapy.

THE FORMAT OF THIS BOOK

Living Groups is organized in four main sections. In the introductory section we have tried to lay the basic groundwork for the other chapters. In Chapter 1, "The Group Therapies and General System Theory as an Integrative Structure," Helen Durkin introduces our subject by taking an historical approach. Since she has been a professional historian as well as a pioneer in the field of group psychotherapy, she is able to provide us with a unique perspective on how the interacting threads of the group therapy field and the modern scientific doctrine of GST themselves intertwine with the intellectual, philosophical and scientific developments of the past century.

As a result of this historical review she comes to the conclusion that the field of group psychotherapy is at a crossroads. On the one hand, the field, as a result of the emergence of new theoretical and professional developments, has become fragmented and in need of a new integrative framework. On the other hand, GST, as one of the products of a new scientific outlook or paradigm which is now beginning to gain ascendence over the classical linear analytic mechanistic paradigm of the last century, seems to offer the possibility of just such a conceptual framework that is called for. Thus she sets the stage for the explorations in the following chapters.

In addition to posing the basic problem with which this volume is to deal, Helen's chapter performs another important function for our readers. The label "systems" and all associated terms have come to carry the double aura of both mystification and intimidation in the eyes of the group therapy community as well as in the eyes of the general public. Helen's personal chronicle, which relates her almost effortless transition from a broad eclectic psychoanalytic orientation to a GST orientation, offers a convivial pathway for others who, though intrigued by the new ideas of GST, nevertheless hesitate shyly at its gates. This chapter functions as a welcome mat and a safe conduct pass for those of all persuasions who would care to join in the explorations of GST as described above and accomplished in this book.

In Chapter 2, I try to articulate the foundational ideas which lie at the basis of GST and to show how GST fits within the paradigm shift which twentieth century science is experiencing. My chapter looks at GST from a philosophy of science perspective while Helen's, in complementary fashion, looks at GST from the perspective of a clinical therapist. There is another kind of complementarity between the two chapters in this section as well. Whereas Helen has taken pains to make the reader's transition from orthodox approaches to group psychotherapy to the new GST approach as gentle as possible, my articulation of GST principles actually breaks new ground beyond the description of GST made by such Model I thinkers as J.G. Miller (1978). Basically, Chapter 2 provides a transition path from Model I to Model II in the sense introduced earlier in this introduction.

Some readers might have a concern about trying to comprehend such a "super advanced" version of GST when they are already afflicted with no little mystification and intimidation with respect to the more traditional Model I. Although it is important for us not to overload our readers, another consideration is also important. Most of us have been exploring the relationship between GST and group psychotherapy for ten years and some of us have been at it for nearly 20 years. GST espouses mutual and reciprocal causality rather than one-way cause-effect relationship, and a good deal of what we know about the content reality of the group therapy field had been "fed back" to the structural principles of GST that we have been developing. The motto of the classical linear analytic mechanistic paradigm of objectivity could be "In reduction is reality," for objective scientists assumed that all reality could be reduced to the simplest reality, the reality of physics. The GST paradigm of autonomy takes exception to this because autonomous living structures create their own reality in their own way at each level of manifestation. I have begun to think the small group level might just be the most resonant level of life for generating fruitful self-descriptions in terms of GST. It is because the field of group therapy as a content manifestation of living structure is so rich that new, more productive formulations of GST can be evolved. Chapter 2 represents for me the distillation of more than 15 years of thought and at least a dozen written revisions. And make no bones about it, the paradigm of autonomy and the phenomenon of autonomous living structure that form the key links between GST and group therapy are ideas which require a paradigm shift, that is, a radical reconstruction of reality. The rock bottom idea of the paradigm of objectivity that has guided scientific effort in the West so well and so long is that every event is caused externally by another event impinging upon it. The paradigm of autonomy, in contrast, has a rock bottom idea that life causes itself autonomously. Shifting paradigms is a harrowing experience. It was for me and it will be for you if you dare attempt the task. To negotiate the transition one must cut loose from the old reality and travel through an insane *terra incognita* before one arrives safely within the region of the new paradigm. This constitutes a warning about Chapter 2, but it also is a recommendation that the intellectual self-injury the chapter invites might lead to healing at a higher level of understanding.

The organizing principle of the second section of the book is that in each of its five chapters a phenomenon or concept that plays an important role in GST overall is applied to the special case of living groups in psychotherapy. In contrast to the chapters in the next section which develop comprehensive systems of group psychotherapy within a GST framework, the chapters in this section operate out of a traditional framework while injecting one or more new GST ideas into their descriptions of the process.

In Chapter 3, Glen Swogger looks at the therapy group in terms of its communication structure and its ability (and inability) to process information. He suggests that the group becomes alive as an isomorphism develops between the pattern of communication that develops between the group members and the patterns operating within each member. In the second half of the chapter Swogger discusses the effects of the therapist's use of self on the group process. He suggests that the therapist's selective ability to *destructure,* that is, to utilize meditative, imaginative and intuitive process, can also lead to flow and change in the emotional life in the group. In terms of the fundamental complementaries of opening and closing that constitute the boundarying operation that plays so central a role in our GST model of living groups, the information half of this chapter deals with closing events and the emotional participation part of the chapter deals with opening events in group therapy.

In Chapter 4, Walter Gruen directly addresses the issue of energy management at the living structure level of groups, group therapists, and group members. He develops the concept of ''nurtenergy'' (nurturant energy) as the physical embodiment of the process that earlier content-oriented theorists called ''caring,'' ''unconditional positive regard,'' and other similar terms. He outlines procedures whereby the therapist can use his or her ''surplus nurtenergy'' as a catalyst for remobilizing group members' energies that are initially brought into entropy through anxiety. He grapples with two knotty issues: 1) whether nurtenergy can be used up like the energy in a battery or whether it can be endlessly recruited through open system mechanisms, and 2) whether nurtenergy is a laser-like structuring force for group memebers, or whether it is more like raw emotional caring that simply gives deep support for group members' own restructuring efforts. Once again, the boundarying issues, the interplay of informational closing and emotional opening are applied in a clinical context with groups.

In Chapter 5, Irvin Kraft also applies the GST concept of matter/energy to living groups, in this case to the process of admitting a new member, a process that every open-ended therapy group has to go through. He introduces the metaphor "swirl" to represent the active emotional energy that can flow amidst a group. Swirl is not an informational process for it does not have attributes such as good or bad, efficient or inefficient, or intelligible or non-intelligible. In boundarying terms, Kraft's essay attempts to articulate how the unstructured opening event is experienced and utilized for therapeutic gains in living groups.

In Chapter 6, K. Roy MacKenzie explores the concept of role to resolve the boundary issues between the subsystem of the individual and the system of the group. With a thorough review of theoretical and empirical literature, he defines the concept of group role, group climate, and role position that forewarns us of the pitfalls of ascribing personality characteristics to a group entity on the one hand, and ascribing role characteristics to individual personalities on the other. He provides extensive examples of group roles including Beck's (Chapter 18) and his own instruments for describing role functions. One of the main functions of group roles is to negotiate the transition over successive stages of group development. MacKenzie utilizes the concept of role as a mediating structure between the individual and the group.

In Chapter 7, David Mendell focuses upon the boundarying functions of the group leader. The *catalyst* function of change agent is related to the opening event of boundarying and the *regulator* function of continuity maintenance is related to the closing event of the boundarying operation. Mendell discusses the group leader's use of his or her own living structure as a therapeutic tool and suggests that the therapist's role is different inside the group boundary than it is outside of it. He explores the usefulness of the ideas of summing and systeming (see Chapters 2 and 13) to account for the process of negotiating therapeutic change between the leader and the members. His clinical case studies demonstrate in concrete terms some of the ways that matter/energy and information, opening and closing, and catalyzing and regulating processes that we have introduced into therapeutic technique from GST can be used to help us lead living groups.

The third section takes all of GST and applies it to whole systems of group psychotherapy. The result of the marriage of GST and the particular system focused upon varies. Some chapters retain the rules and concepts of the traditional system of therapy, some try to integrate GST principles and traditional principles into a new synthesis, and some start almost from scratch and develop a pure GST group psychotherapy method.

In Ulschak and Rath's Chapter 8, the authors define three modes of systems analysis: 1) the hierarchical mode, 2) the entities and attributes mode, and 3) the flow chart mode. They show how the transactional analysis method can be analyzed in terms of these three modes. In Chapter 9, Harris Peck also looks at transactional analysis from a GST perspective. Peck attempts to show how GST operating as a metatheory can reintegrate the individually based TA theory with group process theory. Peck describes therapeutic events in terms of "scenarios," patterned sequences of group behavior. He compares several sets of scenarios as clinical examples and demonstrates how the GST approach provides a framework for analysis within which the strengths of the individual and group system levels can be combined.

In Chapter 10, Helen Durkin presents her dual model integrating GST and psychoanalytic thinking and shows how the problem of behavior change that had been the central limitation on pure analytic technique can be dealt with by means of a synthesis with GST. She traces the natural transition between her early analytic training and her new GST position through a series of clinically dictated expedients. She shows how the boundarying operation embodied in thinking and feeling experiences form the key events in the process approach. The process approach generates a living structure in groups as opposed to the more traditional content approach which generates a meaning structure in groups. She makes a case for Freud being a process thinker whose novel approach was "revised" into content thinking by his more traditional followers. The three new techniques she presents, a product of her GST-analytic synthesis, demonstrate the fertility and practicality of GST for clarifying the theory and improving the practice of group psychotherapy.

In Chapter 11, Bill Gray focuses on system formation and transformation rather than ongoing systems that are already established. He formulates the structure and sequence of the system-forming process and he shows how it can be managed in treating the delinquent offenders he works with. Here is a pattern for therapeutic intervention that works with the complementarity of emotion and cognition, opening and closing, in a manner basic to GST thinking about the boundarying process. While the behavior therapists focus on the symptom as the retrainable habit and the psychodynamicists focus on unconscious scripts as nuclear conflicts, Bill seems to have discovered a method of therapeutic intervention that is analogous to genetic recombination, but at the psychological level. He directly intervenes in the "program language" of the psyche through verbal interventions that are timed and phrased sensitively, in order to lay down the structural basis for a new and better adjusted behavior pattern.

In Chapter 12, George and Vasso Vassiliou describe one of a series of GST-based therapeutic techniques that they are constantly evolving. In the course of the therapeutic work with groups, images (usually paintings) are produced by group members which manifest the living structure of the group. Guided by the Ca-Re (Catalytic = opening-Regulatory = closing/Boundarying) system consisting of the therapists and members who are in a position to operate helpfully, the group members engage in "focus alternation" as they resonate their own inner images with the external image common to them all. George and Vasso Vassiliou have been full-fledged GST therapists for over two decades. Their current efforts demonstrate that using GST as a basic framework for therapeutic intervention can be not only a viable but an enduring catalyst.

In Chapter 13, I try to describe how the fundamental boundarying idea which is a direct outgrowth of LvB's branch of GST can be put into practice in the clinical management of therapy groups. Under the fundamental assumption that living groups, group members, and members' personality substructures autonomously open/close their own boundaries, I enlarge the traditional psychodynamic framework of group therapy by describing a set of interventions on the structural level which can bypass difficulties when impasse occurs at the content level. Opening/closing within individuals, moving inside/moving outside between groups and group members, and systeming/summing between group members or member and leader are all variants of the basic autonomous boundarying event. Achieving autonomy in a group will enhance and restore the autonomy of its members, so that when members can freely move inside and outside the group boundary, they can begin to trust opening and closing to each other. The group leader is made of the same living structure as the group and the other members, so he or she uses his or her own living structure as the chief instrument for catalyzing and regulating therapeutic change.

The final section of *Living Groups* contains chapters that go off into the future of GST group therapy in a variety of directions. The end of our exploratory journey into the ways in which GST can clarify the theory and improve the practice of group psychotherapy is only the beginning of a new one. In these chapters we point to the directions of organization of GST-oriented training/research/supervising subsystems, experiential training for group therapists in GST, the integration of GST ideas with some of the pioneering contemporary intellectual trends, and detailed empirical research in therapy group process and phasing. These final essays signal a bright and growing future for GST applied to the field of group psychotherapy.

In Chapter 14, Helen Durkin shows how the isomorphy between opening/closing at the structural level and feeling/thinking at the content level is harnessed in the therapeutic boundary management of the group, the members, and the leader's own personal structure. As in her previous chapters, Helen demonstrates with salient clinical detail that the transition to and synthesis between psychoanalytic and GST thinking are entirely negotiable. We see here in this chapter, as well as in Helen's other chapters, the actual history of group psychotherapy itself undergoing therapeutic change.

In Chapter 15, I shift my target of focus from what goes on within the therapy group process to the next higher level of the hierarchy of living groups, the group therapy community. Through historical and professional accident, the major subsystems of the group therapy community system, experiencing as clients, leading as therapists or co-therapists, learning as trainees, and observing as researchers or supervisors, have come to be dominated by interaction patterns which, in terms of the concepts developed in this book, can be said to be characterized much more by summing than by systeming processes. A proposal is made in this chapter to develop the relationships between these subsystems of the group therapy community system which have a greater proportion of the open emotional flow of the systeming processes. Videotape observation plays a key role in keeping this system together and alive. A "radiance filter" is described which enables the videotape feedback distilled down to essentials enough to keep the observation current with the ongoing group sessions. Establishing a living balance between summing and systeming at the level of the group therapy community system is likely to threaten the autonomy of each of the subsystems, but it is suggested that this arrangement, or one like it, can create more growth to the community as a whole than has been heretofore possible with preponderantly summing interactions.

In Chapter 16, Don Brown provides a scenario in which, within the constraints of a half- to whole-day workshop format, a group of people can "live" GST. He reports on the GST experiential workshops he has run for the last several years at the American Group Psychotherapy Association's annual convention and other similar meetings. In these workshops GST is presented both didactically and experientially. If the fundamental idea of this book is correct, it follows that living structures at the group level or any other level not only must be understood to be lived in action, but also must be lived in action in order to be understood. In this chapter Don describes an effective procedure whereby individuals with little or no previous understanding of GST as a living structure can come and experience both the information and the energy of this doctrine.

In Chapter 17, Bill Gray resumes his emphasis on the formation as opposed to the maintenance of living structures and scans the intellectual horizon of mid- and late-twentieth century science for resonances with his ideas. He explores the world of closing in living structure by detailing the concept of *autopoiesis* (Varela et al., 1974) by means of which life lives itself in the process of defining and maintaining its own boundaries. He explores the world of opening in living structure by detailing the concept of *dissipative structures* (Prigogine, 1976) by means of which the fundamental principle of order through fluctuation is manifested. He applies these revolutionary modern principles to the group and person level of living systems by identifying the emotional-perceptive cycle where opening and closing, fluctuation and autopoiesis, operate together to make the individual and group system able to achieve change within stability. Finally, in anticipation of Beck's Chapter 18, he shows how steps in Beck's phases in group development are cases of sequential system-forming activity mediated by these boundarying processes. The reader must be forewarned of information overload and noise in the system in this chapter. The ideas Bill deals with are leading-edge ideas, ones which bespeak the immanence of a radically new paradigm of science.

In Chapter 18, Ariadne Beck reports on one of the most extensive and intensive empirical research projects in the group therapy literature. Beck describes the nine group developmental stages and the four different leader roles that have emerged out of her research results. Although her empirical work developed largely independent of GST, she demonstrates that, like organisms, living groups undergo a series of metamorphoses in the course of their development. She anticipates the next phase of our group's work now that the basic ideas have been set forth in this book. Next, we must verify empirically and clinically whether the ideas we have set forth here are valid.

Our explorations of living groups through the focusing lens of GST have led us into areas of both depth and breadth. Our chapters will open up new paths in clinical managment in traditional modalities and they will introduce basically new modalities of group treatment. The chapters will specify minute details of the therapeutic process and speculate upon the broadest philosophical issues. Our committee is living; our group product, this book, is living as well. There are unfathomed complexities and there are unavoidable uncertainties. But we have learned a great deal through our life together and we hope to transmit some of what we have learned about living groups to you so that you may live your groups. We are not through yet and we hope you will not be through with GST whether it be Model I, Model II, Model III, or Model N after you are through with this book.

Living Groups:

Group Psychotherapy and
General System Theory

Part I

General System Theory and Group Psychotherapy

Chapter 1

The Group Therapies
and General System Theory
as an Integrative Structure

By Helen E. Durkin, Ph.D.

Editor's Introduction. As one of the pioneers of group psychotherapy, Helen has observed and participated in this field almost since its inception. Because she was an historian before she became a psychotherapist, Helen is able to cast an historian's eye on the tangled threads of development that evolved in group psychotherapy over the past 50 years and how that development interacted with general scientific and intellectual trends during that period. With this perspective, Helen is able to demonstrate that group psychotherapy has come to a turning point. The field is faced with a dilemma brought on by rapidly changing conditions under which mental health services are dispensed, as well as by a proliferation of new techniques and theories of group psychotherapy. She concludes that the time is ripe in group psychotherapy for the emergence of a new integrative structure.

In surveying the world scientific scene she sees more and more attention being paid to the complexities of life and how they are structured. In the most general terms the scientific study of organized complexity can be termed "the systems approach." Systems thinking in this very broad sense of the term has been applied to the field of psychotherapy several times in the past. She reviews the major systems approach—the cybernetic communications approach which was one of the bases for what is now called family systems therapy. She clarifies the distinction between this important approach to psychotherapy and the specific general systems theory (GST) approach based on the pioneering work of Ludwig von Bertalanffy (LvB) and his colleagues. She concludes that the GST approach, the approach upon which the explorations in this volume are based, holds many advantages as a new integrative framework for group psychotherapy.

Helen traces the early development of the GST committee of the American Group Psychotherapy Association which she has chaired from its inception and which has finally put forth this book. She then introduces the GST perspective in terms of two fundamental ideas: 1) isomorphy and 2) *Fliessgleichgewicht* or flux equilibrium. The idea of isomorphy postulates that beneath the diversity of content among all forms of life there are identical structures and organizing processes. This means that understanding of one level or population of systems can be readily applied to other levels. The idea of flux equilibrium is perhaps LvB's greatest discovery, for it provides a model for understanding the active self-regulating and self-transforming properties of all living structures, including groups, group members, and members' internal personality substructures. She identifies the central operation of these living structures as the capacity for *boundarying,* that is, the selective opening and closing of their own boundaries. She concludes that a great opportunity is now available to synthesize this new knowledge offered by GST with the store of knowledge accumulated in the psychoanalytic and related traditions as the basis of a new, long overdue integration of the field.

She then begins to define the role and techniques of a GST-oriented group psychotherapist. She sees GST as providing a model of functional behavior which complements the psychodynamic model of dysfunctional behavior. She sees the hierarchical model of GST as able to resolve some of the persistent controversies in the group field as to whether therapy is done with groups as such or with individuals. She notes that the GST model considers change and growth as normal phenomena and provides mechanisms whereby such growth is accomplished. She sees the GST model facilitating a focus on dynamic processes and structures as a complement to the content-oriented approach that has gradually drifted away from Freud's original process orientation. Finally, she sees GST as supplying new ways of looking at cognition and emotion in the psychotherapeutic process from a structural rather than a content point of view.

The boundarying idea stands at the center of the new synthesis that Helen advocates for group psychotherapy. At each of the levels at which the group therapy process goes on—the group, the individual member and the personality substructures operating within each member—there are isomorphic structures underlying the diverse contents which generate, maintain and evolve the autonomous capacity for growth and change. These structures are based in one way or another upon boundarying configurations.

The goal of therapy, to help the group members restore or enhance their own autonomy, is concretized into the more practical goal of helping group members more effectively open and close their own boundaries. Helen sees the main function of the therapist as monitoring, regulating, and, when necessary, facilitating the opening and closing of individual and group boundaries. She is able to translate the classical phenomena of resistance and transference and of emotion and cognition into the more tractable terms of opening and closing boundaries. She defines the role of the therapist as an autonomous subsystem within the group who can utilize his/her own ability to open and close his/her boundaries as an effective therapeutic tool. All in all, Helen sees the boundarying process as the governing process in the GST perspective on the group psychotherapy process. She sees no conflict but only complementarity with the classical psychoanalytic concepts and sees a new integration between the two perspectives to the benefit of their field. Helen charts a course which moves smoothly out of the past and into the future of group psychotherapy and into a new era for the field.

THE NEED FOR CHANGE

What is now called the "traditional" method of group psychotherapy was based, from its beginnings in the 1930s, on psychoanalytic therapy, in line with the thinking of its originators, Slavson, Wender, and Schilder (H. Durkin, 1974). It dominated the field for several decades, although other approaches, such as those of Moreno and Pratt, coexisted with it. The first real challenge to traditional group therapy came in the 1950s from group dynamics and then from humanistic experimentalism (existential group therapy). They were followed in the sixties by a proliferation of the then less organized, so-called "innovative techniques," such as the gestalt exercises, encounter strategies, and scream therapy. As a result, group therapy became increasingly fragmented theoretically. Confusion and dissension followed to the point of endangering our credibility with the scientific community.

During roughly the same period, rapid social, economic and scientific changes were taking place, which had repercussions in every field of human endeavor. They led simultaneously to the mushrooming of group therapy and to its fragmentation. Responding to social change, the Federal Law of 1963 extended mental health services to big hospitals and to the community at large. Group therapy flourished, but the traditional analytic approach was not yet readily accessible to these new populations. Certain difficulties in putting psychoanalytic theory into practice in groups had also come to light. Questions and criticisms of the traditional method multiplied, and other approaches were tried out.

Close inspection of the situation gives credence to Edgar Levinson's (1972) penetrating observation that "paradigms are time and space bound." It suggests that we must continually review our group therapy models if we wish to remain responsive to scientific progress, to socioeconomic changes, and to the changing needs of those who come to seek our help.

I was not alone in considering such reassessment. By the seventies a movement had begun among group therapists to search for a means of accommodating valid aspects of the new approaches in order to bring unifying trends into the field. But it seemed to me that what was needed at this point was a more comprehensive framework—a conceptual umbrella which could encompass the major current approaches and could logically incorporate the best of the new techniques. In such a model unifying trends would complement the valid differences that exist among them.

Finding a New Paradigm: Systems Theory and Its Various Branches

There were such paradigms available. During the forties and fifties, while group therapy was struggling with change and dissension, systems theory had become prominent in scientific circles. Ever since the advent of quantum mechanics and relativity theory, scientists from many countries and a variety of disciplines had begun to classify the complex organized phenomena of existence in terms of their organization rather than their subject matter. The body of knowledge it produced came to be known as systems science. This structural approach served to bridge the gap between the physical and the natural sciences. It seemed plausible that it could do the same for the behavioral and social sciences, as well as for the "group therapies."

The complex organized phenomena of existence were called "systems." The several original definitions of "a system" did not vary greatly from that of von Bertalanffy (1968): "a system is an order of parts and processes standing in dynamic interaction." But as the theory developed, so did more modern definitions (see Chapter 17). Each system is composed of parts called subsystems, and itself becomes a part of a larger suprasystem with characteristics of its own, called "emergents." Each category of such interacting wholes forms a hierarchy. For instance, living systems, from the cell to society, form a continuum. Thus, systems thinking is a holistic, synergistic point of view.

Not everything is a system. Sums and aggregates exist as well, and both occur in group therapy. The crucial difference between systems and sums lies in the interrelationship among their parts. Systems are the product of the interaction of their parts. In this they resemble compounds. Sums interact additively. They are like mixtures. Different branches of systems theory have pursued various lines of investigation, but they are in consensus about these fundamental principles.

Systems thinking gradually filtered into the literature of group therapy, as it did into other fields. But the terms, such as interface, input, feedback, and the like, were used in a vague and loose manner. However, two particular branches of systems thinking—cybernetics and general system theory—have had a more organized influence on group therapy.

Cybernetics, which applied information and feedback theory to the study of systems, was the first to make an impact on group therapy. Information theory was strictly mathematical, but Bateson and Ruesch (1951) adapted cybernetics to the study of human and therapeutic communication. They studied schizophrenic communication and introduced the new idea that there are schizophrenic families. The Palo Alto group, including Watzlawick, Beavin and Jackson (1967), Haley (1963) and others, developed a new form of family therapy based on these premises. According to it, the family system as a whole is to be treated, rather than the designated patient, who had usually been considered the "crazy member." Group therapy could not ignore this development. The short-term clinical results were striking. Changes in the family system brought about rapid changes in its members, including the behavior of the schizophrenic patient. Most of the systematic accounts about systems theory in the group therapy literature have until recently referred to this "communications" form of family therapy rather than to general system theory.

While all branches of systems theory hold the above views in common, each branch has certain distinguishing features. For a number of reasons, I feel that GST is more suitable as a framework for group therapy than cybernetics. There are several reasons why:

1) Systems theory as applied to family therapy is concerned primarily with the effect of existing systems, i.e., with the effect of the family on its members. Group therapists have learned, from group dynamics and from the work of S. H. Foulkes (1964), that the group has a strong influence on its members, but they are concerned primarily with restructuring the members' family-induced systems and in forming new more realistic and spontaneous systems of interacting. Family systems therapy has very little to add about how the members' dysfunctional personality subsystems influence the formation of the group.

2) Family systems theory focuses on changing the structure of the family system, but it does not address itself directly to changing the member's personality subsystems. GST, on the other hand, considers that any exchanges between systems have a mutual or reciprocal influence on each other. The cause and effect relationships are circular, not one-way only. This view is more in harmony with the aims of group therapy, which has clearly demonstrated that changing one member's personality structure has significant therapeutic effects. It influences not only his/her own behavior but that of the other members. Indeed, it changes the nature of the whole group. This GST view also adds to the group therapist's technique, for it suggests that he/she examine both sides of any transaction instead of interpreting the motivation of only one of the members. Experience shows that the usual resistance to "being on the hot seat" is appreciably reduced.

3) Family systems therapy employs a mechanistic* model (the steering wheel),

---

*The mechanistic model upon which classical cybernetics and, by extension, family systems therapy is based contrasts with the organismic model upon which our von Bertalanffian model of GST is based. There are some properties both family systems and GST approaches have in common. Both adopt a structural perspective which focuses on configurations of parts and processes that underlie manifest content. Both are holistic in that they focus on families or groups at total configurations rather than trying to reduce them to their parts. Both deal with linear feedback configurations which can often be recruited to stabilize pathology. However, cybernetics does not posit the active organism model that GST does, but only a reactive, error-correcting model. Furthermore, cybernetics does not posit a metabolic process of self-transformation that is characteristic of autonomous life forms. Family systems therapy deals with the family as a whole system and works with structural configurations such as triangulations, but rather than seeing therapeutic self-transformation as an inherent capacity of living systems, family systems therapy sees the patient family as a mechanism

and relies on linear information and feedback theory to bring about change, while group members are nonlinear** living systems. Therefore, GST, which employs a nonlinear organismic model, accounts more adequately for the more complex and less predictable behavior.

The Formation of an AGPA Task Force to Study GST.

I began a more intensive study of the work of Ludwig von Bertalanffy, an eminent biologist often called the father of GST, and that of J. G. Miller, a psychiatrist, who had done ten years of systematic research in order to build a systems view of human and social interaction (see Miller, 1978). LvB viewed the interactions of living systems primarily as metabolic processes which permitted exchanges of energy among them. Miller combined this with the cybernetic view that information was also exchanged.

As I read I felt increasingly that the ideas of von Bertalanffy combined with those of Miller's could provide solutions to a good many problems of group therapy. It was for this reason that I suggested to the Long Range Policy and Planning Committee of The American Group Psychotherapy Association that further exploration of this subject might ultimately have a significant effect on the future of group therapy. The Chairman, then Dr. Harris Peck, promptly set up the GST Task Force. Our directive was to investigate the implications of GST for group therapy. We hoped it might clarify the theory and increase the effectiveness of its practice. The Task Force consisted of interested experienced group therapists and general systems scientists.

We started out as a group of individuals with a wide variety of backgrounds and very different interests, attitudes, and approaches to our common goal. For the next couple of years we pooled our knowledge, greatly widened the scope of our reading, and narrowed the differences in our views sufficiently to perform our task. We began to identify those general systems principles which appeared

---

that has become locked into a dysfunctional state that must be repaired by the entry of the family therapist into the system.

Family systems therapy is probably the most energetic and exciting movement within the mental health professions today. I feel it is riding on the energy of a few great leaders and a small fragment of the total GST perspective as a theoretical basis. I believe that a more complete incorporation of ideas of GST will be necessary if family systems therapy is to keep from eventually running out of this amazing energy. Perhaps this book can begin to show family systems people where they can expand their theoretical base (Ed.).

**The term "linear" has many technical and verbal meanings. In this context of differentiating mechanistic from organismic models, a linear system such as cybernetic feedback is not capable of self-transformation of its own structure. Von Bertalanffy's concept of equifinal dynamic interaction (see Chapter 2, pp. 48-53) is a nonlinear boundary opening process that leads a living system to reset its own set points (Ed.).

to have a significant bearing on the group therapy. During our meetings and "think sessions," we monitored our own intragroup relationships by stopping the task in order to work out the usual interpersonal problems whenever they interfered with the group task. Gradually we became a living group ourselves.

Why GST?

Whereas psychoanalytic and other group theories rely solely on the structure, function, and content of personality sytems, GST is based on a comparative study of the whole range of systems levels from cell to society, regardless of the subject matter. For this reason, GST was able to generate a considerable amount of fresh information about the common features of systems, which has been touched on but never formally elaborated by group therapy. GST thinking and the more traditional group psychotherapy thinking complement each other and provide a more complete account of the clinical events.

What Is New about GST That Pertains to Group Therapy?

GST is an enormous subject. The Task Force had a "tiger by the tail." But let me try to condense the material to what I consider to be essential.

1) The first result of the GST comparative study of systems in general yielded the revolutionary discovery that systems of all categories, across the board, share certain basic structural features called isomorphies and also share common structural laws of operation. This means that whatever one learns about one system will illuminate another particular system one wishes to study. Thus, if group therapists view the group, its members, and their personality structures as three levels of systems, they have access to a most valuable source of new information. (This is called the method of isomorphies and is commonly used by systems scientists.)

For example, heretofore, group therapists thought that individual psychodynamics and group dynamics were structurally different and followed divergent modes of operating. This view had created a problem for the therapist, who felt he had to treat them differently. Moving back and forth is distracting and discontinuous. It detracts from the therapeutic process. A counterproductive controversy of no small dimensions had developed as to whether the individual or the group factors were the "real" sources of therapy (H. Durkin, 1972), but the trenchant discovery of their essential isomorphism allows us to transcend this false dichotomy. Now the therapist may view his group, its members, and their internal personality structures as three systems at different levels of complexity. Focusing on the system boundaries gives the therapist a single uniform approach to all levels which permits him, at times, to cut through the diversity of the content to the underlying structure. He also has the alternative of dealing directly with the content by bringing about changes in the patterned exchanges of energy and information.

In spite of this welcome unifying tendency and the new information, however, we must not forget that GST, taken by itself, is insufficient to account for the special characteristics of human and social interaction. Both LvB and J. G. Miller have pointed out that anyone who deals with a given system will fail to give an adequate account of it unless he/she also takes into consideration the "emergents" or unique characteristics which came into being at its particular level of complexity. Fortunately, psychoanalysis and other current group therapy theories have already provided a good deal of this special information. Using the two complementary characteristics increases clinical effectiveness.

2) Secondly, and of even greater consequence for group therapy, is the *new paradigm of living structure** developed by von Bertalanffy. It provides new information about the special characteristics which distinguish living systems. Up to that time all structure had been regarded as static, but LvB, in his search for a unified theory of biology, discovered that living structure was not inactive and static, but active and dynamic. He found that over time living systems develop a hitherto unrecognized phenomenon which he called *"Fliessgleichgewicht"* or "flux equilibrium." He then delineated the structural features which account for this unique phenomenon. Living, or as he often called them, "open systems" have permeable boundaries which the system is inherently capable of opening or closing. Consequently, each system is able to exchange energy and information with other systems and with the environment. It can close its boundaries to shut out input which is in excess of or inharmonious with its inner state in order to maintain its stability or even its identity. It can also open its boundaries to import energy and information, and process it for the purpose of change and growth by restructuring itself. Thus the phenomenon of flux equilibrium—which by implication constitutes a quasi-disequilibrium—enables us to solve an existential paradox. Can a person be a true individual and a committed group member? The old adage, "Plus ça change plus c'est la même chose," is an example.

To Sum Up

GST does not provide us with a ready-made theory of group therapy. It does provide a new way of looking at our clinical data from the vantage point of a broader perspective and it offers us a solid foundation of new concepts from

---

*See Chapter 2 for more details about paradigms and about the phenomenon of autonomous living structure which many of us in this book utilize as a theoretical basis for living groups. See also the introduction and its contrast of the two GST models (Ed.).

which we may construct a more inclusive model of group therapy and a more effective therapeutic process.

CONTINUING WORK OF THE TASK FORCE

A whole new body of information was opened up to us about the isomorphic structural characteristics of living systems and their common modes of operation. The question before us at that point was: "What does this mean for the working group therapist?" The new information seemed to complement what the average group therapist already knows about the way human and social living systems operate. The hypothesis seemed plausible that our current models could be expanded and/or that a new more comprehensive model of group therapy might evolve which would account more adequately for the complexity, the creativity, and the relative unpredictability of human and social interaction. It also seemed likely that such GST models would eventually provide an integrative framework for the "group therapies."

We were all very much stimulated by the new ideas. Our sessions were exciting, and our discussions very productive, though full of conflict. Our ideas were by no means thought through or well organized. Some new questions emerged: Just how would we be able to make effective use of the new orientation? Would the new information it had generated add anything new to our current methods? Would it really increase our therapeutic effectiveness?

Our next task was cut out for us. We would have to develop some specific hypotheses and put them to the clinical test, so that new models could be constructed and suggestions made about the way in which GST could be applied to group therapy. Doubts assailed us during these difficult times so that we sometimes found ourselves at the very nadir of group experience. It was the same agony of destructuring before restructuring that our groups and their members also undergo. Once a transformation took place, we resumed our task with vigor and enthusiasm.

Some Early Impressions

We were impressed with how accurately the generalized descriptions of how living systems operate seemed to apply to group, person and intrapersonal levels of the therapy groups and how neatly they illuminated the nature of the group interactions. It also seemed to be a distinct advantage to have a single uniform means of bringing about change in these systems through changing the permeability of their boundaries.

It was exciting to realize that the horizons of the group therapy might be expanded within the GST context. The uncomfortable distance between the language of psychotherapy and that of the wider world of science was reduced and the hitherto blurred relationship between our clinical data and the empirical data of other sciences had begun to be clarified. Our communication would improve and collaborative research could now become a real possibility.

We were finding also that we could use the new information to redefine some of our less precise concepts. In my own case, for example, the concept of transference was appreciably illuminated by thinking of it in terms of the early exchanges between the infantile systems and those of their powerful parental systems. In a new assessment of my group members, I could see that some of them in infancy and early childhood had become unable to close enough boundaries to maintain their identity while others had closed so many that their capacity for growth had become limited. The dysfunctional effects were reflected in their patterns of transacting.

The same GST principles seemed to me to provide a structural foundation for the psychoanalytic concept of resistance, which could now be seen as a case of dysfunctionally closed boundaries across which patterns of interaction could not be effectively transported. Thus, the concept of resistance was clarified and the technique of analyzing it was reinforced as one of several good ways of opening boundaries.

When our Task Force met again, we discussed each member's findings and all of us came away with "feedback" on our own work to assess, as well as some new ideas. The result was that some of our members began to make significant modifications in their theory and practice. They reported that these were enriching to the therapeutic process. Ramon Ganzarain was among these (Ganzarain, 1977). Others became interested in some particular GST concept which they considered of crucial importance to the group therapy process. For example, Walter Gruen and Irvin Kraft incorporated the GST view of entropy, which is based on the Second Law of thermodynamics. They found it contributed a great deal to the therapist's attempt to explain and to regulate the redistribution of energy in therapy groups. Their work is reported in Chapters 4 and 5, respectively. David Mendell (see Chapter 7) focused on the application of the principle of isomorphism. Glenn Swogger (see Chapter 3) adapted the cybernetic concepts of information and feedback theory to the level of therapeutic communication.

The Construction of GST Models

A number of us constructed new group therapy models based on the GST perspective. Among this group there were two distinct trends. One was to integrate current models within the context of an overarching theoretical GST framework. My own model, which amounts to an expansion of the analytic model, is an example. The other was to create new, more strictly GST models, which were based on the isomorphic structure of living systems. The latter took note of the special characteristics of human and social systems by regarding them as embodiments of their system structure. Jim Durkin and Bill Gray constructed their group therapy models around the role of the emotional and cognitive exchanges in the intragroup transactions. Jim focused sharply on their implications for the boundarying process (see Chapter 13). Bill focused on their roles as systems precursors and in the formation of new systems (see Chapter 11). George and Vasso Vassiliou, who have long embraced a systems approach, built their model around a group image, which was created by a group discussion of pictures drawn by the members (see Chapter 12).

All of these models differ according to the personality, training, and experiences of their authors, but they share the basic structural features of GST as described above. Consequently, they also share the effects that GST has on the theory and practice of group therapy. In the following section I shall attempt to make some generalizations about the influence of GST on the models now being used. But before I begin, it will be necessary to comment on certain facts that must be taken into account by group therapists who wish to revise their current models or build new ones using GST principles.

The Application of GST to Group Therapy—Basic Assumptions

Applying any new perspective to a given set of data necessarily involves making some basic assumptions. In order to minimize misunderstanding I shall make these assumptions explicit.

1) The group therapist must take into account the fact that GST describes the way typical living systems operate, whereas the therapy group is composed of members who, in the course of their ontogenetic experience, have become dysfunctional to varying degrees. However, the GST emphasis on the autonomy of living systems makes it a fair assumption that the group members, though dysfunctional, nevertheless retain the potential of all living systems for becoming open, active, and autonomous again. The therapeutic process, therefore, will consist of remobilizing these capacities.

2) According to J. G. Miller (1978), anyone who works within the hierarchy systems is entitled to choose the level of system in which he is interested. To avoid confusion, however, he must indicate his choices. For example, I regard the individual members as the "target" system, the group as an ad hoc therapeutic "suprasystem," and the member's inner personality structures as the critical "subsystems." Other group therapists, such as those who follow the Tavistock approach, designate the group as the target system, while the individual becomes the subsystem. GST allows for such variations.

3) GST has intentionally employed the very general terms "matter/energy" and "information" to describe what is exchanged across the permeable boundaries

in all kinds and levels of systems. But at each particular level, energy and information are embodied in terms of the special processes particular to that level. Amoebas do it one way, cows another! Personal and group structures embody their energy and information in terms of their emotional and cognitive processes. From the beginning of life, these processes interact to form a variety of exchange patterns. In the therapy group, energy and information are exchanged. Each member's patterns will sooner or later be revealed in the total group interaction. There they may be experienced by the members, identified, and eventually transformed. The relationship between matter/energy and information and their clinical manifestation in the form of emotional and cognitive processes provides the group therapist with a key to the application of GST to group therapy.

The Necessity for Combining the General and Special Characteristics

Just as LvB and J. G. Miller have pointed out that no one can deal effectively with any given system unless he/she takes its special characteristics into account, so group therapists must take into account the "special" characteristics of personal and group systems. Once such new characteristics have emerged, they become isomorphic to all subsequent levels of systems. Fortunately, this information about human personality systems has already been provided to the group therapist by psychoanalysis, humanistic experientialism, gestalt, and other theories. Group dynamics and communications theory have provided it for the group system. All GST models must devise some way of taking account of this information.

SOME SIGNIFICANT EFFECTS OF GST ON THE CURRENT GROUP THERAPY MODELS AND SOME OF THEIR TECHNICAL IMPLICATIONS

The next section will describe some of the influences and effects that GST will inevitably have on the current models of group therapy. In general, these influences will affect all current models, but will differ with respect to the way GST relates to their particular concepts. My examples will be chosen from analytic group therapy. I would expect examples from other approaches to differ in content rather than principle.

The Influence of GST on the Therapist's Orientation

1) The group therapist who is influenced by GST will view the therapy group, its individual members, and their personality structures, as three levels of living systems—or "wholes"—in continuous interaction, whose open, active, creative and autonomous characteristics he/she will try to remobilize.

He/she knows that the group members are potentially able to reorganize their perceptions and experiences and will be able to restructure themselves in terms of the therapeutic group goals.

2) The operation of equifinality* may be used to increase the group therapist's clinical effectiveness. The therapist will become more aware of the effect which current events in the group or in the environment have in initiating (or blocking) change in the members' modes of interacting. Utilizing these events as a catalyst for change will increase his/her capability as a therapeutic agent. The analytic group therapist who accepts the notion of equifinality will be able to deal with certain forms of resistance more effectively. He will be less likely, for example, to accept the members' rationalizations that their fate is sealed because of the way their parents treated them. He will be sure, in analyzing transference, to show that the past need not continue to determine their present behavior in significant relationships. And, he will use the group interaction to demonstrate that change is possible as a result of immediate group events. Thus, change and growth are enhanced by the concept of equifinality.

3) GST therapists will focus primarily on the flow of the patterned emotional/cognitive exchanges among the members in the group interaction. Consistent attention to process in this way highlights the emotional experience and will be more likely to bring about transformations than would interpretations of content, which can be employed subsequently to consolidate these transformations. Moreover, focusing on the very event which activates change will serve as a constant reminder to the therapist that transference interpretations are intended to serve the purpose of change rather than merely self-awareness.

4) GST highlights the living system's capacity for growth, as well as for self-regulation. Although experience shows that human systems have an extraordinarily high capacity for morphogenesis, traditional group therapists have not yet sufficiently exploited this crucial capacity. There has been an unfortunate tendency to become engrossed in correcting dysfunctional behavior. It has earned these therapists the nickname of "shrinks" rather than the "mind expanders," which the founding fathers of psychoanalysis had in-

---

*According to LvB, one of the characteristics of living systems' metabolic open system exchange of matter/energy with their environments is an unprogrammed but nonrandom goal-directed process called equifinality. Living structure actively moves toward goal states which cannot be predicted from initial conditions as in a linear process, nor can the specific path toward that goal be predicted. Because it is an open system process it improvises ways to utilize opportunities currently available in the environment. The classical example is the sea urchin embryo which, when arbitrarily divided, produces two normal adults. In group therapy the unpredictable interaction process can provide paths which allow open person systems to reorganize their own structures in a therapeutic way. Equifinality provides an alternative within living structures to the strict causal determinism of objective cause and effect (Ed.).

tended us to be. GST can bring about an exciting shift in this direction by stressing the positive and creative aspects of "the unconscious."

The Influence of GST on the Group Therapist's Goal

According to my first assumption, it is essential that we take into account the fact that GST describes the way normal systems operate, whereas the therapy group is composed of individuals whose systems have become dysfunctional to varying degrees.

Viewed in this perspective, the therapist's goal is more broadly conceived. He/she will aim to remobilize the members' full system potentials according to the well-defined GST norms and standards. For the analytic group therapist, this means that bringing unconscious processes to consciousness is no longer the goal but a means of facilitating the members' growth by increasing the input of energy and information from within their personality subsystems. And analyzing transferential and defensive interaction becomes but one way of opening boundaries which have been constricting a member system.

GST Influence on the Therapist's Procedure

The therapist's first step will be to form a new ad hoc suprasystem, the therapy group. With the members' explicit or implicit consent, he/she will set up new therapeutic goals for the group which are intended gradually to replace the members' idiosyncratic (neurotic) goals. In this context "feedback" (in the popular sense* will gradually cease automatically to signal threat to the members. Instead, positive feedback will become a signal to the members to amplify their patterned exchanges while negative feedback will signal the need for changing the pattern, in line with the new goals. When a member reverts to his or her old idosyncratic goals, the group, or a nucleus of its members, will now view the reversion as a deviation and come in to support the group goals of maintaining organization in openness and stability in growth. As the Vassilious have pointed

---

*The term "feedback" and its positive and negative variations has several quite distinct definitions which are often confused. In content terms positive and negative feedback denotes pleasant and unpleasant responses to a person's behavior or statements. In the functional terms of cybernetics, a negatively oriented feedback configuration automatically brings a control system to a normal "set point" by acting to respond in a way which minimizes deviations from the set point, while in positive orientation a linear feedback system amplifies its own deviations from the set point and either disrupts the control system or causes it to oscillate. In structural terms the important distinction is between linear feedback which is structure preserving and nonlinear feedback which is structure transforming. In the arena of psychotherapy a repetitive neurotic symptom is a linear negative feedback configuration that blindly goes on attempting to reduce the deviation experienced as anxiety. Helen is talking mostly about nonlinear feedback where the individual, presumably neurotic feedback systems of the members are temporarily replaced, and therefore restructured by nonneurotic group norms (Ed.).

out (see Chapter 12), there is always such a nucleus of members who are able to act in this way to fulfill their function as partners in the therapeutic systems.

GST provides a powerful new rationale for employing the group as a therapeutic suprasystem. It provides an excellent arena in which the entire repertoire of the members' exchange patterns will unfold and can be amplified to the point that they can be fully experienced by them and identified as functional or dysfunctional by the therapist. These patterned interactions, which are either too rigidly or too loosely bounded, can eventually be transformed. Secondly, the group, itself a living system, will develop its own morphostatic/morphogenetic balance or steady state with the help of the therapist's interventions. Its influence on the member will be greater than that of any single member, including the therapist. It will put pressure on the members to conform to the group goals. As Jim Durkin once pointed out, it is, paradoxically, the morphostatic state of the group cohesion which encourages morphogenesis in its members.

The Function of the Group Therapist: Regulating the Exchanges Through Boundary Control

Next we come to the influence of GST on the role of the group therapist. How does he/she implement the goal of remobilizing the members' full potential for autonomy? Here, he/she takes a cue from the way normal systems change themselves. They are able to restructure themselves by regulating the permeability of their intra- and interpersonal boundaries. It stands to reason that the therapist may temporarily assume the role of the organizing subsystem in which he/she serves the boundarying function for all three systems. Thus, GST provides a more comprehensive governing principle to guide the therapist in selecting techniques. The therapist's function, however, will be limited to catalyzing, facilitating or stimulating the system's potential capacities. Even the dysfunctional system retains the capacity and the right to accept or reject the therapist's input.

The flow of the exchanges in the group transaction will provide clues to correct boundarying. For instance, exchanges which show very little mutual influence on the participants suggest that the boundary region between them is too impermeable, too closed. When the participants flood each other to the point of becoming unstable, then the boundaries are too open. Opening boundaries in constricted systems will enable them to increase their input, process it, and restructure themselves. Closing those that are unstable prevents excess input and gives the system time to stabilize its internal interaction. It is important to emphasize that the events of opening and closing are not inherently good or bad, but depend upon the context.

The concept of flowing equilibrium represents the holistic nature of the GST approach. The therapist makes his clinical decisions not in terms of any single boundary, but in terms of the openness and closeness in whatever system requires therapeutic intervention. He consistently keeps his eye on the total context.

How to Change Boundary Permeability

The work of Jim Durkin and Bill Gray provides us with further guidelines to carrying out this boundarying function. They independently came to the conclusion, on the basis of their clinical experience with the new models, that genuine spontaneous emotions (in contrast to the "cover-up" emotions which attend defensive interactions) embody boundary opening. Cognitive input serves to reinforce existing boundaries or to create new ones after a basic shift in the personality subsystem has been experienced and processed through emotionally based transformations. The complementary processes of emotionally based transformation and cognitive consolidation are both essential to more durable structural change (see Chapters 2, 13). Cognition alone is sterile; but emotions alone are too evanescent to permit structuralization of the transformations. When the patient can himself articulate the change he has experienced, he is in a better position to regulate his own boundary changes. He has taken another step toward autonomy. I have tested these hypotheses clinically and find them valid (for examples see Chapter 10 and 14), but further work is needed.

The Use of Already Established Techniques Reexamined in GST Terms

GST also gives us a new look at existing techniques. Upon close examination, most of the current techniques may now be understood anew in terms of their capacity to open and close boundaries. The therapist is therefore not limited to the technique of any single theoretical approach. His technical options are markedly increased.

For example, an analytic group therapist may continue to analyze transference and resistance as his major techniques, especially to open intrapersonal boundaries which will change a member's mode of interacting. GST will reinforce the analytic principle of intervening at the point when the emotions reach a peak in a transferential interaction. But when the boundaries are exceptionally "sticky," it will also offer the alternative of using other techniques such as role-playing, gestalt exercises, or encounter tactics. Such situations are frequent in those members who are orally or anally regressed. However, once the emotional shift has occurred, the therapist will see to it that cognitive input is used to create new boundaries. Without this consolidation, the transformations will prove evanescent.

Or, the therapist may use an ego-psychological technique to close boundaries when members reveal a weak sense of identity because they are too open. Questions such as "How do you feel?", "What is your opinion?" and "Why don't you feel entitled?" help the group member change his/her stability as a system. Thus, the generalized GST framework provides the therapist with more technical choices without destroying its own internal consistency.

New Techniques Derived from GST

GST does not provide ready-made new techniques. However, the model of the living structure, with its concept of the boundarying process as the change agent, is bound to inspire the creative therapist to devise new techniques which he can then test out clinically. Certain innovative GST techniques have already been developed. (See Chapters 10, 11, 12 and 13.)

GST Takes a New Look at Countertransference—The Therapist's Personal Organization

Since not only the group members, but also the therapist, constitute self-referential systems, it goes without saying that the structure of the therapist's personality plays a key role in determining the nature of the therapeutic process. He is constantly engaged in a rigorous procedure in which he is required to be open enough to listen empathically to the members' communications, and closed enough to maintain his own identity, so that he can withstand their dysfunctional infantile demands. Whether he engages these members' communications with his own feelings or uses them only to understand what is going on, the therapist will find it necessary to remain as aware of his own feelings as possible. Thus, he will be aware of the state of his own boundaries and of how they affect those of the members. Under these conditions the therapist will change and grow in his contact with the patients, yet the firmness of his identity will be maintained. An important part of his task will be to become increasingly aware of undue internal stresses that distort his own perception so that he can avoid unwittingly promoting his own idiosyncratic goals. Sometimes consultation with a colleague or supervisor is required.

It is often said that the therapist's effectiveness derives not from what he says, but from what he is. GST transcends this false dichotomy and helps us to realize that his thoughts and feelings are normally reciprocal. When they are, he will be able to find the most facilitating way to make the right interventions. His feelings, which are most often expressed nonverbally, will be in accord with what his cognitive training has taught him is appropriate. The therapist's primary tool for catalyzing the growth of autonomy in groups and group members is his own autonomous living structure.

CONCLUSIONS

Because GST is based on the comparative study of the organization rather than the content of the entire range of living systems, it has been able to generate new information which adds significantly to our understanding of human and social interaction. Its discovery of the isomorphic structure of all systems has made possible a uniform approach to the three major group therapy systems. Its wider perspective has enabled us to transcend a number of counterproductive dichotomies, such as that between individual versus group factors, between emotion and cognition, and between biology and culture. The new science of living systems has brought to light and conceptualized certain phenomena not hitherto recognized, such as the theory of energy, equifinality and flux equilibrium. Thus, the territory of group therapy has been extended.

GST offers us an opportunity to add to the productivity of our current theories, to reorganize our current theories, and further to incorporate this new information. It suggests the possibility of employing GST as an overall integrative theoretical framework which encompasses our various current approaches without eliminating their valid differences. Unity in diversity can, with effort, replace our current dissension. Thus, communication among us will be improved and collaborative research will become at last an attainable goal.

The Position of the Therapist in the Group

The therapist is, in my view, at the psychological center of the group. As we know from psychoanalysis, the members, who necessarily look to him/her for help, place him/her in that position, partly because he/she is realistically the expert, and partly because they irrationally impute their omniscient and omnipotent fantasies to him/her. He permits this, but does not himself play out this role. Indeed, it is one of his goals to help them eventually see him in a more realistic light. From his knowledge of GST the therapist is constantly aware that his aim to remobilize their autonomy cannot encroach on their right to self-determination. He is aware that he cannot change them, but must limit himself to facilitating their own capacity to change.

He is, as I see it, a full participant in the group interaction on the level of their latent communications. But he only rarely expresses his personal reactions verbally. Instead, he maintains the analytic attitude of concerned neutrality, and uses his own feelings and perceptions to try to comprehend what is going on at all three levels of the group interaction.

The Function of the Group Therapist

The reader is by now familiar with the fact that the GST therapist temporarily assumes the responsibility for the boundarying opening/closing function in order to regulate the exchanges among the members until they develop their own steady states and are ready to take over their own boundary control—in other words, until they have achieved autonomy. In order to insure maximum efficiency, he may alternate between facilitating the flow of exchanges in the members' personality subsystems and that of the group as a whole. As he works, thus, on the structural level, he is frequently able to save considerable time by cutting through the diverse content to the structural basis of dysfunctional systems.

At other times, he may need to prepare the members for opening or closing their boundaries by exploring their transferential modes of interacting. Analyzing these and the resistance which resides in them has in my experience proved to be one of the surest ways of facilitating boundary change. Moreover, once a boundary has opened and new input has been processed by a member, he/she tends to slip back into his/her accustomed behavior. One swallow does not a summer make, and often working-through is necessary. However, using the structural GST approach in concordance with analysis seems to cut down appreciably on the tedious follow-through.

But there is an even more important reason for dealing with analytic content. We must not forget that the therapist is interacting with human systems who experience their identity and their relationships with others in terms not of structure but of content. It is a sine qua non that the therapist make genuine person-to-person contact with the members. To do that, he must talk with them in terms of their thoughts, feelings and interpersonal behavior. By dealing with this content, in which the underlying structure is embodied, he is able to put flesh and bones on the skeletal network of the boundaries. Again, we note a complementary interplay between the two approaches.

Moreover, psychoanalytic interventions enable the members to increase the crucial input from what Freud, interestingly enough, called "the system unconscious." Coming to undersatnd their transferential behavior, their primitive fantasies and, consequently, their irrational fear of giving up their defenses is a crucial factor in the willingness of human systems to restructure themselves. In my experience, the most poignant and moving moments in treatment occur while the patient is in the process of remembering the past instead of acting it out. It enables him to close his temporal boundaries and move into the present. In this unique experience he becomes reacquainted with the spontaneous child he once was and regains a sense of his own continuity.

Chapter 2

Foundations of
Autonomous
Living Structure

By James E. Durkin, Ph.D.

Editor's Introduction. By probing deeply into the foundations of general system theory (GST), this chapter gives us a more profound understanding of the structural characteristics common to all living systems and provides a basis for understanding the way in which they can be applied to expand the horizons of group therapy and to increase its clinical effectiveness.

Living systems are autonomous because their structure provides them with the inherent capacity to become self-defining, self-organizing and self-transforming by means of exchanging energy and information with the environment. The author points out that this autonomy is indeed the primary characteristic of all living structures. He takes particular pains to show that the features which lead to their autonomy cannot be accounted for by the old paradigm of objectivity. They seem to require the very constructs which are furnished by GST. Furthermore, the foundational ideas of GST coincide with those of the new paradigm, which has been emerging for some time in various forms. For this reason, he calls it the paradigm of autonomy.

Using the action language he believes to be appropriate to this new paradigm, he then attempts to show how it accounts for the autonomy of living structure. His discussion begins with von Bertalanffy's original contributions about open systems, the boundarying process, and *Fliessgleichgewicht* and goes on to the more recent developments in general system theory in which process is increasingly emphasized and heretofore unexplained phenomena of self-reference and paradoxical bipolarities in living structure, which had been relegated to "the position of perverse anomalies," are finally taken into account. Considerable time is then spent in showing how the new notion of the complementarity of irreconcilable but inseparable aspects of living systems is successfully woven into the fabric of the new paradigm to account for the autonomy of living structure. Boundary opening/closing, energy/information, individual/groups are examples.

With this new information, he then attempts to build up an operational model which accounts for the structure of autonomy and may be used to incorporate group therapy theory and practice into the new paradigm of autonomy (H.E.D.).

INTRODUCTION

All of the authors in this volume have utilized general system theory (GST) as the foundation of their studies of living groups. The goal of this chapter is to clarify the foundations of GST itself. The enhanced perspective on GST provided by this investigation is intended to add a certain depth of understanding to our application of GST to living groups. The scope of inquiry of GST is broad, including all forms of life from the simplest prototypes of biological life to the most complex social organizations. Groups, group members, and group members' inner personality substructures are, of course, included within this range. One of the great insights of GST is that, although life is made manifest in a wide diversity of particular embodiments, there are structurally identical or isomorphic self-organizing structures common to all forms.

In this chapter a central concept will be introduced which recognizes the fundamental isomorphism underlying all forms of life. We will call these isomorphic self-organizing structures—together with their diverse embodiments which characterize the full range of life forms—*autonomous living structure,* or living structure for short. We will consider GST to be the scientific investigation of living structure, as we consider living groups and their members to be particular embodiments of living structure. Thus, the concept of living structure will be used as the key to the connection between GST and living groups.

Living structure is alive because it has achieved autonomy. In this chapter we will show just how autonomy operates. Autonomy is usually defined at the content level in terms of its effects. An autonomous individual is self-organizing or self-governing and executes actions that can be responsible to, but are ultimately independent of, environmental influence. But such approaches to explaining autonomous processes beg the question because they do not specify the operations by means of which the effects are achieved. One of the chief contributions of GST is that it focuses on the structure of autonomy; that is, it identifies the processes and configurations which mediate the achievement of such basic autonomous characteristics as wholeness, self-regulation and progressive self-transformation. A GST-based analysis of the structure of autonomy in group and group member living structure provides an explanation of how living groups can therapeutically restore or enhance their own autonomy.

Autonomous living structure is a new kind of idea. As we proceed in our explanation of the structure of autonomy, it will rapidly become clear that the traditional scientific framework of the *paradigm of objectivity,* which has guided scientific inquiry for at least several centuries, is inadequate for our exploration of this phenomenon. Many of the basic pillars of the concept of autonomy will be found to lead to complementarities and paradoxes when seen through that objective perspective. As a result of this impasse, we will find it necessary to generalize from the paradigm of objectivity to a more general *paradigm of autonomy,* as we shall call it, in order to encompass our findings about living structure within a self-consistent framework. Expanding the very basis for inquiry in this way is, of course, a risky step, but it appears necessary if we are to comprehend the foundations of living structure and, ultimately, to understand how groups and group members achieve their living structure through the exercise of their autonomy. We gain autonomy by talking about autonomy.

GST AS PART OF A NEW SCIENTIFIC POINT OF VIEW

The emergence of GST from its roots in biology was only one of a number of parallel growths in scientific thought in this century that were interested in phenomena exhibiting organized complexity. Parallel metatheoretical doctrines such as French structuralism (Piaget, 1970) rising out of anthropology, linguistics and cognitive psychology, dialectical humanism rising out of political thought (Wald, 1975), and existential phenomenology rising out of philosophy and religion (Poole, 1974; Polanyi, 1958) were all systematically exploring the underlying structures of living organizations and their products. A number of new technologies grew rapidly during this period, including cybernetics, operations research, systems engineering, and theories of computation and artificial intelligence. Their newly developed powers of analysis and modeling asked questions that could not even have been asked before. At a less technical level, a number of social/political movements arose that were weaving new interconnections between the science of knowing and the politics of winning. Such groups as blacks, gays, grays, women, consumers, and environmentalists were using the tools and the knowledge of science in new ways (J. E. Durkin, 1980a).

Are there some common threads in this tapestry of new growth being woven during the middle years of this century? Four basic departures from the standard approaches of traditional science are apparent in these new doctrines, technologies and movements:

1) *Holding to holism rather than reductionism.* Rather than trying to divide up the objects of scientific investigation into smaller and simpler units, the new emphasis is on the complex patterns of interrelationship that integrate the parts into a whole.
2) *Espousing an ecological rather than a technological perspective.* Rather than casting the scientist in the role of an external, personally neutral investigator, the ecological perspective plants the person of the scientist in the midst of his or her field of study, thus requiring personal responsibility and value commitment to the scientific work.

3) *Accepting intrinsic uncertainty rather than demanding determinism.* In the last few hundred years, mathematics and physics in particular, and the other sciences in general, pursued the Laplacean ideal of acquiring enough data to predict the future with certainty. But recent discoveries, such as the Heisenberg uncertainty principle (1958) and Gödel's incompleteness theorem (1931), suggest that completeness and consistency are incompatible with descriptions of the world. New generation methodologies, such as Catastrophe Theory (Thom, 1975) and Fuzzy Set Theory (Zadeh, 1976), are beginning to integrate such essential uncertainty into formal analytic tools.

4) *Seeking deep or "virtual" structure rather than grounding fact exclusively in direct observation.* There is a definite post-empirical trend in modern science which attributes reality to forces (such as the virtual particles of modern physics [Capra, 1975] and the chreods of epigenetic development [Waddington, 1970]) that are directly observable only in their embodiments. The phenomenon of "structure" for structuralists like Lévi-Straus (1963) is an "unconscious reason" that cannot be seen directly.

Each of these new strategies of science, both singly and in combination, bespeaks a fundamental alteration of perspective on what is to be investigated and how the investigation is to be conducted. In short, a paradigm shift (Kuhn, 1970) is taking place. As new ways of looking at reality are developed, new realities are being discovered. GST is right at the center of this paradigm shift. In the most general terms, the aim of GST can be said to be the investigation of organized complexity. During the first 30 years of its existence, GST's accumulating theory and practice have gradually become harnessed in the service of control. GST became a control technology, the purpose of which was to take on a complex target "system" and, with its tools of analysis or modeling, achieve control over the power and productivity of that system. It could then be utilized more efficiently by those interests in charge of that system. In terms of the distinction drawn above in point 2, GST's initial control stance was a technological approach rather than an ecological approach.

Now, a vigorous new stance is rapidly emerging within the ranks of GST, in part stimulated by new theoretical discoveries, and in part stimulated by a new awareness of relationships between scientific knower and known. This new stance, which will be called the autonomy stance, represents a reunion with the original roots of GST in the theory of life (von Bertalanffy, 1952). There is a new focus on natural systems, that is, configurations exhibiting self-organized complexity, rather than complexity that is organized externally. Several fundamental discoveries lie at the nerve-center of this evolving autonomous branch of GST:

1) The *principle of autopoiesis* (Varela et al., 1974) demonstrates operationally

how certain configurations of elements can generate their own unity and wholeness.* It is an extension and an improvement of LvB's original open system model because it is spelled out more operationally. Parallel to this model is Prigogine's work with self-developing "dissipative structures," which won him the Nobel Prize in 1977. This operationalization of autonomous organization is comparable in its profound implications to the discovery of the linear feedback principle by Weiner (1948) several decades ago.

2) A logic can be seen as the formalization of a paradigm (Günther, 1962). Traditional logic (Russell & Whitehead, 1908) has always been restricted from application to self-referential situations, but a new *logic of indications,* begun by G. Spenser Brown (1972) and developed by Varela (1975), has opened up a formal basis for self-description and self-transformation, the primary capabilities of autonomous living structures.

3) Traditional analytic procedures, even those which deal with highly complex target systems, are geared to deal with only one level of organization at a time while disregarding other levels. And yet, one of the primary characteristics of natural living structures is that they organize themselves into hierarchical configurations which involve important interactions between levels. There is considerable new work on *hierarchy theory* (Pattee, 1976, 1978) which addresses just such problems of multilevel controls.

4) Although the "molecular revolution" in biology is now dominating the headlines, many GST people (including, especially, Waddington, 1970) have steadfastly pointed out that the phenomenon of epigenesis, by which genotypes are transformed into phenotypes, poses problems that cannot be solved by cracking the genetic code. The major GST hypothesis—of latent or *virtual self-organizing principles* which guide the pathways of the development of living structures—is receiving more and more general attention as the ambitious hopes of DNA's double helix being able to explain everything about life gradually fade away.

These new theoretical and methodological developments in GST have made it possible to see a new kind of object of scientific investigation, the phenomenon of autonomous living structure. Individual embodiments of this phenomenon of living structure have been seen before as objects, but now self-organizing cells, organs, organisms, persons, families, groups, human organizations, ecologies, and societies can be seen in a different and more general light. The secret of the underlying structure of their observed autonomy is beginning to unfold. The term autonomy is gradually being transformed from a content label into a structure variable upon which operational measures can be performed, tests made, and theories built.

---

*See Chapter 17 for more detail on autopoiesis and dissipative structures.

The discovery of the structure of autonomy—and it was indeed a discovery—is opening up a new relationship between the GST knower and the GST known. The earlier goal of GST control over the "system-object" has to be questioned in the light of the newly discovered fact that such living structures exhibit a fundamental autonomy through which they essentially control themselves. The ascription of autonomy to the objects of general systems research mandates a redefinition of the research situation.* The working relationship between the scientific knower and that which permits itself to be known inevitably becomes a two-way street with the autonomous researcher engaged in a cooperative effort at self-description and self-transformation with the equally autonomous system under investigation. In the earlier definition, the appropriate strategy was simply to utilize the best tools in the best way to complete the job of getting control over the system-object. But now, a more ecological perspective has to be maintained wherein the investigator and the investigated are mutually responsible for each other, and in that sense are peers in autonomy (J. E. Durkin, 1980a). The subtle interactions between living structures working together are nowhere more apparent than in the field of psychotherapy.

It is clear that our study of living groups in this book must be aligned with the newer autonomy-focused branch of GST, rather than with the more traditional control-object branch. In terms of this distinction, it would be fair to say that the GST approach that underlies our study of living groups in this book is that which is focused on the investigation of autonomous living structure. It is part of the GST tradition that different GST writers autonomously define the scope and aim of their field in different ways. A fundamental distinction has been made between abstract systems which can be investigated with mathematical tools and concrete systems for which empirical investigative techniques are required. A further distinction has been made between living systems and non-living systems. J. G. Miller (1978) has focused on living systems and has defined the scope of GST as a hierarchy of living systems that is similar to the concept of living structure put forth in this chapter. However, Miller's aim is more functional than structural, more descriptive than explanatory, more anatomical than physiological, and less focused on the dynamic structures of autonomy and how they work. In terms of the distinction between the autonomy stance and the technological control-object stance made above, Miller's work seems to be more aligned with the latter.

In this chapter, we are defining the hierarchy of living structure as the scope of investigation of GST. The goal of the chapter is the investigation of the working configurations by means of which living structure achieves its autonomy. The investigation of living structure includes particular embodiments at the level

---

*Quantum physics had to face a similar redefinition when it found that the process of observing influenced what is observed (Heisenberg, 1958).

of human groups, group members and their inner personality structures, but it extends beyond that range to include all living structures from cell to society. The kinds of autonomous functions that have to be accounted for within this definition of GST include the various abilities of living structure to generate itself, maintain itself, evolve itself and, finally, dissolve itself. It will become apparent as we proceed with our investigation of living structure that some of its properties do not fit comfortably within the paradigm of objectivity upon which traditional science rests. Characteristics of living structure, such as its complementarity of manifestation as both action structure and language structure, its capacity to hierarchicalize itself, its self-referential control structures, and its ability to engage in boundarying operations, indicate that a new, broader paradigm is necessary for comprehending the phenomenon. The foundations of this new paradigm of autonomy will be discussed in the remaining sections of this chapter.

ASKING OBJECTIVE QUESTIONS ABOUT AUTONOMOUS LIVING STRUCTURE

In the last section I showed how our study of living groups, group members and members' personality subsystems fit comfortably within the conceptual framework of GST, particularly that emerging branch of GST that focuses on the structure of autonomy in the extended range of all life forms. In this section I will explore this goodness of fit in more detail by examining the phenomenon of autonomous living structure, the collective name suggested for this wide spectrum of living processes. As an initial step I will assume the framework of the paradigm of objectivity and try to describe living structure as an objective phenomenon. We will see that the normal questions asked by an investigator from the objective perspective yield paradoxical answers when applied to the description of living structure. I hope that this *reductio ad absurdum* procedure of inquiry will lend support to my assertion that the phenomenon of living structure can be grasped only with a new set of questions emerging from the perspective of a new paradigm of investigation.

Assuming the objective perspective, to call living structure a phenomenon implies that it is an objective entity. One of the primary assumptions of the objective perspective is that there is a world of space and time "out there" that exists independent of our subjective observations of it. How do we set the spatial boundaries of living structure? Living structure includes every living individual from the lowliest virus to the whole world civilization of animals and plants. Let us also consider that, as living structure has evolved through time from the beginning of the first autonomous embodiments in some primordial soup to the world family evolving into the future at this moment, it has acquired language structures* concurrent with its physically embodied action structures. The self-knowledge in our genes guides the building of our material bodies. The knowledge in our brains guides the building of our works of art and science, and the artifacts of our world. Where do we draw the dividing line in space to designate the limits of life? Isn't this very document—which is an encoding of the language structure of my own living structure—describing itself as a part of life? These considerations lead me to define living structure as a space which breaks out of its own space, a temporal process which determines its own future and thus breaks out of its own time. The normal objective categories of time and space just simply cannot contain living structure.

Another primary category of the objectively defined world is the process of cause and effect. Our most significant contacts with the objective world "out there" occur when we directly apprehend event "A" as a necessary and sufficient cause of event "B." It is through such a network of remembered, perceived and anticipated causal links that we know about, act within, and act upon the world. But our experience of our own and others' living structures slips through these cause-effect linkages. Living structure autonomously causes itself. It behaves under the influence of, but is ultimately independent of, external causes. It regulates itself and maintains a stability in the face of disturbances from the outside. It evolves itself into progressively more adaptive forms. Living structure chooses. The determinism of the cause and effect perspective is transcended in both small and large ways by the capacity of living structure for autonomous action and self-knowledge.

Four More Dilemmas

The objectivity-minded investigator, when apprehending the phenomenon of living structure, would proceed in a typical fashion to ask several other basic orienting questions to determine just where the phenomenon lies in terms of the dimensions of the world defined by his paradigm. As we shall see, the application of these straight either-or dichotomies to this autonomous phenomenon yields only equivocal or paradoxical answers, suggesting once again that the paradigm of objectivity is ill-equipped to cope with living structure.

1) Is living structure *a real or an ideal* phenomenon? Any and all embodiments

---

*Language structure need not always be articulated in verbal terms. If it were defined as such, neither a cell nor an infant would have a language structure. It is considered here to be a more general property in which some encoded reflection of the physical structure is contained within that physical structure. In this context, an infant "knows" how to acquire food through its sucking instinct, and a cell "knows" how to reproduce through its genetic code. Autonomy is not automatic; it slowly emerges, sometimes fails, and always occurs through transforming interactions with other parts of the environment such as mother, society, radiation, etc.

of living structure are real world constructions embodied from matter/energy. But the organization of these concrete configurations is guided by self-organizing principles which cannot be observed independently of their embodiments. The self-organizing principles do not simply carry out a preformed plan, for the variations that happen to be in the internal and external environment during the history of the structure can profoundly influence the path of its epigenetic development. The local encounter between an individual with an impulse for growth and an environment with its particular response to this impulse is constrained by general laws of interaction and growth which open up some pathways and close others in all such encounters. The circular interactions between these properties are so interwoven that it is impossible to classify living structure one way or the other.

2) Is living structure *a whole or a part* phenomenon? Living structure is both, because the term applies both to the whole spectrum of life ranging from cell to society, and at the same time to every individual embodiment in every population of every order of this spectrum. It is both, because life proliferates and develops, and any cell could, in time, produce any organism or any person or any society. It is the property of living structure—that the whole resides in each of the parts—that raises the difficulty of answering the whole/part question simply. Whole and part are complementary to each other in living structure, irreconcilable but inseparable. But, it is also characteristic that emergent wholes that arise autonomously from a set of parts exhibit new characteristics not found in the parts. A person cannot be totally accounted for by his biology, nor a community by its individual inhabitants.* Thus, living structure, because of this complex interaction between the wholes and parts which constitute it, cannot be clearly classified.

3) Is living structure *a stable or a changing* phenomenon? Living structure autonomously opens and closes its own boundaries. It generates closing configurations that serve the function of morphostasis, which is maintenance of an internal constancy in the face of a disturbing environment. It also generates opening configurations that serve the function of morphogenesis, which is the regulated transformation of structure. Once again, there is a complementary relationship between change and stability. Only within a stabilized structure is ordered adaptive change possible. But only a structure that adapts to changing conditions and evolves to higher orders by changing its own structures to do so can maintain survival under pressure. Living structure cannot be characterized objectively as either only stable or only changing.

4) Is living structure *a subjective or an objective* phenomenon? Objective means "out there," independent of the observer, taking up time and space, causing effects and being effected by causes in the world of action. Living structure

---

*A hologram has much the same whole/part structure. See Varela (1976) on Star Trinities.

as a whole, and in each of its embodiments, is "out there," a concrete objective action-structure phenomenon. Subjective phenomena reside in the world of language structure encoded in some kind of symbolic form within the physical action system of the knower. Language can be used to guide or select action, but it is not the same as action, objectively speaking. Living structure exhibits self-knowledge as an essential part of its autonomy. Even a cell has self-knowledge encoded into its own genetic structure, while social institutions have isomorphic knowledge structures independent of those which its human populations can articulate. Language structure has the capacity, using its self-knowledge, either to maintain stability or generate change, to proliferate into parts or integrate into wholes. But once again, subjective knowledge, encoded in language structure, and the objective embodiment of that knowledge in action structure are complementary. Thus, the attempt at clear distinction fails.

The objective orientation questions asked here—real-ideal? whole-part? stable-changing? subjective-objective?—are representative of ways of seeing the world and of organizing its constituents that have served us well for at least several centuries. When the paradigm of objectivity was established, the distinguishing of these categories and the making of these assumptions behind them served to settle a number of profound issues: The community of scientists could go to work unencumbered by the paradoxes and dilemmas raised by a close examination of the issues involved. But now it is late in the life of the paradigm of objectivity, and those long-ago buried issues are now beginning to crop up again due to the questioning of the authority of the objective perspective. Life was no mystery when there was a clear subjective part and a distinct objective part (Descartes, 1955). But now, as a sign of an impending paradigm shift, scientists are examining phenomena such as living structure which subvert and question the old categories. What must be done, if we are to gain an understanding of phenomena which go beyond the perspective of objectivity, is to look at autonomous phenomena on their own terms. We will do this in the next section.

AUTONOMOUS ACTIONS: LIVING, WHOLING, OPENING/CLOSING, BOUNDARYING

We distinguished the phenomenon of autonomous living structure as the organizing process behind the embodiments of all life forms from cell to society. We attempted to define this phenomenon more clearly in terms of the reality specified by the paradigm of objectivity. Objectivity cannot encompass autonomy. Living structure cannot be contained completely by time and space. It both causes and effects itself. It is both real and ideal, whole and part, stable and changing, and subjective and objective. But, just as our lively phenomenon is difficult to assimilate into the traditional dimensions of reality, it is equally difficult for us to accommodate ourselves to a paradigm which offers new perspectives with which to see the phenomenon. The categories of the new paradigm of autonomy, as we shall see, will still appear evanescent and paradoxical to our objectivity-bound thought processes.

To tread the pioneer's path between the absurdity of the old objectivity and the elusiveness of the new autonomy requires patience and fortitude. Living structure is difficult to embrace as a palpable and coherent whole. And yet I believe that we all intuitively understand living structure because we are a part of it. I believe that we are all deeply aware from our personal life experiences that a purely objective view cannot adequately account for the living phenomena within us and around us. In this section we will describe living structure in terms of its own autonomy. Living structure engages in action on its own terms. Because of this, I will describe what it does for itself in terms of action verbs, rather than trying to describe what it is in terms of objective nouns. The self-referential form in which these assertions about how living structure acts, e.g., it lives itself, etc., will be semantically awkward, but the words are chosen to help us break out of the objective model. It will be noticed that there is a certain correspondence among the four either-or objective questions of the second section, the four assertions of autonomous action reviewed in this section, and the four foundational ideas examined in the next section of this chapter. Their issue-by-issue correspondence does not quite add up to a formal theory of living structure, but the similarity of concern formulated over these three different analytic perspectives suggests a common line of focus and a coherent set of basic components of the phenomenon of living structure and the paradigm of autonomy which cradles it.

Living Structure Autonomously Lives Itself

The objective facts of birth and death in individual organisms hardly seem autonomous acts, but they do if they are seen in the larger perspective which involves the whole species and whole continuum of evolving life. The entire hierarchy of living structure with all its parts and wholes, individuals and collectivities, goes through rhythms of waxing and waning, of emergence and extinction, of development and stabilization. But is there something isomorphic in all these living individuals going through all these rhythms, something that is not simply a passive reaction to external forces or passive adherence to innate rhythms? Is there a common denominator of the expression of autonomy in all of these living forms, a basic act of living?

As I see it, the basic act of autonomous life is activity itself. Living structure is essentially defined by its activity. A cell acts, an organism acts, a person acts, a group or family acts, and a community acts. They initiate and terminate their own activities within the sphere which they regulate by opening and closing their boundaries.

The range of autonomy is limited in every living structure. Each individual has only a narrow band of autonomy surrounded by many layers of hierarchical constraints over which it has virtually no control. This narrow band of autonomy can be compared with the tiny gap of *kaios* which emerged as heaven and earth parted in the Greek myth of creation to form a fertile field of creative energy from where cascaded the phenomenon of life. Let us consider, by way of example, the band of autonomy attainable at the psychological level of living structure—the level of the person. The person can do little to alter the physical forces impinging upon him. Ultimately, gamma rays shot upon us will cause death no matter what we do. Until recently, the chemical forces within our organisms were beyond our control, but the field of psychopharmacology is beginning to make inroads in that area. Our ability to control our inner biological environment has increased rapidly as well. Here we see developments such as organ transplants, antibiotics, biofeedback control and even genetic recombination.

On the "top side" of the hierarchy of living structure, we find that we have relatively little autonomous control over our sociology, economics, politics and history. The constraints imposed by phenomena covered in these disciplines give us relatively little freedom to choose our own destinies. But at our own psychological level we have a distinct freedom. We have autonomous control over what we open our personal boundaries to and what we close them to. In the face of tremendous pressures of a social nature from above and of a natural kind from below, we can open and close to almost anything we please. Operationalized as *boundarying,* autonomy accounts for the great potentials and the great limitations of our personal structures. At other target levels of living structure—biological, group, community—there is the same narrow band of autonomy surrounded by many layers of constraint.

The non-living world does not originate action, but rather reacts to the surge and flow of impinging external events. The non-living world is guided by Newton's first law of inertia which states that things at rest stay at rest unless moved, and moving things continue moving unless stopped. Living structure, in contrast, starts itself and stops itself without external cause. It is intuitively hard for us to "compute" the idea of such causeless action because our objective perspective does not let us countenance such events; nevertheless, living structure causes itself actively.

Each living structure is real and inevitably involved in physical embodiments built from matter, which requires energy for action. There must be some way for living structure to recruit the energy resources of the non-living substrate in order to support its autonomous action. The working configuration that living structure generates to supply the energy needed for its activity is clear: It is LvB's open system configuration. Its particular embodiment is quite different in different life forms, but the underlying structure is isomorphic among all populations and orders of life. Life achieves activity through its metabolism, the process of importing rich materials, utilizing what they have to offer, and expelling them when depleted to make room for more. Through this process, living structure has available a constant potential for work to allocate to the maintenance of its integrity or to the transformation of its structure into more highly adaptive forms. Non-living structure consists, for the most part, of closed systems without metabolism, and as such, must be ruled by the law of entropy which states that energy and organization can move only downhill to dissipation and disorganization. Living structure is negentropic in that it counteracts and even reverses this downhill path with its persistence in living form and evolution. By feeding upon metabolic material it becomes locally negentropic.

LvB has called his generalized metabolic process *Fliessgleichgewicht*. We can call this "steady state control" where, by metabolically maintaining itself at a point just off equilibrium, living structure can harness the inherent physical tendency to strive toward equilibrium to perform work. It is like the water mill which borrows the downhill energy of the stream to move its gears and stones to perform the useful functions of the mill. The obvious example of steady state control in open systems is the feeding of organisms. It must be stressed, however, that isomorphic fueling processes are operating at all orders of living structure. A personal structure might feed on interesting experiences or on being cared for, while a town might feed on community spirit or commitment. Experimentally, establishing these isomorphies is one of the tasks of GST research. The main point, however, is that steady state control is the mechanism which living structure has established to engage in continuous autonomous activity.

Living Structure Autonomously Wholes Itself

We all have deep intuitions of wholeness or unity, both within ourselves and in the living and non-living things we perceive in the world. We have a built-in ability to distinguish figure from ground in our perceptual apparatus. This probably goes far in shaping our view of the world as made up of populations of unified wholes that can change but always come to rest again. Less biased perceptions from the world of physics now see the world more in terms of energy fields in flux than in terms of separate objects. At another level, ecological and system-oriented thinking sees interacting patterns of relationships in balance and flow as a more reliable reality than physical objects isolated in space. This brings up the question of whether living structures are seen as wholes because we who perceive them feel more comfortable seeing them that way or whether there are "wholing" forces actively working within living structure to develop and maintain wholeness.

I believe that a good part of the activating energy available to living structure is spent on the autonomous action of organizing wholeness. I see a process of striving to achieve self-organization as a whole which can function within its environment as an inherent directive process in living structure. Wholing* means achieving function through self-organization. Functioning in living structure involves maintaining and developing oneself in the face of environmental forces which work passively or actively against such adaptation. Living structure takes action to differentiate itself, to simplify itself, to regulate itself to achieve internal consistency, to transform itself into more highly adaptive structures, and to integrate its parts so that they all contribute to the whole. Detailed in the next section will be some of the mechanisms by means of which these functions are accomplished. The point is that all such self-organized wholing structures are autonomously generated and maintained, rather than externally imposed or developed through passive natural selection processes.

How can achievement of functional wholing through autonomous self-organization be distinguished from non-autonomous prewiring of function on the one hand and non-autonomous environmental control on the other? Genetic control of inherited traits in individuals seems to be an example of non-autonomous prewiring if individuals are seen not as the fundamental biological units, but as part of the epigenetic landscape of the population gene pool within which individual organisms function as temporary carriers. The shaping of behavior through selective reinforcement, on the other hand, is an example of environmental control if we disregard who or what shapes the shaper at the next higher level. GST and other autonomy-focused views are beginning to discover new principles of organized action that are distinct from both of these causal processes.

The only way to articulate autonomous laws is to employ autonomous language such as the self-referential forms used in this section, and these do not compute well within an objective perspective. But objective language is all we have to negotiate the paradigm shift, so it must do. If left to act together, any group of living parts will autonomously form themselves into a whole. In actively striving to achieve individual function they will improvise and consolidate group functions. As the group functions develop, the individuals will fall autonomously into greater degrees of interdependence and specialization. The group will autonomously generate self-maintaining configurations to strengthen the "boundary" between the inner and outer world. Strengthened by self-organization, the whole will be more free to develop in new directions that are more adaptive. The unity of the whole will strengthen as functional equivalence arises where any of a number of parts can be recruited alternatively to do a needed job for

---

*See Varela's "The Arithmetic of Closure," 1978.

the whole. Inherent life activity will happen upon and come to harness laws of self-organization which increase the probability of forming a whole. The specifics of some of these laws will be discussed as foundations.

Living Structure Autonomously Opens and Closes Itself

The path of autonomy is the path of uncertainty. The price that life at all levels must pay for its partial freedom to decide upon its own fate is the risk that the choice may lead to non-survival. Thus, autonomous control is by definition incomplete control. According to the model of the structure of autonomy presented here, the primitive events which lie at the basis of all living structures are the autonomous acts of opening and of closing one's own boundaries. Opening/closing may be enacted in vastly different ways at different levels of embodiment of living structure, but as far as the distinction between the individual and the environment goes, the events are isomorphic, i.e., structurally identical.

Closing a boundary around oneself insulates and isolates that closing individual from the change and flow of its environment. The effect of boundary closing is morphostatic, that is, it tends to preserve and stabilize structure. Boundaries in living structure tend to be resilient rather than rigid, so that adaptive variations in behavior in the face of environmental disturbances are typical. However, closing events tend to be conservative events. Opening up the boundary around oneself, on the other hand, dissolves the distinction between the individual and environment and permits free flow and interchange with it, which may result in a transformation of the individual's structure. Opening processes are difficult to describe systematically because the function of description itself is to achieve closure. On the other hand, the nature of the open flow process is to move unconstrained by boundaries and not to be directed in advance toward an explicit goal. Flow mandates the moment-to-moment improvisation on a path of least resistance. This opportunistic process is what LvB calls *equifinality*. Much of the creativity of open system functioning depends upon such spontaneous equifinal actions of living structure. The outcome of such opening events cannot be predicted, except to say that some basic structural transformation will take place before closing comes again.

Opening and closing are the key events in the continual struggle of living structure for adaptation within its environment. The environment is on the outside and the autonomous individual, organism, person, group, community, or any level of self-organized structure is on the inside. The active agent, the individual, opens and closes its own boundary with a selectivity and timing that promote its survival and growth within that environment. The adaptive process has two complementary aspects which correspond to opening and closing events at the structural level. The *assimilation* process is a boundary *closing* process where external influences are altered to suit the internal structure of the individual.

Verbal communication is largely assimilative, because the receiver of a message decodes it in a way that might be quite different from the way it was encoded by the sender. The boundaries between individuals prevent the passage of each sender's message to be received on the sender's terms. In contrast, the *accommodation* process is a boundary *opening* process where the individual restructures itself to suit the environment's terms. Mutual emotional encounters between persons are largely accommodative because each person's personal structure is transformed to some degree by the experience as it moves along its equifinal path in a way that could not be predicted at the outset of the process.

The process of embodiment, wherein a living structure such as a person or group moves through its history from birth to death, is an adaptive struggle between an individual and its environment where the autonomous events of opening and closing, accommodating and assimilating, are actively employed by the individual to achieve wholeness, stability and growth. The outcome is not predictable, for the equifinal process will be influenced by the specifics of the historical time and space within which the process immediately occurs. But, in any case, the basic events can be boiled down to the opening and closing of boundaries.

Living Structure Autonomously Boundaries Itself

The primitive events of opening and closing operate in a complementary relationship that make them irreconcilable but inseparable. Open flowing is chaotic, unless constrained by boundaries and thus channeled in one direction or another and at one rate or another. By the same token, the organizational constraints imposed by boundary distinctions would pulverize living structure without the energy of open flow to press boundaries to their limits. In verbal communication the strict semantic meaning prescribed by the set of formal boundary distinctions in the lexicon of a language is impregnated by the emotional energy imposed by the communicators as they exchange messages which are built up of these formal language distinctions. A living boundary must always be united with a living flow of energy in autonomous structures, which balance their stability and change through boundarying operations.

An exclusively closed or an exclusively open living structure could not thrive or even survive. The maintenance of a living autonomy requires a judicious shifting back and forth between the open and closed configurations. But who or what within living structure decides who or what to open or close to, and when to do it? To claim that there is a "decider subsystem" (Miller, 1978), the function of which is to make such decisions, merely begs the question, for who decides what the decider decides? The objective viewpoint is limited to either an environmentalist explanation which suggests that opening or closing occurs under conditions for which it has been rewarded in the past, or a nativist explanation which suggests innate or prewired decision-making processes. A third explanation for the choice of opening or closing is that the choice represents a new kind of action, an autonomous action, for which a new framework of explanation must be built. What would constitute such a framework, and what would justify its replacement of the more traditional explanations?

Let us attempt to face this difficult question by looking at a particular situation at the level of personal structure. At the psychological level, where living structure is embodied as a person, boundary closing operations are embodied in thinking or cognitive functions. In the thinking process, an adaptive struggle is resolved by drawing boundary distinctions among alternatives and evaluating which of those alternatives is of higher value. Boundary opening is embodied at the level of personal structure as a structure-dissolving emotional activity. For example, rather than maintaining the distinctions posed by the horns of the dilemma, whatever those distinctions may be in content terms, the person may break down in anger or tears and essentially circumvent the issue involved, or at least circumvent dealing with it on its own terms. The rationalist policy of facing issues squarely may not always be the most effective way to resolve a situation, for sometimes an emotional outburst can restructure the situation in such a way that the dilemma no longer holds and movement in another dimension may flow more easily toward resolution.

How does the autonomous individual decide whether to break up or to see it through? There could be strongly predisposing personality traits which call for strongly conditioned responses of one kind or another, but within a great, broad range there is no intrinsic determinant which directs the response to the stressful dilemma. There might be residual anger from a totally independent situation in the individual's immediate or distant past which will facilitate an angry outburst. There might be recent successes in reasoning through a dilemma which will influence the individual to choose the cognitive alternative. The important and difficult point is that within a broad range the autonomous individual is capable of opening or closing boundaries for any of a number of reasons, or as a result of any influence selected as relevant. The whole complex of memories, evaluations, and attitudes within the person will gain a momentary configuration at the point of decision-making and result in a response of the total person which no external assessment could have predicted under most circumstances.

FOUNDATIONAL IDEAS BEHIND LIVING STRUCTURE AND THE PARADIGM OF AUTONOMY

Our scientific efforts over the past few centuries have been guided by the paradigm of objectivity. In this century science has centered its focus on the phenomenon of life and its various orders of manifestation in the biological, psychological, and social spheres. Paradoxically, the path of following the canons of objectivity in the pursuit of understanding the nature of life has led to the discovery of a number of phenomena essential to life, the understanding of which can hardly be contained within an objective framework. Objectivity prescribes externally verifiable descriptions of phenomena, and yet, all life forms internally generate self-descriptions. The procedure of objective validations is inappropriate in subjective descriptions. Reliability of these validation procedures is questionable. Objectivity assumes a single perspective of reality, and yet all life forms are embedded in hierarchies in which they operate at several levels of reality simultaneously. Objectivity aims at establishing cause-effect relationships, and yet all life forms utilize circular causal feedback configurations wherein causes cause themselves and effects effect themselves. Objectivity strives to achieve closure by providing complete and consistent descriptions and explanations, and yet life processes are characterized by openness to essentially unpredictable self-transformations. All in all, the outstanding achievement of the paradigm of objectivity—in its investigation of the wide range of life forms, the phenomenon we have called autonomous living structure—has been its demonstration that the autonomous characteristics of life transcend the capacity of objective descriptions to account for them.

The miracle of living structure pervades the world. From obscure beginnings in some primeval soup, living structure has activated itself, organized itself, proliferated itself and evolved itself into a hierarchy of complex and ingeniously adapted structures able to survive in and sometimes even subdue the non-living environment out of which they have arisen. What are the fundamental facts of this amazing phenomenon which can enable us to understand the processes through which living structure has achieved these characteristics? GST has taken on the task of accomplishing this goal. As a scientific endeavor, GST expects to formulate a consistent and complete picture of the phenomena it is attempting to explain. However, as I have illustrated above, the attempt to grasp living structure as an objective phenomenon leads to inevitable paradoxes and complementarities. In order to deal with living structure we must consider its deviant paradoxical properties as central to the phenomenon, rather than merely as incidental perverse anomalies.

In the next several sections we will build up an operational model of living structure from four foundational ideas, each of which exhibits one or another paradoxical property when viewed objectively. Out of these paradoxical configurations will arise an accounting of the structure of autonomy and an explanation of how living structure achieves wholing, self-regulation and progressive self-transformation.

The Complementarity of Action and Language in Living Structure

The first foundational idea is that living structure operates on two complementary modes of manifestation. Because of this complementarity, a scientific description of the phenomenon must accommodate itself to this inherent duality by formulating its descriptions in two complementary modes. The profound idea of inherent complementarity has pervaded Oriental thought for centuries. The Chinese concept of Tao, which might be described as the living structure of the universe, can be apprehended in time and space only by observing the interplay of its two complementary embodiments, Yin/Yang. Yin, the dark receptive feminine principle, and Yang, the light creative masculine principle, are irreconcilable but inseparable. The interplay of Yin/Yang is experienced as a dialectical progression with one principle falling to the other just as it seems to dominate the situation. The shift is not externally caused by some agent; it is an autonomous motion of an invisible Tao.

These complementary dialectical processes were considered mystical analogies at best to Western science until the advent of modern quantum mechanics in the early part of this century. Niels Bohr (1915) articulated the complementarity principle in which radiant energy had to be described both as waves *and* as particles in complementarity. Complementary descriptions are not descriptions of different parts of the same phenomenon which has some unitary objective existence in itself, but are total descriptions. Complementary phenomena operate simultaneously at different levels, and can be experienced phenomenally only as fluctuating spontaneously between their dual states. If we are to understand the phenomenon of living structure, we must suspend our logical assumption that something cannot be more than one thing at once, and try to cajole ourselves into seeing complementary dualities pulsating back and forth autonomously between their half-realities.

Every individual living structure—every cell, organism, person, group, community and society—manifests itself through *two* complementary structures. The term "structure" is used here in the sense of a working configuration of parts and interconnecting processes organized to achieve a particular goal or function in the environment. We will split up the integral duality of living structure only to facilitate exposition and speak as if there were two separate structures that stand as distinct parts of a larger whole. We must utilize the language and logic of the paradigm of objectivity, which adheres deeply to the assumption that any given entity can be only one thing at a time and not two. At the same time, we must hold to the paradoxical proposition that all of living structure is both one thing and another simultaneously.

Living structure is composed of 1) action structure and 2) language structure operating in a complementarity relationship. Action structures are *embodied* physically in time and space, while language structures are *encoded* virtually as meaning which is not locatable in physical time and space. Action structures are configurations of matter/energy, while language structures are configurations of information. Action structure carries out acts which perform the functions of distinguishing the individual as a separate whole, maintaining the stability of the individual in the face of a fluctuating environment and generating growth toward more highly adaptive states. Language structure reflects descriptions of the individual's own action structure, together with descriptions of the environment within which the action structure operates. The term "description" here is employed in a much more general sense than the usual sense of a verbal articulation in conventional language that is characteristic of person-level descriptions. The operation of self-description can go on at all levels of living structure. For example, the genetic code encoded in arrangements of the elements of the DNA molecule in every cell is a self-description of that cell that does not utilize verbal language. The self-descriptions of living language structures, though varying widely with respect to the media in which they are encoded, are isomorphic as self-descriptions.

Pattee, the biologist, asserts that no science of living structure can achieve explanatory power without resorting to this complementarity:

Fundamental models of living systems from cells to societies require the simultaneous articulation of two formally incompatible modes of description in order to provide explanatory power. Biological models are autonomous, epistemological subject/object systems; that is, they contain models or descriptions of their environment and of themselves; and their characteristic behavior depends upon the interplay of their physical environment and their own description of their physical environment (Pattee, 1976, p. 146).

This complementarity model of living structure superficially resembles Descartes' psychophysical parallelism of mind and body, *res cogitans* and *res extensa* (Descartes, 1955), but this classical view does not articulate the complementarity principle, nor does it specify operations by means of which autonomy is achieved through the interplay of these dual structures, as we shall do in the following sections. Like Yin/Yang, neither action structure nor language structure can stand alone. The information code of self-description must be embodied physically if it is to persist in time. Furthermore, an action structure must be guided and stabilized by an underlying plan organized by the language structure. The duality is irreconcilable but inseparable.

On the other hand, there are operations that distinguish action and language structure, and which enable their cooperation in the establishment and maintenance of autonomy. The principle is that *laws* guide action structure and *rules* guide language structure.

The Interplay of Rule and Law in Life's Self-simplifying Hierarchies

Living structure constructs itself in hierarchical arrays. Cells group themselves into organs, and organs group themselves into organisms. Organisms generate psychological configurations that in the human species call themselves persons.

Persons form themselves into groups and groups form themselves into communities. All of these self-hierarchicalizations serve the aims of autonomy in living structure by promoting stability and growth. Living structure, thus compartmentalized into semi-independent hierarchical substructures, achieves more stability than a monolithic structure can achieve because when one substructure is disturbed or destroyed, the total configuration is not pulled down. In fact, substitute functions often emerge equifinally during such fluctuations, opening up new pathways to growth. Furthermore, if new growth is piecewise rather than global, the new exploratory structures will have an even better chance to emerge, stabilize and thrive. It is unlikely that the evolutionary process would have developed as far as it has without the benefits of hierarchicalization.

Is self-hierarchicalization an autonomous process that happens of itself in living structure? If so, what are the operations by means of which it is accomplished? The second foundational idea behind the phenomenon of living structure is that living structure utilizes its complementarity structure to move back and forth between hierarchical levels of organization. Through its definition of itself as a dual action and language structure, it can use simple rules to control complex internal interactions guided at a lower level by laws. The result is a hierarchical structure in which complex partial operations at one level are balanced against simplified whole operations at the next higher level. Pattee offers a succinct description of the law-rule distinction:

Laws are (a) inexorable, (b) incorporeal and (c) universal. Rules are (a) arbitrary, (b) structure dependent and (c) local. In other words, we can never alter or evade the laws of nature. We can always evade or alter rules. Laws of nature do not need embodiments or structures to execute them; rules must have a real structure or constraint if they are to be executed. Finally, laws hold at all times and places while rules exist only when and where there are physical structures to execute them (Pattee, 1976, p. 146).

Laws and rules work in complementary fashion to organize the autonomy of living structure at every level. The genetic code is the self-descriptive rule that guides cell development while the dynamic processes of epigenesis, whereby cells differentiate into specialized organs in unplanned but systematic interactions with their environment, are guided by laws. At a higher level, the policies and norms of larger social systems are rules, while the natural processes of birth and death and other population dynamics are examples of natural laws which affect living structure. Rules can constrain laws, as, for example, the establishment of birth control policies in China. Runaway demand dynamics can generate inflationary pressures that are countered by rules which tighten credit. Nevertheless, rules and laws influence each other only indirectly because they operate in two complementary domains which do not speak the same language.*

---

*An analogous assertion is that sums and systems themselves sum together. See section on boundarying.

A basic distinction between laws and rules is that laws are rate-dependent and rules are rate-independent. Laws operate in the physical world of time and space where their rate of action makes a difference in the result. In neural transmission, the rate of firing generates the quality of psychological experience. The arbitrary rules of a particular language, on the other hand, convey meaning regardless of the rate at which expressions in the language are articulated.

The law/rule, action/language complementarity provides a resolution of the dilemmas encountered earlier in this discussion where we applied the basic orienting categories of the paradigm of objectivity. Rules provide ideal patterns which are then embodied in reality. The whole describes itself by a general rule, which then constrains the lawful interplay of the dynamically interacting parts. Rules maintain stability as the laws guide the changing process. Rules are subjective formulations, while laws impersonally determine the path of objective processes. The complementarity of action structure and language structure makes the process of life intrinsically uncertain, for rule events or law events can intrude out of the blue to change the course of an individual's path. Sudden discontinuous shifts from rule control to law control, or vice versa, are "catastrophes" (Thom, 1975) which occur frequently in the lives of all individuals. This essential indeterminacy provides a niche for the operation of autonomy. In the group psychotherapy process, for example, the key events usually involve sudden shifts from cognitive rule-bound thinking to the opening up of law-bound emotional flow. The next foundational idea describes how such law/rule shifts can lead to the emergence of hierarchical structures which foster the evolutionary development of living structure.

Self-hierarchicalization Up and Down Levels of Organization

Living structure is negentropic; that is, it is inherently active and activates itself to counter the entropic tide that pervades the non-living universe and constantly disperses the organized state of complexity into simple random chaos. The energy for this activity is harvested through the *Fliessgleichgewicht* configuration in which living structure selectively opens its boundaries to exchanges with living and non-living structures in its environment. Because of its activity and its openness to interactions from outside its boundaries, living structure also has an inherent tendency to complicate itself, that is, to become involved in networks of relationship with other structures which become increasingly complex. Population explosions at the biological level and knowledge explosions at the psychological level are examples of this negentropic process of self-complexification.

The achievement of autonomy is the achievement of freedom, and the achievement of freedom is linked with living structure's achievement of control over the internal and external environment. The growth of complexity within living structure provides such capacity for control, as more interlinked resources become available to generate more sophisticated input, output and processing configurations which can deal effectively with these internal and external environmental demands. The naturally occurring linear feedback configurations discussed in the next section are examples of these. But there is a cumulative cost to be paid for the increasing complexity of organization. In general, complexity expands more rapidly than its capacity to control because the complexity itself must be controlled by more complexity. There always comes a point where the task of coordinating the interaction dynamics that arise between the complex components get bogged down by the weight of their own complexity. Thus, a complementary process of self-simplification is necessary if a living autonomy is to endure.

It appears that living structure does have the capacity for autonomous self-simplification. There are periodic "catastrophes" of self-redefinition where living structure redefines itself at a higher or lower level than before. Some of these quantum leaps are irreversible. When single-celled organisms evolved into multicellular organisms, the complex laws of interaction of the parts were substituted by a simplified rule of the whole. Other hierarchical transformations are reversible. We move from a set of individuals to a single solid group and then back out again. As individuals, we join in simplified sexual union and back out again. In both irreversible and reversible hierarchical shifts, there is the same shifting across complementary law-guided and rule-defined structural organization.

The autonomous "vertical" shifting up and down hierarchical levels, our second foundational idea of the paradigm of autonomy, is thus connected with the first foundational idea of "horizontal" shifting back and forth between law-guided action structure and rule-defined language structure. Since both vertical and horizontal shifts are involved in these self-caused autonomous acts, the process might be called a "diagonal dialectic." Living structure is arrayed in a vast hierarchy of levels of complexity. Every individual operates within dual intersecting structures. On the one hand, he/she operates as a part of a higher level structure, and on the other, he/she operates as an organizing whole for an interacting set of parts. Our objective logic attempts to follow the rule that everything is either one thing or another and cannot be both at once (*tertium non datur*). Living structure, when described within the constraints of this logic, seems to violate this canon and thus appears as a paradoxical phenomenon. But this complementarity of being a whole of parts at one hierarchical level and a part of a whole at another is a limitation of our way of seeing rather than a defect in what we see. The logic of objectivity does not allow us enough dimensions to see autonomy completely and consistently.

Pattee describes the mechanism of the shift of control from one hierarchical level to another in this way:

A hierarchical constraint is established by a particular kind of new rule that represents not merely a structure but a *classification* of the microscopic degrees of freedom of the lower level which it controls. . . . In other words, hierarchical controls arise from a degree of internal constraint that forces the elements into a collective simplified behavior that is independent of the selected details of the dynamical behavior of its elements (Pattee, 1973, p. 93).

Our own perceptions of living structure, constrained by *tertium non datur*, apprehend a process of fluctuation. First we are a group at one level, then we are a set of individuals at a lower level. We attribute external causes for each shift of levels: We lost the group when we began to mistrust each other. The group coalesced when one of our members asked for our help in coping with a crisis.

An example of this process is the formation of the self-description of a human group as a group, the consequent formulation of rules, and the subsequent control of group process by the formulated group rules. In the initial stages of group process, each of the individual group members circulates within the group space, independently defining his/her own presence. In time, the interaction dynamics thicken and the group atmosphere seems to become encumbered with cross purposes. But sooner or later, and usually through a shared emotional experience which solidifies the situation, a "catastrophe" of redefinition occurs in which the group begins to see itself as an integral unit. There is a selective loss of detail whereby everyone present becomes an equal "member" regardless of differences. A guiding constraint or rule controls the interaction dynamics, namely, each member has an equal right to work and an equal right to be helped and is entitled to equal time. A hierarchical transformation has taken place.

Thus, in the operation of self-hierarchicalization, living structure utilizes its complementarity of structure to move autonomously back and forth between levels of organization. By moving from the dynamic interplay of parts guided by the natural laws of action structure, to the constraints of rules generated as part of a knowledge structure, living structure is able to engage in self-simplification. Paradoxically, this simplification is entropy in the service of negentropy.* The selective loss of detail through self-redefinition at a second level and the control through a generalized rule provides an offsetting balance to living structure's tendency toward generating complexity. There is a dialectical process always operating in living structure between simplifying wholes and complicating parts. At the group level, the rule-guided synthesis usually comes apart after a time, and the group moves back into a turgid convoluted process where everyone seems to be moving at cross purposes again. This, in turn, is a prelude to new

---

*Actually it is an autonomous process of generating "tibs" of negative information.

synthesis.* In the next section we shall see how two-level configurations involving the interplay of rule control and law control can be harnessed by living structure for both stability and growth.

Morphostatic and Morphogenetic Self-referential Configurations

Here is the famous liar's paradox: "This statement is a lie." Looking at this self-descriptive statement from a logical point of view, that is, with a mind to evaluating whether it is a true or a false statement, we must conclude that if it is true it is false and that if it is false it is true, assuming the word "lie" to mean a false statement. This statement exhibits an intractable autonomy with respect to our efforts to comprehend its meaning precisely because it is self-referential. It is a configuration which reenters its own boundaries so that it is both subject and object, both cause and effect of itself. The inherent uncertainty and contradiction are not just a trick of language, as had been thought for years. In mathematics, Gödel's proof (1931) demonstrated that no mathematical system could be proved both consistent and complete within its own boundaries, and in quantum physics the uncertainty principle shows that the process of measurement (description) puts limits on the accuracy of measurement. All in all, there are absolute limitations on the description and control of self-referential structures.

The third foundational idea is that all embodiments and encodings of living structure are endowed with self-reference and, therefore, subject to the limitations and benefits of self-description. Every level of living structure describes itself. A cell describes itself in its genetic code, a person in his or her self-concept, and a city in its official policies and charter. The paradox is that such self-descriptions reside in complementary fashion both inside and outside the boundaries of the individuals they describe. Persons generate their own self-descriptions internally from an ordering of their experiences, but then utilize them as an external guide to further experience. There is always inherent uncertainty as to whether an external or internal description is operating.

In addition to describing itself, living structure also has the fundamental ability of autonomously transforming its own structure, presumably in the direction of more highly adaptive forms. This self-transformation process works both in the long term, as in evolutionary ascent, and in the short term, as in individual accommodative processes of coping with day-to-day challenges. Psychotherapy is a person-level self-transformation process that is ultimately an autonomous action that the person achieves for him- or herself regardless of who or what is recruited as an external aid. As usual, paradox is involved in such self-referential

---

*See Chapter 18 in this volume on this dialectical group process.

actions. The paradox here is that the selfsame structure that opens itself up for transformation is the structure that is initiating and controlling the transformation process. There is excitement and uncertainty in every such autonomous metamorphosis. Those who guide such processes, such as parents, therapists, and presidents, have to tread a narrow, winding path between overcontrol and undercontrol in order to be facilitative.

Living structure has harnessed these self-referential capacities into working configurations which serve the cause of its autonomy. Two such configurations will be presented: *linear feedback,* which performs a morphostatic or structure-preserving function; and what LvB has called *dynamic interaction,* a nonlinear process which performs a morphogenetic or structure-transforming function. The point of leverage in self-referential structures, the point which is also the point of paradox, is that processes of self-describing and self-transforming and the products of these processes are complementary aspects of the same thing. Paradox, logical contradiction, and complementarity are similar concepts, and it is difficult for us, immersed in the anti-contradictory logic of the paradigm of objectivity, to appreciate the impact of the self-referential idea.

What is the working structure of linear feedback configurations, by means of which self-regulation functions are achieved? Linear feedback configurations incorporate both the property of complementarity of language and action structure and the property of hierarchical interplay in its operation. Although each particular linear feedback structure is embodied or encoded differently, they all have the same general structural characteristics. They are dual structures in that they combine an action structure and a language structure at two different hierarchical levels. At a higher level, there is a rule of the whole which states in terms of a simple rule what the ideal state of the system should be. This encoded rule is often called the set point. In a home thermostat the set point is the 72° setting. At the lower level, there is an action structure which engages in lawful interactions with its environment. In a home thermostat the action structure is the bimetal band wound in a spiral so that it coils and uncoils with temperature and causes the switch to go on or off. The configuration is self-descriptive at both levels, the set point describing itself in language structure and the working input/output part living itself in action structure.

The key aspect of the linear feedback configuation is its circular causal structure. There is a most confusing verbal ambiguity here because the term "linear" is often taken to mean unidirectional, that is, noncircular, causality. We will try to clarify how a circular causal feedback system can be linear. Part of the law-guided energy output of the configuration is "fed back" in a loop to become one of the inputs to the system. This loop is the critical self-referential structure. The two self-descriptions are then set against each other and compared. The discrepancy between the set point and the fedback output, that is, between the ideal and the actual, is called the *error signal.* The linear feedback configuration is constructed in such a way as to act on its own error signal. If the error signal is great, that is, if the distance from the ideal state is great, the action of the system will be great. If it is zero, that is, if the system is now in its ideal state, it will remain inactive until disturbed by the external environment.

All linear feedback configurations are isomorphic, whether they are man-made or natural, living or non-living. A home thermostat, a toilet bowl water-level controller, the pupillary reflex system of an eye, a mammalian body-temperature control system, and a self-stabilizing self-concept—all have a set point which generates an error signal when the system's action output is discrepant and an effector actuated by error. There is some conceptual confusion between positive and negative linear configurations and linear and nonlinear feedback configurations. A negative feedback system is arranged so that the error signal is wired to reduce itself; that is, it activates the system to behave in such a way as to reduce the discrepancy between the set point and the output which, circularly, is what causes the error. Thus, when too much light enters the pupil and activates an error signal, the error signal acts to close off the pupil so that less light enters. The functional result of negative feedback wiring in linear systems is the morphostatic function of continual convergence on the set point.

A positive feedback system is arranged so that the error signal is wired to increase itself; that is, error adds to error rather than subtracts from it. For example, if the neurons in a pupil were crossed so that more light would open the pupil even further, the excess of entering light would soon saturate the receptors and wash out perception. In this way, a positive feedback configuration is unstable, but it is not morphogenetic in the sense that it generates a controlled transformation of structure. Positive wiring on a linear feedback system often leads to oscillatory behavior, such as the neurotic pattern of building up to the same kind of crisis again and again without learning. A therapist who emphathizes too closely and tracks the patient's cycles repeatedly is not doing an effective job.

Well then, just what *is* linear about linear feedback? The concept has a mathematical definition called superposition, which states that the output of any linear system is the sum of the independent inputs. This more closely approaches the fundamental idea that, when entities or processes are combined linearly, they do not open their boundaries to each other or transform each other's structures, but rather pass through each other as if the other were not there. Ross Ashby (1956), the cyberneticist, gives an excellent example of a linear relationship which I will paraphrase here. If a few pebbles are thrown into a quiet pool, each pebble, upon impact with the water, will generate concentric ripples moving out from the center of each impact. Assuming each expanding circular wave to be one inch higher than the surface of the pool, when the waves from two pebbles cross, the combined waves will suddenly jump to two inches in height as they superimpose upon each other, but as soon as they pass on their separate courses each will lose the temporary deformation caused by the linear interaction between them and resume its one-inch-high travel as if the other had not existed. In considering linear feedback configurations or the more general idea of linear summing interactions, we can say that each component behaves as if the other were not there. This does not mean that there is not a reciprocal effect upon each other; such a linear effect is, however, simply conceived as a temporary deformation rather than a boundary-breaking mutual restructuring process such as those to which we are about to turn.

A linear feedback controller is linear because the two self-descriptions—the action description of the output and the language description of the set point—are linearly combined to generate the error signal which ultimately activates the behavior of the system. Such linear interplay results in a blind and single-minded struggle to continue converging on the set point regardless of the quality of context. Neurotic defenses have this linear quality in that they blindly pursue the set point of reducing threat regardless of whether the threat is potentially helpful or not, as psychotherapeutic interventions might be. The advantage and disadvantage of linear feedback are that it is automatic and morphostatic.

The complementary nonlinear open-boundaried self-referential control configuration is more difficult to discuss because it is difficult to enclose the ideas of openness in language. LvB (1968, pp. 150, 161-163) defined a nonlinear boundary restructuring process that he called *dynamic interaction*. The path and outcome of dynamic interaction are not defined in advance by a fixed set point, as they are in linear feedback control. Rather, they are improvised serendipitously along the way as they meet pathways of transformation that happen to be available during the process. LvB called this process *equifinality*. In linear feedback configurations, the two hierarchical levels—the simple rule of the whole and the lawful dynamics of its parts—are isolated from each other. In the nonlinear dynamic interaction process, a fusion of action and knowledge, of law and rule, occurs. This fusion is the key to the equifinal process of morphogenesis, as well as the solution to the paradox of how living structure can autonomously control its own transformation.

LvB (1968, p. 150) has this to say on these two forms of control:

The basis of the open-system model is the dynamic interaction of its components. The basis of the cybernetic model is the feedback cycle, in which by way of feedback of information, a desired value (set point) is maintained, a target reached, etc. The theory of open systems is a generalized kinetics and thermodynamics. Cybernetic theory is based on feedback and information. Both models have, in respective fields, been successfully applied. However, one has to be aware of their differences and limitations.

The open-system model in kinetic and thermodynamic formulation does not talk about information. On the other hand, a feedback system is closed thermodynamically and kinetically; it has no metabolism.

An open system may "actively" tend toward a state of higher organization, i.e., it may pass from a lower to a higher state of order owing to conditions within the system.

A feedback mechanism can "reactively" reach a higher state of organization owing to "learning," i.e., information fed into the system.

In summary, the feedback model is preeminently applicable to "secondary" regulations, i.e., regulations based on structural arrangements in the widest sense of the word. Since, however, the structures of the organism are maintained in metabolism and exchange of components, "primary" regulations must evolve from the dynamics in the open system. Increasingly, the organism becomes "mechanized" in the course of development; hence later regulations particularly correspond to feedback mechanisms.

Two or more living structures autonomously open their boundaries to each other, and in doing so they temporarily abdicate their individuality-defining rule structures and define themselves as a single united system. Unstabilized by the dissolution of their self-defining rules, the newly united parts *fluctuate* dynamically within their collective boundary. It is within this unruly flux that the divergent and spontaneous process of equifinality holds sway, for the convergent process of rule guidance and hierarchical order gives way to a metabolic morphogenetic process in which order is created from the chaos of the interplay of the formerly separate structures. Prigogine (1976) has demonstrated this phenomenon, which he calls a *dissipative structure,* in the process of an unstructured liquid coming to a structured boil. Gray (this volume, Chapter 11) has noted the same kind of resonance phenomenon; he calls it *thematic fluctuation,* when a system structures itself out of a chaotic mix of interactions. Subsequent to this catastrophe, the complementary process of reclosing individual boundaries consolidates this spontaneously generated structure and sets a new perspective and direction in each of the former participants of the open encounter.

The fluctuation process just described—where boundaries, hierarchical levels, and even identities fluctuate wildly—may seem strange, but we are faced with the problem of accounting for the paradox of controlled openness. At the human level we have the phenomenon of the emotional encounter where we seem to lose both control and awareness, and fall into a dynamic fluctuation process in which individual identity structures are temporarily opened up to the group structure at the next higher hierarchical level. This opening-based process of dynamic interaction necessarily involves a shift in hierarchy levels of the living structure. It is only through a jump in levels that a true restructuring can take place. The jump is reversible, in fact inevitable, for every opening closes of itself and without external cause.

The complementary pair of control configurations, linear and nonlinear, is general across all levels of the hierarchy of living structure. To establish this generality, a complementary pair of concepts will be introduced, *summing* and *systeming.* Summing is linear, information-based, closed boundary contact between living wholes, while systeming is metabolic, open boundary contact between living wholes. Summing between living structures is reciprocal—two one-way streets; systeming between living structures is mutual—one two-way street.

Summing is assimiliative in that the exchange of influence, by passing through boundaries, transforms action into messages that are encoded in the sender's terms, but decoded in the receiver's terms. Systeming is accommodative, because in opening to each other the participants mutually transform their structures in a metabolic, that is, matter/energy, process. Thus, the function of summing is the preservation or consolidation of individual structure, while the function of systeming is the transformation, that is, destructuring and restructuring, of individual structure. Summing and systeming themselves sum together. They operate together as a linear mixture, like salt and pepper, rather than in a nonlinear compound, like sodium and chloride.

A linear feedback control configuration within a single individual can now be seen more clearly as self-summing, or rather a summing situation between two or more substructures within an individual. Because boundaries are not broken nor structures transformed, summing between individuals and within individuals is isomorphic. On the other hand, since "boundaries" are opened in systeming, there is necessarily a hierarchical jump or catastrophe between levels. The individuals who open to each other vanish and the superordinate boundary that encompasses the flow between them becomes the new higher level individual within which mutual transformations take place in the process of dynamic interaction. Autonomous change, then, must be seen structurally as a dual process of open transformation and closed consolidation of structure. Opening is an autonomously controlled event, but the dynamic interaction resulting from the opening event cannot be controlled. The transformation process of psychotherapy involves an opening process experienced as an emotional encounter among people. Some or all of the members of the group become one with each other in emotional openness, and a transformation takes place in the heat of encounters which must subsequently be defined, that is bounded, so that their lessons can be applied outside of the therapy room. We will see in my therapy chapter (Chapter 13) that the prescription for the group leader—"be open to opening and closed to closing"—can be expressed in terms of summing and systeming.

Boundarying Operations Generate the Structure of Autonomy

The fourth and foremost foundational idea is that of boundarying. The boundarying operation may be defined as the dialectical process whereby living structure opens/closes itself. The typographical slash (/) represents a complementarity of structure which will be explained below. Opening/closing is a pair of primordial events which, because there simply are not any deeper level concepts in terms of which to define them, must stand as undefined terms within this conceptual scheme. We can say only that in living structure opening *is* and closing *is*. We can say what sorts of external events are caused by opening/closing, but we cannot say what causes opening/closing because it causes itself, even though some external event might well be the occasion for it to do so, or some internal process might be recruited as an instrument for carrying out such a boundarying event. Autonomous living structure is responsible to external events, for autonomy is ultimately responsible for what it does, but autonomous events are not caused by other external events in the sense of causality, which stands as the cornerstone of the paradigm of objectivity.

The other three foundational ideas lying at the basis of the phenomenon of living structure and the paradigm of autonomy are derivatives of the boundarying operation. The complementarity of action structure and language structure—of law-guided and rule-guided behavior respectively—has its basis in the horizontal, dialectical alternation of opening and closing as the inherent autonomous activity of boundarying. The "vertical dialectic" process of moving up and down the hierarchical levels of living structure has its basis in the boundarying operation, in that restructuring at a higher level is essentially closing a whole around a set of parts, and restructuring at a lower level is essentially opening the whole to liberate the parts from their constraints. Finally, the achievement of self-referential control configurations is boundarying-based, with linear feedback developing out of the interplay of closed self-descriptions at two hierarchical levels, and dynamic interaction developing out of the opening of wholes to each other.

The language and logic of objectivity are not competent to describe the phenomenon of autonomy as operationalized in boundarying. Objectivity rests passively in dichotomies, while autonomy pulsates actively through complementarities. Objectivity focuses on one level at a time while autonomy perambulates freely up and down hierarchies of parts and wholes. Objectivity cleanly separates the observer from the observed, while autonomy observes itself in the observation. Boundarying simply cannot be described as a living process in the language of objectivity. There is no "it" sitting out there in objective space that has appeared as a result of a closing event called "boundary." There is no "it" sitting out there in objective space that has appeared as a result of an opening event called "flow." If there were such objects, we could represent autonomous living structure as a set of concentric and eccentric circles (the boundaries) enclosing and dividing areas of space (the flow). But such a representation could not capture the active complementarity, self-hierarchicalization, and self-referential control configurations in action, even though they are all essential embodiments of the boundarying idea. The best that can be done with objective language is to speak about opening and closing events and the various boundarying configurations and, in doing so, attempt to expand the self-consciousness of the language to fit the new data.

Another path to the development of a descriptive language for autonomy leads through logic. A logic is an explicit formalization of the implicit foundational ideas of a paradigm (Günther, 1962). A rigorous logic for the paradigm of autonomy has been presented by G. Spenser Brown in his seminal book, *Laws of Form* (1972), and developed by Francisco Varela (1975, 1978). Brown, descending to levels deeper than that of the true-false logic of objectivity, focuses upon the primordial act of *indication,* that is, the act of designating mere presence or absence, whether that which is indicated is true or false. The single logical operator of the system, a distinctor, is signified with a mark "⌐ ." The two basic states or values of indication are 1) the marked state also indicated by "⌐ " and 2) the unmarked state signified by a blank "   ." With the two states of the form, the single operator and two axioms, Brown constructs an arithmetic and a calculus of indication which represent all four of the new foundational ideas of autonomy within their scope. In fact, the metaparadigmatic act of drawing a distinction, together with its complement of removing a distinction, is isomorphic to the boundarying operation that plays such a central role in our model of living structure.

Brown's indicational logic provides rules of concatenation through which complex hierarchical structures can be represented and operated on to build up or to simplify hierarchical levels. Self-referential structures are as intrinsic to Brown's logic as they are anomalous for classical true-false logic. At the level of indication, a self-referential configuration merely reenters its own indicative space. Brown demonstrates that such reentering structures have the logical characteristic of bi-stability; that is, they autonomously pulsate back and forth between the marked (bounded, closed) and unmarked (unbounded, open) states. He interprets this active, logical alternation as the process of time. In this chapter we interpret this bi-stability as life.

Varela (1975, 1978) has followed up on Brown and cleaned up several bugs in Brown's system. At one point, it seemed appropriate to Varela to add a third fundamental state to the marked and unmarked states: a self-referential state which indicates itself, that is, indicates indication. Since this state can be interpreted as moving back and forth dialectically between open and closed, he calls it the *autonomous state* and signifies it with "⌊⌋ ."

The Brown-Varela logic of indications provides a formal language, both for the description of the action of living structure in describing and transforming (boundarying) itself, and for a description of the language of living structure by means of which living structure describes its own action. The primary canon of objectivity is that the properties of the observer shall not enter into the observer's description of the properties of the observed (von Foerster & Howe, 1975). Since the logic of autonomy indicates indication, describes description, defines definition, observes observation, and delineates the boundaries of boundarying (all equivalent assertions), the primary canon of both the paradigm of autonomy and the Brown-Varela logic of indications, which stands as the language structure of that paradigm, is that the properties of the observer shall be revealed by what the observer chooses to observe. To quote Varela:

The starting point of this calculus following the key line of the calculus of indications, is the act of indication. In this primordial act we separate forms which appear to us as the world itself. From this starting point we thus assert the primacy of the role of the observer who draws distinctions wherever he pleases. Thus the distinctions made which engender our world reveal precisely that: the distinctions we make—and these distinctions pertain more to the revelation of where the observer stands than to an intrinsic constitution of the world which appears, by this very mechanism of separation between observer and observed, always elusive. . . . Autonomy is seen in this light to *engender* the two stages of the form [opening/closing—Ed.] when this ceaseless process is broken into its constituents. By the introduction of a third autonomous state into the form, we do nothing but restore to view that which was there at the beginning, and which we can only see now reflected as segments of the world [action structure—*Ed.*] or in language itself (1975, p. 23).

By giving us an indication of boundarying as an autonomous pulsating cycle (Whyte et al., 1969) of opening/closing events, marked/unmarked events, or observer/observed events, the Brown-Varela logic frees us from the paradoxes imposed by the limitations of the paradigm of objectivity when dealing with autonomous living structure.

Let us reflect upon the primitive autonomous events of opening/closing. *Autonomous living structure closes itself.* Such closing events are acts of drawing a distinction between the inside of oneself and the outside of oneself. Living acts of closing are language acts in the most general sense—acts of observing, measuring, and naming oneself—as distinct from the environment created by that closing act of distinction. Closing oneself is a rule-making event that creates information, but which does not in and of itself alter the matter/energy on either side of the distinction. Closing oneself often engenders boundary objects, such as the skin of an organism, the walls of a group room, or a city-limits sign, which are in general called "boundaries." But living boundaries are made of information and are encoded, not embodied. The material products of closing a "boundary" are no more living than the surface of a stone or a lake.

Our first foundational idea asserts that living structure exhibits two complementary structures: a physical action structure and a language structure. These dual structures stand in a complementarity relationship and require two alternative descriptions. The language act is achieved by a closing event. Living structure encodes a description of itself by drawing a boundary around itself which defines itself. The act of definition is self-referential in that it refers to both the action structure it describes and the action of its own describing process. The closing act also makes a hierarchical jump because the description is on another level than the action it describes. Within a human group, interactions among individual members reach a critical point of intimacy, at which point the members open to each other and define themselves as a group. This alternative description of the individuals as a group can then function as a rule for various self-regulatory functions. As a language structure rule, the closing act functions to stabilize the living structure until its complementary opening process unbounds it.

Autonomous living structure opens itself. Such opening events are acts of dissolving boundary distinction between what is inside and what is outside oneself or between formerly distinct parts of oneself. Defining opening is a paradoxical act because, as indicated above, the act of defining is a closing act. Defining opening entails making an "it" out of it and giving it a name. If we named the "it" of opening and the "it" of closing, we would call them "flow" and "boundary." But we have argued that the visible physical boundaries are only the by-products of the informational rule that constitutes the living act of closing. To conceive of flow as a "thing" standing between boundaries within "things" called living structures is as misleading as conceiving of boundary as a "thing" standing between flows. Such a view would make objects of both, would lose sight of their complementarity, hierarchy and self-reference properties and, in short, remove their autonomous life. There must be another approach to describing opening.

Although somewhat unorthodox, the notion of boundary closing as an informational act is appealing because it unites the world of matter/energy, which is necessary but not sufficient to life, with the world of information, which is also necessary but not sufficient to life. We know that closing "boundaries" is negentropic, that is, it creates more improbable and more complex structures in the world. We might argue that opening is an entropic act in that it dissolves structure. This implies that only closing is a living function and that opening is a property of the non-living substrate, the dull clay out of which life springs. But the essence of our argument is that boundarying is the basic operation of living autonomy and that boundarying is dually defined as complementary opening/closing. The symmetry of opening/closing must be preserved. To preserve this symmetry, opening—though an act of self-simplifying and structure-dissolving—must be defined as a living act in its own right.

Boundaries are made of information. Information is measured in units called bits, which is short for binary digits. Thus, a bit of information is created when a single boundary distinction is drawn to separate a whole into two parts. Information is a dimensionless quantity and, therefore, is incapable of being physically represented at some particular location in time and space. Consequently, no one has ever seen a bit, nor has anyone ever seen a boundary. What we see all around us is not in the rule-structure domain of informational boundaries, but the action-structure embodiment of the autonomous act of boundarying.

From the perspective of the paradigm of objectivity, information is a property of "the world out there," naturally occurring boundary distinctions which we as subjects simply name and measure. These boundaries exist only because we, for the moment, do not. This bi-stability between subjective and objective, between knower and known, leads to paradox when viewed objectively (see page 32). From the perspective of the paradigm of autonomy, however, this paradox of fluctuating opening/closing is the central starting point. The world of autonomy begins with a Brownian act of drawing a distinction and then dissolving it in endless logical dance. The primary reality defined by the paradigm of autonomy, then, is not what is bounded or unbounded, but the boundarying process itself.

The fundamental idea of creating structure by closing informational boundaries around oneself, within oneself, or upon one's environment sets easy on practical, progress-oriented Western eyes. However, the symmetrical idea of an active opening, self-simplifying, or destructuring process, where boundary distinctions that once seemed important become less important, is difficult for us to even countenance. This goes against the grain of objectivity in the same way as the idea of an invisible or virtual Tao which manifests itself only in the embodiment of a ceaseless alternation between the Yin/Yang complementarity. Boundarying and Tao are isomorphic.

When applied to autonomous living structure which boundaries itself, the symmetry of opening/closing must be preserved by expanding the concept of information to include both primordial events. I would like to interpret the act of opening oneself as a process wherein *negative information* is autonomously created. Negative information is not entropy as it appears to be from the objective perspective, even though boundary distinctions are dissolved in both the living act of opening and the non-living process of entropy production. Autonomous opening is an active creation of negative information. In what units can this generalized negative information be measured? In the domain of electricity, resistance is measured in ohms; its inverse, called admittance, is measured in ''mhos.'' I would like to define the unit of negative information created when a single boundary is opened a *t-i-b*. A new particle has been discovered, or, to be more autonomous about it, created. At the cost of multiplying entities against the prescription of Occam's famous razor, the symmetry of the primitive complementary constituents of the boundarying operation is now preserved. On the other hand, the symmetry between information and entropy is now restricted to the objective measurement categories used before Spenser Brown and Heisenberg when the observer was not yet construed as part of the observation.

How shall we interpret the act of ''tibbing''? A number of processes that were not readily accepted as part of the domain of positive information can now be integrated into the extended bit-tib domain. In the West we assume that the process of learning is limited to creating internal boundary structures, while Oriental wisdom sees the process of meditation as one of learning by emptying. Such disciplined self-simplification is a process of tibbing. I would also assert that acts of feeling, both within and between people, are boundary-dissolving acts of autonomy which create tibs. Let me hasten to point out that we usually indulge our cognitive biases by equating feeling with the cognitive boundaries with which we label our feeling experiences, in order to store and evaluate them. But while we are experiencing the self-transforming processes of loving, fearing, angering, or paining we don't deliberate over which of these labels to apply to our experience; that would be creating bits of self-description rather than tibs of self-transformation. If we are correct in describing feeling as an opening event creating tibs, we must learn to see feeling, not as an objective process where a thing called a feeling moves through a stable person, but as a self-transformation process where we move through the path of feeling to which we open ourselves.

The complete formalism of autonomous information theory has not yet been worked out. Such an exercise would certainly bring forth some interesting and possibly unexpected results. For example, in positive information theory the quantity (T) is defined as the amount of information actually transmitted after correcting for what was in the sender and receiver before the transmission occurred. What would be the equivalent concept in negative information? It would be the exact measure of the boundary-dissolving the sender and receiver caused in one another. The concept of systeming described elsewhere in this discussion is probably isomorphic to the concept of $(-T)$. The development, interpretation, and application of this extended positive/negative information theory as a formalism for describing boundarying should prove a fruitful methodological aid for investigating autonomous living structure.

Summary and Conclusions

Our investigation of the structure of autonomy manifested by the range of living forms from cell to society has converged upon the boundarying operation, the operation whereby living structure opens/closes itself as a complementarity in dialectical fluctuation. It is through the boundarying operation that autonomous living structure generates, maintains, evolves and ultimately dissolves its own structure and thus achieves the basic life functions of wholeness, self-regulation and progressive self-transformation. Boundarying autonomously describes itself in such language structures as the Spenser Brown/Varela logic of indications, the genetic codes, and, of course, in the living structure of this presentation to you the reader. These living processes and others like them in which the autonomy of life manifests itself can be described only in self-referential terms. The fundamental proposition that autonomy causes itself is considered an ill-formed or paradoxical statement within the framework of the currently orthodox paradigm of objectivity. The introduction of a wider paradigm within which the phenomenon of autonomous living structure can be scientifically predicted, controlled and understood has been the principal intent of this chapter. This model of the structure of autonomy has its roots in the GST model of LvB and develops organically, autonomously out of it.

Part II

Some Systems Concepts
Applied to Group Psychotherapy

Chapter 3

Human Communication
and Group Experience

By Glenn Swogger, Jr., M.D.

Editor's Introduction. This chapter is presented in two main sections. The first deals with information-processing within groups and shared patterns of communication. The second focuses upon the personal involvement of the therapist in the group.

Dr. Swogger's thoughts regarding group communication are based on the premise that groups develop as they come to create and comprehend their own shared patterns of communication. As information-processing is utilized by group members to develop states of conditional readiness to respond, group stability grows by building up a common set of such states which structures future interactions. As patterns of communication change, the structure of the group transforms itself.

The second part of the chapter deals with an expanded attitude of psychotherapists which calls our attention to the similarities between therapists and patients rather than focusing on the patients' pathological behavior symptoms. Instead of a one-way casual relationship where the therapist affects the patients, the author proposes a mutual process of discovery where the patient and therapist influence and touch each other. The interaction between the two works at the unconscious as well as the conscious level, rather than on a constantly rational cognitive plane.

In this chapter we see the embodiments of a number of GST principles. Both in the first section where information-processing leads to structuring interactions and in the second section where the therapist's use of self is increased, we witness living structures transforming themselves therapeutically. Furthermore, we see exemplified the isomorphy between the personal world of the therapist and the ongoing issues and events in the group. Finally, a good example of the GST proposition of complementarity is seen in the way that the cognitive and intuitive modes dealt with in the two parts of the paper mutually enrich each other.

The value of systems concepts for group therapists is in providing us with a more comprehensive and accurate map of the terrain of group experience. The map directs our attention to the pattern of communication in a group, which forms its structure as a living system. Realizing that each group is a whole in which the members are parts enables us to understand the impact of the group on individuals, the nature of group transformation, and the role of the therapist's person in the group. These are the issues which I wish to discuss briefly in this contribution to a general systems approach to group therapy.

THE ISOMORPHISM BETWEEN PERSONAL AND INTERPERSONAL INFORMATION-PROCESSING

One way of developing a systems approach to groups begins with a concept of human communication—the individual as an information-processing system. We process information which comes from outside our skins—stimulus is an inadequate term, because it implies passive reception. We select and transform parts of the outer world into our own codes of information. The shape or form of a message—be it a gesture, a word, an odor, or whatever—is used as we transform it internally into other codes of information. We also use what happens inside our skins—changes in our own posture and muscle tension, "gut" changes mediated by the autonomic and related nervous centers, hormonal changes, and an awareness of our own information-transforming processes such as in dreams or biofeedback. These "happenings" inside us are transformed and recoded in more than one way as we become aware of them, verbalize them, picture them, feel them, secrete specific hormones, and so forth.

The information-processing concept of personality changes our picture of the person from that of an organism *reacting* to stimuli with behavior to a person *acting* on the environment to select and capture messages and create new internal structure. People may take in messages which change them but do not immediately change their behavior. For example, you may act on my messages to you by some observable behavior—you may shout "Eureka!" or you may leave the room or you may fidget. Or you may do something internally, which involves classifying, recoding, comparing, and creating new inner dimensions, so that you change yourself in such a way that you behave differently in the future when you confront a given message or situation. These inner states which lead to changes in future behavior may be called *states of conditional readiness* for behavior—"What I will do *if* "—if I get a certain message or am in a certain situation. All of us have a repertoire of states of conditional readiness for behavior. For example, we enter a new group with many possible ways of relating to the group and its individual members available to us. Furthermore, our repertoire is not completely fixed. We can modify and recombine old modes of relating and develop new ones on the basis of experience. But we usually begin in new situations by falling back on our tried and true previous styles of behavior.

With this picture of persons as communications systems, capable of a variety of alternate modes of relating to others, let us try to conceptualize a group as a system. A group is obviously more than a collection of people in the same room. And the members of even the most cohesive group will often be separated from each other, and will most likely be members of other groups as well. Groups show varying degrees of stability, distinctive patterning of relationships, clarity of boundaries, and other characteristics. We can describe these phenomena in systems terms if we accept the definition of a system as a set of elements whose states or behaviors are in some way interrelated or interdependent. If the communicative behavior or even the mere presence of others makes a difference to you in some way, which leads to reciprocal behavior on your part which influences them, then in a rudimentary way you constitute a group. This broad definition of the system properties of a group makes it clear that there are degrees of relatedness or systemness, and helps to prevent us from thinking of a reified concept of "the group" as a single entity with a single set of properties. It also allows us to define an important dimension of groups—the degree to which patterns of communication or relatedness are confused, chaotic, ambiguous, and transient, at one end of the spectrum, or clear, coherent, purposeful, and stable at the other. Groups of individuals become a system, and distinguish themselves from other groups, as they develop a distinctive pattern of communication—in other words, a shared pattern of relatedness, a set of norms.

This shared pattern of relatedness is a distinctive, unique pattern of communication, with its own jargon, taboos, etc. (It is impressive how even a brief experiential group quickly develops words with special meanings, preferred modes of speech, norms, etc. Such shared, distinctive communicative experience is the germ of the development of widely different groups and cultures, as well as language differentiation.)

The shared pattern of communication represents the degree and manner in which individuals have united to form a larger unit—a group. Viewed from this perspective, a group can be observed and its patterns of communication and their transformation described. To take a very tiny segment of interaction as an example, suppose that in a therapy group Member A looks at the leader and says he has a stomachache, whereupon Member B looks at his watch and says he has to leave the meeting early. One can make a number of speculations about this sequence, but if one focuses on the group communication system rather than the individuals, then instead of commenting about the meaning of A's stomachache or B's having to leave, one could observe the apparent discontinuity between A's and B's comments and explore that. If, instead, B followed A's comments with a description to the therapist of his headache, one could observe not only the discontinuity between A and B, but also begin to infer a shared norm: "We will compete to be cured by the leader."

Another example illustrates a change in the group pattern of communication and how it occurred. It involved an inpatient group on a hospital admission unit, led by two male co-therapists, one a psychiatrist who worked on the unit (the author), and the other a senior social worker.

In the first of the two group sessions reported here, the patients were passive and their activity was oriented toward asking questions of the two therapists. To the psychiatrist they often posed medical questions, to the social worker questions about family or life problems. The leaders tended to respond by answering the questions and somewhat uncomfortably but feebly trying to shift the focus away from this pattern. There was a sense of discontinuity in the process of the group as one or another type of question was asked to one or another of the group leaders. In a rehash meeting after this session, the co-therapists began by expressing their dissatisfaction with the way the session had gone and with the patients, but gradually shifted to their own competitiveness with each other, their feelings of being put down and one-upped by the other both inside and outside of the group situations, their anger at each other and their competition for the allegiance of the nursing staff and other staff members who were involved in the group therapy program. They became uncomfortably aware of how much the behavior of the group was dictated by their own struggle. They then tried to decide how to intervene in this process. It was agreed that the best solution lay in openly discussing their competition and their feelings about this with the patients, so that it could no longer function as a covert structuring element for the group and so that in the process the structure of the group might be changed.

The next session began much the same. After again pointing out the passivity and leader-directedness of the patients (the group had been confronted with this before without effect), the therapists turned to each other and began to discuss their conclusions about what they had been doing and their feelings about this. They talked of their need to be loved and admired by the patients, their feelings of competitiveness and rivalry, the ways that these were reinforced by their different professional backgrounds and institutional roles, and the ways that this led them to interact by answering the questions in their "specialty." As they did this, they began to experience an increased sense of activity, aliveness and significance about what was happening in the group. Their comments complemented and supplemented each other rather than being on separate tracks. The therapists experienced feelings of embarrassment, but also some laughter at the predicament that they found themselves in, and a sense of relief at having broken through it. The patients listened to this, at first shyly, and then with some confirmation of what had been happening from their own observations. They gradually became more active. In part, this took the form of their feeling free to express directly their own feelings and observations about each of the leaders, positive and negative. They felt freed of the constraint to have to preserve a neutral attitude toward the therapists in the fact of their struggle, and could say that they liked or disliked certain things about one or the other therapist in particular. Without any effort at interpretation or structuring on the part of the leader, this shifted to reactions toward parents and parental conflict. The whole atmosphere of the group was much more one of sharing and activity than had previously been the case.

In the first session, the flow of communication had been patient-therapist, along certain rigid lines. Later, this flow became more open and flexible. Thus, change in the group, i.e., transformation of the structure of the group, occurs with change in the pattern of communication. This is because the pattern of communication *is* the structure in the group. This pattern is partially determined by *whom* people talk to in the group. It is also influenced by *how* people communicate together in the group. This *how* can include not only what sort of behavior is the predominant channel of communication, i.e., verbal, nonverbal, etc., but also the constraints or rules or grammar of communication. For example, in the stage before the transformation, the rules were related to roles, namely the doctor/patient role. Personal experiences were cast in the form of questions and symptoms. After the transformation, the grammar of communication was one of sharing of experience—relatively less cast in terms of role relationships and seen as valid in its own light and in its own terms. Accompanying this was a heightened sense of arousal, involvement and feelings of significance. In other words, the emotional or nonlinguistic modes of communication were more actively involved.

In this instance the transformation was initiated by the therapists, but this is not always the case. It was the case in this instance because the fact that the two senior therapists/consultants were actually together in the group, rather than having alternate roles as they usually did, made them more aware of the conflict (or had they scheduled themselves to be together because they were ready to deal with the conflict?). Immediate feelings which led to the transformation in the therapists' behavior had to do with their sense of unhappiness and dissatisfaction about what was going on in the group.

This example also illustrates that rules and patterns of communication create boundaries—they make certain issues and subjects acceptable or taboo. Although the therapists had verbally presented the problem to the group in terms of the content of the problem, namely, "You are too passive and we are always answering questions," a transformation could not occur until they broke the old rules of communication in the group and reformulated a new set of rules, initiating this new set by practicing it themselves. The old rules of communication in the group had acted as a boundary which effectively kept out certain types of communication and experience from the process of the group.

To generalize: One can imagine groups as dealing with a whole variety of inputs from many sources and via many channels—events in previous meetings, the state of the individual members, the state of the institutional or cultural suprasystem, etc. Some of these inputs are present before a group meets, others develop during a meeting, others are unknown to some members. How the group processes these inputs can be observed. This processing may range from primitive and rigid to rich, warm, sophisticated, and creative. The output depends on the goals of the group, linked, of course, to the nature of its information-processing code. The output may involve the performance of a work group, the reflexive development of knowledge about the group itself, or whatever. No actual group is characterized by one pattern of communication—there are competing and conflicting modes of functioning, and groups can be observed to vary in terms of how well or consistently they deal appropriately with their tasks.

The concept of groups as having degrees of systemness or ordered relatedness is of value in understanding the reactions of individuals as they enter or form a new group. Bion (1959) and others have described primitive anxiety-laden reactions to the group situation. These reactions appear to be maximized by the ambiguity and lack of structure of a new group, and to be relieved by the development or successful imposition of structured patterns of communication within the group. In other words, these primitive anxieties appear to be aroused by the lack of systemness of the group. I would like to suggest an explanation for this phenomena, based on a contrast between group and dyadic relationships and some characteristics of human information-processing. In a dyadic relationship, the individual has a relatively greater sense of conviction, even if illusory, of being able to control and influence the other, of some equality—of being able to grasp, hold, fight, have sex with, or in other ways physically interact with, another person. This conviction is also fostered by the reality that it is possible to receive all communication channels from one person, e.g., sound, sight, smell, touch, etc. (even if one cannot describe or articulate all that is perceived). Also, one can maintain ongoing, relatively uninterrupted and coherent communication loops (e.g., a conversation, a dance). All this is grounded in the experience of early parent-child relationships, as well as in sexual and aggressive acts and fantasies. The possibilities for real control via communication in various channels are greater. In contrast, in a group situation it is more difficult to maintain the illusion of control over the other persons and over information input, because 1) the group exists independently of the individual and will continue to exist even if he or she leaves, unlike the dyad; 2) the rest of the group is usually physically stronger than a given individual and can't so easily be grasped and held, etc.; 3) the individual cannot simultaneously have a dyadic relationship with all; 4) there is chronic input overload—the individual cannot simultaneously pay attention to all other members and channels of communication. In this connection it is important to note that information-processing in the human brain, at least in its more conscious and verbalized aspects, appears to deal with inputs serially rather than simultaneously; 5) there are more possibilities for disorganization in a group, i.e., more individuals who can manifest unpredictable or unwanted behavior, to say nothing of the possibilities for irrational behavior by the whole group.

Some of the work of Harold Schroder (1973) and his associates is relevant here. They found in experimental teams given a task with varying degrees of complexity of information input that, as the input load increased, the teams performed their task with ever greater degrees of skill and sophistication. After a certain point is reached, however, further increases in information load result in a reversion to more primitive and stereotyped modes of thought. What I am suggesting, in contrast to Schroder's work, where the variable is the increasing complexity of an assigned task, is that in small groups generally, but particularly in new, unstructured groups, the input from the group itself can constitute an overload.

Primary among the feelings induced in the individual in an unstructured group situation are feelings of helplessness, passivity, subordination, neediness, fearfulness, and lack of control. Also present are concerns about being looked at, exposed, judged, and attacked. The individual feels in the presence of something larger. Along with the fears, the group as a powerful and independent unit can elicit hopes of succor and strength, and a wish to belong. There is also in the perception of the inevitable (greater or lesser) disorganization of the group a fear of chaos and uncertainty as to purpose and task, a sense of arbitrariness. In terms of the life experiences of group members, one can say that the realities of the group situation duplicate certain aspects of the infant's relation to the mother and may therefore induce regression in individuals.

Consider these feelings in terms of the communicative behaviors which lead to the development of the group as a system. If we imagine a new group, we might imagine X individuals attempting in X different ways to relate to each other—a psychological Tower of Babel. However, from the moment of meeting, intense and multiple attempts at coupling into larger systems are being made. In the case of therapy groups, we know this happens in waiting rooms and even in fantasies of prospective members before meeting. The attempts to relate to the group may involve a variety of *primitive control behaviors*. By this I mean maladaptive, inappropriate attempts by an individual to control information input, processing, and output, and to influence the communication patterns of other individuals in the group to the same end. The concept of primitive control behaviors might be clarified by listing a few examples, with no attempt at completeness. Silence, or blandness, or conventionality reduces output and often is also an attempt to reduce feedback or input. This usually requires relatively little change in the behavior of others, as long as they are sufficiently inattentive. Other forms of primitive control behavior require more of a joint effort. There may be demands for conformity, for the avoidance of difficult or upsetting topics, to reduce input overload. This may be accompanied by attempts to hamper the development of the group, or to weaken others in order to control their output, attacking strengths and competence.

Many of the types of primitive control behavior involve a denial of group realities and a substitution of illusions of dyadic relationships. Thus, we have the paradox that certain kinds of phenomena traditionally called group-as-a-whole phenomena are actually attempts to deny the reality of the group as a whole. Here may be included attempts to focus the entire group on oneself, so that the effective unit is dyadic; a group that is collectively bent on this approach does a lot of advice-giving. Similarly, scapegoating is an attempt to simplify complex problems into a good-versus-bad-one-to-one relation: "If it weren't for him. . .". Attempts to foster some sort of magical group unity also betray a wish to relive a dyadic fusion. The simplification of information-processing in these situations is often manifested by redundant chants, slogans, and other stereotyped behaviors. That group leaders are often central figures in attempts to recreate the group as a dyad is not surprising in view of their special role and association with parental figures.

In an ambiguous group situation where individuals cannot "lock in" to an ongoing dyadic communications loop and be guided by it, each person is thrown back on his or her own inner models of relating to others. This reveals the person's internalized object relations, in the terminology of the object-relations school—which is equivalent to the repertoire of states of conditional readiness. This phenomenon is the basis for part of the diagnostic and therapeutic usefulness of groups. We "become ourselves," with deep and far-reaching consequences, in groups, and we also defend desperately against that process.

Success in our efforts to become related to each other in groups depends on our common humanity: My internal world of remembered and meaningful relationships with others is crystallized into a conditional readiness to respond to you. Thus we recreate past internalized relationships in current ones. This structural correspondence between one system level (intrapsychic) and another (group, interpersonal) is referred to in systems terms as isomorphy. However, the processes by which isomorphic relationships are negotiated and transacted are complex and constitute much of the process of the group. Sometimes harmony prevails and we agree that "I'll let you be in my dream if I can be in yours"; often, though, we experience a feeling of pressure or suction to fulfill roles subtly demanded by other group members or even the whole group (scapegoating). We have the experience of being "hooked" (TA) or manipulated by someone else's fantasies (Bion, 1959). Horwitz (1978) has discussed these processes in detail, using the concept of projective identification. The isomorphic "fit" or "mismatch" between each member and the group is a reverberating, dynamic process which allows individuals to change internally through participation in the group process.

THE ISOMORPHISM BETWEEN THE FLOW OF FEELING WITHIN THE THERAPIST AND WITHIN THE GROUP

The systems approach to groups here described has important consequences for the group therapist or consultant. Just as there is isomorphy between individual members and group, so there is an isomorphy between the inner world of the therapist's experience and the events in the group, an isomorphy which has practical consequences for the therapist. The therapist is viewed as much more inside the group and a part of the group system than previously. This change of perspective has many roots. Our society has witnessed a rebellion against impersonal technical knowledge. In contrast to the emphasis on objectivity in the past, which increased the distance between the knower and the known and required that the knower remain anonymous, we now demand that all knowledge be accompanied by a personal signature. We do not see the observer as distinct from what is observed, and we ask of the scientist, "Where are you at?" We now understand that objectivity has often involved excluding parts of ourselves that were essential to the process of knowing.

However, this shift has not been without its problems. At times we seem to accept the personal and authentic uncritically. We lapse into a placid tolerance of different viewpoints, rather than using self-knowledge for the purpose of critically comparing our biases and perspectives with others. We thus lose the opportunity for integration and synthesis of viewpoints and the development of a more holistic view of reality. In the field of therapy, this intellectual trend has provided the basis for charismatic leaders, with great needs for power and adulation, and corresponding harmful effects on their followers.

The implications of a systems approach to groups for the group leader can best be clarified by examining the psychoanalytic concepts of transference and countertransference. A change has gradually occurred in these concepts which has clinical implications. Just as resistance and transference were first seen as hindrances which needed to be gotten rid of or circumvented, and later seen as major—and inevitable and necessary—components of the treatment process, so countertransference has undergone the same evolution.

The term countertransference traditionally has been used in two senses. Originally, it referred specifically to the effect of the patient's transference on the therapist, stirring up unconscious conflicts in the therapist which arose from the therapist's unresolved infantile conflicts and fixations. Later, countertransference was broadened to all feelings and reactions of the therapist to the patient. Here I will refer to the "use of self" instead of countertransference in the broader sense, because the original definition of countertransference gives the term a connotation of pathology that I wish to avoid. The "use of self" is more neutral and leaves open the question of whether in a given instance the self is used therapeutically or not. Sometimes our focus on self-examination and pathology leaves our patients with little sense of what normal emotions are like. We have a concept of adaptation—of normal functioning—which we model as therapists. Do we model what normal passions are like? Our fears of recognizing our similarities to our patients can lead to a subtle scapegoating of the patient, with the therapist taking a superego role. Avoidance of normal emotionality and a realistic use of self-revelation reinforces an unconscious identification with the patient which can have harmful consequences.

The basic shift in the paradigm of the therapist's relationship to individual patients, or to the group, is from a linear concept—A causes B which causes C, with the therapist unilaterally acting on the group—to a systems concept, which sees A, B, and C as mutually influencing each other. For our purposes, this involves paying some attention to the influence of the group and its members on the therapist.

In trying to describe the significance of this paradigm shift for the therapist, I always think of the Charles Schultz cartoon in which Charlie Brown is asked, "Do you ever get in over your head?" Charlie pauses, then answers, "When I get up in the morning, I'm in over my head." From the moment a group begins, therapists are "in over their heads"—faced with the input overload of the group and the impossibility of processing this input consciously and verbally, with the "head." They are caught up in the process of the group, unable to act unilaterally, as much influenced as influencing. The therapist, along with other group members, is swimming in a sea of human communication. This sea includes multiple codes and channels, interrelated hierarchically. The therapist is faced with the same task as the other members of the group—how to integrate this experience in the service of the therapeutic task of the group. The role of the therapist thus shifts from seeing oneself as performing operations on the group to participating in a mutual process of discovery and description of the experience of the group, the formation of human relations in the group, and the use of experience and involvement in furthering the task of the group.

How do we as therapists integrate what we perceive? I would suggest that a significant portion of these data are nonverbal, i.e., behavioral, and that the processes of perception and integration of these data are largely unconscious (in a descriptive, not necessarily a dynamic, sense). For us to use these data, we must temporarily dispense with our objective, verbal consciousness, and allow ourselves to be receptive, influenced by the processes occurring in the group. We must enter a meditative state, aware of the spontaneous processes going on within us which organize our experience of the group. What happens in the group as a whole, as well as its members individually, is transformed into an isomorphic set of happenings within us. Our first awareness of group process phenomena often takes the form of a vague, hard-to-verbalize feeling state, to which we must attend. These inner happenings are not necessarily identical to the group process, but they are always meaningfully related. The therapist must have an attitude of patience and self-acceptance and be able to tolerate uncertainty, in order to allow time for this spontaneous inner organizing process to occur.

Here is a brief clinical example: A group appeared to be functioning well. The members were open about their feelings and took initiative in tackling problems themselves. During the session, my initial pleasure gradually faded and I became aware at first of a feeling of restlessness and irritation. After several exploratory questions got nowhere, I told the group that I felt excluded. At first the members joked that I was the patient, and then revealed some of their suspicious and counterdependent attitudes towards me which had been excluded by the initial pattern of communication.

Freud (1957) emphasized the importance of the therapist entering this state of "evenly suspended attention." He saw this as allowing the therapist's unconscious to tune into the patient's. He described how the therapist must banish from his mind therapeutic goals and preconceived ideas about the patient's behavior.

The similarity of this state to that described in meditation is striking: the admonition to shift the focus from the ego, to give up desire and activity, to give up focus on the self. However, the therapist's meditative state is not narrowed to a few internal stimuli (e.g., breathing), but remains spread over a wider range. Robert Ornstein's (1972) work on the psychology of consciousness is helpful in relating the concept of meditation to the evenly suspended attention of the therapist and his use of his own inner states. Ornstein sees meditative states as attending to the right hemisphere functions of the brain: spatial rather than verbal, nonlinear, simultaneous rather than sequential events, dealing with holistic, organized patterns of relationship. These mental functions and the meditative state would be most appropriate for picking up and integrating the complex, multichannel, organized patterns of communicative behavior of a group.

It has been pointed out that the translation of right brain modes of thought into the verbal mode corresponds to the psychoanalytic picture of the process of making unconscious material conscious. This approach suggests that in some sense *feelings* are *perceptions*, even if they are derivatives that are distorted by many other influences. Paula Heimann (1950) puts this very neatly when she says, "Our basic assumption is that the analyst's unconscious understands that of his patients. This rapport on the deep level comes to the surface in the form of feelings which the analyst notices in response to his patient." In order to integrate the experience of the group and make decisions about therapeutic interventions, we must use our awareness of our own inner state as one of our major guides.

Although Freud was well aware of the importance of the meditative state and of unconscious communication, his linear concept of technique led him to react negatively to his awareness of the effects of the patient upon the therapist. The countertransference might bias the therapist and cause him to use poor judgment or misunderstand the patient. It is a source of error which the therapist must weed out, or he should give up treating the patient. This view of the therapist and his need to maintain himself free of neurosis and of countertransference distortions undoubtedly contributed to the difficulties in discussing countertransference, as shown by the fact that in the ensuing 40 years after Freud first described countertransference very little was written on the subject. In the last 25 years, however, there has been more open discussion of countertransference, which has modified the concept and is of relevance to us as group therapists.

The pioneer in this work was Heinrich Racher. In his book, *Transference and Countertransference* (1968), he explored the many and varied phenomena of countertransference and their significance for therapy. Two of his most important conclusions are as follows:

1) Countertransference is not an occasional contaminant of the therapist's activity, but a regular component of the therapeutic process.
2) The therapeutic activity of the therapist, i.e., his efforts to heal the patient, must be paralleled by efforts to heal his own related countertransference—the "internal splits," as Racher called them. There is a process of self-analysis and healing in the therapist which parallels the development of the group. When patients say that the therapist has changed in the course of a group, this is sometimes not due to a changed perception of the therapist, but to this parallel process.

A further expansion of awareness of the therapist's enmeshment in the therapeutic situation has come through the concept of the working or therapeutic alliance, and through Leo Stone's view of the psychoanalytic situation (1961). Here the emphasis is on the fact that the therapeutic relationship cannot be encompassed in the transference-countertransference paradigm, but must equally account for the basic human relationships involved and the human relationship which develops around the task of therapy itself. Another development has appeared in the work of Guntrip (1969) and Winnicott (1965). They assert that the specific conflicts of certain patients reflect basic dilemmas of human life and significant problems in our current culture. Guntrip (1969), for example, sees schizoid patients as manifesting in more profound form a major cultural trend of our times.

These developments point up a basic problem in psychoanalytic theory in this area. On the one hand, the importance of the therapist's unconscious is repeatedly acknowledged. On the other, countertransference is stigmatized as evidence of professional failure, and personal and public awareness of countertransference is accompanied by feelings of shame. When we refer to a colleague's countertransference, we rarely mean it as a compliment: "What a beautiful countertransference!'' Nevertheless, there has been a gradual change in attitude toward countertransference, and I would like to carry the process further by generalizing these findings.

As described earlier, each of us has an internal repertoire of states of conditional readiness for behavior. I believe these can be equated with the internalized object relationships described by Guntrip (1969) and others. An interpersonal relationship involving two or more people is accompanied by an activation of internalized object relationships. An awareness of that inner state is essential to understanding of and involvement with others, particularly in therapy groups. In fact, the therapist may exclude himself from the group by splitting off certain aspects of himself. It is impossible to designate a subset of those inner states as countertransference because they are an amalgam of personal history, basic human themes, and specific responses to the immediate situation. The question of whether the therapist's countertransference is pathological must be dropped in favor of a regular and systematic exploration by the therapist of how internalized object relations are activated in the therapy situation, and what implications this has for therapeutic efforts.

The considerations presented here have many implications for the therapist; I would like to mention a few of them.

1) The importance of the meditative state has already been described. How does one enter it? Of course, this touches on the broader question of how open and comfortable the therapist is with himself or herself generally. This will depend on to what extent, through therapy or other liberating experiences, the therapist has healed inner splits and blind spots. Experience with meditation and altered states of consciousness may be of value. In a narrower, more immediate sense, the therapist needs to be aware of personal body states and feelings, postural responses to events in the group, feelings of anxiety and tension. We must allow ourselves to react inwardly to minor events, to be distracted by them, even if this means losing track briefly of the verbal content. We must allow ourselves to be dumb, confused by the events in the group. We need to hang on to this inner state until it makes the group meaningful to us. At times it is helpful to ask oneself, ''What would I need to do or say in order to make myself comfortable with this group?'' The answer may give a clue about the leading issue in the group at the moment, although the therapist usually will not express or act out these conclusions without further evaluation.

2) The model presented here provides a rationale for greater flexibility in the therapist's choice of active and passive therapeutic techniques. In linear models, silence tends to be equated with neutrality, with doing nothing. No action, no reaction. The therapist's silence presumably denies gratification and builds up pressure for change, but it just as often allows defensive maneuvers to go on unperturbed or lapses into a stubborn stalemate. An axiom of the communications model is ''You cannot *not* communicate.'' Silence is a communication. This

confirms what therapists already know and have reported: The therapist's silence may communicate unobtrusive interest; rejection and withdrawal; timidity and uncertainty; or a sadistic attack on the patient. Silence may manifest a sense of peaceful relatedness, of communing, of being "alone together." Silence may communicate the therapist's respect for the group's autonomy. At other times, the therapist's silence may show a refusal to accede to the suction of the group into a form of relatedness which he feels to be inhuman or inimical to the group's task. In such instances, the therapist may model a crucial aspect of maturity, the capacity to be alone.

Activity, on the other hand, has been too exclusively identified with gratification of patients' instinctual and defensive needs. We are trapped here in the transference-countertransference paradigm, and in our cultural prejudice in favor of the verbal and the mental. What has been ignored is that at times active techniques, such as structuring the therapeutic situation via guided imagery or Gestalt, or active discussion of sublimations, or touching, or other forms of behavior, may promote therapeutic work and not simply amount to a transference gratification or a concession to ego defects. Not to use these possibilities may lead to identification of the therapist with the superego, a sort of aversion therapy where the therapist only speaks in response to pathology.

3) The same considerations argue for greater flexibility in therapist self-revelation. To consistently avoid self-revelation displays omnipotence on the part of the therapist, because it denies the group's influence on the therapist and insists that transactions will be unilateral. In our culture, there is a deep-seated and pervasive fear of being unilaterally manipulated and exploited, a consequence of our ruthless utilitarian technology. This is a cultural component of the male struggle against passivity which Freud (1957) found so pervasive. Therapists cannot effectively interpret this struggle if they inadvertently adopt the same model for therapy.

Freud advised against self-revelation and said, "The doctor should be opaque to his patients and, like a mirror, should show them nothing but what is shown to him." At the same time be advised that ". . . he must turn his own unconscious like a receptive organ towards the transmitting unconscious of the patient." Could we not reconcile these two statements by suggesting that "mirroring" involves not a bland smooth exterior, but an active process in the core of the therapist's self. When patients dance in front of us, we, being *human* mirrors, must inwardly perform a similar or complementary dance—and this is what must be reflected back to the patient.

The two clinical examples mentioned previously are instances where the therapist's self-revelation in the group was useful. In unstructured groups where dependency needs are frustrated, the group may often wish to exclude the therapist. This often goes along with a pseudo-independent, pseudo-therapeutic façade which functions to avoid issues. Pathology is projected onto the therapist, whose interventions are seen as intrusions and interruptions. The therapist's expression of feeling excluded, wondering about feeling so lousy and uncomfortable when everything is going so well, may be an effective intervention. Similar to this are states of denial or avoidance of a broad area of importance to the group. Issues around the relationship of co-therapists are an example. Another example is as follows:

In the early stages of a therapy group, the group focused on Rebecca's need to keep distant and remain in control. I pointed out the group theme of privacy and distance vs. intimacy and helpfulness. After some resistance, Rebecca accepted the interpretation and explored some implications of this trait in her relationships with others. Toward the end of the meeting, she turned to me and said, "You know, you're like me—you like distance and control too!" I gradually became aware of my own shyness and anxiety in this new group, and a few minutes later acknowledged these feelings. This led several members to reveal painful experiences of being excluded in high school. The shift toward greater openness in the group and toward seeing me as less distant then led to exploration of fears that greater intimacy would lead to greater hostility and hurtfulness in the group.

A patient's denial of his or her effect on others in the group or the group's denial of the effect of such a patient may require self-revelation on the part of the therapist. Such a patient may "hear" feelings, but not hear abstract interpretations. In these instances the therapist must understand his own hostile feelings for the patient, both because they may need to be conveyed to the patient and at the same time because there is the risk of traumatizing or scapegoating the patient. Therapist self-revelation may be helpful in working through subtle forms of intellectualized denial, in which the patient agrees to a correct interpretation but limits its impact, as though saying, "Yes, I agree, that's very interesting, but I'm not involved." Therapists' expression of their own reactions to or similarities with the patient may help break through this barrier. Of course, patients may demand that therapists reveal more of themselves as a resistance, to shift the focus away from themselves and gratify dependency needs, or to play an accusatory and guilt-producing role toward the therapist.

The question arises whether there is something about groups which promotes the involvement and self-revelation of the therapist. I think there are several factors, in addition to the input overload mentioned earlier. The group situation deviates from the traditional doctor-patient relationship in that there are several patients who can compete or collaborate with each other to disrupt traditional roles. Thus, it is a less structured situation and the therapist is bound to reveal more of himself. In addition, patients can observe and compare their transference reactions to the therapist and their observations of the therapist's personality. Thus, the question of the therapist's use of self may come up more acutely in groups, although it is an issue in all forms of therapy.

Ernst Ticho (1974), in discussing the work of Winnicott and Martin Buber, once explored the possibilities and limitations of an "I-Thou" relationship in therapy. He warned that such a relationship hinges on the maturity of both therapist and patient and that therapy cannot simply be relabeled an I-Thou relationship; rather the relationship must be achieved. In many instances such a goal will never, or only partially, be reached. But an awareness of the existence of these dimensions is always important to therapists in understanding themselves and the therapeutic situation. We must ask ourselves how much of us do patients want—and how much of us can they use—in service of the therapeutic task. This must be our guide, rather than the exclusive gratification of our own needs, or arbitrary rules of procedure based on outdated concepts of objectivity.

In this chapter I have described two complementary routes to the understanding of small groups and the use of this understanding by the group therapist. Systems and communications concepts provide a comprehensive "map" of the complex, interrelated events of the group. In the actual experience of the group, however, events are so numerous and rapidly changing that initially they cannot be perceived and integrated consciously. Instead, therapists must utilize the deeper layers of their selves to apprehend the flow of group experience. This allows for a sensitive and holistic comprehension of a wide range of human concern and relatedness, in multiple intertwined systems and levels of systems. Systems theory provides a rationale for this process by stressing the specific isomorphy between the inner world of the therapist and the events of the group. These two modes of knowing, theoretical and intuitive, may then mutually enrich each other.

Chapter 4

Group Therapy as a
System of Energy
Transformation

By Walter Gruen, Ph.D.

Editor's Introduction. General system theory has described the process of organization and reorganization of systems in terms of patterns of energy exchange. This chapter focuses on that energy exchange as a necessary condition for systems change in psychotherapy groups.

Freud, Maslow, Fromm, and Erikson all refer to an availability of energy beyond mere maintenance of equilibrium. Here, Dr. Gruen illuminates the use of energy in movement, growth, and self-transformation of systems.

Therapists must better understand the energy operations within their groups, the author contends, in order to grasp the evolution occurring within the group, to perceive accurately group changes that occur from moment to moment, and to aid patients in their own energy efficiency.

Dr. Gruen hypothesizes a concept called "nurtenergy," a specific psychic energy operating in groups, which combines aspects of the nurturant group environment with energy and information. His work also includes a discussion of the negentropic nature of living structures; that is, living systems progress to new stages of organization as they maintain an ongoing energy exchange with their environments.

Also included here are data corroborating Gruen's view that nurtenergy should be available from the therapist, focused on the patients, identified by them, and finally utilized by them for optimum negentropic self-transformation.

Gruen relates nurtenergy to the boundarying process, illustrates the catalytic nature of nurtenergy, and lists practical implications for the therapist. Some insightful statements herein help the reader understand the often discussed, but usually poorly explained, phenomena of therapeutic warmth and faith in the patient.

It is generally accepted that in order to recognize, understand, and reorganize the interaction in the group and the forces within each group member, the group therapist needs the following skills: 1) a thorough knowledge and an expert command of a theory of personality organization; and 2) a theory of group dynamics. His personality theory allows him to fit diverse behavior manifestations and feelings into a meaningful pattern which he selectively feeds back to the group members as interpretations.

It is also generally understood that the therapist must learn and practice certain behavior patterns that are characteristic and even unique to his role as therapist. These role characteristics are correlated with some well-known laws of behavior change or relearning, so that they are seen as necessary leverages for patients' behavior change. For instance, he must be maximally permissive in order to allow negative and self-deprecatory feelings to surface. He must be maximally nonjudgmental to create a neutral and even friendly climate for examining the most antisocial and disapproved emotions. He must show interest in the patients' revelations so that they feel encouraged to discuss the most hidden and trivial matters. He must have some knowledge about repressed capacities for change so that the patients can identify these coping forces and take new hope that there they can change.

It has also been generally recognized that the therapist needs to muster and exhibit some form of warmth (called, for instance, "unconditional positive regard" by Rogers, 1951, and "caring" by Angyal, 1973) to help the patient feel accepted and worthwhile. It has recently been demonstrated that this warmth is more than a mere desirable characteristic. Several studies (Truax & Wargo, 1966; Lieberman, Yalom, & Miles, 1973) have tried to show that its presence may be correlated with accelerated change in patient behavior, while its absence may be correlated with a lack of change or even deterioration. However, not much is known about the operation of this warmth in the actual interaction process between the therapist and the patient. Hence, its exact operation as a force in the process of behavior change is not known. We have loosely equated it with "love" or "TLC," which is also seen as a necessary force from parents for the adequate personality development of their children.

I am proposing that the principles of GST offer us a rationale for the characteristics and the workings of this warmth. From this perspective we can understand this warmth as a vital and necessary force working along with the therapist's cognitive input and his well understood role characteristics in the successful therapy group. Since GST has also described the process of the organization and reorganization of subsystems in a living system in terms of patterns of energy exchange, we obtain a new understanding of the nature of warmth as a source of energy that obeys definite system characteristics in both the therapist and the group. The application of GST principles to this energy exchange process further allows us to view the specific forces in the group that partially promote behavior change as a direct consequence of the therapist's well managed warmth. From this theoretical understanding of warmth, I shall try to deduce some specific recommendations for the clinician to become a more effective therapist.

GENERAL SYSTEM THEORY PRINCIPLES OF ENERGY EXCHANGE IN LIVING SYSTEMS

GST sees the living system as a system of forces which can progress to new stages of organization so that the energy from physical-chemical inputs is available for more complexity of the system as a whole. Hence, the living system has the potential for decreasing entropy, if entropy is defined as energy in a form unavailable for work and is associated with maximum disorder and disorganization. A non-living system, such as a windstorm or a gasoline engine, reverts to a state of maximum entropy—or disorganization—as soon as the energy within the system is used up. At that point, the closed system attains a state of equilibrium in which energy is no longer available and in which the forces acting upon or within the system are randomly organized. GST utilizes the concepts of thermodynamics by calling this state "the reversion to maximum entropy." The living, open system, on the other hand, can maintain an energy exchange with its environment in such a way that input is reorganized to allow for an active exploration of the environment for more input and for the continuation of the energy exchange. By reorganization of its components, the living system can transform itself into a dialectic sequence to new levels of organization in which more usable energy is available for more complex activities.

E. Schrödinger in *What is Life and Mind and Matter* (1967) has stated that an open system feeds on negative entropy. This process involves the importation of complex inputs full of energy and ready for use. In this way, the organism performs its work function, as well as maintains itself in a steady state, by the importation of materials rich in free energy. Under some forms of component reorganization, more complex interactions with the environment (beyond mere maintenance of the steady state) are needed. For example, when the organism takes insufficient nutrients to maintain a resting state, the interaction might include greater procurement and catabolism of energy sources. In this way, disorder or death can be averted for a while while entropy is reduced. Hence, growth is a result of the counteraction between anabolism and catabolism of the building material. The system includes an instant potential for energy expenditure that can be mobilized in surplus quantities from the energy necessary to maintain the steady state. Examples of the investment of energy that accumulates from negentropic processes in the organism are found in the most primitive forms of behavior, as well as in brain function and physiological processes of higher animals. In higher organisms, including man, these autonomous activities embody themselves as play, exploration, invention, creativity, and self-realization (von Bertalanffy, 1966).

Energy can be combined, reorganized, rechanneled, or transformed to allow complex consequences. Lack of such reinvestment may allow energy to be wasted or to be depleted, for instance, when the organism covers up or compensates for deficiencies or tension. Grinker (1973) reminds us that living organisms are involved with their environment in a circular process. Their energy systems are in a constantly changing state of activity. They use energy to receive and transform input from the environment. By doing so, they create new organizational patterns which may later liberate usable energy.

To summarize, even though we can look at system change along other dimensions, energy exchange is a necessary condition for systems change. For instance, we can focus on new organization of components through a change in boundaries within a system, or we can focus on the creation of a new, reorganized system by breaking the boundaries of the original and reintegrating the components. Energy exchange is further illuminated by a GST approach because it allows us to appreciate the use and application of energy in the production of homeostasis or in movement and growth.

EVIDENCE FOR THE UTILIZATION AND TRANSFORMATION OF ENERGY IN PSYCHOTHERAPY

In psychology, we already possess numerous references to the availability of energy that is not needed for mere maintenance at minimal subsistence level. Freud (1957), for instance, recognized that growing older is correlated with a striking diminution in the movement to form cathexes and that the general ability to form mature object cathexes is based on relatively smooth psychosexual personality development. Maslow's theory (1954) of personality development tries to show that energy can only be invested in a hierarchically more complex level of needs when previous need levels have been adequately satiated. Fromm (1956) has pointed out that one cannot love another person unless one can accept, that is, love, oneself first, because true object involvement requires perception of the other in a new and more complicated experiential context. Finally, Erikson (1964) has postulated a theory of complex levels of organization of the ego forces. Investment of psychic energy into a more or less permanent (sexual) friendship is only possible if this more complex form of energy emerges after an adequate sense of ego identity has been developed. Similarly, reorganization of energy forces resulting from solving the intimacy conflict in the ego's development is a necessary step before new energy is available for "generativity," that is, the stage where one generates one's own continuity through producing and caring for either creative activity or living offspring or both.

The study and explanation of psychopathology are replete with references to energy concepts. The excess expenditure to solve various conflicts saps energy sources from the person so that he shows various deficiencies in his capacities to function normally. Hence, individuals are unable to love, to observe accurately, to work, to feel certain emotions, or to even perceive reality. This is especially true if the organization of their various emotional and perceptual components leads to need frustration or to retaliation by others or to both. In addition, the existence of psychological conflicts and of need frustration leads to secondary disorganization; this disorganization has been described by such terms as anxiety, tension, depression, or stress. In such instances, we see clearly how the development of such reactions as anxiety can further inhibit efficient, negentropic organization and can then lead to the disruptive accumulation of entropy. It is perhaps premature to equate anxiety with entropy, but whatever the breakdown of energy forces is like, their presence is heralded by correlated forms of energy and tension. The experimental literature is full of studies that show how excessive tension or anxiety inhibits the ability to carry out both moderately simple and complex cognition tasks and behavioral sequences.

In the dyadic therapy system, the process is reversed. The therapist provides a sanctuary-like situation where the faulty organization can be examined in quasi-slow motion under the nutrient support of an energy field coming from the therapist. In this medium, accelerated reorganization of psychological forces is possible so that the patient can shift his reinvestment of energy for need satisfaction and eventually proceed to a more complex form of energy transformation. The therapist also supplies a cognitive framework or theory by which the patient can reorganize his faulty need investments and understand where he has gone astray. When the patient adopts the theory's important fragments and the cognitive organization of his own psychological forces within it, he has further gained a tool by which he can understand his needs and his priorities. In this system, the markedly developed state of entropy or disorganization with its correlated anxieties can be first stopped and then reversed until reorganization to a new steady state is possible. This new steady state can then allow for the investment of saved energy into new need-gratifying channels.

A therapy group is an even better example of a social system in which entropic accumulation occurs at the beginning and is slowly reversed. Finally, it results in a hierarchically more complexly organized steady state. When this negentropic organization has endured for a while, the very social system (the therapy group) becomes less necessary for each individual member's maintenance of negentropic processes. The group then terminates and each member can reinvest his energy reorganizing capacities outside the group.

In the beginning of a therapy group, there is an unorganized aggregate of patients who have all accumulated entropy from the faulty organization of their psychological forces. Each patient's entropy state has made it doubly difficult to interact with the others in the group situation. Each group member fears exhibiting his faulty functions because they might alienate him from the others, who are strangers to him, in a permanent way, as he has experienced in previous encounters. Hence, patients carefully avoid contact and confrontation. This accumulation of entropy is further accelerated in the first few meetings because involvement in the group is feared due to previous social disasters, and because the newness of the therapy group is threatening. The accumulation of correlated tensions and other disruptive feelings occurring at the beginning process of group therapy is well documented in the literature.

As the group progresses, the therapist can again decrease this anxiety by pointing to it as a normal and understandable manifestation of a beginning group and of the patients' psychopathology. Hence, this disruptive anxiety acquires meaning and becomes material for cognitive reorganization under the guidance of the therapist's theory of personality and theory of group development. Eventually, the reorganization of need systems and channels of expression in each person leads to a new social organization in the group, after it has gone through a sometimes very rocky roller-coaster ride. Sometimes this final stage is referred to as group cohesion or the working stage of a therapy group, although it too may have its ups and downs. Here, the increasingly negentropic organization of individual forces leads to new behaviors within the group and to new types of contacts with other group members. When the negentropic forces within each patient become stabilized so that successful interactions can be made with others outside the group, the group loses its function of merely promoting reorganization in each member, and group dissolution occurs. Each member has now achieved a steady energy state, which allows him or her to accumulate some negentropic forces for potentially even more exacting and complex personal investments.

Hence, the group is a good example of a short-lived system which goes through a stage of growth and evolution similar to the growth and evolution and maturity of living systems at other levels. We see its negentropic potentials and the achievement of more complex energy investment by changing components and reorganization.

To recapitulate on the existence of the energy, I would like to contrast the entropic with the negentropic use of available energy in group therapy. Let us assume for the sake of argument that each of three patients comes to a group meeting with 100 units of energy that is available for investment to satisfy his or her needs. This pool of energy can be spent quickly in an interchange as follows: One patient becomes slowed down in a depressive mood by emphasizing how hopeless he is. The second yells and screams at the depressed one for frustrating the screamer's needs. The third patient becomes anxious and tense on a motoric level because he sees no chance to inject himself into this interchange. Hence, the energy of the three patients is literally used up and is not available anymore. The interchange has caused the individual patients an additional expenditure of energy, leaving them virtually depleted. We are assuming, of course, that for some reason the therapist in this example has allowed the situation to occur in this way so that nothing else has happened to the three patients except what has been described here.

On the other hand, it is possible that these three patients could meet with a high level of therapeutic involvement in the group. For instance, the easily depressed patient is yanked out of the inevitable investment to face the depression and to accept his good points from the group. The yelling patient can work through his yelling and eventually choose an alternate path towards his needs. The anxious patient can get an opportunity to inject himself and become helpful to the other two patients and thereby maintain at least his previous energy equilibrium. With such a high level of involvement, energy can be saved for at least the depressed and yelling patients in this example because their energy was utilized for a more complex purpose. Both patients in this example can now invest the same amount of energy in a new way of relating that will be satisfying and growth-producing rather than depleting. They can invest the available energy in such a way that the returns are satisfying to their needs and will provide them with the potentials for new and more complex, but also more creative and, therefore, even more satisfying, purposes.

This development is even true if their insights and their involvement in the group may have been exhilarating enough to be physically exhausting. When this physical exhaustion is recharged with rest or a night's sleep, the psychological reorganization that took place at the group meeting can sustain these people in new and more complex involvement. This involvement is not possible for the depressed or anxious patient when he arises from a physical rest or from sleep without this reorganization. He is still depressed or tired. We need only remember here that an anxiety-ridden person usually cannot eat a good meal to replenish his physiological or psychological resources adequately. However, the two patients described above may develop a heartier appetite for a good meal after a group meeting than was possible for either one of them before. Hence, the 100 units of energy can be either spent or transformed into a different form of energy able to function at a different level. At that level the energies may be isomorphically equal to each other in strength, but completely different in phenotypic characteristics, and hence can be used differently and integrated differently in the reorganization.

Coming back to the examination of forces in the group, we know that the therapy group's increasing complexity of organization is perceivable in the process of norm-building. This has been adequately described by a variety of observers (Hill & Gruner, 1973; Martin & Hill, 1957; Meador, 1971; Schutz, 1958). Usually three or sometimes four stages have been recognized which represent different plateaus of more complex involvement after the entropy-producing conflicts have been solved at previous stages (Braaten, 1974; Tuckman, 1965). The attainment of a cohesive, work-oriented stage allows the group to resolve a number of group issues and individual problems with sustained energy. This energy was previously dissipated either toward the leader or toward other group members in the middle stage, or dissipated in escape channels in the introductory stage, in which the initial anxiety was too great. From these studies and observations, guidelines have been prepared for clinicians which indicate what signals are diagnostic of the various stages. These guidelines allow the clinician to accelerate the group's movement to the most negentropic, work-oriented phase (Gruen, 1977a, Yalom, 1975).

So far, most of these observations about groups have been couched in terms of disorganization or organization. There has been a dearth of emphasis on the input and interchange of energy sources such as therapist feeling efforts and the reception, transmission, and effect of these sources. The energy source allows this transformation from a disorganized aggregate of anxious and minimally interacting patients to a negentropic cohesive group. The latter has all the earmarks of a well-functioning team and tackles its own interactions in such a well-defined and goal-oriented way that members' surplus energy is now available for new involvements outside the group. Only when we understand the energy that is operating at the group interactional level—including the targeting and utilization of this energy—can we fully grasp the evolution occurring in a therapy group and the system changes that occur from moment to moment.

THE SEARCH FOR A CONCEPT OF ENERGY IN PSYCHOTHERAPY: NURTENERGY

In another paper I have made an attempt to identify and trace the energy component (Gruen, 1977b). Even though such a force must originally have been derived from physical-chemical energy along the catabolic-anabolic principle proposed by von Bertalanffy, the next higher or more complex isomorphic expression of energy into a psychological form of energy may well be channeled through the firing of nerves. I have tentatively traced the specific psychic energy operating in the group to help transform its elements and called it "nurtenergy."

Nurtenergy was first described as being isomorphic with nerve firings. They become goal-oriented when they are organized as "information" after a pattern of nerve fibers, which become organized as a pattern because of learned and associated experiences. Also, the increased understanding of the right hemisphere as a locus of nonverbal emotional signals (among other functions) made me speculate that this energy might be regulated and amplified in this structure. The evidence that has accumulated about force fields emanating from living bodies and being captured in both psychokinetic phenomena and in Kirlian photography gave me an indication of the possible manifestations of this energy beyond the skin. I further reasoned that this energy can either be diffuse or highly concentrated like a laser beam and then targeted more functionally toward selected persons. For instance, I cited various studies on child-rearing in both animals and man as an example that this targeted energy is necessary for the development of physiological and psychological well-being in infants and children. Finally, I pointed to the effect of therapist warmth and caring on possible positive outcome in psychotherapy as more indirect evidence of the presence and concentrated effect of this energy. While nurtenergy as an energy medium has thus been indicated to exist by circumstantial evidence, it must remain a hypothetical concept, because specific sending apparatus, communication medium, and receptor sites are not yet known.

Nevertheless, I felt that the conceptualization of an energy force like nurtenergy made it possible to understand the negentropic processes in the transformation of an aggregate of anxious patients into a coherent and cohesive working group. I also used it to help the therapist understand his part in the process and to provide him with better guidelines for accelerating the process of change. First of all, I saw him or her as an organism with nurtenergy to give and to invest because of his or her own negentropic functioning and because of his or her knowledge of the dynamics of change. He concentrates his nurtenergy into a coherent beam that then temporarily energizes the patients' energy-depleted systems. In this way, patients feed off this surplus nurtenergy, which acts as an auxiliary force to help in their own reorganization. In this article (Gruen, 1977a), I cited various authorities on the psychotherapeutic process to substantiate this catalytic function of the therapist.

Furthermore, I saw the rules about having no agenda and no direction in group therapy as a fertile soil for the therapist's nurtenergy to become noticeable and usable for the patients. Not only does this loose mix in a therapy group allow a more leisurely examination and realignment of previously nonrewarding, rigidified interaction systems in and among the patients, but it also slows down the interaction so that the patients can tune into the excess energy available from the therapist.

I also felt that the speculation about the existence and properties of nurtenergy as a guided catalytic force and as a lubricant of the group forces would have implications for the therapist. A therapist without surplus nurtenergy most likely cannot propel a group to its final stage of cohesive working-through. Also, the therapist has to withdraw or make more diffuse his nurtenergy injections as the group moves out of its first phase and begins to tackle its problems with newly generated nurtenergy from its own component members. The patients, of course, come with potentials of surplus energy and even with remnants of investable nurtenergy which they may reveal quickly, even if fleetingly, to others in the more liberating and sanctuary-like moments at the beginning of a group. Eventually, patient nurtenergy grows as the patients' own entropic organization of forces changes. It is then available for each other and becomes a symbol of growth and a source of new gratification for the investor. In this change, over time, the leader becomes less of an energy provider and more involved in the task of supervising the encoding and channeling of information.

I would also like to emphasize at this point that I see the utilization of nurtenergy as a catalytic process. The energy must indeed be available and visible to the patient but may be used very differently in various transformations among patients. It should not be seen as an energy "beam" that is borrowed in its totality or adopted in its present form by the patients. The latter idea of simple transfer would again imply a closed system in which the energy is either used up or not used up. In such a closed system the process becomes a mere introjection or identification with the therapist's characteristics by the patient, which would deny the system organization of people within the group. The therapist does indeed inject nurtenergy into the process in a concentrated form, but it becomes an organizing focus which hits different patients in very different ways and becomes utilized in terms of very different components by each patient's psychological system. Also, the component is only hooked into when the patient is ready for it. It is not "used up" or "taken away" by the patient, nor is the therapist depleted of it. It may be seen to function more like a trigger, somewhat analogous to coupling a car with a dead battery to a car running with a full battery. Here the resting engine is momentarily triggered into action by the charging battery of the running car and then generates its own energy back into its dead battery via its motor and generator. The therapist functions as a catalyst in several ways by supplying a reservoir of nurtenergy as well as interpretative connections from his storehouse of personality and group theory. Both of these reservoirs are integrated in new and even changed manifestations by the patient in his own use of them within his own reorganization.

Also, the providing of nurtenergy by the therapist is, of course, not a one-way street for him. The therapist also draws energy from the group, insofar as his involvement with the group is part of his work identification, role definition, emotional gratification, and self-concept. The comfort provided by verification of familiar concepts in the sequence of events in the group, the reinforcement of the effects of his skills, the joy at surprises and the success of dealing with these as challenges, the joy of being able to give and receive feelings and to promote change and growth within the context of knowing and experiencing other people intimately—all are important reinforcements for the therapist. They recharge his own negentropic organization so that he in turn can generate nurtenergy both within and outside of the group.

With this focus on an energy force that has been defined as nurtenergy and described in terms of important properties, I specifically include the group's system properties, which have been called the group leader's "social-emotion orientation function" by social psychologists (Bales, 1958; Fiedler, 1967). Various studies have identified two major leadership functions. *Task orientation* or *work orientation* is the more prominent and important one in so-called task groups in the community. In contrast, in therapy groups, the second function, *dealing with the management of the emotional climate,* is more prominent and necessary because the group initially has no well-defined task or agenda. Nevertheless, the developing system of interactions and norms could not function without the leader supplying some task functions. We have alluded to these when we touched on the rules and role characteristics the therapist sets up for himself and for the group members in the therapy group. Among these are the implicit rules he injects when he attaches meaning to feelings and interactions from his own theory of personality dynamics and group functioning. These task functions promote information exchange, and can facilitate system transformation and major group transformation to reorganized steady states.

NURTENERGY AT WORK IN THE GROUP

Other chapters in this book examine processes and rules for system changes (see Chapters 5, 10, 11, 13 and 18). I would like to focus here a little bit more microscopically on the nature and manifestations of this nurtenergy which I have postulated as an important energizer in the transformation process. In the previously cited publication (Gruen, 1977b), I have already referred to the nurturant characteristics of this force and have equated its energy component with those generally associated with "love," "concern," "caring," and "protectiveness." In order to be maximally useful for the practicing group therapist, I want to identify the optimum nature of this force in group therapy and particularly the manifestations of the raw energy that should be available from the therapist, then targeted to the patients, perceived and identified correctly by them, and finally utilized for optimum negentropic self-transformation.

Three recent studies contain some data that can help us focus on those manifestations that are uniquely relevant to group therapy, rather than individual therapy or child-rearing or even friendship. Palan et al. (1974) helped to isolate the "sleeper effect" in group therapy patients. This has been assumed to exist for some time but has been difficult to pinpoint, because of the methodological difficulties of assessing outcome and change over any length of time. They found that some patients continuously improve after therapy. These patients are more often associated with a "positively active therapist." He or she is described in terms of being caring and actively injecting positive concern. These core conditions were seen as seedlings which are planted by the therapist, "flourish in a fertile and self-nourishing soil as the continued gainers provide themselves with their own high level core conditions to facilitate their own growth and development" (Palan et al., 1974). In this sense, they had taken over as their own therapist and were reinforcing themselves and improving in terms of qualities borrowed from a model therapist.

Azima (1976) applied the Bales interaction categories to therapy groups and found, among other differences, that therapists' inputs are much more frequently found in the positive reaction category (shows solidarity, shows tensions release, and agrees) than had been found earlier with discussion groups. Hence, therapists supply more emotional support than leaders of discussion groups. A final piece of evidence for the working of our energy force is the modeling research that has been conducted by Bandura and associates (1969). While these studies have addressed themselves to individual patients with more narrowly circumscribed behavior problems, the modeling effect of a therapist who exudes a quiet confidence that the patient can carry out the feared task and then positively encourages the patient to imitate him or her has been demonstrated to result in relatively quick learning.

At this point, the reader should be quite aware that I am not dealing with the interplay of cyclical, evolutionary, or boundary forces of the subsystems that flow within the larger group system of group therapy. I am, however, looking at the group as a larger system which starts with certain energy balance and moves to an end stage with a structurally very different energy balance, in which the reorganization in the new steady state has produced negentropic characteristics. These negentropic characteristics allow the group and each patient to invest liberated energy in more complex ways. I am, therefore, not concerned at this point with the blow-by-blow transformation from the beginning to the end state. I am also not looking more microscopically at some of the processes and elements that make this major transformation and energy exchange possible such as the cognitive or interpretative inputs from the therapist and patients, or the specific understanding and consequent gatekeeping that come from the therapist's knowledge of group dynamics and personality dynamics. I am also leaving out any discussion about the therapist's perceptual sensitivity that would allow him to sense when a patient is coasting or emotionally responding to another patient, or even expressing his own needs or a basic group issue. These issues all become boundary problems in more cross-sectional slices through the group process, and these are dealt with in other chapters (see Chapters 5, 12 and 13). These slices, of course, are also energized and may even borrow from the catalytic nurtenergy force from the therapist.

Let us consider, for an example, a patient who has acquired a negative view of himself from his parents' evaluation and treatment of him. Let us assume that this negative self-view is further fueled and buttressed by four additional sources: 1) an oedipal relationship to his mother who needed to see the patient as weak in order to assist her with her own wishes; 2) his relationships with others, who, because he has used this script, have agreed with some of his negative self-descriptions on the basis that he knows himself best of all; 3) rejection by others and subsequent reinforcement of the script; 4) adoption of an ideology that "people are no damn good" and association with people and groups who share this view.

Let us assume that the therapist has made available his surplus nurtenergy with the informational content, "You can change your adjustment and your self-concept." This nurtenergy force has been bombarding the boundary of the patient over several meetings. Finally, there is a point where a repeated demonstration of the helpfulness and interest of other patients and the therapist makes the patient realize that the other patients in the group are "good people," contrary to his earlier conceptions. The therapist senses this minor transformation and makes sure that the patient verbalizes and strengthens this realization with some show of feelings. This breakthrough may then allow the therapist to summarize the views of other group members about the patient as being opposite to that of the patient. Perhaps later—in another session—this can be followed by interpretation of the oedipal underpinning and of the parental origins of the patient's negative self-evaluation. When the various pieces of the former self-view are thus fragmented, there first may be some disorder, after which the patient reorganizes his view of himself, of his parents, of others, of the world. The patient changes in his own way, rather than borrowing from the therapist's energy or value system. Transformation for the patient follows his own realization that he can change. He has been shown, not told, that his negativism toward himself and others is inappropriate. For instance, he may now acknowledge positive qualities and his attraction to some people, but maintain dependency and more self-inhibiting qualities toward needy, female authority figures and may still gravitate to world-hating people in situations where he feels somewhat inadequate.

I am not considering where and how the initial breakthrough occurred. I recognize that the bombardment, the forces leading to the break, and the system qualities surrounding the precursors and the focal point of the break all exist. It would be beyond the scope of this general introduction to an energy model in GST terms to trace its momentary flow to specific episodes in one segment of the group. Such an exposition would take several more chapters. In the next section I will give, however, a specific example of the catalytic effect of nurtenergy on a patient's self-esteem.

FURTHER PROPERTIES OF NURTENERGY

The studies mentioned in the previous section and other observations about the forces acting in therapy (Frank, 1973) indicate that the information content associated with nurtenergy is the therapist's faith in his patient's restitutive and coping process. The therapist keeps before himself a constant and emotionally tinged hope that each patient will sooner or later get in touch with old or hidden strengths and resources, that he or she will become aware of these, and that he or she will eventually use them experimentally and then more habitually. It is, therefore, a form of trust in the process qualities of the human being as another example of the living system with its negentropic potentials toward growth and self-fulfillment. It should not be construed as mere concern or caring or even love for another human being. Caring implies stretching out a hand to another and indicates that the therapist is coupled with him or her in some way because there is some acceptance and even admiration. The major focus of nurtenergy, however, rests on an admiration of potential or very embryonically appearing qualities—that is, faith in the inherent system quality and potential of the human being. In addition, nurtenergy implies an active force that not only assumes the presence of coping but also pushes for it and helps realize it. A mere passive, emotional quality such as, "I am with you," or "I contemplate or bask in your admirable qualities," which is eminently characteristic of caring, is not the major component. It would imply that the caring individual is inherently frustrated if he cannot maintain contact with the other. This break of contact is minimized between caring individuals, but it is a carefully practiced rule in group therapy. Nevertheless, the therapist may translate his nurtenergy into mere caring at the beginning of the group, when members are still unable to cope and are instead filled with anxiety and other signs of disorganization. Then the translation of nurtenergy to a caring response is a way of translating the faith in eventual growth into the message, "I am with you while you suffer and are weak because I know that you can do better."

This energy from the therapist can only penetrate to his patients if the boundary maintained by the patient is broken. Jim Durkin (1976a) has shown how the neurotic, watertight boundary system may flow around and against someone else's boundary system so that only information is exchanged. Energy is only exchanged if the boundary is actually broken so that the energy can flow in and affect the whole system, including the information contained in the boundaries. It is, therefore, this faith of the therapist—concentrated in a beam of nurtenergy—that can affect the thinking or informational content of the patient when he previously insists on maintaining a negative self-concept or the myth of a helpless person who is afloat without direction in a sea of trouble.

I would like to illustrate more specifically the whole process in which the patient borrows from the therapist's nurtenergy in order to develop his own nurtenergy potential. Let us suppose a patient says to himself and also tells the group that he is worthless and helpless and is completely beyond knowing any other way out except to insist that he is nothing and to beg for their sympathy. At some point, the therapist will turn his attention to the patient and ask him questions about this view. Let us assume further that the therapist's request for information also contains the nurtenergy beam. This energized beam can be expressed either in references to the therapist's faith that the patient can be helped to see himself differently, or in "little seeds of doubt" about the absolute necessity for the patient to see himself this way. These doubts may be contained in the request for further confirmation of the patient's helplessness. The patient then may begin to react in the following sequence: "I am worthless, but the therapist asks me questions and is warm." "I am helpless, but the therapist does not rescue me, and, in fact, he tries to reassure me when I talk or when I try to think through my problem." "I cannot solve my problem without massive help, but the therapist has implied that I helped myself in situation X or in group session Y." "I don't understand my miserable self, but the therapist says and implies that I can learn to understand myself if I only try again slowly and listen to my feelings."

The transformation that is slowly beginning to take place in this patient requires, of course, the cognitive content illustrated above. This content can be specified further by interpretations which encode and reorganize diverse elements in these messages. However, the negative message, "I am nothing," is suspended by the nurtenergetic faith of the therapist from his reservoir of available energy. In this way, one boundary in the patient around his consistently negative self-image is broken, so that he can at least listen to different feelings and alter his vaguely formed self-concept. Eventually, there may be a transformation to a new steady state where the patient can say progressively: "I must be worth a little more because I formerly ignored qualities A and B in myself and these are valuable." "I am something, because I now understand the origin of my efforts at defeating myself." "I underestimated my own power to try again and experiment." "I now have faith that some things work for me, and I can try again with the hope that I will get some positive feedback." As this feedback becomes reinforcing, the reinvestment process accelerates.

We can also see here that the energy of the therapist is not used up by merely flowing from the therapist to the patient. It becomes instead a catalytic force which energizes the initial movement of the transformation within the patient. The nature, direction, and final organization of the transformation are uniquely the patient's and do not contain recognizable "units" from the therapist's nurtenergy.

When the patient can say, "I am something," he must first of all say, "I am something because I felt and heard the therapist say so—or heard other group members say so at the instigation of the therapist." Later, the patient can move through messages like: "I am something because I can see my own good points." "I am something because I can sense my own strength flowing from me and affecting others in the group." "I am something because I can reach out and do more for others and for myself." "I have recontacted other people and situations for mutual benefit, and I have developed my own (nurt)energy". In summary, he may say something like: "I have sensed and reacted on a transformation within me which has allowed me to develop accurate sensitivity to myself and awareness of feedback from others; the positive feedback allows me to invest more and more and gain more for myself and for others." Therefore, there is a negentropic open system in formation* that shows efficiency in its investment and harvesting potentials.

In order to illustrate the catalytic action of nurtenergy, I would like to contrast two different uses of it by two very different patients in the same group. Let us

---

Editor's note. See Gray on system-forming (Chapter 11).

assume that one patient sees herself as so vulnerable that she has erected a strong castle around herself and only looks at the world through tiny gunslits without ever lowering the drawbridge to let another human being come across. She is resisting the attempts of other group members to approach her and she maintains hostility toward the therapist with a message: "Who are you to tell me what I should think or feel?" However, her self-imposed isolation has also caused her much pain, so that she feels lonely and abandoned. The therapist's energized message of faith in her ability to change and to give as well as to receive may finally allow her to lower the drawbridge for a fleeting moment to allow perhaps one group member to come through. Even though this first encounter may produce a catastrophic reaction, it may also allow further experimentation in extending herself or in allowing more contact, until she can look at her jealously guarded treasure chest again and discover that it is far fuller than she had believed. A transformation of her vulnerability and of her power to invest and harvest may result. In contrast, another patient needs to fill up his low reservoir of himself by demanding succor. He begins to ask the therapist for help and quickly tries to become dependent on him. The therapist denies this dependency. Instead, he uses his nurtenergy to imply that the patient does not need this help because the therapist has faith that the patient contains raw forces of his own potential autonomy. If the patient finally begins to act upon this faith, he may develop his sources into new ways of behaving that are, however, not dependent on or borrowed from the nurtenergy beam of the therapist. In these two patients, the same surplus nurtenergy from the therapist is catalytic to two very different developments of patients' utilization of their own energy. Hence, I do not imply that the patient borrows from the therapist's energy or depends on him. Instead, nurtenergy energizes and activates the patient's more-or-less spontaneous discovery of his own resources for reorganizing his energies.

These examples also afford me the opportunity to show how energy processes are involved, rather than the mere passage and receipt of information, in these transformations. I consider the intensity and the emotional coloration of the therapist's remarks expressing faith in the patient's capacity to change as an important accompaniment to the content. It is, for instance, quite conceivable that a therapist could learn the message of hope and transmit it consciously via cognitive signals. He may do so because he believes that such a message is therapeutic, is part of his role and represents one of his tools. If he does not *feel* the message, he cannot tailor it into a befitting translation to a given patient. The message will come out instead as a general "advertisement." In this form it does not have leverage and the patient can easily relegate the message to the scrap heap of previous messages of similar tone that he has heard from friends or associates. They may also have said, "Oh, you'll also get over this," in order to get the patient out of their hair or to offer the person some canned reassurance as a way of satisfying their own needs to be helpful.

We must remember that the patient has invested a good deal of energy to maintain the entropy-producing self-esteem in order to give in to masochistic tendencies toward self-defeat. A closed system like, "I am no good," must be reinforced and protected to serve other needs (for instance, punishment needs, low-key involvement, getting attention through pity, etc.), or to protect against shattering surprises. Hence, information to the contrary may not be enough to pry open this boundary around a tight and relatively closed system. I would argue that the informational message must be laced with emotional energy like nurtenergy, that is also perceivable, repetitive, and felt at the impact site, before any message can penetrate.

I am postulating, therefore, that it is not enough for the therapist to merely subscribe to a positive faith and to have inner concern for his patients. The systems analysis of the dynamics of the force fields which I developed here suggests that the therapist should inject this force consistently and make sure that it is perceived and manifested. He can thus facilitate a breakthrough of his energy flux into his patients' systems. This requires that the therapist quite consciously look for opportunities to inject this energy into the group processes and that he find ways of translating the force into appropriate information. In this way, it can be perceived and understood cognitively, as well as being received on an as yet poorly understood emotional or even extrasensory level.

The therapist should become aware, therefore, of concentrating this narrowed beam of nurtenergy during the therapy meeting as he checks the content constantly against the cognitive map of his preferred theory of personality. It requires that the therapist be alert for tiny cues when the patients first deviate from their helplessness script and make attempts to try a new coping device or emit some faith in change. He should listen for such cues and magnify them or freeze the process by pointing the attention of the group to them. He might also express his own pleasure at their occurrence. Further reinforcement needs to occur when new and more positive behavior patterns emerge among patients. Liberal injection of the therapist's feelings of pleasure and even joy can sometimes be helpful here, especially when patients begin to sound more hopeful or venture forth with less self-defeating behavior patterns or feelings. In addition, the therapist can explain and, therefore, neutralize feelings of anxiety or disappointment in the group by pointing to them as inevitable manifestations of the group process. In this way, these forces do not become obstacles that overwhelm the group or discourage negentropic transformation. In another publication, I have illustrated in more detail how the group therapist can reinforce and accelerate this process of self-generation of new energy for change (Gruen, 1977b).

PRACTICAL IMPLICATIONS FOR THE THERAPIST

In conclusion, there are implications for the therapist inherent in this model of a therapy group's energy processes. First of all, the assumption that a force like nurtenergy is a necessary component to bring about a negentropic, cohesive stage requires that we train and encourage therapists who are capable of generating and sustaining such a force throughout the duration of their group. Besides implying their own availability of surplus nurtenergy from their essentially negentropic personal functioning, they should not have needs invested into the group or into their role as a therapist which would inhibit the production and visibility of nurtenergy. Hence, power needs, needs for friendship, love and acceptance, needs for personal relevance, etc., should not be operating in the therapist in such an overwhelming way that he is constantly looking for gratification from the group.

Also, the therapist should have faith in the healing power of therapy and in the changeability of human beings. Undue pessimism here may inhibit his nurtenergetic faith in his patients' coping resources. This implication points to a researchable assumption regarding therapist's confidence in his patients as it is related to outcome. According to my formulation about the nature and direction of nurtenergy, the therapist who has the greatest realistic confidence in his patients' coping power and potential for change should show better results—all other factors being equal. Hence, a therapist who is pessimistic about human nature, who feels that individuals are basically determined by forces operating in childhood or controlled only by fate, or who believes that people are necessarily constricted by defensive systems cannot generate much nurtenergy. Therapists must be aware of self-fulfilling prophesies. Hence, the dimension "belief in the plasticity and growth of the human being" versus "the leopard cannot change his spots" may be a meaningful correlate of the amount of nurtenergy available to a therapist and therefore the amount of such energy usable for his or her patients. Also, if the therapist is too exclusively tied to a cognitive orientation which requires him to diagnose the patient's behavior in theoretical concepts at the expense of letting his feelings also guide him, he could seriously jeopardize his free release of any excess nurtenergy toward the group.

Another implication is that transformation or working-through in patients is not possible without the generation and availability of therapist's nurtenergy. Take, for example, a therapist who makes and maintains a good systems contract with this patient, who is sensitive and alert to the important variables in his patient's pathology and character, who can invest them with adequate meanings from his knowledge and experience, who has learned the right techniques of dealing with personality and group manifestations and who applies them at appropriate, choice points. He still cannot adequately provide a focus for patient transformation unless he also can rely on available nurtenergy and can inject it as an organizing focus (see Chapter 11). Without this, his tool of sensitivity, his theoretical understanding, and his knowledge of the use of tools become sterile techniques. The energy must be available as a catalytic leverage for change before other skills and tools from the therapist can be applied.

A final implication is that the therapist can magnify the availability of his surplus energy and encourage its perception and use by the patients during the initial stages by always being alert to special opportunities, by reinforcing the patients' correct perceptions and use of this energy, and by reinforcing the tender beginning of negentropic forces, especially the emergence of surplus nurtenergy in his patients. In this way, the process of transformation to group and individual negentropic systems can be accelerated and brought under the therapist's, and eventually the group's, conscious guidance.

Chapter 5

Entry: A Study of
Energy in Groups

By Irvin A. Kraft, M.D.

Editor's Introduction. In this chapter Dr. Kraft examines how the entrance of a new member into a group might alter energy flow. Kraft's ideas are predicated on two basic assumptions: 1) Groups exist in order to process emotional energy and 2) Swirls of emotional energy (patterns of energy flow) are generated by the co-mingling and co-production of energy by group members. There is great similarity between Kraft's concept of swirling and the concept of opening as discussed in Chapter 2.

Kraft's emotional flow of energy is an exciting construct which reflects the nature of living systems. Along with his explanation of this process in groups, the author relates entry to the overall boundarying process and looks at group role assignments for new members.

In the course of this work, Kraft reemphasizes the four hierarchical levels of structure (or organization) of energy: biochemical, intrapsychic, interpersonal and sociocultural. Group energy results from the processing of energy by each group member at each level.

Kraft builds his energy-oriented framework and then poses trenchant questions dealing with energy transactions in the acceptance of new members, and new sources of power for groups. While he answers these questions, he couples GST with the specific issue of entry into psychotherapy groups. In his ingenious presentation, Kraft has formulated an explanation of a powerful force that can be utilized to help achieve autonomy in living groups.

To study a phenomenon in science, the analytic mode simplifies it to the point where presumably we measure solitary factors. How can this analytic procedure work with the complexities of a group, even one as small as a therapy group of eight with two co-leaders? Of the various analyses attempted in group therapy, a typical procedure assumes sequential episodes in the group's saga, as if the therapists started with eight or so members at one time, everyone met at each session, and the group ended at a given point in time.

Since this does not fit what I have experienced and studied, I asked certain questions: What in reality (as I "know" it) really happens in my adult groups? I chose that form of group therapy, for I despaired of describing adolescent or latency groups within this format. First, my groups are open-ended, having a life of years and years (!), comprising perhaps 20 or more persons over a period of 24 to 36 months. The group encounters entries, departures, absences, changes of co-leaders, and deaths. The actual number of the eight patient members attending a given session might be as low as four and as high as eight, depending on the time of the year (e.g., Christmas holidays), vacations, and other factors. Some members wholeheartedly agree at the time of the recommendation of group therapy to a minimum trial of three months, and they leave before or just after the time contracted for.

Other writers about therapy groups have catalogued their impressions under the two classical titles of process and content. In the process framework, the groups examined a new member at several levels of interaction: "Tell us your problem. Why are you here?" As the new member's narration ensued, various members would respond with reference to their own experiences and perhaps to those of the group: "I had that kind of problem with my spouse, so I thought, and then the group helped me see that I really was doing something else, like being a rescuer." As the old members and the new one interacted, the group tested him as to his group suitability, often by throwing directly at him a feeling statement. "You just disgust me the way you go on and on and don't see what we put right to you!" In the content framework, on the other hand, group members would focus on the story of the new patient and deal more with its details and intricacies than with how they perceived his or her interpersonal style.

A therapy group lends itself, as do other groups, to different models that explicate its structure and functions. In general system theory, the group occupies the niche of an open or living system in which its parts undergo replacement without altering the group's continuing structure. The group, as an open system, exists for the processing of energy more than for its information content. We designate the energy processing procedures at the group level as primarily involving a form of energy, emotional energy.

To illustrate this usage of an energy concept in groups, I asked myself: How do I distinguish one group from another of the five or more that I have going at any one time? Do I name it by the day of the week on which it meets? By the composition of membership at a given time: all women, mixed gender, act-outers? Pursuing this relentlessly with myself, I realized I disregard diagnoses, types of problems, numbers of patients, and other factors, and I basically consider each group as to its present state of working, of effectiveness and of tenor. In essence, then, my real description, emotionally and intellectually, is how the flow of energy goes in each.

This brought me to a crisis of how do I really further picture or develop an image of each group? The answer turns out to be a sort of Dow-Jones Group Energy Average with an ample supply of peaks and valleys (see Figure 1).

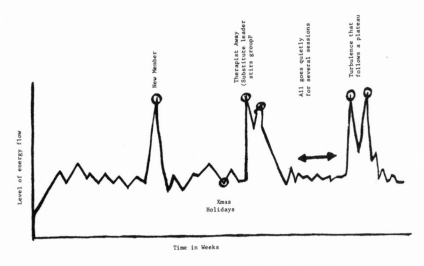

Figure 1. Level of energy flow over time in a typical group

Thus, to return more specifically to the theme of this paper, the continuity of a group requires a structure, a framework that identifies it over a period of time and which attends to the variegated, changing patterns unique to that group. Since content or even themes change from session to session and over periods of time, energy flow traits become fundamental identifiers to both the rational and intuitive processes of the leader. Transformations do occur in parts of the group—the patients and the leader—as do isomorphisms.

To depict these ideas more vividly, we shall first visualize interactions in a group by the more traditional mode of arrows, indicators of contact and exchange (Figure 2). We suggest that the same sequence of group events, when viewed from the perspective of energy flow, would be as shown in Figure 3.

Thus, A and B do not just vector a line of a message to each other and to C, but each emits energy that mutually affects all members of the group, including the leaders.

If this is so, we confront a number of implications. For our purposes, we shall differ from the concept of emotional energy as Gruen (1977a, b; Chapter 4)

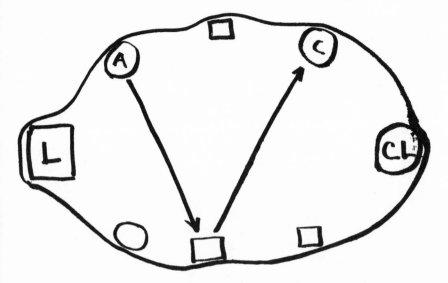

Figure 2. Leader decides patient has fitability for the group

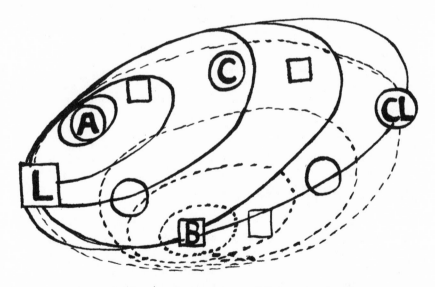

Figure 3. Picturing the group as a swirling energy structure

describes it. We assume that emotional energy is neither good nor bad, positive nor negative, efficient nor inefficient, intelligible nor non-intelligible. Swirls of emotional energy become known and detected by group members and yet not necessarily tagged or identified. Intensity and quantity furnish qualities to which an individual patient can then attach content markers and react according to his or her own particular perceptual screen. In effect, the receiving person processes the overt and covert behaviors of the other group members, as well as his own internal processes, for identification or naming the energy. Somebody has to move, speak, moan or alter his body expressions to offer content information. As a patient receives an impact of emotional energy, he may find himself confused; that is, he senses the energy impact but can't translate it adequately and accurately at the cognitive level.

To carry this description to an extreme, picture a therapy group that meets silently in total darkness without touching each other. Emotional energy will swirl and encompass its members, surely to be detected—but how to be interpreted? Processing of emotional energy requires the use of sensory modalities and time. Most episodes in a group occur in the immediate present, yet we know of other instances when a patient realizes hours or days later that something transpired in him in the group meeting.

Ed had learned in the group how he intellectualized his life actions, thoughts, and feelings. This had been very ego-syntonic in his engineering work where his colleagues jokingly called him the Mr. Spock of their enterprise. He came to group psychotherapy after a lovely young lady told him heatedly that she wanted his feelings and him and not just thoughts. Once in the group he felt accepted but puzzled by the other members' insistence on sticking with feeling expressions. Three days after a very intense emotional confrontation of several members, Ed with his woman friend watched a television show and felt tears in his eyes and on his cheeks. She wouldn't let him wipe them away, and, as this occurred, he flashed to the group scene and realized he had been deeply penetrated by the level of emotional energy in that session. And now he connected it with his own life. He finally began to attach self-referent words or markers to some of the emotional energy he had deflected previously.

Emotional energy does possess the characteristic of intensity which is later qualitatively dealt with by the various patients' boundaries. Roles, transferences, countertransferences, outbreaks, retreats, regressions, etc. all demonstrate some usage and marking of emotional energy.

Gruen (Chapter 4) tackles the leader's therapeutic behaviors of good will, love, empathy, and caring and calls them nurtenergy. He compares it to a laser beam, while in this paper we see emotional energy in general as a widening series of concentric circles with some specific markers or directors, such as, "John, I like the way you let out your feelings then." All members of the group know the leader addressed his emission of emotional energy to John, yet each can also share it within the receiving capacities of his boundary subsystem.

So, the core pattern for each member of the group is that of the leader and his consistent emanation of energy by his own living system (Lieberman, Yalom, & Miles, 1973). He is a central swirler. He reflects this in his patient selection, although, in private practice groups, fee payment ability strongly determines patient choice. Within that constraint, the leader selects patients who need to recognize and more effectively deal with emotions. The leader's patterns of energy flow, which change with his age and other factors, such as his life experiences, remain central. At the same time, the other group units and the co-leader determine certain patterns of flow despite what the leader might do. This persists independent of techniques and theory and personal styles.

Energy in a group never exceeds a certain total. We know of an energizer role some patients portray. Therefore, a total or even a median level of energy stays higher for that period of time. Or, if there is a series of crises, the group keeps its level increased.

We see also that in this context there exists group emotional energy, which, however, is not created by the group, a construct, but by the co-mingling and co-production of energy by the various group members. They then invest this into a time-space-limited organization, the group. This swirl of energy, whose intensity, quality, and quantity vary from moment to moment, accretes, refurbishes itself, adds to or divests itself of markers and identifications, and then redistributes its net energy back to its individual members when the session ends. We do not see the group existing as an entity or living system beyond when it meets with its members. They refer to it as: "Our group . . ." "The Group . . ." "My group . . .". And meanwhile, once the energy flow that crossed boundaries gets marked and embedded in individual memories, it lives on in their demarcated energy storage systems.

Let us follow this model through with other of the general system theory concepts. A basic perception consists of hierarchical levels of structure or organization of energy. In this volume we view four such levels in each individual of the group: biochemical, intrapsychic, interpersonal, and sociocultural (see Chapter 6). Any movement of energy involves these levels, and the group energy swirl ultimately resides value-wise in how the individual group member processes, utilizes, and reflects it at each level.

For example, the group has become intensely involved in Mary's highly charged expositions of her anxiety attacks. She has known and dwelled with them for over 20 years, polishing and burnishing them in previous therapy to be her shining self-presentation of the chalice of discomfort. The leader asked the group members to consider their own experiences with anxiety and tension, and then, using this information, arrive at how to detect and to measure this variety of emotional energy. They agreed that a biochemical level of energy was involved, as in heart rate, respiration and pupillary size. They conceded that Mary at an intrapsychic level perceived herself as anxious and having an attack. They accepted that they too would be involved in Mary's episode, since its emotional energy should spill out to be detected and processed by them. With such energy levels in mind, they concluded that direct inspection of Mary, combined with their introspective observations of themselves, failed to substantiate Mary's chronic claim to acerbic fame: her true, classical anxiety attacks. She had a phantasmagoria of signs and symptoms that in reality remained within herself, not showing externally except with her reported, verbalized introspection of her intrapsychic level of involvement.

This paper deals with entry from the viewpoint of energy flow, as required by the definitions and assumptions of general system theory. Other chapters have defined general system theory, levels of energy involvement, and multiple facets important to viewing therapy groups in GST terms. In this framework we pose a number of questions: What is the nature of emotional interchange? How do we describe the group's acceptance of a new member in energic terms? Can a group be an open system without additional sources of energy? Is entry a form of acquiring additional energy in a group?

ENTRY

Entry means here that the group witnesses a person, hitherto not so considered as a member, coming to the meeting of the group. He arrives obviously because the leader suggested that he join the group. Procedures for this vary from leader to leader, yet, ultimately, in the kind of group defined here, the entry of a new patient derives from a decision by the leader. Should this prospective member be discussed with and by the group prior to entering? Do the group members have any true decision-making powers? Can they reject a newcomer?

Since no single answer exists, but variation abounds, we can illustrate this with the example of Tom, a moderately paranoid architect, depressed with his loss of work. From a general systems viewpoint, the leader in our example determines that Tom will enter the group, and the group members at least physically alter the group boundary to permit Tom to enter and to sit among those already initiated. Immediately, the internal energy flow of the group changes as the members assess Tom. The options before them consist of some sort of struggle with the leader or with Tom to reject him or to change the decision. Or, the group can treat Tom more as an inclusion body within the structure of the group but not truly transact with him (see Figure 4). Thus, Tom may not be playing a role active enough by group criteria for them to say he has been accepted by them into the group system.

Tom may intercede with his energy flows, interfering, directing, obstructing or increasing the energy quantums of the group, and still the group consensus denies him membership. Perhaps then we see the paradox of a system denying part of its own existence and structure. It is my impression that, regardless of how the group may consider itself, realignment of energy flows begins the moment Tom physically enters, regardless of what signals members emit to negate or affirm his membership. Whether refusing or affirming his presence, each member nevertheless encounters Tom, utilizes energy to demarcate and to identify him (his maleness, sexuality, ideas, problems, etc.), instigates energy circuits intrapsychically at once, and evidences the existence of additional emotional energy in the group. Functional energy flows and interacts regardless of the nature of the signals of communication.

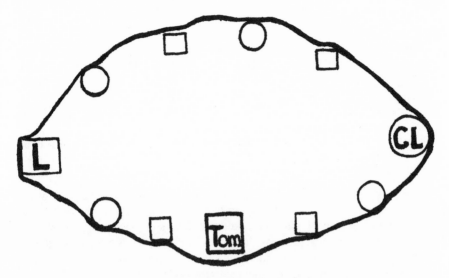

Figure 4. First group meeting with physical entrance

Tom sat silent most of his first session, but his almost unblinking stare, his intense near-glaring at speakers, his stiffness of posture, and his obvious positive transference to the therapist served as stimuli. Some members responded to Tom verbally. Others looked at him frequently and some spoke up at times in ways that were designed to see if Tom reacted.

Essentially, the group struggles with the realization at some level of awareness that Tom enters the group at a different stratum of perceptivity and operational communication than theirs. Along with the customary immediate estimates of Tom's craziness, intellectual brightness, and caring capacity, they really concern themselves with whether he displays his emotional energy capacity primarily in an analog, a digital or in a combined manner. Is Tom going to intellectualize or will he be a high-level emoter?

By this I refer to the crude dichotomization of left and right brain communications. This classification bases itself on recent work with patients after surgery that severs the commissure that connects the two sides. Left brain comprises digital, analytic, arithmetic summations, black-white, and deductive reasonings. Essentially, the right brain shows analog, synthetic, gestalt, intuitive, and polychromatic thinking. Most of my groups function more with the latter emphasis, although both formats find utilization at the times most appropriate to the focus of communication of the group. For example, episodes of high emotional content tend to be "irrational," "colorful," using basic language, and very impressionistic (right brain). The group as an open system decides on what level of interaction and perception to enclose Tom with its boundary. As Figure 4 suggests, Tom seems in and yet out.

Another example might help here:

Rosemary, whose boundary system reads the world as dangerous unless placated by crippling rituals and compulsions, entered a therapy group, with many misgivings, after a period of individual therapy. She rarely spoke, cried frequently, and always came late by 15-30 minutes. She described her fears and concerns personally, yet somehow from her left brain. She resisted crossing her own and the group boundary for eight weeks and then failed to show up thereafter.

In contrast, Rose Ellen entered a group without any preliminary sessions other than one connected with her son's consultation, and she became an involved member in the initial session, as she operated with them on a right brain level with high intensities of feeling.

After a period of intense outflow and interflow of emotional energy, the group often lapses into a lower level of energy output, as if weary from the processing of so much input by each member, and the members become aware (sometimes quite abruptly) that much time has elapsed. A therapy group's boundaries always operate with a time frame, especially as the group is usually structured in advance to meet for one and a half to two hours with the leader. Entry tests this traditional allocation, for the group must decide on the new member's entrance during that session, or it might arrive at a pattern of taking perhaps four or five sessions for boundary penetration.

The time for penetration remains flexible in duration and is relative. Also, the boundary mechanism may vacillate with a new patient: in-out; partially in or out. If the new patient pulls back and retreats as the boundary opens for him, some of the group's energy escapes and is lost. Closure of a boundary entrance may be accompanied with irritability by group members or the system may generate bursts of energy, as the members wax with wrath over the new member's withdrawal behavior.

Thus, boundarying processes themselves become an important second phase of entry, after the leader's initial decision, which is phase one. Has the leader primarily enacted the role of decider in the first stage of entry for the boundary subsystem? Perhaps he assumed more the decider-initiator function and then a decider-follower role as the group itself processes entry. Part of this duality involves considerations presumably beyond the group as a system per se: "Do I need another group member? For group psychodynamic reasons? For money? I'll look over the group and my candidates and decide on fit. Do psychodynamics dominate which individual to select for which group? Or do I pay more heed to right-left brain considerations? I assume any of the new ones can afford my fee." Ultimately, fit follows the form that the energy distribution of the group now takes.

The leader, having pursued his questions to an answer, offers the new member to the group's processes for transiting its boundary. He becomes the system's initial ingestor. We saw above that the group might encapsulate new members for a time as inclusions. Recall, of course, that the new patient possesses his own boundary subsystem, which undergoes processes isomorphic to those of the group. Thus, we have a major system, the group, boundarying with a new prospect's boundary subsystem. I suggest that "fitability" emerges as a consequence rather than as a pre-entry condition.

"Fitability," a not too elegant term, describes how a new member rates or ranks according to the numerous criteria in the minds of the group members. As mentioned above, entry involves phases of fitability (see Figure 5). The initial or first phase rests with the leader's evaluation of the patient and his subsequent decision to place the patient in the group. In phase 2 the new patient begins the physical and emotional process of boundarying with the group members, who know the leader's approval resides as a given. Depending on past experience in

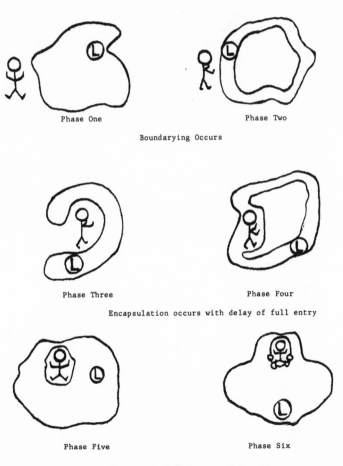

Phase One　　　　　　　　　　　　Phase Two

Boundarying Occurs

Phase Three　　　　　　　　　　　　Phase Four

Encapsulation occurs with delay of full entry

Phase Five　　　　　　　　　　　　Phase Six

Entry accomplished as systeming occurs

Figure 5. Phases of the entry process

the group, such as the rare episode when a group has in effect denied membership to a newcomer, most members believe the new one will eventually be a good, reverberating colleague. Still, however, they process him, each according to his own perceptions.

In phase 3, the group scrutinizes him over a number of sessions, averaging at least three to ten weeks, as to how congruent he is with the ongoing passage of the group. This evaluation can involve not only those functions while the leader is present, but after-group, leaderless sessions as well. Phase 4 finds him firmly entrenched in the group.

Now, examining the same sequence in energy and system terms, fitability essentially connotes that the newcomer's system of emotional energy contains the capacity to receive and to emit energy at levels commensurate with the leader's estimate of the baseline level of the group.

Tim, a 53-year-old married engineer, was referred to the therapist for depression and dissatisfaction with his marriage. These complaints emerged after his 14-year-old daughter entered an adolescent group for her dissident behavior, including runaways. Tim requested group therapy because "I know I won't talk or reveal much to you individually; I find myself like a clam that way." With misgivings by the therapist Tim entered the group. In phase 2, Tim obviously strove to maintain his boundary like a Maginot Line, and group members over the next three or four sessions underwent summing with him (see Durkin, Chapter 13). Finally, Tim agreed to attend an after-group dinner meeting. One of the women members sat next to him, proceeding to talk intensely to him, closely, eye-to-eye, of how she believed he could release himself from behind his wall of compulsive reiteration of his wife's sexual coldness. Tim haltingly and softly said to her, "I'm so alone!" In subsequent meetings Tim dressed more casually, spoke of himself, and felt part of the group as they underwent systeming.

Another clinical vignette illustrates how quickly one can transit the boundaries when a patient's psychological readiness pours out emotional energy to the group from the moment of physical entrance.

Connie came for consultation after her husband and his lover had been seen in a panic state with significant psychopathology bathing all three. She and her husband of eight years had shifted their group spouse-sharing, swinger activities to a menage à trois which cracked open. After one individual visit, Connie entered a group as a scared, seemingly intimidated, monotoned, shy woman. About halfway through that session, the leader turned to Connie and related the current group interaction to her situation by asking her how swinging behavior fitted with it. As she replied, she gazed primarily at the therapist with the group's attention riveted on her. Her plea for responsiveness touched the group and entry to it occurred quickly with concurrence of both boundary mechanisms.

OTHER ROLES AND FUNCTIONS OF LIVING GROUPS

Entry spotlights various facets of the group's structure and its matter-energy processing subsystems. The process of entry foreshadows many other functions in the group. Structure itself emerges from the arrangements of system elements in the three dimensions of space and the one of time. Variable rates of change also characterize structure. A therapy group derives structure from the varying topology of its members, the setting usually prescribed by the leader, the time of and duration of the meetings, and the physio-psychologic characteristics of the leader and the group members—all, in effect, relating to the dynamic functional flow of emotional energy. This brings alive and makes familiar the rather rigid, anatomically structural terms of Miller (1978).

As mentioned above, group process delineates how the members act, think, and feel with each other and within themselves. The group system delegates nonverbally to various members certain functions, sometimes seen as role-task assignments. One interesting and constructive trait definition is that often pridefully assumed by the borderline or pseudoneurotic patient. Often I'll turn to that person and ask him to translate what the group seems to be undergoing at that time. He will usually define in terms of himself how the emotional energy flow of the group goes and what it means. By this and similar techniques, the leader rewards certain actions and energy transactions, thereby assigning values to them. Another of his functions is to regulate and to direct the energy flow when he judges it to be too intense for a particular patient or even destructive for the entire group. One technique of this lies in using humor to plateau and to lower the energy intensity; another is to utilize a special facility of one of the members whose wit either affords release for the group or helps channel energy flow.

Jim quickly became the overt humorist of the group. His warm but dry wit illuminated certain moments, often helping an energy eddy resume a viable connection with the main energy flow of the group. For instance, Jim might say, "Gosh, if I could just express a feeling the way you do, I'd be right in the middle of this group on that point."

The group usually assigns its processes and working to its own members, not to outsiders. Part of that is confidentiality. The members feel more comfortable in not disclosing group content or transactions to spouses or others.

Entry of a patient and the leader's actions illustrate the assignment process. The leader might assign directly or nonverbally certain tasks of the group to the new member. If the group does not agree with the leader's assignment, it might well make its own delegations. Conflict, usually not verbalized, can occur, and the leader might believe his cogent decider functions supersede those of the group's noncompliance. In the following example, Rosy was like a black hole in astronomy, and the group took over her "fate" with them.

Rosy came to the group looking harried and haggard in the almost immediate aftermath of breaking off a seven-year sadomasochistic affair with her woman lover and resuming her wife-mother roles with her husband and two children. She mentioned in her one-to-one consultation interview that despite over six years of couple therapy she would probably be reluctant to discuss in a mixed adult group these past experiences. Her depressed, drained appearance in her first group session elicited approaches by group members, and her meager responses brought on an attack by Mary, "I talk to you and try to help you, and all you do is swallow up my words and sympathy. When will you get enough to move and let us in?"

Other system functions can be examined in an anatomical framework (Miller, 1978) to obtain more information about our initial questions. Despite limitations of being structured and limited for process, we can suggest that the producer subsystem organizes the stable intrasystem relationships which carry on for satisfactory episodes of time. The producer subsystem becomes evident and glaring as the group struggles about when to do what with the new member. Seating arrangements, dyadic and triadic alignments—all of these and others, as the new member is processed, express the functions of the producer subsystem. Usually the group itself, with the therapist's leadership, tends to fulfill this role.

Elizabeth always seated herself as close to the leader as possible, usually in the chair just to his right, and she dangled her hand provocatively close to his body. She had staked this position so definitely that, even when she arrived late, that seat remained hers. The group tacitly assumed a producer role-function, assigning topology according to the implicit claims of each member, primarily with reference to the leader and his energy flow. Secondarily, the dyads and triads of member relationships decided who would sit where.

Other subsystems exist, according to Miller (1978). In his more formal delineation of subsystems, the storage of matter-energy strongly plays into the system's survival. These elements for deposit comprise in our group the ideas, behaviors, modes of access to right brain data, and the triggers for emotional outbursts. Prior to entry these role and task assignments have been nonverbally agreed upon by the leader and the group members. For example, the group cynic or humorist has an assignment to store his tricks and talents for use when the group wants to call them for release, exposition or elucidation. Entry of a new member as a new subsystem poses the question of what storage capacity, talent or capability he has. Will he be assigned tasks formerly done by group member A or B because it turns out that he does certain ones better? Is he a competitor?

Fanny entered the group looking sad but friendly. After about an hour of interaction, during which she was alertly silent, Fanny suddenly interrupted Charlie's pontifications of his insights with a very pungent question. This startled Charlie and the other members. "Wow!" "This gal really shoots from the hip!" "Where do you go now, Charlie?" asked John, one of the oldest in membership. Fanny then marked herself as the person who'd remember everything and put it back out with deep insights referable to herself and others.

Miller (1978) includes an extruder subsystem entity which deals with the wastes created by the suprasystem. In a therapy group waste would be either a member of brief or even longtime membership who shows behavior intolerable to the group and its rules. The entry of a new patient who becomes quite unacceptable to the group may bring on extrusion or expulsion, as if he were a splinter or a foreign body, rather than even a waste by-product.

Bob entered the group and left three weeks later without a word to the leader in the group. He dominated his first session with comments about himself and others that showed fear and contempt: "If I decide to do something, I'll do it, like not getting drunk." Betsy softly asked, "Then why are you here?" Bob ignored her. He refused rather loudly and strongly to join in after-group dinner sessions. When his absence was definite, the group never mentioned him again.

Among the subsystems processing information, the input transducer involves both the leader and other group members, for this sensory function brings markers conveying information into the group. Signals from the extero-group world cross the boundary in the form of verbal narrations by its members of outside events that affect one patient or another, and which then service other group members. Entry amplifies this, for a new member brings new experiences, traumas, and other accounts for the group to process via each one's perceptual screen (boundary).

Bedford came because his extramarital affair with a young woman had begun to possess him to the extent that he had become much less productive and increasingly perfunctory at work. "Shape up or out you go!" was the dictum from his superior. Confusion, despair, and depression pushed him to consultation and the group. He narrated hesitantly and circumstantially to the group the tragic ins and outs of his previous adventures. The rapt attention of group members indicated that Bedford had effected entry immediately and that he brought some facts and significant fantasy that amplified the energy level of the group. Lots of swirling energetic interplay gave Bedford a strong feeling of belonging and directives for actions toward his friend.

Another subsystem, the associator, forms ". . . enduring associations among items of information in the system" (Miller, 1978). A group within a short period of its own life as a system develops its own history of shared events and seems to have a need for some connections with its own past. Even though there might well have been departures of most members, continuity exists via the leader and remaining patients, who clue in newcomers by amplifying references to previous events in or after the group session. When a new patient initially senses this continuity and shared past of the group, he may feel isolated. Part of group integration of the newcomer consists of sharing these associations, thereby also reducing isolation. Entry, therefore, points out how much stored and associated history and recollection is almost taken for granted.

Miller (1978) indicates that a system may not have all of the above and other features, yet the one essential subsystem is the decider "in the sense that a system cannot be symbiotic or parasitic on another system for its deciding."

When, for example, a member insists on talking about the actions and deeds of an outsider, such as his wife or his boss, the group decides and informs him to talk about himself.

Kent, as one of the seniors in service in his group, "obsessed and compulsed" endlessly until Tim challenged him on it. "I dare you to contract with us for the next five meetings to tell us only good things about yourself and none of that stuff about your boss, the business, and your mother." Everyone chimed in supporting the proposal and Kent acquiesced. In effect, he agreed that his energy expenditures in the group would be more meaningful when concentrated on his here and now with his co-members.

Other features of the group as an open system also reflect the impact of entry. Feedback phenomena, both negative and positive, become enhanced by a new member entering the group. Feedback describes the two channels by which a portion of the output data from the system returns to the input, take-up point of the system. The returned information can be used by the system either to stay steady or to deviate from its previous pattern. The former is termed negative feedback and the latter positive feedback.

Tom feels impact from the group almost immediately during his first session in it. This unnerves him, as his system gropes with this input new to him. Tom reflects to the group a highly emotionally charged outburst about himself: "I don't know what you really mean, but I really feel put down. You people don't realize how smug you are in your way of dealing with me, and I don't like it!" The group responds by checking on itself, its behavior and its verbal productions. As this occurs, one person comments: "Tom is right; we have become smug. Look at the way we ignored his signals." This becomes positive feedback to unsettle the group and to alter its output patterns.

SUMMARY OF ENERGY AND ENTRY

Thus, we see that the entry phenomenon highlights for group therapy in energy terms a number of the premises of general system theory. We imagine and detail somewhat the extensive complexity of the group system; yet, large areas remain to be examined. As the group psychotherapist applies his own psychodynamic theoretic framework to his groups, casting his observant eye and third ear on the same phenomena may prove fruitful in the mode of open, living systems. Emotional energy flow proves a fascinating construct to patients as the leader openly shares it with them and reinforces a leader's tendency to therapeutic self-insight.

Chapter 6

The Concept of Role
as a Boundary Structure
in Small Groups

By K. Roy MacKenzie, M.D.

Editor's Introduction. This chapter contributes guidelines from a GST perspective to help organize the complex, continuously changing relationships in a therapy group. Dr. MacKenzie proposes that role positions are not only useful as organizing measures and valuable tools for understanding group dynamics, but also essential for the therapeutic group process. As individual members discover roles in which they function well, they engage in a process that focuses on the boundary that distinguishes their individual personalities and their specific role requirements. This concept may be useful in understanding the transformations of individual group members.

After reviewing the social psychological literature on small group roles, the author discusses various roles and dimensions of groups. He also explains systems, suprasystems, and subsystems and suggests an examination of the boundaries between these organizing units. Dr. MacKenzie focuses on GST principles of isomorphy, levels of organization, and the idea that group members are not simply results of their contexts but actively participate in the development of their own contexts.

General system theory properly emphasizes the delineation of system units, together with related suprasystems and subsystems. By thus organizing the field of action, it becomes possible to identify the boundaries among these units and the nature of the transactions which occur across such boundaries. In the context

The research program from which this paper originated is supported by an operating grant from the Alberta Mental Health Advisory Council and the National Institute of Mental Health, Grant No. RO3 MH34901.

of small group psychotherapy, it is conventional to speak of the group as the system, and its individual members as the subsystems (Gray, Duhl, & Rizzo, 1969). Traditional psychotherapeutic approaches have focused particularly upon the subsystem of the individual and the interactional patterns between a given individual and others, either in a dyadic context or in a group setting (Bales, 1950; Rogers, 1961). Another orientation has been to consider the group-as-a-whole (Bion, 1961; Ezriel, 1950; Whitaker & Lieberman, 1967), while still others have emphasized the place of the group in a larger organizational context (Kernberg, 1975).

In this chapter, I would like to look in some depth at the boundary between the subsystem of the individual and the system of the group. Many of the existing concepts regarding these two levels in the hierarchy of organization have unintentionally served to blur the distinction between the units involved. This has resulted in terms suited to individual psychotherapy being inappropriately applied to the group-as-a-whole. I would like to review these traditional concepts of the group and contrast them with more contemporary ideas concerning the group as a social system. This will include a review of the concept of group norms and climate, as well as a consideration of group roles and group development stages. I hope this will highlight the inappropriate use of the term "role" to label personality features and lead to a reconsideration of the concept of role as a resolution to the boundary issue between the subsystem of the individual and the system of the group. It is suggested that the designation of group role and the incorporation of an individual member into that role is a result of the developmental needs of the group interacting with the qualities of the individual. It thus highlights the general systems focus upon discrete systems and subsystems and the transactions across their mutual boundaries.

TRADITIONAL CONCEPTS OF A GROUP-AS-A-WHOLE

The study of the group as a social system, that is, as an organizational entity, has been hampered by the language generally chosen to describe group-as-a-whole phenomena. A group is not an individual, and terms used to describe it must be appropriate to a group level in the organizational hierarchy. The group as an entity is at a different level in the organizational structure with its own group boundary, within which are located the individual boundaries of the member subsystems. To be more specific, a group has no cerebral cortex and cannot think. What happens in a group may cause each of the members to think and, indeed, their thinking may at times have some commonalities, but it is the individuals, not the group, who are managing information in a symbolic fashion.

Bion's (1961) concept of "basic assumptions" implies that the group "en masse" has a common pattern of thinking which transcends the individual. Bion assumes that all members of the group, whether or not they demonstrate their adherence to this common theme, must be reacting to it. The vagueness of his language betrays the difficulty in applying individual psychological concepts to a group system.

In short, I shall insist that I am quite justified in saying that the group feels such and such when, in fact, perhaps only one or two people would seem to provide by their behaviour warrant for such a statement, if, at the time of behaving like this, the group show no outward sign of repudiating the lead they are given. I daresay it will be possible to base belief in the complicity of the group on something more convincing than negative evidence, *but for the time being I regard negative evidence as good enough* (1961, p. 58, emphasis mine).

I mean to indicate, by its use, the individual's readiness to enter into combination with the group in making and acting on the basic assumptions; if his capacity for combination is great, I shall speak of a high valency, if small, of a low valency; he can have, in my view, no valency only by ceasing to be, as far as mental function is concerned, human. Although I use this word to describe phenomena that are visible as, or deducible from, psychological events, yet I wish also to use it to indicate a readiness to combine on levels that *can hardly be called mental at all but are characterized by behaviour in the human being that is more analogous to tropism in plants* than to purposive behaviour such as is implicit in a word like "assumption" (1961, p. 117, emphasis mine).

Investigation shows that these aims are sometimes hindered, occasionally furthered by emotional drives of *obscure origin*. A certain cohesion is given to these anomalous mental activities if it is assumed that emotionally the group acts as if it had certain basic assumptions about its aims. These basic assumptions, which appear to be fairly adequately adumbrated by three formulations, dependence, pairing, and fighting or flight, are, on further investigation, seen to displace each other, *as if in response to some unexplained impulse.* (1961, p. 189, emphasis mine).

Whitaker and Lieberman (1967) have developed the concept of group focal conflict from the same theoretical tradition. Their arguments are perhaps best summarized in their key propositions.

Proposition 1. Successive individual behaviors are linked associatively and refer to a common underlying concern about the here and now situation.
Proposition 2. The sequence of diverse events which occur in a group can be conceptualized as a common, covert conflict (the group focal conflict) which consists of an impulse or wish (the disturbing motive) opposed by an associated fear (the reactive motive). Both aspects of the group focal conflict refer to the current setting.
Proposition 3. When confronted with a group focal conflict, the patients direct efforts toward establishing a solution which will reduce anxiety by alleviating the reactive fears and, at the same time, satisfy to the maximum possible degree the disturbing impulse.
Proposition 4. Successful solutions have two properties. First, they are shared; the behavior of all members is consistent with or bound by the solution. Second, successful solutions reduce reactive fears; the individuals experience greater anxiety prior to the establishment of a successful solution, less anxiety after the solution is established (p. 17).

These examples of group level conceptualization incorporate a basic failure of boundary definition. It may well be that a number of group members are struggling with a similar psychodynamic issue. However, each of them is doing this in his own fashion, utilizing his own past experience and own typical cognitive style. To describe the group as having these thoughts would be inaccurate, as it might be misleading. All of us have found ourselves, from time to time, resonating to common dimensions in group discussions. To say that in such a situation the group is thinking these thoughts is, in essence, to deny the unique individuality of each member and to distort the concept of the group.

THE GROUP AS A SOCIAL SYSTEM

A group becomes a group and not a "heap" of individuals, to borrow a term from physics, only when it becomes organized. Organization implies the recognition of nonrandom events. Once patterns of behavior become evident, these patterns provide handles for describing and categorizing events. Attempts can then be made to understand the significance of such patterns and allow at least modest prediction of future behavior. To quote Watzlawick et al. (1967):

The search for pattern is the basis of all scientific investigation. Where there is pattern, there is significance—this epistemological maxim also holds for the study of human interaction (p. 36).

All of this implies that a group becomes a group from the systems organization standpoint when it begins to function in such a way that the behavior of one individual has predictable implications for the actions of others. Thus, an organizational system of mutual interdependence emerges in the sense that no one individual can act entirely autonomously. His behavior is both a partial result of the context in which it occurs and contributes to the ongoing development of that context.

Group Norms and Climate

To understand behavior, it is not enough to understand the individual actor. One must also assess the context in which the behavior is occurring. A particularly important aspect of context for the group psychotherapist relates to group norms. "Group norms" may be defined as:

rules of behavior, proper ways of acting, which have been accepted as legitimate by members of a group. Norms specify the kinds of behavior that are expected of group members. These rules or standards of behavior to which members are expected to conform are for the most part derived from goals which a group has set for itself. Given a set of goals, norms define the kind of behavior which is necessary for or consistent with the realization of these goals. (Hare, 1976, p. 19).

The term "group climate" may be used to characterize certain aspects of observed group behavior which reflect the impact of norm expectations upon the behavior of individual members. (MacKenzie, 1978)

Considerable data from social psychology literature suggest that once an organization such as the small group becomes established, its functional operating principles remain remarkably consistent over time. Even though the individual membership may change, the overall characteristics tend to persist from generation to generation of members. From a GST standpoint, this may be seen las the result of homeostatic mechanisms working within the group system. To some extent, one can control contextual variables coming from outside the group by proper selection criteria, for example, sex, age, and socioeconomic status. However, many of the extra-group variables are relatively fixed, for example, service delivery system characteristics, institutional policies, or hospital location. In contrast to these more distant aspects of context, group norms or group climate can be specifically and directly influenced by the group leader. I have introduced the term group climate in part because it relates to observed behavior and partly because I like the analogy of the group leader functioning in one of his capacities as a thermometer, gauging the strength of various aspects of group climate much as a meteorologist reports on temperature, humidity, and wind velocity.

The term "environmental press" originates with Murray (1938) and refers to the influence of the environmental context on the behavior of the individuals within a given situation. A sizeable literature suggests that environmental characteristics are as effective in predicting individual behavior as personality variables (Goffman, 1961; Mischel, 1968). In a particularly relevant application of the same theory, Moos (1974) has studied treatment environments in a variety of psychiatric service settings. He has been able to document the influence of various environments on the behavior of their inhabitants and correlate this with outcome change. He has demonstrated, for example, that treatment programs tend to have enduring characteristics, even though the actual patients and staff within those programs may change. He has documented high dropout rates in wards which were scored low on the dimension of "patient autonomy" and "order and organization." Programs having a good record for community tenure following discharge tended to promote an atmosphere characterized by the "free and open expression of feelings," coupled with a high emphasis upon "personal problem orientation" and "patient autonomy." This type of study provides sound documentation of the importance of "environmental press" in shaping behavior and inducing persistent change effects. Its relevance to group psychotherapy is clear.

The encounter group study by Lieberman, Yalom, and Miles (1973) has suggested similar findings in the small group arena. Their findings document the complexity of group process and the possibility of a variety of pathways towards change induction in group members.

In sum, it appears that diverse normative types can lead to high yield at termination. Moderate to high approval for loose group boundaries, however, seems systematically important. Groups with tighter boundaries, but with moderate to high approval for emotional intensity, tended to achieve lower yields. Negative outcomes seemed more likely when approval for peer control was low. Groups which highly approved confrontation without regulating emotional intensity or boundaries or with little peer control tended to have more dropouts (p. 285).

The same study also identifies the relationship between the leader's style and group norms. This area is of particular concern for programs training future group therapists.

Our findings do not deny the importance of the leader in determining the course and outcome of the group. They suggest, however, that the nature of his role may be more precisely described. The leader has both a direct and indirect role: he attempts to change members by his personal interaction with each individual in the group, and he has a social engineering function in which he indirectly contributes to outcome by helping to construct a group which is an effective agent of change (p. 429).

In summary, the relatively few studies available based upon clinical small groups tend to confirm the impression from the social theory literature that the characteristics of the environment exert important pressures upon the members in that environment, in terms of both present behavior and enduring change. Furthermore, there are data to suggest that an important function of the small group leader is to create a group atmosphere which is conducive to member change.

An important but inadequately researched area concerns the type of norms or climate dimensions which are most relevant in assisting and understanding the effects of group psychotherapy upon change in the individual members. For example, one can speak in relatively general terms such as the degree of interpersonal openness and the degree of leader control, or alternately focus on more mechanistic concepts such as language structure, specific reinforcement patterns, and continuity/discontinuity of topic content.

One approach which seems to have promise consists of rating groups on a variety of diverse behaviors. These ratings may be made by either group participants or observers. The results in turn may be subjected to such statistical treatment as factor analysis. Ideally, this should identify clusters of descriptors which tend to move together as various groups are rated. For example, one might predict that an item such as, "Members of this group feel very close," would be associated with an item saying, "Members of this group feel very warm towards each other."

This approach, of course, is dependent upon the initial spectrum of questions. These in all likelihood have been chosen for their conceptual significance and are subject, therefore, to the theoretical bias of the investigator. There is further danger that one might find factors consisting of a cluster of terms which may be related mathematically, but which may make precious little sense conceptually. If the original data base was not diverse enough, for example, one might find a misleading clumping of terms because of extraneous influences. For example, a dimension of "leader challenge" may be associated with a dimension of "leader control" because the groups were all taken from a locked ward.

Despite these difficulties, we have some interesting examples of this type of approach. For example, in the Lieberman et al. (1973) encounter group study, the application of factor analysis led to the formulation of five normative dimensions:

1) intense emotional expression;
2) open boundaries—expression of outside and personal material;
3) hostile judgmental confrontation;
4) counterdependence/dependence;
5) peer control.

Moos and Humphrey (1973) have developed a Group Environment Scale (GES) based on clear theoretical concepts. The final version of the 90-item scale has ten subscale dimensions based around three broad areas:

A. Relationship dimensions:
    1) cohesiveness
    2) leader support
    3) spontaneity
B. Personal development dimensions:
    4) independence
    5) task orientation
    6) self-discovery
    7) anger and aggression
C. System maintenance and system change dimensions:
    8) order and organization
    9) leader control
    10) innovation

In recent work with a similar instrument, MacKenzie (1978) has identified eight dimensions, each based on a theoretical concern and supported by factor analytic studies.

1) *Engagement.* This dimension relates to the psychological "glue" holding members together. Items on this scale tap the members' desire to attend the group, the importance of the group to them, and their sense of close, intense

participation. This dimension is equivalent to the concept of cohesion as it is commonly but somewhat loosely used in the group therapy literature. The dimension has been identified as important for effective group therapy (Yalom, 1975) and has theoretical interest as a marker of the state of the external group boundary.

2) *Disclosure*. Items on this scale describe the revelation of material, including events, feelings, and attitudes, pertaining to extra-group experiences which are of a sensitive personal nature, of considerable importance to the individual, and not generally revealed in a social setting. It should be noted that this definition deals with external material and does not include the quality of interpersonal openness which is sometimes covered under the general term self-disclosure. This dimension relates in part to the "self-disclosure" literature (Cozby, 1973) but in such a way as to monitor Lieberman et al.'s concept of internal versus external content as a predictor of therapeutic change (1973).

3) *Support*. These items refer to the expression of feelings and attitudes indicating warmth, empathy, and genuineness among the members in general. This scale is specifically focused upon these Rogerian dimensions which have a lengthy documented relationship to effective treatment as necessary, if not sufficient, ingredients for change induction (Rogers, 1961).

4) *Conflict*. Here items relate to the expression of feelings and attitudes indicating interpersonal friction, disagreement, and anger among the members in general, as opposed to general acquiescence and attempts to muffle conflict. Together with Support, this dimension focuses on the interpersonal boundary and has direct application to group development stages (Beck, 1974; Dugo & Beck, 1977).

5) *Challenge*. The focus here is on resolving problems and difficulties within the group. This is conceptualized as being based upon interaction which serves to reveal issues and provide constructive observations. The two key concepts are feedback and confrontation, but this is to be distinguished from Conflict, which has a negative interpersonal connotation. This dimension is seen as reflecting an attempt to pursue interpersonal psychodynamic work.

6) *Practicality*. The focus in this dimension is on resolving problems and difficulties which are located outside the group, for example, discharge plans, marital difficulties, work/social/recreational involvements. While these topics may entail considerable emotion, the scale is designed to measure the focus of concern as lying outside of group interaction. Together, Challenge and Practicality form two broad criteria for differentiating the work atmosphere of groups.

7) *Cognition*. This scale deals with the degree of emphasis upon understanding behavior, the use of interpretation, theories concerning mental health, and the supplying of reasons for why people act the way they do. These theories

may be applied to the individual, to the interaction between individuals, or to the group-as-a-whole. Several sources emphasize the importance of cognitive control in maintaining behavioral change (Lieberman et al., 1973; Meichenbaum, 1977).

8) *Control.* This scale relates to the control of behavior exerted by the group-as-a-whole. This may, of course, indirectly reflect the influence of the leader or a particularly prominent member. We are concerned here with the resultant effects, that is, the amount of pressure to adhere to group expectations a person in this group would experience.

While there are clearly many areas of overlap in the instruments described, it would seem evident that the task of adequately exploring the methodology for measurement of group norms has only just begun. In particular, there is a need to apply this type of conceptualization to longer-term therapeutic groups.

Group Roles

Groups, as organizational entities, may also be characterized by the role structures within them. Before describing some key organizational roles, it is important to emphasize that we are here concerned with descriptions of the individual as an organizational component in the group system. There is a conceptual danger in this area similar to that discussed in the group-as-a-whole section of this chapter. We have many examples of psychodynamic concepts being used inappropriately as role designations. For example, the transactional analysis literature is replete with interesting and potentially useful behavioral descriptions such as "the help rejecting complainer" or the "kick me, I'm down" script (Berne, 1961). These may be effectively utilized in a therapeutic context but, from the standpoint of the present discussion, it is critical that one understands these descriptions as referring to individual behavioral patterns. They should not be confused with formal role designations.

One definition of role offered by the Webster dictionary is: "a socially prescribed pattern of behavior corresponding to an individual's status within a particular society." Just as we have already alluded to the use of group norms to achieve explicit or implicit group goals, so group roles are conceptualized as necessary functions to be executed by group members to further the growth and development of the group as a social system. It is intriguing that the word role comes from the same Latin root as "roll," which contains among its definitions "to cause to take shape as a mass by turning over and over," and "to put a wrapping around." These descriptions have striking application to the tumbling turbulence of group interaction which evolves role assignments and the propensity of these role designations to become encapsulated and resistant to change.

While there is considerable scope for further exploration of role terminology, certainly a short list of critical group roles which have some research support would include the following (see also Chapter 18):

1) *Designated Leader*. The convener of the group and the participant who most straddles the boundary between intra- and extra-group considerations in his capacity as a participant/observer; he functions as a task guide and communication expert, and ensures that necessary ingredients for constructive group functioning are present and activated. Since the role of Designated Leader occupies a unique organizational position within a group, and one which may contain considerable authority, his or her behavior is of particular relevance in describing the group system. There is important evidence that the role model of the leader is a significant determinant of group characteristics, especially in the early stages (Lieberman et al., 1973).

2) *Scapegoat*. The member who crystallizes, by his deviancy, issues concerning group goals, adherence to norms, and conflict/competition. He is, therefore, frequently the object of attack, but in the process he becomes the vehicle by which the group clarifies and resolves differences within its ranks.

3) *Emotional Leader*. The member who is perceived as most exemplifying the supportive function of the group. He is able to focus on emotional issues, models an attitude of concern and involvement and may become the spokesman for the group. These qualities and functions ensure a nonthreatening atmosphere conducive to change and also render the emotional leader as the group member most ready to initiate personal growth.

4) *Defiant Member*. Whereas the Scapegoat struggles on the external group boundary of acceptance/rejection, the Defiant Member activates the boundary between individual autonomy and fusion into undifferentiated groupness. This member is sensitive to the possibilities of engulfment and, therefore, resists the pull of group cohesion. A common pattern is for this member to seek assurance of individual worth through attempts to negotiate a "special contract" with the Designated Leader; thus, the group is led to a consideration of each member's dependence on/independence from the group.

5) *Task Leader*. In addition to the Designated Leader, a particular member may take over many of the functions relating to problem focus and resolution. In doing so, this member enhances the ability of the group to deal in a persistent fashion with important issues.

Role Position

As a practicing group therapist, I have been uneasy about the designation of group roles when these are applied as if only one specific member could occupy one specific role. In some groups, for example, there is one individual who clearly functions as an Emotional Leader, and often one who functions as a Scapegoat. However, in many groups it appears as if these role functions are held to a significant extent by more than one member. On the one hand, there is danger of reinforcing rather than utilizing group role designations. For example, a leader who unwittingly reinforces a Scapegoat role is likely to lose that member from the group. These are the persons who report even many months later that they have been actively harmed by the group experience. On the other hand, there is a danger of properly identifying a member on a group role dimension, properly focusing on the importance of the role to the group, but in the process failing to recognize other members who might also have potential on that particular dimension. An idea current in the family therapy literature helps to resolve these difficulties.

In recent years, some writers have focused on the concept of family position (Blood, 1972; Nye & Bernardo, 1973). Thus, they speak of the husband/father position, the eldest daughter position, the only child position, etc. For each position, one can then develop a behavioral role repertoire which fits that position. One index of family dysfunction is a member who possesses only a limited role repertoire for his position. For example, a husband/father who is well equipped to fill the breadwinner aspects of his role position may be seriously lacking in the support dimensions also necessary for successful occupation of that position. By applying this thinking to the group as a social system, I believe we can usefully clarify the application of social system role concepts.

By moving one step back from the actual members in the group, one may conceptualize role positions as critical organizational axes within the group. Each of the roles described above must be represented in a group if it is to develop through its necessary stages. Each of the members may be considered for occupancy of the positions. Such an approach allows the therapist to keep the concept of roles firmly in mind and to specifically consider the functioning of those individuals who are high or low on a particular role position. The introduction of role position as an intermediate concept allows us to more simply explain the common phenomenon in groups whereby several members in turn may function in a single role capacity. For example, we have all had the experience of the role position of an absent Scapegoat being quickly occupied by another member. Even within the context of a single group session, some degree of role exchange may occur.

However, the concept of role position may be taken further. I have already suggested that the presence of these role positions is a necessary component to group development. A group without a Scapegoat, for example, can never really come to terms with variation and the uniqueness of the individual. The group is stuck in a more preliminary phase of member uniformity, each basking in the support of a non-differentiated group mass. Once a group has recognized its existence, as a living system, it seeks to develop internal structure. Since the role positions are critical to this development, there is specific suction upon the group members to seek out occupants for each role position. To be fanciful, one might imagine the group encircled by a number of role position vacuum outlets. Each member will be pulled by these various vector forces and find himself positioned in the theoretical organizational space of the group according to his suitability to fulfill the role criteria for each position. It is this process which highlights and dramatically focuses upon the boundary between the individual personality and the changing role requirements of the group as a developing, living system. The clinical literature has clearly focused upon the role of personality in understanding individual function in a group. However, this perspective may be misleading since it disregards the organizational requirements of the group as a dynamic social system. Hence, the concept of role position stands as a mediating structure between the individual *and* the group.

ISOMORPHISM OF GROUP DEVELOPMENT, ROLE POSITIONS, AND INDIVIDUAL CHANGE

I am indebted to the work of A.P. Beck, who has creatively linked group roles with group developmental phases (Beck, 1974; Dugo & Beck, 1977). In a comprehensive review of the literature on group development, she has identified nine phases which can be seen as epigenetic in the sense that successful completion of one is required before the next can be fully resolved. She has identified important role functions necessary for the proper resolution of each phase. The role positions described earlier are derived in part from her work. Her model offers some important ideas for further research validation.

An important concept in general system theory is that of isomorphy. Through the identification of similar internal structure/functions in different parts of the system, the operation of general principles can be identified. This concept has not been an easy one to apply to the group psychotherapy situation. It would be particularly useful to identify isomorphism between the group developmental phases with their attendant role positions, as defined by Beck, and the process of therapeutic change in the individual member. While it would be premature to suggest a comprehensive theory, there are some intriguing parallels. By way of illustration, I would like to work through one particular situation and wonder aloud if a similar approach might not be applied across the spectrum.

Beck, in agreement with many others in the group development literature, has identified the second phase of group development as one in which the focus is on the establishment of a group identity and direction. It is characterized by stereotypic relationships and considerable interpersonal friction and competition. Beck has identified the role position of Scapegoat as a particularly critical dimension in this phase of group development. The Scapegoat, being an outsider, a deviant from the consensus, serves as the polarizing factor to resolve the goals of this stage of development. Through the person of the Scapegoat, the group is able to come to terms with the idea of acceptance and incorporation of difference among the members.

In a similar fashion, for the individual group member, an important developmental phase in therapeutic change is the recognition that he as an individual is a complex person with multiple facets, not a unidimensional entity. Some of these characteristics are acceptable and some unacceptable; some are recognized as being strengths and others as weaknesses; some are evaluated as positive and others as negative. The recognition and delineation of such patterns for the individual are often necessary in coming to terms with his own unique characteristics. Once that task has been accomplished, then the process of integration of diverse parts and the relationship between them can be constructively approached. The concept of role position, I believe, has been helpful in my own understanding of this dimension of change for the individual. Further studies of such possible isomorphisms between the group and the individual member are being actively pursued in our research program.

Further ideas may be generated by an understanding of the relationship between role position and the individual group member. It is well established that the Emotional Leader not only puts the most into the group, but also derives the most from the experience. Consistently, the Emotional Leader is the one who benefits most and demonstrates the most dramatic change through the course of therapy. Similarily, the Scapegoat is at greatly increased risk for premature termination or for a harmful group experience. The Defiant Member must struggle specifically with dependency issues. Since each of these role positions involves a critical learning dimension for the individual holding that position, as well as for the group-as-a-whole, therapeutic leverage can be exerted by purposeful attempts to develop role position flexibility. To some extent, each member should be encouraged to function as the Emotional Leader, as a Scapegoat, etc. Thus, each individual can come to terms with the "developmental crisis" related to that role position. Just as a healthy family should be characterized by role flexibility, the same is true for a healthy, growth-promoting group.

SUMMARY

This chapter has attempted to apply a number of concepts of general system theory to small group functioning. Particular attention has been focused on the boundary between the individual and the social system of the group. The necessity of using terms appropriate to each level has been stressed. The concept of role position has been highlighted as a critical structure which offers useful insight into the relationships between group development stages and the needs and abilities of individual members. These theoretical approaches offer some useful guidelines for the researcher and the clinician in organizing the often bewildering complexity of the continuously evolving relationships in a functioning therapy group.

Chapter 7

Isomorphy in Group Therapy: The Leader as Catalyst and Regulator

By David Mendell, M.D.

Editor's Introduction. Dr. Mendell's chapter examines the therapist's role in psychotherapy from a GST perspective. Clearly, this experienced group leader's use of isomorphic images and analogies aids in his discussion. Examples from the natural and mechanical worlds help us understand GST principles such as boundarying, summing, systeming, feedback and isomorphy.

Specifically, Dr. Mendell's work deals with the catalytic and regulatory nature of the therapist in group and family therapy. The reduction of patient anxieties and the reinvestment of valuable energy are the immediate goals the therapist strives for as he tries to provoke change in the current state of the group. Also, the therapist attempts to assist patients to achieve greater organization and to emerge as autonomous individuals as they discover and regulate boundarying processes.

The group therapy leader is both an agent of stability and an agent of change. As change agent, helping to initiate the change desired by the patient, he is the group's catalyst. As the agent of homeostasis, he is instrumental in maintaining the integrity and continuity of the group—in part through his being the continuing element, in part through the group's relationship with his integrity and continuity (meaning) as an individual, and in part through his valve-like regulating of boundaries.

"Group catalyst" and "regulating valve" are isomorphs of chemical and mechanical processes, an isomorph being a similar or parallel structure or operation. Isomorphy is an important concept in general systems theory. It enables usable information to be carried over from one system or discipline to another where information is different or lacking, for instance, from one family system to another in a therapy group, or between the physical sciences and the less exact social sciences. Such an operation is negentropic in that by increasing information it increases the energy available to the system. The patient who sees how a particular problem is handled in another family and applies that approach successfully in his own family system is freed to tackle another problem area. The group therapist, in applying patterns and relations from physics and chemistry to group dynamics and therapy, can gain in understanding and mastery of his task.

This paper examines from a general systems perspective the process and the negentropic effects involved in the group therapist's acting as a catalyst and as a boundary regulator, as well as related isomorphies.

THE THERAPIST AS CATALYST

A catalyst is an agent that provokes change or causes change in rate of reaction, without itself being essentially altered in the process. Enzymes, for example, are biological catalytic agents in the processes of digestion and fermentation. The group leader has a similar capacity in psychotherapy. Like the digestive enzyme that converts complex foods to simple units absorbable by the bloodstream, the group leader helps to break down "indigestible" elements of the group's complex input of information and energy into simpler substances that can be reintegrated by the patient in a more useful and constructive manner.

Like the enzymes that act on glucose to release the energy locked in the glucose molecule, the leader seeks to reduce the patient's anxieties which are bound up in conflicts that act to decrease his available energy. Like the enzymes that synthesize, or build up, complex compounds from simple ones, the leader assists the patient to reinvest the energy formerly tied up in anxieties and conflicts into more complex, growth-producing patterns. As in catalysis, the leader preserves his integrity (in the face of seductive transference, for instance), while acting as an agent of change for the patient.

Group members act in the same catalytic mode in areas of their competency and in addition make an auxiliary contribution, much as do minerals or trace elements that accompany and facilitate enzyme action.

The catalytic function of the leader initially expresses itself in the selection process in the forming of the group—in the bringing together of representatives of families with related problems who have at once sufficient homogeneity for cohesion and sufficient heterogeneity in variety and quantity of resources to cover the gaps or deficiencies of group members lacking those essentials. The group process—how the group works—may be explained as follows: Each family has areas of weakness as well as areas of strength. As the members of the group identify the weak areas in their respective family systems, they become able to realize others' strength and avail themselves of other families' methods of coping in those areas. The change required by the common need/goal is then fueled by the similarity/diversity available in the so selected group.

This aspect of the leader-as-catalyst—his ability to put together a group having the proper balance between homogeneity and heterogeneity—is directly related to his capacity to diagnose, quantitate, and project future behavior in relationships. It is also related to his ability to explain and persuade. Patients must be convinced of the desirability of participating in the group if their fullest cooperation and energies are to be elicited and involved.

Once the group is set up, the leader, drawing on his technical and personal systems, then transmits a catalytic model to the members via his total personhood, as exemplified in his "doing" and "being." This process potentiates movement in their own circles (systems). He does this primarily by modeling a systeming mode for the group and by regulating boundaries.

Catalysis is to start something (or someone) in a specific direction. Actually, the catalytic process of group psychotherapy may be said to begin with the leader's professional and personal reputation, for it mobilizes the patients' trust, anticipation, and hope, which are essential parts of therapy. Their inertia, their resistance to change, is partially compensated for or overcome by their heightened expectations. We have learned clinically that resistance and stasis in the individual patient stem from blocks to growth occurring in his relationships with significant members of his original family. These intergenerational blocks are to be differentiated from the transient ones that develop in the group (e.g. transference). The therapy group promises a new family-like situation where these blocks are absent and will not develop. As in marriage, where one chooses a mate "like home but with improvements," so the therapist as group leader is seen, in part, as a parental figure but with improvements, one who has, for example, greater mastery, insight, objectivity, and respect for the patient's individuality.

A number of these catalytic factors can be seen at work in the following case history:

R. E., the mother of an extremely disturbed patient, was unwilling to enter therapy with a colleague of mine who was treating the family. When he transferred the case to me, I in turn called the mother to come in. Because she knew me from having been in attendance, as a volunteer in the Children's Hospital, at a large pediatric psychiatry conference which I had headed, she came in without any resistance and was amenable to my suggestions, which included an evaluation and her subsequently going into group therapy.

R. E. appeared to be a small, pleasant woman. Her daughter, the patient, was a severely overweight young woman with two small children, who, as a result of her mother's dominating behavior, had taken to sitting on the edge of the bed in an almost catatonic stupor. The mother had assumed control over the children, and unendingly criticized her daughter for what she did not do. These actions had only increased the daughter's inertia. (She, like her mother, was unduly sensitive to criticism.)

Although the first two groups into which I put the mother included, in the first group, some older women, also mothers, and, in the second, some very tolerant people who might understand her situation, in each instance she protested to me after a number of sessions that the group was not suitable because the others did not like her.

I then transferred her into a third group, which had some younger people who were having problems with their mothers. After she had been a short time in this group, and I observed that she was impervious for the most part to what they were implying about their mothers and her, I directly questioned one young woman who was dealing with some similar traits in her own mother. I asked her, "How do you feel about this mother [R. E.]?" She replied, "I feel like running away and killing myself." R. E. was truly taken by this reaction; as a result, her attitude toward her own daughter began to change.

Initially, I had given R. E. support in the evaluation, in that I was not critical, for I could understand her situation from her family background. Neurotic tendencies are transmitted from generation to generation, and each neurotic area is but a link in the chain. So I did not blame her in any way. I had shown further support by being sensitive to her feelings about the first two groups and transferring her to a third, although I did not share her belief that the members in groups one and two had disliked her. Ordinarily, I do not transfer a patient so readily. However, inasmuch as the basic principle of a group is to get seven or eight other viewpoints, which are more convincing than one or two, transferring a patient to a second group would provide 16 viewpoints, and so on, the value of which would speak for itself. There is an old saying: "If one man says you're drunk, disregard it; if a second man says the same, wonder about it; but if a third says it, lie down." I thus served a catalytic function in initiating a process without being, in this instance, the process myself.

Unlike the individual therapist who has to do himself whatever therapy is to be done for the patient, the leader in a therapy group prepares or sets things up so they can happen. He is like the person who focuses a convex lens in bright sunlight on a piece of paper to initiate the paper's burning—but he himself does not burn the paper. By my putting R. E. into selected groups and then directing a specific question to a specific group member at a specific point in her expressing herself and in the unfolding of R. E.'s own situation, I identified and put into focus the intersection point of potential constructive contact between the two. The group's input of information and energy could then flow through the channel available at an optimum time. At that point, the emotional-cognitive gap that had prevented R. E. from empathizing with her daughter was bridged, and she became able to organize feeling and thought negentropically into constructive action.

The Leader as a Growing System

A catalyst has been defined as an agent of change that remains unchanged in the process it facilitates. However, it is not wholly true that the catalytic agent in a therapy group situation undergoes no change. Because the therapy group is a living system whose elements move and grow, and the leader is a member of the group as well as its catalyst, he does change. Like everyone else, the leader has a continuing need to explore and grow as a psychodynamic system, not only in breadth but also in complexity and flexibility. The interchange with patients is one source of growth and information for him as he continues to learn more about his patients, himself, and the world in general.

The therapist's change, however, must be in his own pattern, toward his own goals and identity, in accord with his own priorities, and not in the defective pattern of the patient's family. In the complex therapeutic interrelationship, eternal vigilance is necessary lest the therapist change in response to some manipulation of the patient and get drawn into the patient's family system. It is equally important that the therapist not fall into some pattern of gratification or exploitation at the expense of the patient, either as the seducer or the seduced or both, and in that way become inextricably linked with the exploitative family of the patient. If the therapist loses this capacity to maintain his autonomy, i.e. boundaries, he cannot function as a model of a consistently growing, effective organism or system for the patient. Even such experienced and distinguished therapists as Ross Speck and Lyman Wynne have noted that at times they have had to fight off "going crazy," e.g., when involved with the family of a schizophrenic adolescent.

But this is not to say that the leader's movement and growth, as a therapist and as a person, are not related to the patient's system. In fact, it is an important element in the patient's organizing effort that his system, his personhood, be recognized and responded to by the therapist as being meaningful. The growing tip of the patient's roots is received and nourished by the therapist and the group isomorphically.

J. N., a struggling artist and an extremely sensitive and intelligent young man who was having problems with his identity, particularly in his relationship with his father, in a way operated as his therapy group's antenna. He sensed and responded to the most delicate of cues, in an involved, heartfelt, caring manner. He was initially quite hesitant about voicing his perceptions, but with my encouragement he began to speak out more and more strongly. I labeled this the artistic prerogative and pointed out that a committee organized to "plan for the future of the United States," with outstanding leaders, educators, and business people, also included an artist. The function of the artist—one might call it his area of leadership or unique capacity—was to sense or foresee trends and the future in an intuitive way, dealing with subliminal stimuli that would be missed by less sensitive people. In other words, here was a systems concept in operation, sanctioned by eminent authorities, that validated the contribution of the artist. I deliberately drew attention to this in the group, because of their beginning jealousy over my "favoritism" toward this patient, to make my strong support for his contributions understandable and acceptable.

In time, the "favoritism" became that of the group, for J. N. never made use of his vantage to one-up them. Because his insights consistently manifested sensitive, loving attitudes toward all the group members, they ultimately could not fault them, and they learned to cherish him and his contributions. A regressive sibling-rivalry mode, bounding out J. N., was bridged. This enabled an exchange at the interface in which the group and the leader got caring and perceptivity from him and he got recognition and self-esteem from them—to a sufficient degree that he could relinquish the dead-end quest for such recognition and self-esteem from his father. In the course of this group affirmation, J. N.'s resolve to be an artist and not to go to school, as his father had wished, was strengthened, and he married a warm and supportive woman, a graduate student; when he left therapy, his life seemed well ordered. He also was able to relinquish his demands on his father, and to go his own way.

The therapist's respect for the patient and learning from him are basic aspects of the therapy, for they enhance the patient's self-esteem (not only has he, the patient, grown through interaction with the therapist, but the therapist has grown through contact with him) and the patient's increase in self-esteem powers his growth. The therapist's acceptance of valid observations from his patients confirms their sound and unique elements as well as separating out the distorted ones from their family system.

THE THERAPIST AS BOUNDARY REGULATOR

The system under examination is a psychotherapy group. My working definition of a group is an organized number of people with a common goal and recognized leadership. The group has a boundary between those in and those out. The boundary, the goal, and the leadership define the group.

A system cannot be changed wholly from within—or wholly from without. There can only be change where there is a growth-producing overlapping with another system—in the case of the therapy group, the systems of the leader and the other members. An outside point of reference or assistance is needed, as in the case of a mired jeep, which can winch itself out of its predicament if there is a tree nearby to which a cable can be attached. An individual's capacity for physical movement is predicated not only on initiation of the process within his body, but also on his having a firm footing on something solid. An astronaut can do many things standing on the ground that he cannot do when suspended in the air. Archimedes said of the lever, "Give me a place to stand on, and I will move the earth." There must be a leverage point, a point of attachment that provides a base or stability, for change to take place. An outside point of reference is also essential if a system is to acquire new information.

As change agent, the leader is outside, separate from the group. As a group member, he is inside the group and a necessary constituent of the group. For overview, for regulating, he must position himself outside the group. An isomorphic example: Testicles function inside and outside the body. If too much inside, they are incapacitated by the higher body temperature, and their reproductive function, essential for growth and continuity of the family group, becomes inoperative; they need to be "cooled." Yet the testicles must be sufficiently a part of the body to receive warmth, nourishment, protection. That is, they must be close enough to survive but separate enough to preserve their vital and unique function. Similarly, the group leader who is too close to the group will lose his objectivity and overview and may appear threatening to the members, like a dominating or devouring, possessive parent. The leader who is too distant, on the other hand, will give the group members the feeling of not being "with" them; in self-defense they will isolate him entirely. To fulfill his function, therefore, the leader must be able to listen and share the members' feelings, yet remain sufficiently objective not to be overwhelmed by their emotions or impeded in defusing misdirected or excessive emotion on the patients' part.

The ground rules for the therapy group (demarcating its boundaries) are set out and agreed upon by the group at the outset, the leader being guided by his own rank-ordering of value orientations. These ground rules, intended to abet constructive, creative communication and living, bound in the group's activities by bounding out loose and destructive modalities carried over from defective family structures and outside activities.

Transactionally setting and regulating boundaries also has catalytic value. This approach, when handled in such a way that the group members, as well as the leader, become actively interested in and involved in their maintenance and/or necessary change, allows the members greater freedom for "being and becoming" and permits their "leading" quality to emerge—the necessary step for growth as well as the goal in therapy (Mendell, 1975).

The constructive model of group climate provided by the rules becomes in turn the model for the individual to bound out the "noise" from his own family (i.e., family block) which deters his development and individuation. The rules also prophylactically bound out some possible parental transference; e.g. requiring members to pay for missed sessions and stipulating that habitual violators will be dismissed or asked to change groups establish a boundary between the therapist and the guilt-ridden parent who indulges his child's transgressions.

An essential part of the ground rules is the understanding and agreement among the members of a group that, in its interactions and mutual relationships, the group itself has priority over any of its subgroupings (for example, those involved in confidences, secrets, sexual affairs) and over isolated, individual actions. Sharing is not two against one. Subsystems within the group create eddies, circularities, because they lack the advantage of a true group. When they do occur, as they occasionally will, the hindrance is minimized if they are shared fully with the group. This may even be to the advantage of all concerned as "grist for the mill." Thus might be heard, "I sure wanted to go to bed with her after the last session, but when I thought of going over all the details with the group, it really cooled me off." In this way, the boundary is preserved between therapy and friendship or social activity, which cannot maintain the pressure for change, but becomes like a "hole in the bucket."

Monitoring boundaries is both a catalytic and a regulatory function of the leader. As a catalyst he highlights and energizes (brings to life) relevant boundaries and their significance. When boundaries are violated, the leader points out the self-defeating aspects of such behavior, allowing the patients to make the decision independently as to whether they want to discontinue old patterns and stay within the boundaries or give up the therapy. This ordering of priorities is a supplemental and parallel operation to the family's ranking of values.

The following case history illustrates how confrontation, a direct mode of boundary regulation, can catalytically initiate a new course.

V. A., who had experienced years of depression and hospitalization, as well as E. C. T., was the mother of a very difficult schizophrenic adolescent youth. V. A. had recently been forced to hospitalize her son. There followed many months of combined family, group, and individual therapy, during which she would break down and weep miserably and interminably. This behavior continued even after the family had improved considerably (although there were still occasional impasses with husband or son or both).

One day, in the midst of an intolerably long crying spell on the part of this patient, I felt myself becoming bored and angry, and as V. A.'s tears continued I realized I felt she was "doing a number on us in the group." The group was responding rather diffidently and exhibited some restlessness. This affirmed my own feeling and I decided to risk verbalizing my reaction. "What a lot of shit!" I exclaimed. "I feel inundated." I gave my anger full rein as I saw the patient accepting it with amazement but not with excessive anxiety. "My God," I continued, "I don't know when I've heard such a lot of shit!" The patient paused, sniffled a little, and gradually quieted down. The group, which had reacted with some surprise to my outburst (unusual for me), made a few supportive observations to her and then went on to other things. (Generally, leadership function is best expressed by permitting the group to lead wherever possible, part of the catalytic function being to stimulate the leadership potential of the group members. However, this time I took the lead, because the situation seemed ripe, even overripe, for it.) V. A.'s weeping spells did not recur, although occasional moderate grief reactions came and went. She felt able to leave therapy not too long after.

The characteristic patient manipulation is a sum relationship, learned from his family suprasystem, which he imposes on the therapist and the group to ensure the response he wants. This push-ahead, which, like the parental taking over of areas properly left to the child, is intended to advance the parent-child progression, has the obverse effect from systeming. (In a sum relationship, the parent takes over part of the child's autonomy; there is a one-way boundary, controlled by the parent. In systeming, by contrast, there is a shared two-way boundary to which each can contribute.) Embodying the message, "sum or be summed, penetrate or be penetrated," this intrusive manipulation represents an attempt by the patient to suck the group into his family system by intruding the help-me mode (see Figure 1). (Because being-summed is what he is used to, it constitutes security.) Like his intrusive parent, he can then say, "Look what you're doing to me," when in reality he is doing it to them. Such passive hostility could be

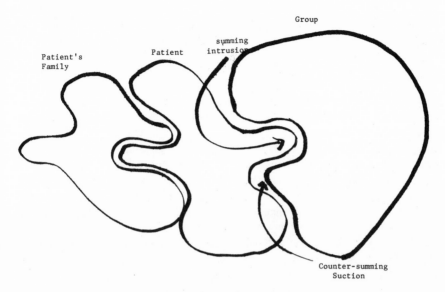

Figure 1. Patient's summing effort in therapy group

called counter-summing. I also call it the One-upmanship of the Underdog.

As in judo, where an aggressive attack is diverted and the attacker's energy and momentum are utilized to bring his aggression under control and into a more mutually agreeable relationship, the group responds to the patient's aggressive or exploitative summing effort by 1) confronting or disregarding his intrusion, and 2) systeming with him at other points of interaction (Figure 2). By failing

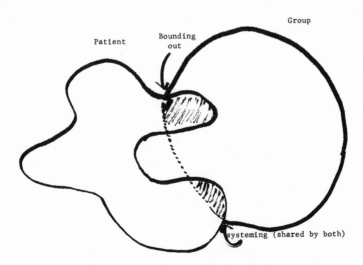

Figure 2. Group's response to patient's summing attempt

to respond to the intrusive behavior in the manner of the patient's family, they bound it out. By systeming with him, they reward his real self. (This is opposite to the family's mode, which disregards the true self and rewards the "fronting" self.)

In the instance just described, the rejection by the group and myself of reactions inappropriate to the relationship as we felt and understood it, i.e. a progressive, therapeutic, constructive association or system, bounded out reactions related to an earlier, still functioning remnant subsystem of the family of origin, a foreign body or intrusion (a sum) into the ongoing group or system. By our clearly and unequivocally (without guilt or ambivalence) bounding it out, V. A. had to make a choice—this one or that one, remaining in the group system with its present-day benefits or returning to the original family system with its distorted benefits and symptom maintenance. By accepting the group's reaction as valid, she chose this one. At the time, of course, V. A. had strong roots of trust and identification in the group to buttress such a decision and make it possible. This bounding-out also represented confidence that she could stand on her own. It was an "easing her out of the nest," a belated adolescent rite of passage into adulthood.

My son Jeff, who has co-led some of my groups with me, has at times a playful but considerate manner. He initially goes along with the patient's summing effort but with the tiniest smile, implying, "We are playing your game, but I don't believe it," a metacommunication (a message about a message). Then, as the operation of intrusive manipulation is laid bare and the patient takes a square look at it in a climate of humor and acceptance of him as a person, he can allow himself to give it up, the control and attention it is meant to achieve being clearly unnecessary in the situation. It gets bounded out—i.e., redesignated as garbage rather than food, as something to be thrown away rather than something useful to retain. New actions then become possible for the patient.

Boundary Regulation in the Process of Individuation

As a regulator, the leader, in the transactions among individuals in the group, clarifies boundary conflicts, helps to resolve them, and works to keep them resolved. Isomorphically, he also seeks to integrate and harmonize the various subsystems within the individual members. His functions can be compared, in some respects, to a filter or valve regulating flow at the various interfaces in which his systems participate. His goal is to help his patients achieve a greater degree of organization and more efficiency as psychodynamic systems—to emerge as more fully individuated individuals.

The therapist's capacity to regulate begins with the capacity to distinguish the functioning of various systems and to focus on them with some precision in relation to the individual patient and his boundaries. Only then can the patient begin the process of separating his real self from his "façade," which represents the defensive accommodation to the distorted boundary areas of his family (garbage). The chrysalis of the butterfly pupa initially serves a protective functioning, but becomes an impediment to the growth and individuation of the butterfly as it emerges. Only if the butterfly frees itself completely from its former protective "façade" can it fully realize its function, i.e., to live. The intense struggle to free itself, appearing almost desperate to the human witness, is no more difficult than the isomorphic effort required by its human counterpart. Likewise, that which in the human had served at first as a needed protector of life, such as downgrading one's own value in deference to parental need, can later be the barrier to relationship and communication.

The bounding-out of the summing or "bad" parent occurs through the patient's participation in the group, utilizing the group boundary as a supportive systems interface with his individual system. This provides a base for building up his own systeming capacity and for extruding the sum intrusion of the parent and replacing it with a systems-type interaction area. There is a struggle because of the conflict with the old system—self/parent, with parent in charge—and because of the intrusion of the parent into the patient's territory, which affects parts of all his perceptions of the outside world, and causes him to reject conflict in the latter through loyalty to the former. As the ties with the group negentropically strengthen the patient's self, the reinforced self can begin to dismantle the parent-intrusion and rebuild the replaced self in the area reclaimed from the intrusive parent.

In identifying the self with the group goals, the patient and the group form a system with a goal of extruding the "bad" self or the "bad" parent. The anticipated violent reaction or rejection from the parent, which prevented any contemplation or confrontation and dealing with the parent, also prevented any resolution and maintained a status quo. When the self is strengthened with the backing of the group or new system, it becomes able to do this. It is also able to tolerate the close scrutiny, the close contact, and the struggle to separate elements involved in the process of individuation. The first steps involve pointing up the bad parent area within oneself and retaking possession of it by extending the group/patient systeming movement into it—with confidence that one will ultimately come out in charge rather than be consumed. The confrontation is necessary because of the parent's power and because of the parent's having been the primary model.

For example, a daughter has a model from her intrusive mother of how a woman can have power. By expecting it, living it, identifying with it, even though figuratively holding her nose while doing so, the daughter can take the defective model over and then redirect it and recalibrate it for more constructive and suitable relationships. In systems terms, the intrusive "summing" mother is absorbed by the increasingly systeming daughter, the sum (summing, intrusive area) thereby being depsychotized, digested, and utilized as energy and power by the daughter as she increasingly assumes the systeming mode of the group.

This process of individuation is illustrated in the case history that follows:

Because B. N. was generally exceptionally quiet and passive in his group, I had his wife A. R. attend his group as well as her own. (If individuals do not communicate much in the group, they probably follow a similar pattern in the marital relationship and are not enjoying the sharing potentialities of the marriage. Placing husband and wife in the same negentropic system of the therapy group may help open the way for greater sharing.) Toward the end of one session he said to her, "I am trying to think of what you are expecting me to do. I feel so wrong and guilty, sitting here and not doing it." He thereby demonstrated the mutuality of their problem at this point. Each was summing and counter-summing the other.

She responded, "I feel I have to be a bitch, because I get angry about the way you act. Things you do I don't like, and things you don't do, I wish you did." This was from a woman who had entered therapy so anxious and so overidentified with others' pain that she could never assert herself.

I had previously pointed out to A. R. the gradual acceptance of her identification with her bitchy mother as the avenue to her own assumption of power for her own goals. That is to say, by overcoming her fear and her feelings of repugnance toward her mother and thereby changing her personal process from bounding out the bad mother to systeming with her, she would be able to draw on the energy and information of her mother as model. She had subsequently been struggling ambivalently about allowing the "bitch" to come out as opposed to living up to the expectations of those around her (equivalent to bounding in the powerless child to please the mother and thus the world). She felt her relationship with her husband was getting nowhere, and she was sinking deeper into frustration and despair over the outlook for their marriage. She was afraid that if she truly expressed how she felt, her husband would leave her.

Since only a few minutes remained before the end of the hour, I felt I had to take advantage of this opening. I condensed her situation to two alternatives: "Do you want to not be yourself, trying to please everybody else, letting your marriage deteriorate, and continuing in your uncertain state? Or would you rather let the 'bitch' out so your husband knows where you are, giving him an opportunity in his own way to join you in dealing with the 'bitch'?" In systems terms, was she willing to risk systeming with her husband, relinquishing the safety and old vengeful satisfaction gained from bounding the mother out while allowing herself to be victimized? My alternatives bounded in so-called bitchy behavior by showing that in this instance it was goal-directed and not destructive. In psychoanalytic terms, it was in service of the growing ego.

A. R. finally admitted she could see the point, although she had professed confusion over my often repeated rank-ordering of personhood, which is: First you are a person, then you are a man or a woman, then you relate with another man or woman as a mate, then you are a parent, then you have a vocation and/or a profession or calling. Being a person is the primary system and foundation for adequate and conflict-free participation in the other systems. Otherwise, one cannot successfully resolve the progressive conflicts as they occur in other areas of growth. Making an explicit statement of this rank-ordering provides the patient with reinforcement (information plus energy) in choosing the more appropriate course of action, that which promotes individuation.

My alternatives forced A. R. to face the fact that she had been projecting her negative feelings toward herself onto others, in order to avoid the unpleasant connotations associated with being a person. Presented in a climate of humor, with the group joining in with her and my laughter, and with firmness on my part in nailing her down as she tried evasive tactics, they bounded out her façade, her presenting a substitute for her real self, her accommodations to her earlier environment. By systeming with her "personhood," the group and I provided information and energy for her extending the systeming into the interface with her mother, growing into and reclaiming the area summed out by the mother (like reforestation of a burned tract of land).

Some sessions later, after another member of the group, a young woman resentful of her dependent relationship to her parents, had triumphantly told of confronting them with a request to come to a family counseling session, to which they had readily agreed, A. R.'s quiet husband (B. N.) commented: "That's great. Think I should talk to my father? What would I say? Not 'Go to hell,' but something to let him in, rather than to close him out. And only then would I confront him with my feelings as to why I was not allowed to feel." Because of the young woman's input, he could conceive of accepting his hostility and exclusion of his father and could also conceive of attempting to open boundaries to him for needed communication.

Several weeks earlier, I had suggested that B. N. try imagining his father on the empty chair in front of him and expressing his feelings without restriction. His wife had added at the time, "This is harder for me than when I went through it with my own mother. I am carrying it for him—relating with his father. My mother was a bitch, but she was easier to confront than his father's passive aggression. The broken voice, and so on. That is harder for me." She bowed encouragingly to her husband's talking to his father in the chair (a graphic example of the mountain-climbing marital pattern, which is discussed below.)

I then sat down in the chair and had B. N. address me as his father. The wife said afterwards, "He sounded much better than usual. He generally talks so softly with his father I cannot hear him. This is the first time I've heard him. I used to get mad at the way he did with his father. Actually he was ignoring him by not talking clearly—it was as if he didn't care—not that he was angry or sad as he was today."

Another member of the group said: "I know how powerful it is to stand up to one's family—like life and death—almost like an amputation. Like his father would die. For a new life for himself."

The regulatory function of the group therapist is to clarify, identify, and build up firm boundaries for the group within which the members can feel free to release emotions which have previously been ruled out of bounds, which are feared, which are unfamiliar and frightening as to management, and which have been judged destructive to the individual and his relationships. (It might be noted that the anxious repression of any one strong emotion tends to suppress contingent or related emotions, through fear that expressing one will, like opening Pandora's box, lead to their all escaping.) This allows the individual to experience his emotions within a protected situation. Once he experiences them, he can integrate those emotions for use. Through trial and error, and through application of more validly cognitive judgments based on previous experience, and as gathered or reformulated in the therapy group from the various other family models available there, he begins to system successfully in the group and in the world. (This is to be differentiated from intellectualization, which is seemingly related but is actually a defense and diametrically opposite, being a circular subsystem rationalizing the blocked progression, i.e., a pseudomorph.)

By encouraging B. N. to confront his incorporated father in the group, I helped him to identify and express the hostility which he had been suppressing. I bounded in what he had been bounding out. Bounding his hostility toward his father into the group and providing an avenue for its release reduced it to manageable proportions. B. N. could then utilize it constructively with and for his father (systeming), as opposed to his previous mode of passive hostility (counter-summing).

The group setting, when judiciously matched to the patients, gives them the opportunity to both observe and emulate others from different family systems and to express their own feelings more freely than they would be likely to in the family. They are thus given a model (information), as well as protection and facilitation (energy in form of support), for testing and confirming those feelings (increasing information). The therapist, by displaying clarity and firmness in boundary formation, not only produces the boundary for this kind of work, but also gives the patient a model for building his own personal boundary and related interpersonal boundaries, such as in the family and his other groupings.

The interchange pattern in passive hostility, as between B. N. and his father, seems to me to be isomorphic with the condensor in an electric circuit. There tension builds up on each side, on each plate, with a gap in between, and only at extremes does it discharge across—in contrast to the bridging operation of communication in systeming, which is continuous and not disruptive or excessive. Because of inadequate feedback, caused by the rigid bounding-out, the relationship remains a crippling circularity.

When interchange of information and energy becomes possible at the interface of systems in opposition, the target system can be energized to new capacities, much as the sun's energy causes fruit to ripen. There is a breakthrough from flat circularity. The upward spiral of increasing complexity, which is the normal process of individuation (isomorphic to biological maturation), is reactivated.

In the group therapy process, feedback loops from member to member, from unconscious to conscious and vice versa, from one of the families represented to the others—and back again in an incremental way. A benign cycle, goal-directed, it gains velocity and power (like a cyclone) as the mutual reinforcement potentiates each group member. This sweep overwhelms and wears away the various deviations and inappropriate family patterns which are also represented in the group. Emergent new patterns are subsequently tested for appropriateness and utility, first in the group, then at home with mate or family.

The feedback model is a continuous cross-section of the whole concept of communication. Applying it to group and family interaction makes the quality and presence or absence of reciprocal input, as in the disregarding or disqualifying of one of its members or subgroups, more real and evident. It also clarifies the concept of mutuality in the system formation and maintenance in any one of its members. This then helps point the way for its amelioration.

In the marital relationship, the corresponding operation is what I call the "work of marriage." I compare it to two (or more) mountain climbers joined by a rope. The first climber initiates action and secures an advanced position so that his partner can climb with support and diminished risk; the partner then does likewise. This action is repeated again and again in an alternating pattern of input and feedback of information and energy. This growth or progression in marriage is isomorphic to the therapy group in its reciprocal sharing of resources and advantages.

Transactions proceed concurrently at various systems levels—therapist/patient, therapist/group, patient/family, patient/patient. The negentropic increments in each help catalize the other. The therapist also interacts with the next higher levels, the professional suprasystems of his discipline. The isomorphy of progress and growth, evident in the former transactions, is equally present in the latter.

Psychotherapy is systems in interaction and movement. The leader's input of information and energy functions both as a catalyst and as a regulating valve (to draw on isomorphic transactions in other disciplines where the proportion of science to art is greater than it is in psychology). The effect, under optimum conditions, is synergistic: The whole (the group) becomes more than the sum of its parts (the individual patients in the group and the leader), facilitating the therapeutic process of individuation.

Part III

General System Theory
Models of Group Psychotherapy

Chapter 8

General System Theory
Approaches for the
Group Therapist

By Francis Ulschak, Ph.D.
and Gustav Rath, Ph.D.

Editor's Introduction. Although the authors of this chapter were not working members of our task force, we were glad to incorporate their work, which corroborates our own view that GST may serve as an integrative framework. Aware of the self-referential nature of the interaction among living systems, they begin by pointing out their basic premise—that the boundary between any system and its environment is determined by its definer and his/her purpose. In this case, the definers are two group therapists who employ a transactional analysis method. They then proceed to describe three approaches to systems analysis which they have applied to their work: the hierarchical structural (i.e., the relationships among the components of the system), the entities of the system, and the flow chart approach. The weaknesses and strengths they have discovered in each of these are noted. Finally, they illustrate the specific ways in which each of these systems approaches may contribute to the work of the group therapist who is confronted with a given situation. It is apparent from their case illustration that they have been able to increase their clinical effectiveness by moving harmoniously back and forth between systems and analytic interventions, which supplement each other. As pointed out in other chapters in this volume, it is clear that a GST perspective enhances the autonomy of the group member.

In this chapter we first define our use of general system theory (GST) and present three approaches to viewing systems. A major emphasis of our approach is the role of the definer of the system and his/her purpose in defining the system. The boundary between a system and its enviroment is determined by a decision of the system analyst. We then present a case study to illustrate how a group therapist may use the tools presented to view his/her group.

Throughout this paper, when we speak of GST, we are referring to "open systems," i.e., systems which influence their environments as well as being influenced by their environments.

SYSTEM REFLECTIONS: THE DECISION MAKERS

For this chapter, a system will be defined as a set of entities, attributes of the entities, and the relationships between the entities that are deemed significant to the purpose for which the system is being defined (Thompson & Rath, 1972). Implied in this definition is the role of the definer and his/her purpose in defining the system. The definer in this case is the author. It can be the therapist.

The questions of who is defining the system and for what purpose are crucial to a study of systems. Hall and Fagen (1956) allude to the significance of the definer when they state: "In a sense, a system together with its environment makes up the universe of all things of interest in a given context. Subdivision of this universe into two sets, system and environment, can be done in many ways which are in fact quite arbitrary. *Ultimately it depends on the intentions of the one who is studying the particular universe as to which of the possible configurations of objects is to be taken as the system*" (p. 83, emphasis ours). Later, in an example, Hall and Fagen again emphasize the intentions of the one studying the system when they state that splitting a set of related objects into system and environment "depends essentially on the points of view at hand" (p. 84).

Whyte, Wilson, and Wilson (1969, p. 219) echo Hall and Fagen in their use of the following analogy in discussing a definition of systems:

It's a bit like the umpires discussing their efforts. The first one said with some satisfaction, "Balls and strikes, I call them as I see them." The second, a little more arrogant, said, "Balls and strikes, I call them as they are." The third one, of greater experience and wisdom said, "Balls and strikes, they ain't nothing until I call them."

The person defining a system determines what is a "ball" or a "strike," i.e., the definer determines what is inside the system and what is outside the system (environment). Using systems language, the definer determines the boundaries separating the system from the environment.

The significance of the definer of the system and his/her purpose in defining the system can readily be seen in viewing a therapy group as a system. The objects within the system are the members of the group. The attributes of these members are listed and the relationships between them delineated. A gestalt therapist may select one member of the group and define that one person as the system to be worked with. The rest of the group becomes the environment. A group therapist might view the whole group as the system to be worked with and the environment is all that which falls outside of the group boundary. The sociologist may define the community or ethnic group of which the group is a part as "the system." The group, then, becomes one of the sets of objects in this larger system.

The importance of this for this paper is that the definition of a system is dependent on the intentions and purpose of the definer. A psychiatrist with a certain purpose will define the system one way; the family therapist, with another purpose or intention, will define it still another way; the sociologist another; and the group therapy member will define the system in still another way. For example, Eric Berne (1966) offers five formal ways to describe a group.

In the group therapy setting, various decision makers can be identified. The client may be seen as the decision maker in a decision to be involved in the group. Or, if the client is "assigned" to a group, e.g., a court referral, the agency or individual assigning may be seen as the decision maker. The therapist is involved as a decision maker in the decision to accept the client into the group. Other group members may be seen as decision makers in how they decide to relate to another group member. And, if the group therapy is a treatment mode of an institution, then the institution may be the decision maker when the purpose is to evaluate the effectiveness of various treatment (modalities). All of the actors in group therapy system, then, may be involved in being the decision makers at various points. The critical question becomes: Who is defining the system and for what purpose?

SYSTEM TOOLS

There are a variety of tools available to the systems analyst. We present three common approaches. Each approach will provide the system definer with a little different perspective on the system.

1) The Hierarchy

This approach is essentially a hierarchical approach to systems. The discussion concerning the group represents a hierarchical approach. Systems are seen within a framework of suprasystems and subsystems. Figure 1 illustrates the hierarchical approach. The circles could be extended on the "macro" side to the universe, and to particles of the atom on the "micro" side. Shawchuck (1974, pp. 144-147) provides an excellent visual illustration of hierarchical systems. The hierarchical approach to systems allows us to concentrate on understanding one internal system at a time without becoming immobilized by complexity of the total universe. Some systems can be treated as external environment, some as producers of internal effects, and some in the full complexity necessitated by the nature of our goals, responsibilities, and skills.

The strength of using a hierarchical approach to looking at a system is the

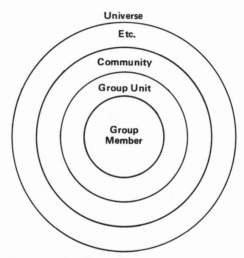

Figure 1. Hierarchical Approach to Systems

ability to isolate one subsystem for analysis. The therapist may find the hierarchical approach very useful in establishing a group and reflecting on the authority structure. By viewing how the group fits into other systems, the therapist will be able to have a more explicit contract for the group. The hierarchical approach can also be useful in thinking about possible levels of intervention, e.g., intrapsychic, interpersonal, family, etc. The therapist may use it to develop various intervention options (see Chapters 1 and 10).

The major weakness of the hierarchical approach is that it does not provide process information readily. It will not be useful when trying to understand a sequence of behaviors and how they interrelate.

2) The Entities of the System

Another approach to systems is to look at the entities of the systems, the attributes of the entities, and the relationships (structure) between the entities. Again, the element of choice on the part of the definer is significant. The system is identified by someone identifying the significant elements of the system. An example of the entities and the attributes of the group mentioned above are:

ENTITIES	*Person 1*	*Person 2*	*Person 3*	*Person 4*	*Person 5*
ATTRI-	Member	Member	Member	Member	Therapist
BUTES	John	Mary	Tom	Jane	Martha
	Blonde	Brunette	16 yrs.	40 yrs.	Brown hair, eyes
	6′ tall	140 lbs.	shy	aggressive	confrontive

The relationship between the entities (structure) may be as shown in Figure 2.

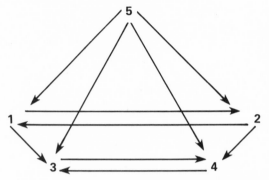

Person 5 has a direct relationship to all the other parties. Persons 3 and 4 interact a good deal, as well as persons 1 and 2. Person 2 tries to interact with person 4 but person 4 does not reciprocate, etc.

Figure 2. Relationship between the entities (structure)

On this view of systems, someone is making decisions about what are significant entities, attributes, and relationships. For a group relating to women's consciousness and issues, sex may be a very significant attribute. In another group, sex may not be a significant attribute.

Another useful concept in looking at the relationship between the entities (structure) is Berne's group imago (Berne, 1966, p. 153). The group imago is the private structure of the group as seen through the eyes of each member of the group. Thus member 2 may draw the group image as shown in Figure 3.

In this case, person 2 has a place for person 1 and the leader in his/her structure (e.g., transference of mother or brother). However, persons 3 and 4 are undifferentiated in the private structure.

The major strength of this approach to systems is the analysis of a specific *level* of a system. The therapist who chooses to use this as a tool of analysis will have an excellent "snapshot" of the system being analyzed.

A major weakness is that it does not provide a dynamic view of the system.

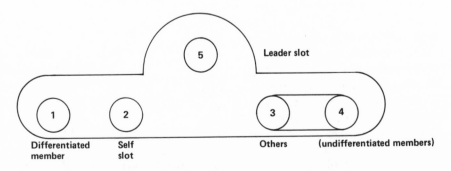

Figure 3. Group image as drawn by member 2

The word "snapshot" fits appropriately. Once the system is identified, this provides a picture of a moment in time.

3) Flow Chart

Another method of defining a system is to view the flow of energy, matter, and information through the system. Thus, the system is seen in terms of the input into the system, the transformation of the input in the system and the output. And, as in the other two tools, a crucial role is played by the definer of the system. In flow chart form, this might appear as in Figure 4. The input, transformation, output may be seen as a "black box." Elements are introduced into the black box, transformed and emitted (see Figure 5).

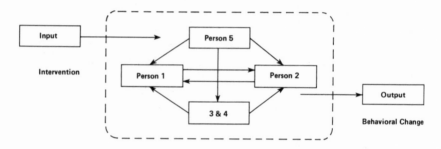

Figure 4. Flow chart

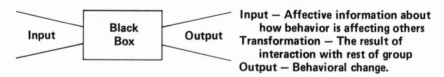

Figure 5. Transformation takes place in the "black box".

A major strength of the "black box" approach is following the sequences which happen in the defined system. It provides a good deal of information about process, e.g., when x happens, a, b, and c follow and the final result is y. The "black box" will prove useful in understanding how a person (group) begins at "one place," e.g., feeling relaxed and comfortable, and ends at "another place," e.g., feeling uptight and nervous.

The major weakness is that it does not provide a good analysis of the components of the system.

Again, all three of the above are ways to approach systems. Since the delineation of a system is very dependent on the purpose of the person defining the system, these three approaches take on different value in different situations. In one situation, the hierarchical approach may provide the most useful information for the therapist defining the system. In another setting, the flow charting may be most useful, etc. And, in another setting, a therapist may incorporate all three. For example, in setting up a group, the therapist may use a hierarchical approach to clearly define how the group relates to other suprasystems, e.g., a hospital. The therapist may use the entities approach to define clearly the components of the system in order to provide predictive material about how the group members may interact. And, finally, the therapist may use the flow chart to understand specific sequences of behavior which happen between individuals or within an individual in the group.

A CASE STUDY AND EXAMPLES

The purpose of this section of the chapter is to show how the concepts presented above have very useful, practical application for the group therapist. Again, the usefulness will depend on the purpose the group therapist has and the problem he/she is defining. In one setting one approach may be more useful than another. The case is presented and then various models are used to approach the case.

The primary treatment mode of the group under consideration is that of transactional analysis (Berne, 1961, 1963, 1966, 1972; Steiner, 1974). Transactional analysis can be seen as a therapeutic system including structural analysis (ego states and what happens internally in a person), transactional analysis (looking at what happens when two people are interacting), game analysis (viewing repetitive patterns acted out transactionally which result in bad feeling payoffs for the persons involved) and script analysis (looking at the assumptions persons have made about themselves and how these assumptions become the operating rules for their view of themselves, others and the world).

Specific concepts referred to in this case study and their definitions are:

1) *Parent Ego State* contains attitudes and behaviors which the individual incorporates from external sources. These are learned and imitated decisions. Parent may have a critical and controlling view of the world, e.g., "you should never do that . . . ," and/or a nurturing and supportive view of the world, e.g., "here, let me help you with that. . . ." These two aspects of Parent Ego State are referred to in the literature as Critical Parent and Nurturing Parent.

2) *Child Ego State* contains the impulses and feelings which come naturally to a child. In a Child Ego State the individual acts and feels childlike regardless of his/her age. Child Ego State is composed of behaviors and feelings which are free and spontaneous, or which involve either attempting to please the other person (compliant) or rebelling against the other person. The free spon-

taneous aspect of Child Ego State is referred to as Free Child and the compliant or rebellious aspect is referred to as Adapted Child.

3) *Script* (Holloway, 1973, p. 2) is an unsatisfactory life plan prematurely decided on by a child under stress at an early age and is characterized by repetitive, unpleasant, emotional experiences and recurrent dissatisfying relations with others. The script affects both intrapsychic and interpersonal workings of an individual.

4) *Contracting* is a process of defining tasks and relationships (Ulschak, 1978). Typically, contracting will involve questions like: (a) What do the parties involved want? (b) What are the parties willing to do to get what they want? (c) What are the criteria for success of those involved? (d) What "goodies" are there in achieving the "wants"?

Clinical Case

G. begins her work in a group by telling a story of a problem she is having at work. She is employed as a school counselor. One of the students she works with has come into conflict with the institution's truancy rules and is about to be put on probation. G. will be having a meeting with the student and her "irate" father. The starting point in the discussion is how to conduct an effective meeting where the school rules can be explained adequately and information communicated to the parents of the student.

Initially, the group offers ideas about how to design the meeting so as to communicate the information effectively, as well as deal with the potential conflict. Then the focus shifts to G. and how G. can handle her fear of the meeting and, specifically, the father's anticipated "irrational anger." The question becomes how G. can take care of herself in a conflictual setting.

The next shift in focus is to what G. is feeling in the here and now. G. reflects she has sweaty palms, fear, and an anticipation that she will do poorly in the meeting. As a counselor, she is supposed to do everything right and to successfully resolve the conflict. G. recounts a scene with her family from the previous night which involved her sons and her parents. Through the use of a double chair technique, G. gets into an internal dialogue between her Parent and Child Ego States. There is a conflict between an internal Parent message of "Be Perfect" and the Child feelings of fear and inadequacy. Through the dialogue, there is a resolution that G. does not have to be "perfect" (and, indeed, is not perfect) and she gives herself permission to be effective in the meeting.

Approach 1: Hierarchical Approach

The hierarchical approach simply involves the therapist viewing various levels of intervention. Each system involves multilevels and multi-goals (Mesarovic, 1964).

The case of G. illustrates the hierarchical concept very readily. The therapist has various options for interventions. The initial level for an intervention may be at the institutional rules-counselor interface. Here, an evaluation of the reasonableness and effectiveness of the school rule might be looked at. The counselor might take on the role within the school of an internal change agent. The next level that may be looked at is the meeting-counselor interface. Here the question might well be how to design an effective meeting. The question may be posed: How does one design a meeting such that the potential conflict can be productively dealt with? A third level that could be viewed is the interface between the counselor and the irate parent. Here a question concerns how the counselor handles conflict, or how to deal with an angry person. Finally, another level is how the counselor interprets and perceives conflict internally. This gets into the intrapsychic level. An intervention here might be designed to get the person into an internal dialogue.

A summary of some levels and possible goals for each level is presented in Table 1 (many more levels could be added, of course).

TABLE 1

Level	Goal(s)
1. Intrapsychic	Resolve fears of conflict, past learning about conflict
2. Interpersonal	To handle conflict and anger effectively
3. Meeting	Designing for effective conflict management
4. School	To develop rules and regulations appropriate to setting

For each level, there may be one goal or a series of goals for the therapist and client. It is through a contracting process that the therapist and client arrive at the appropriate level for intervention. Ethical problems arise when interventions are made at a level inappropriate to the one agreed upon in the patient-therapist contract. Thus, for example, concerns arise if the level of intervention contracted for is the organizational level but interventions are made at the intrapsychic level without a conscious agreement to shift levels.

The therapist and client must decide what is the appropriate level of intervention as well as evaluate the outcomes of an intervention at that level. Our philosophy is to intervene into the system at the lowest level possible while still achieving the desired outcomes. The purpose of this is to minimize the disruptive side-effects of the intervention on the rest of the system. By intervening at the lowest effective level, there is less chance of producing major negative side-effects in other segments of the system. Thus, for an example, an interpersonal conflict within an organization will probably be most effectively dealt with on the interpersonal level. To intervene by bringing together the whole organization in a confrontation meeting will increase the complexity of the intervention and the possibility of negative spillovers. Consequently, our view is—intervene at the lowest level possible which will still produce the desired results. This could be a guideline for the group therapist.

Approach 2: Entities, Attributes, and Structure

An initial decision when approaching the group as a system using the entities, attributes, and structure approach concerns the level of intervention. Once the level is decided upon, the next step is to define the entities, attributes, and structure at that level.

Entities are things, people, children, messages, chairs, groups, etc. Attributes are the characteristics of the entities which distinguish them from one another. Structure shows the rules of how one entity relates to another and how the attributes of entities are changed.

Assuming that the level of intervention which is decided upon by the therapist and client is the interpersonal level of the client, the concepts of entities, attributes and structures are clearly seen. The group is composed of four men and four women. The entities of the system, then, become the members of the group as well as the physical surroundings. Thus, the type of seating, lighting, objects around the room, etc. are all entities of the system. Attributes of the entities include such things as being male or female, age, height, weight, role (therapist or client), expectations, projections, etc. The critical question for the person using this systems approach is to differentiate the insignificant attributes from the significant attributes. A significant attribute in this setting is that G. is an exile from a Latin American country and still has a good deal of identification with that country and culture. Structures, i.e., the rules by which entities relate, determine what is permissible to say, feel, and do within the group. An interesting experiment in an ongoing group is to ask the members: What are the explicit and implicit rules that are functioning in the group? What is it OK to feel and do and what is it not OK to feel or do? These questions make the group structure explicit.

The therapist who takes time to identify structures, entities, and attributes may develop a variety of intervention strategies.

Approach 3: The "Black Box"

The "black box" approach is also most effective at the point where the level of intervention into the system is identified. Then, the various inputs into the system, the transforming of these inputs, and the outputs can be clearly defined.

In considering our client, G. receives as input that a father of one of her students will be coming to visit her. G. takes the input, runs it through her inner

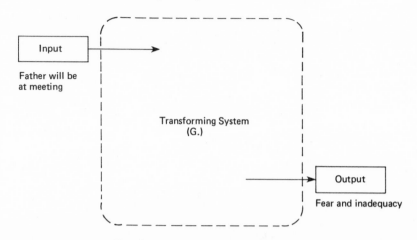

Figure 6. Flow chart for Client G

world (transforming system) and ends up with the output of fear and inadequacy (see Figure 6).

The rules of her script are the ways that she makes sense of the world. One rule that G. lives with is that "I'm not OK—others are OK." Consequently, whenever there is conflict or the threat of it, G. feels she will end up at fault; she is the one who is wrong. Another rule in G.'s script is that "as long as I am helpless, and can't think, others will take care of me." Instead of dealing with the situation at hand, G. gets scared and helpless, which invites others around to "take care of her." Other rules that operate in G.'s script include: "You must always remain in control," i.e., cut yourself off from your feelings because expressing feelings means a loss of control; "Be perfect", i.e., there is no room for "mistakes" and, consequently, you are to feel inadequate and try harder continually; and, "Be pleasing," i.e., take care of others and disregard yourself.

Thus, when G. gets the input that a father is coming to a meeting, the father becomes an "irate father," the internal rules begin to function and G. is feeling inadequate and scared. Figure 7 reflects what happens internally to G. after the input.

By looking at inputs, outputs, and the transforming system, the therapist can develop clear understandings of how information and energy flow through the client system.

CONCLUSION

The material in the case study is presented to demonstrate various ways of approaching systems. The models presented can also be readily integrated.

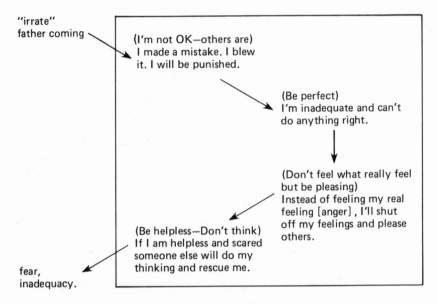

Figure 7. G's internal transformation

An example of a multi-goal multilevel hierarchy can be seen in our client G. The goal of the ''Be perfect'' Parent message may be to keep the client responding to a now internalized Parent. The creation of a guilt cycle means G. stays in an ''I'm not OK'' position. The inadequate Child goal may be to elicit support and rescue from others around. G.'s goals for being in the group are for both personal and professional growth. In turn, the overall goals of the group, personal and professional development, are seen within the context of the society.

Throughout the hierarchy, there is the potential for conflict and competition as to what goals get met. The ''Be perfect'' message is in internal conflict with a sense of inadequacy, as well as with Adult realization that it is not possible to ''Be perfect.'' In the group, one individual's desire to do personal work may conflict with others who want professional growth. A person's desire or personal goal to be a part of the group may conflict with a family goal, which is to have time together. The values and norms of the greater society may be in conflict with both individual and family goals.

The group, as many groups do, builds solidarity. And with the solidarity is a wish to retain its existence over a long period of time. The retention of the group over a long time may be in conflict with the hospital goal of discharging patients to maintain a high turnover rate. The high turnover rate itself may be in conflict with societal goals, regarding those patients who society wants to keep in the institution because they are uncomfortable, unpleasant, etc. to have around. By understanding the potential for conflict between goals at various levels, it becomes possible to understand how one level's activities may be frustrating another level. Interventions can then be designed appropriate to the level of the problems involved.

On thinking about entities, attributes, and structure, consider the patient, Mr. A. (an entity). His attributes include demographic data such as age, sex, race, past history. The nutrition psychiatric program (another entity) has the attributes that include Mr. A., the number of patients, the admission criteria (e.g., they all have nutritional problems), the ward as closed and the therapy group. The attributes of the group include that it meets twice a week in the dayroom for 45 minutes. Two aides run the group. In addition, there is a part-time group member who is a psychologist. One structure is that the group is physically organized in a circle. A structure rule is that persons ask for strokes. Another structural rule is that patients are not allowed to hit each other and that if a patient attempts to strike at another, the aides will act to restrain the patient. At the individual level, we have attributes of the patient, which include the distribution of energy (the data one might get from the egogram), contamination and isolation of ego states, games, rackets, decisions, etc. The script might be seen as a listing of attributes of the client.

Structures are rules the system operates with. Again, the script workup within TA provides excellent insights into the internal rules a client may function with. Some rules might include such things as: "If I get close to someone, I will be hurt. Therefore, I will not get close." "If I feel my feelings, I will be sad (angry). So I will not feel." "If I accept positive strokes, then I cannot continue putting myself down."

The flow chart approach may be usefully integrated with the entities approach at this point. A member of the group may understand the "rules" with which he has decided to live. However, he may not be aware of the sequence of behaviors which right at that moment triggers the "rules." For example, someone in the group may compliment Mr. X. Mr. X immediately discounts or discards the compliment and feels angry at the person who gave the compliment. The therapist may then invite him to walk through the sequence of events that resulted in the anger. The end result will be an awareness of how Mr. X specifically acted out the rule "If I feel close to someone I will be hurt. Therefore, I will not be close." The end result is Mr. X has specific information about his internal rules and external behaviors which keep him in a "not OK place."

The purposes of this chapter have been to present various views on systems and boundaries, and to suggest some practical uses for the concepts discussed. General systems theory provides some concepts which can be extremely useful for the group therapists in developing intervention strategies.

Chapter 9

Some Applications of Transactional Analysis in Groups to General Systems Theory

By Harris Peck, M.D.

Editor's Introduction. The value of Dr. Peck's article is that it eases the reader into a position where he can see the useful application of GST to the popular TA approach. Not only does the chapter demonstrate the integration of these two theories, but it also suggests the view that GST is a potential metatheory acting as an overarching set of suppositions under which we might find TA, encounter, psychoanalysis and other emerging models of the psychotherapeutic process. Peck reminds us that groups have delineated developmental stages in which certain events can be expected. Other suppositions of the GST outlook suggested here are to focus upon events rather than on entities, to focus on structure rather than content, to integrate complementary communication of groups and individuals and, finally, not to expect a neat and foreseeable outcome to group psychotherapy.

Besides reviewing basic TA concepts, Peck uses group scenarios as a springboard to a GST perspective in therapy. He compares methodologies and claims that greater group autonomy results from this particular perspective.

Group psychotherapists must sometimes wish that they had two heads, one to look at what is happening to individual patients in the group, and another to observe the behavior of the group as a whole. If alternation between these two ways of looking at the group therapy world does not produce actual vertigo, it is generally because most therapists tend to favor one view over the other. Thus, in any given situation, they tend to either (a) explain group phenomena in terms of the actions, thoughts, or feelings of a particular member or several "in interaction," or (b) look to the status, development or behavior of the group as a whole as the primary determinant of what has transpired. General systems theory suggests some approaches to integrating these disparate views and lessens the need to either alternate between theoretical models or to cram untidy fragments of data into one or another conceptual box. This presentation will review some selected aspects of both group process and transactional analysis and demonstrate some ways general systems theory can contribute to their integration.

Of the many recurrent themes or principles embraced by general systems theory, this presentation will refer to only a few. GST will be utilized as a "metatheory by means of which a variety of substantive areas can be explored or explained" (H. Durkin, 1974). The specific theoretical areas to be explored are selected aspects of transactional analysis and group process theory.

Transactional analysis is a theory of personality developed by Eric Berne as a conceptual tool for group psychotherapy. TA is based on the analysis of transactions, seen as consisting of a stimulus and response proceeding from specifically defined ego states of the individual participants.

Those aspects of group process theory to be considered in this presentation refer particularly to concepts about group developmental phases commonly utilized in the group psychotherapy literature,* as well as incorporating some of the original work conducted by our group at the Albert Einstein College of Medicine (Kaplan & Roman, 1963; Peck, Roman, Kaplan & Bauman, 1965). These theoretical formulations attempt to explain the movement of the group as a whole from a loosely organized aggregate of individuals into a well-defined entity capable of (a) establishing goals and direction, (b) providing a context for the differentiation essential to effective therapeutic work, and (c) achieving the autonomous functioning which facilitates the productive culmination of therapy.

The introduction of GST as a metatheory integrating the TA and group process approaches permits the elimination of agents or entities (be they groups or individuals) as the crucial elements in the performance of events. The focus is rather on the self-organizing process, which can be seen directly as events succeed each other in time and space.

GST does not postulate a theory or a model of either the specific content areas covered by TA or group process theory. As a metatheory, or a theory of such theories, it transcends particular contents and lends itself to a study of the general structure of group/individual relationships. Within this structure the two theories may be seen as a complementary pair, providing two fluctuating perspectives of both individual and group as alternate levels of a self-organizing hierarchy.

A second theme to be emphasized in this presentation is the approach to space and time suggested by Miller (1978) and reflected in the idea of Scheflen's (1976) sequences of behavior, which will be referred to as scenarios.

---

*Theories and systems conceptualizing and categorizing developmental phenomena in therapy groups were all heavily influenced by the pioneering work of Bales (1950), Bion (1952) and coworkers at the Tavistock Clinic (Ezriel, 1952). Significant elaborations and later innovations were introduced by Bennis and Shephard (1956), Schutz (1958), Stock and Thelen (1958).

Individual behavior as manifested in the transactions between therapist and patient or among group members will be dealt with in terms formulated by Eric Berne (1963, 1966) and such co-workers as Claude Steiner (1974). Transactional analysis has the enormous advantage of lending itself to the description of observable behavior in terms which have a high degree of reliability even among untrained observers. Since it is not feasible to incorporate a comprehensive summary of transactional analysis within the body of this paper, the presentation will deal primarily with relatively self-evident TA terms and concepts. Some brief definitions of a few commonly used terms are as follows:

The "Child" ego state refers to behavior essentially preserved in its entirety of early childhood and may, as the name suggests, appear in such forms as that of the "Frightened," "Sad," "Angry," or "Free" Child. These are considered "Natural" Child states in which the individual responds to his or her own biologically-based needs, as distinguished from "Adapted" Child behavior which is primarily shaped by parental expectations through such mechanisms as compliance, withdrawal, or procrastination.

The "Adult" refers to the computer aspect of the personality which exchanges information and utilizes such information in decision-making.

The "Parent" is essentially made up of behavior derived from parents or authority figures. The most commonly identified Parental states are the "Critical" and "Nurturing" Parent ego states, embodying behavior of the sort suggested by their names.

Discussion of group process phenomena will be largely limited to a consideration of developmental phases in therapy groups, utilizing concepts as formulated by Bion (1959) and the Tavistock group and later elaborated at the Albert Einstein College of Medicine (Kaplan & Roman, 1963; Peck, Roman, Kaplan & Bauman, 1965).

The idea that a group, any group, passes through a sequence of more or less consistently recurring developmental phases in the course of its history is not a new one to social scientists. It is, however, only recently that group therapists, even those of different theoretical persuasions, could employ relatively objective criteria and achieve some degree of consensus about the phase of development of any given group. Such consensus requires that the observers share some common criteria and categories for describing group behavior in answer to the question, "What happened?"

Various systems for describing and categorizing developmental phases in groups have been suggested. For purposes of this presentation we will employ concepts and terms which enjoy a high degree of consensus in the literature regarding gross, basic, and more evident manifestations of change from one group phase to another.

The initial phase of a group's development is characterized by a tendency for transactions to occur primarily between therapist and individual patients. Dependency and protection are common themes. Among the more frequent types

Therapist   Group Member

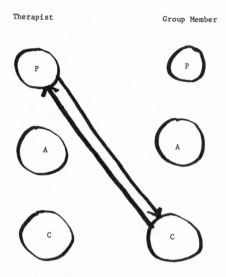

Figure 1.

of transactions are those between the therapist's Critical or Nurturing Parent and the individual group member's Scared, Helpless or Confused Child (Figure 1).

During this group formative phase, overall goals and a general agreement about the group's mode of work are arrived at between the therapist and the group, and individual patients begin to develop various types of therapeutic contracts. Most therapists are acutely aware that the way in which this process takes place will frequently determine how patients become engaged in the treatment process, as well as the overall therapeutic effectiveness of the group. It is generally considered an undesirable situation when the patient ends up with a recitation of his complaints or concerns, helplessly waiting for the therapist to either come to his rescue or correct his unacceptable behavior. A more desirable outcome prevails when patient, therapist, and other group members establish some contractual understanding of what each will contribute to assisting the patient to make changes which he considers desirable in his thinking, feeling, and behavior.

If the therapist employs the group process model for explaining either of these developments, he may point to the tendency of groups in the formative goal-setting phase to assign to the leader magical and omniscient powers and for the initial lines of transaction to be primarily between the designated leader and the patients.

The same phenomena viewed in transactional terms may be described as a patient in his Helpless or Confused Child "hooking" the Critical or Nurturing

Parent of the therapist. If the therapist does not allow himself to be hooked and engages the patient's Adult, both may be able to utilize the group in eliciting information. This will enable the patient to establish a therapeutic contract reflecting his situation realistically and to engage with the therapist and other group members in formulating plans for change.

Although some common elements may be discerned in these two views of the process, most therapists are likely to approach the matter either in terms of their effectiveness in assisting the group to establish its goals and boundaries, or as a question of whether the patient and therapist have effectively engaged each other in formulating a meaningful therapeutic contract.

One of the attributes of general systems theory which the group therapist may find helpful is the way in which it transcends the familiar patterns of linear causation, wherein phenomena tend to be dealt with as objects or things, or in terms of their intrinsic nature. Ludwig von Bertalanffy (1968), generally regarded as the founder of GST, was very heavily influenced by the principles of the Einsteinian revolution, which focuses primary attention on events as they occur in space and time. From this orientation, the phenomena described above may be seen as a programmed scenario commonly associated with the early stages of group formation.

The remainder of the presentation will be devoted to the study and discussion of illustrative scenarios, based on typical situations encountered by group therapists. The purpose of introducing these scenarios is to demonstrate the usefulness of GST as a metatheory. The scenarios could be viewed from either a TA or group process perspective, each of which is incomplete without the other. The scenario form lends itself to a demonstration of the GST emphasis on events rather than entities or agents. The scenarios deal with the several events as programmed sequences of behavior in a way which enables the therapist to see the interrelationships between the group process and TA perspectives without requiring the choice of one over the other.

In the section which follows, two greatly oversimplified alternative scenarios (L and M) from the initial phases of a group will be outlined. These scenarios will illustrate the possibilities of what Helen Durkin (1974) has referred to as the group therapist's role as a "decider subsystem," if "he chooses to restrict himself to catalyzing their [the group members'] self-regulatory process and cultivates wherever possible any emergent sign of growth potential."

In the second set of scenarios to be offered in this presentation (X and Y), we will assume the conditions existing in the group in a middle phase would be different depending on whether the initial phase had followed scenario L or scenario M. Scenario L would be more likely to lead to X, and M more likely to lead to Y, but all things are possible, particularly if a therapist is able to facilitate an equifinal jump, which is "how a self-regulating structure can radically transform itself even though what was to be transformed is the very structure that has to regulate the transformation'' (H. Durkin, 1975).

SCENARIO L

A. The Initial Structuring of the Group

The chair of the therapist is placed apart from that of patient group members, and all chairs are more directly facing the chair of the therapist than they are each other.

B. The Assumption of Complementary Roles

Event 1: Comments are initiated by the therapist.
Event 2: Therapist signals patients prior to their speaking.
Event 3: Comments by patients are addressed to the therapist.
Event 4: The therapist continues to direct his comments to individual patients, who respond primarily to the therapist during the remainder of the session.

C. The Establishment of Contracts

Contracts are established between therapist and patient with minimal participation of other patients.

D. Diagram of a Typical Pattern of Interaction—see Figure 2.

SCENARIO M

A. Initial Structuring of the Group

Chairs of therapist and patients are placed in a circle, more or less evenly spaced from each other.

B. The Establishment of Complementary Roles

Event 1: Comments are initiated with comparable frequency by both therapist and patients.
Event 2: Patients and therapist all signal each other in eliciting responses.
Event 3: During the remainder of the session, comments are directed from patient

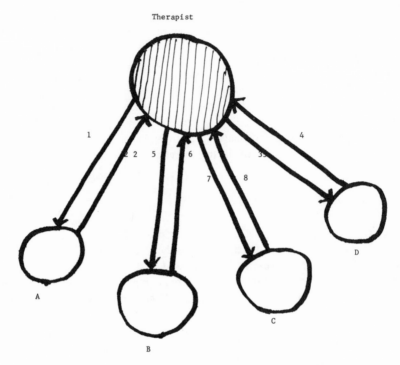

Figure 2. Diagram of a typical pattern of interaction

to patient and by therapist to both the whole group and to subgroups as well as to individual patients.

C. The Establishment of Contracts

Contracts are established by individual patients with the participation of both therapist and other patients.

D. Diagram of a Typical Pattern of Interaction—see Figure 3.

Although the end products of both Scenario L and Scenario M may be viewed either in terms of the group as a whole or of the individual patients which comprise it, it is evident that neither perspective is complete without the other. In the above sequences, behavior of the group, the therapist and patients are all various aspects of a series of interlocking events. These events have been presented in somewhat oversimplified, diagramatic form in the scenario to illustrate several points.

Therapist

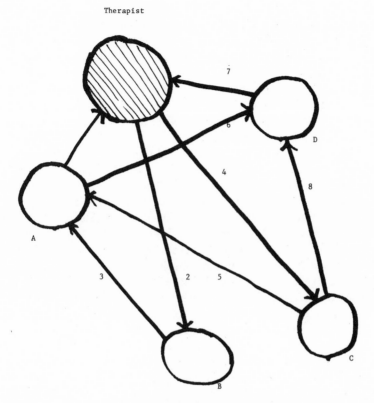

Figure 3. Diagram of a typical pattern of interaction

Designating the location of phenomena as inside or outside a particular boundary is an arbitrary or culturally determined convenience which may be dispensed with when it serves no useful purpose. Scenario L or M need not be thought of as originating exclusively (a) in the individual psyches or transactions of either patient or therapist, or (b) in the collective structure or phase of development of the group as a whole. Perhaps Goffman's (1959) concept of ''defining a situation'' offers one of the more useful models for referring to the essential conditions of a situation in which a given program is to be followed.*

It is evident that the one item, the position of chairs, which has been identified

---

*In *The Presentation of Self in Everyday Life*, Goffman states: ''When an individual appears before others, he knowingly and unwittingly projects a definition of the situation, of which a conception of himself is an important part. When an event occurs which is expressively incompatible with this fostered impression, significant consequences are simultaneously felt in three levels of social reality, each of which involves a different point of reference and a different order of fact'' (p. 242).

as significantly contributing to the initial structuring of the group, may be but one indication of a cluster of other possible elements defining the situation. These might include the therapist's posture, lighting arrangements, greeting patterns, or the manner in which seats are assigned or selected. Any and all of these items may be viewed either as "internal" transactions determining the initial shape and formation of the group, or as ways of "externally" structuring the group which influence the nature of the initial transactions. However, both "inside" and "outside" are different aspects of the way in which the situation is defined in the first of the three sequences.

Designation of the sequences as A, B, and C implies an orderly time progression with a beginning and an ending for the various segments of the scenario. However, Sequence C, the Establishment of Contracts, is both the termination of one scenario and the beginning of another. Indeed, the events located in Sequence A (Structuring the Group) will probably be repeated in some altered form in a subsequent scenario such as that seen in Scenarios X and Y described below. Thus, not only do adjacent sequences overlap and impinge upon each other, but they also are generally repeated in modified form time after time during the life span of a group (see Chapter 18). Such boundaries as space and time, which define the group, its members and subsystems, are nevertheless sufficiently discernible so that there can be some consensus about them. They also circumscribe and define the universe to which the therapist, patient, or observer will attend. A general systems approach contributes to our understanding of how boundaries are formed and thus extends our awareness of the variety of options for defining or intervening in any given situation.

SCENARIOS OF INTERMEDIATE GROUP PHASES

A somewhat more complex illustration of some of these principles is encountered in the recurring debate among group therapists about whether the individual patient or the group should be the primary focus of therapeutic intervention.*

Group therapists are often confronted with what seems to be such a choice early in the middle phase of a developing treatment group. As the group emerges from its formative stage and begins intensive therapeutic work, a frequent occurrence is the appearance of subgroup formation and the emergence of indigenous leaders. Such subgroups and their leaders are reflections of the differentiation essential to the performance of any complex human social endeavor. Conflict in this stage may assume such forms as the following:

---

*These issues were addressed in the papers by Foulkes and Schwartz and Wolf in the 1960 volume on *Topical Problems of Psychotherapy* and are still very much in evidence in the papers by Anthony and by Wolf and Schwartz in the compendium, *Comprehensive Group Psychotherapy* (1971).

1. Those patients who prefer an intellectual approach to their problems versus those who lean toward "gut" type experiential efforts.
2. The patients who consider themselves sick and in need of treatment versus those who think of themselves as well and in need of opportunities for growth.
3. The oldtimers who profess to know their way around versus the new and uninitiated who proclaim their bewilderment.

Often these disparate directions will be prominently reflected in the statements or participation of a group member who emerges to carry the banner of one or another subgroup.

Let us assume that the conflict is between patients who favor the more intellectual mode versus those who are inclined toward the gut experience. The leader of one subgroup may confront his opponent with the charge that he is "afraid to feel" or to "let himself go," or that he is "all talk and no action." Such charges may be countered with measured expressions of concern about the failure of the first to "think things through" or to "generalize from experience" or urging to "get into your Adult" and "consider the options."

Either of these positions may coincide with the therapist's own view or bias and he may well be inclined to engage one or both of the protagonists in terms of the material elicited by the conflict. If, on the other hand, the therapist is primarily concerned with the need to further the development and differentiation of the group, he may direct attention to the transactions between the two indigenous leaders or their subgroups. As noted in the previous illustration, a general systems approach can serve an integrative function and avoid some of the limitations inherent in the exclusive use of either the group process, intrapsychic, or transactional approaches to such a situation.

A format similar in structure to the previous L and M scenarios will be utilized in describing the developments associated with the following drama in a therapy group, in which it is assumed that a scenario L-type group is more likely to lead into a scenario X, and scenario M-type group is more likely to lead into a scenario Y.

The Drama

John: (screaming at Jane) I am furious at you! You're piling the same kind of putdown shit on me that I get from my wife.
Jane: Have you ever considered what other options you have besides screaming at either me or your wife?
John: Don't give me that "options" stuff. Stop running away from your feelings about what I said.
Jane: Why don't you get out of being angry all the time and get into your Adult?

SCENARIO X

A. Expressions of Conflict Between Members

The scene described above continues as an interchange between John and Jane without participation by other members of the group.

B. Interruption of Conflict

The therapist finally intervenes by either supporting the expression of feelings by John or facilitating Jane's attempt to elicit Adult information from John.

C. Reaction to Intervention

The therapist's intervention is accepted by John, Jane, and the other group members as helpful and therapeutic.

D. Typical Pattern of Interaction—see Figure 4.

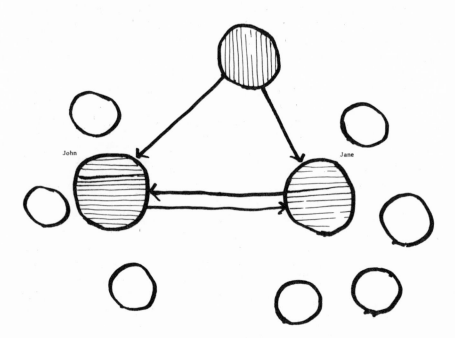

Figure 4. Diagram of a typical pattern of interaction

SCENARIO Y

A. Expressions of Conflict Between Members

The conflict between members is supported and modified by members of John's and Jane's subgroups with interactions both within and across subgroup lines.

B. Interruption of Conflict

Members of both subgroups begin to reduce and resolve the conflict prior to intervention by the therapist, who may direct attention to aspects of the process relating to: 1) John's and Jane's roles as indigenous leaders of their subgroups; 2) the interaction between the subgroups; 3) the interrelations between 1) and 2).

C. Reaction to Intervention

All members of the group experience a sense of the resources available to them from other members of the group, and emerge from the conflict with both individual members and the group as a whole achieving a higher level of autonomy.

D. Typical Pattern of Interaction—see Figure 5.

Although the above scenarios have been greatly condensed for purposes of illustration, it is apparent that there is a greater degree of complexity in scenarios Y and M than in scenarios X and L. In terms of group developmental theory it may be said that a scenario Y-type group has achieved more differentiation than an X-type group and thus displays a capacity for more effective therapeutic work by its individual members and is more likely to achieve a higher degree of autonomy for the group as a whole.

Complexity in systems is associated with their degree of openness and the utilization of positive feedback, which may in turn increase confusion and complexity. Levinson (1978) points out, "An open system is one which is in continuous exchange with its environment. . . . Depending on the level of openness, it can either maintain its level of organization (homeostasis), or it can actually increase in complexity. If its commerce with the environment is extensive enough, it can change the environment, in essence creating its own ecosphere."

These formulations in general systems terms appear to be directly applicable to the illustrative scenarios and embrace the various levels of discourse related to the group process, transactional, or intrapsychic happenings.

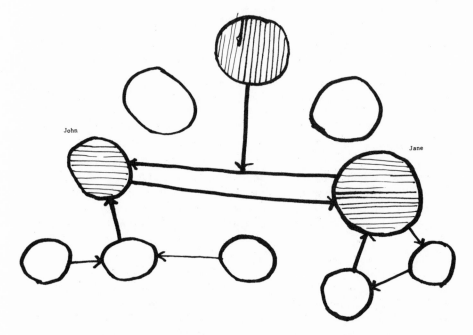

Figure 5. Diagram of a typical pattern of interaction

The relative complexity between the L and M scenarios is perhaps most evident in their differing patterns of interaction. Scenario X is confined largely to therapist-initiated transactions with one patient at a time. The more complex interactional patterns of scenario M suggest in Levenson's terms that "the group will continue to shift and change, by itself, and most important, it will develop its own directions. The outcome will not be necessarily predictable to the therapist, or controllable."

Perhaps it is the essence of the therapy group viewed as an open system that the therapist may lose certain kinds of control and predictability and accept a higher degree of confusion in return for greater therapeutic effectiveness and autonomy.

It is evident that the more active participation of other patients in the contract-setting process in the M scenario is likely to be more confusing and less predictable than the more restricted therapist-to-patient transactions of the L scenario. These differences set the scene or, in Goffman's terms, "define the situation" in the Y scenario, in which conflicts are resolved by the group rather than the therapist, and indigenous leaders begin to take over some of the therapist's prior functions. Under such conditions there is likely to be more variation in the trajectories through which patients fulfill their contracts or by which the group achieves autonomy. Levenson, citing von Bertalanffy on "equifinality," states, "The system will develop along certain inherent trajectories, arriving at the same endpoint from different beginnings."

Beginnings, trajectories, and endpoints may all be viewed in either group process or transactional terms. The general systems approach in this presentation is offered as a metatheory which can assist group therapists in reorganizing the ways in which they view their data, and perhaps provide additional options for more effective therapeutic intervention.

Chapter 10

The Technical Implications
of General System Theory
for Group Psychotherapy

By Helen E. Durkin, Ph.D.

Editor's Introduction. Perhaps the most fundamental and far-reaching criticism of psychoanalytic therapy is that it provides no clear path from insight to behavior change. In this chapter Helen shows how the synthesis she proposes between psychoanalysis and GST can be brought to bear on this problem. Over the years of her group practice, Helen reports that she found herself coming up with *ad hoc* intervention techniques which seemed to violate some of the sacred precepts of orthodox psychoanalysis, but seemed to be effective in facilitating behavior change. Then, as she began to come into contact with GST ideas, she saw that this new conceptual framework could provide a theoretical basis for utilizing these techniques that she had discovered. Thus, Helen found that she had gradually become a GST therapist without even knowing it.

Helen reports that her early training in psychoanalysis had been somewhat unorthodox in that she was trained by people who were quite process-oriented rather than being content-oriented. With this perspective Helen was able to see that although Freud originally presented his ideas and insights in process terms, his followers gradually shifted the emphasis back into content terms. Freud, according to Helen, was in tune with the most modern thinking of his day, such as the process thought of the new physics which thought in terms of dynamic fields of forces rather than in terms of objects causing effects in other objects. His followers, on the other hand, held to "Aristotelian" thinking which focused on nouns rather than verbs. The new techniques she had developed out of clinical necessity were much more in harmony with the original orientation of Freud than of the psychoanalytic orthodoxy established by Freud's later followers and, as she discovered, directly within the scope of GST.

What characterizes the "process approach" that Helen aligns with her own technical changes, Freud's original orientation, and the GST framework? How is it to be distinguished from the "content approach" which she suggests has come to dominate orthodox psychoanalysis? Although trying to distinguish between such terms as "process," "structure," "content," and "function" often leads to more confusion than clarification, I would like to try and answer these questions and show why the dual GST-psychoanalysis model that Helen arrives at leads to the practical solution of the perennial behavior change problem. I see the difference between the process approach and the content approach that Helen is trying to distinguish in the following ways: The process approach strives to create a *living* structure, while the content approach strives to create a *meaning* structure out of what goes on in the relationship between therapist and patients. A meaning structure is a language formulation describing or encoding the personality as a target object, but not embodying it. A living structure—and here the term "living" is used in the verb sense rather than the adjective sense—is an embodiment in action structure which includes a self-referential language structure within it.

The meaning-living distinction can be further clarified by distinguishing two basic modes of human interrelationship, thinking and feeling or, if you will, cognition and emotion. How does a content approach to thinking and feeling differ from a process approach? A content approach observes thinking and feeling events as they occur in the room during the session and tries to extract the meaning of what it is that has been thought and felt. It does this by lodging small units of meaning into a larger, more comprehensive hierarchical structure of meaning. Both types of events are equally items of behavior to be observed and analyzed in terms of such objective criteria of meaningfulness as completeness and consistency. In this situation the persons of the patient and the therapist are more or less off stage, for each is an instrument for generating the meaning structure. The patient is a data-generating instrument while the therapist is a data-analyzing instrument.

The process approach to thinking and feeling exchanges in psychotherapy calls for a different definition of what is on stage and what is off stage. The persons of the therapist and of the patient are not mere instruments in the process approach, but living wholes whose action structures are as essential as the information they exchange. Process happens in the here and now. Thus the therapist as well as the patient must be physically present to each other as members of the same field of influence. Cognitive exchange is not sufficient, for the flow of emotional energy between the participants is also necessary. In the process approach, thinking events must be taken on their own terms, but feeling events must also be dealt with on their own terms and not just as a clue to meaning.

The new technical changes that Helen reports in this chapter all involve the process of fluctuating between thinking and feeling events. It is for this reason that the GST model of living structure, which focuses upon the interplay of thinking and feeling events as the normal living process, was such a fortuitous discovery for her. The operation of boundarying with its alternation of opening and closing, which lies at the heart of the GST model, provides a powerful tool for understanding and dealing with the living interpersonal process. At the human level, boundary closing can be interpreted as thinking and boundary opening as feeling. Living structure transforms itself by opening up feeling flow and consolidates the trans-formation by closing boundary structures around it. Thus the GST model gives equal focus to thinking and feeling, each on its own terms.

As Helen points out, GST does not in and of itself prescribe a method of group psychotherapy. But it does provide a model of living structures in living relationship that can serve as a complement at the process level to the analytic work of gradually constructing the pattern of meaning in a person's life. Helen's "dual model" takes the strengths of both approaches and opens up a path from insight to behavior change through her theoretical and clinical discoveries.

GST AND ANALYTIC GROUP THERAPY: THE DEVELOPMENT OF AN INTEGRATED MODEL

In Chapter 1, I described some of the external conditions which led me to expand the psychoanalytic model of group therapy and I outlined the principles of the overarching GST framework. I also summarized the changes GST would bring about in the orientation, the goal, and the function of group therapists. The present chapter explains why I undertook the search for a more generalized theoretical framework for the field of group psychotherapy, and traces the steps I have taken in the still ongoing process of integrating the two theoretical approaches. The technical implications of the new, more comprehensive and unifying theoretical framework will be discussed and clinical examples will be given of those technical changes I made which led to the reorganization.

The Author's Starting Position

I have frequently been asked, "What is different about the way you work with groups now that you use GST?" Unfortunately, the answer is not as simple and straightforward as the question, for my work started out somewhat differently from most analytic group therapists. Dr. John Levy, under whom I began my training, put primary emphasis on what was going on in the relationship between the therapist and the patient. In other words, I was process- rather than content-oriented from the start. A large percentage of what went on in the therapy groups consisted of transference and resistance behavior. So it was easy to adopt a psychoanalytic model* when we later (1942) came under the direction of a well-known analyst, Dr. Geraldine Pedersen-Krag. Her teaching was always on the growing edge of psychoanalysis. Like John Levy, she was process-oriented. She had incorporated psychoanalytic ego psychology and object relations theory in her thinking and was interested in working with the preoedipal character structure. Finally, she believed in helping the patient take responsibility for his participation in his current dilemmas and his future behavior. The process orientation and the focus on the very early parent-child relations,** during which the patient's modes of interacting are formed, made me receptive to the GST point of view. I felt

---

*And so did my colleague, Dr. Henriette Glatzer. We have followed parallel paths from 1938 to the present time.

**These very early formative events occurred before much capacity had been developed to process content-coded experience. Therefore, they centered around structural experiences such as forming boundaries and the like where the structural perspective of GST might supply a needed basis.

at home in GST territory. GST seemed to me to open up the next logical path in my growth as a therapist and to lead me to some vital new ideas.

Since 1938 I have been employing this progressive analytic approach in the practice of individual treatment and, with certain modifications, in group treatment. I found analyzing transference and resistance as it occurs in the group process to be dynamic and quite effective. As time went on, however, I became increasingly aware that certain of its theoretical inadequacies impeded the effectiveness of psychoanalytic psychotherapy.

THE EFFECT ON OUTCOME OF CERTAIN THEORETICAL INADEQUACIES IN PSYCHOANALYTIC THEORY

Psychoanalytic theory has been one of the great leaps forward in the history of modern thought, yet it has rarely been free from criticism. Much of the criticism has been the result of misunderstanding on the part of the critics and of the misuses on the part of clinicians. But other criticisms were quite warranted and must be examined because the results of analytic treatment have not been as far-reaching as had been anticipated. It had been assumed that explicit behavior change would naturally follow from genuine insight. The strategy of analyzing transference and resistance had seemed adequate for the hysterical patients who were treated in the early years (with the possible exception of patients who had underlying character problems). At that time no new techniques seemed to be required. In the long run, however, it became apparent that while analyzed patients excelled in self-understanding, the ability to change their behavior too often lagged far behind.

Because of its heightened interaction, analytic group psychotherapy improved the situation somewhat, but there remained a tendency among the members to talk about feelings rather than to express them directly to one another. Moreover, the number of character problems increased—and so did the problem of turning insight into changed behavior. Because of the influx of narcissistic, borderline, and orally or anally regressed patients into groups, the need for new techniques has become urgent. These patients are themselves unable, without further help from the therapist, to initiate new behavior patterns. More than ever the gap between insight and changed behavior had to be narrowed.

By the 1970s criticism of psychoanalysis had mushroomed, and many new approaches and techniques began to be employed in group psychotherapy. Again, some of the criticism was warranted, but much of it was the result of misunderstanding and should have been aimed at the misuse of analytic technique in group therapy.

The conceptual dilemma in which group therapy finds itself today can best be understood if we examine the historical and human context in which it developed. Psychoanalysis was a product of the revolution against Cartesian reductionism, 19th century empiricism, and substantive Aristotelian thinking. In that spirit, Freud boldly set about investigating the invisible dynamics of unconscious motivation. His technique of analyzing transference and resistance as it occurred in the therapeutic interaction clearly reflected the new significance which was given to process.

There were several reasons why this innovative technique did not bring about as much changed behavior as had been anticipated:

1) Unfortunately, Aristotelian thinking, with its tendency to use nouns rather than verbs, to emphasize content rather than process, was deeply entrenched in the thinking of the scientists, writers, and the laity of the day. They did not fully register the profound shift toward process that had occurred. Even Freud's followers were not fully cognizant of its meaning for therapy. The psychoanalytic literature was replete with static substantive terms such as "the unconscious," "the transference neurosis," and the like. For this reason, practicing analysts and later group analysts who had not fully comprehended the shift continued to make too many static content interpretations of transference phenomena rather than process interpretations of the event. Content interpretations tended to produce information and lead to insight, whereas process interpretations led to change. Content interpretations failed to render Freud's brilliant innovative technique of analyzing transference behavior as it was experienced *in vivo* as effective as it could have been. In other words, the fact that psychoanalysis came into being during a period of radical change in scientific ideas was responsible for its lack of complete effectiveness. The transition took a long time and is, in fact, still interfering with the production of sufficient changes in behavior.

2) Even more troublesome for the analytic practitioner was the fact that the content of unconscious processes constituted a veritable Pandora's box of frightening primitive unacceptable feelings. Both patients and therapists gave evidence of a strong tendency to avoid these feelings. They unwittingly joined in resistance against bringing them to light in the therapy session. This avoidance of critical emotions had the effect of binding the energy that was needed to bring about change. Only directly expressed emotions freely release that energy.

3) Both patients and therapists perceive the group exchanges in terms of their personal experience. There is regularly a discrepancy between the "objective events and their subjective perception." To put it another way, this self-referential nature of the clinical material confused the interpretive process and made it less effective.

4) Therapists were expected to tolerate their formerly repressed feelings, yet they were simultaneously warned that these very feelings could lead to "noxious countertransference." Psychoanalysis provided at least a partial solution to this predicament. It required the therapist to undergo a personal analysis

in an attempt to minimize his neurotic countertransference. But experience proved that there was no end to self-referential cycles, and hence, to countertransference interference with the treatment process. It was not until the late fifties that psychoanalysts began to accept the fact that "countertransference" (in the broad sense) was the very basis of both the analyst's empathic and critical attitudes to the patients (Racher, 1968). Now the best solution seemed to be for therapists to try to be as open as possible to their feelings and impulses in order to reduce the tendency to act them out. It must be admitted that this problem was not fully resolved and that countertransference management continues to be the greatest source of technical error.

5) Lastly, a number of inadequate concepts led to technical errors. The intricacies of psychoanalytic concepts are difficult enough to translate into down-to-earth interpretations which help the patient come to understand his subjective distortions of what is going on in the treatment situation (transference). When these concepts are ambiguous or imprecise, the margin for error rises sharply. Yet because of the unfamiliarity of the newly discovered unconscious feelings and impulses, it was difficult to conceptualize them accurately. It is not surprising that a number of the analytic concepts were indeed ambiguous.

Clearly then, both individual and group psychoanalysis make stringent demands on their practitioners. Freud transcended substantive Aristotelian thinking with a new emphasis on process, but his followers' thinking lagged behind him in this respect. The paradigm lag in group psychotherapy was even greater because it was based largely on the followers of Freud who did not fully appreciate the new focus. Moreover, analytic group therapists had been unable to get rigorous analytic training in the early days of the movement before the new modality had been successfully established. Consequently, there were great variations in the techniques which "analytic group psychotherapists" used. In spite of its basic efficiency as an agent of change, analysis of transference and resistance in the group situation was not as satisfactory as had been anticipated.

General system theory, on the other hand, insisted on process interpretations from the beginning so that it proved to be a logical extension of Freud's therapeutic approach rather than that of his followers.

Before I go on to demonstrate this proposition, however, I shall continue with the theme of how, step by step, I introduced technical modifications in analytic group therapy as I practice it, which ultimately took me right to the front door of GST.

Some Common Errors Which Grew Out of the Inadequacies of Psychoanalytic Therapy

I had discovered some of the theoretical pitfalls in my own practice and made a few technical modifications to correct for them. A few years later my experience in supervising trainees and less experienced group therapists confirmed my hypothesis that certain theoretical inadequacies and imprecisions of psychoanalytic theory acted as a deterrent to optimal clinical effectiveness. The supervisee's most common errors seemed to be linked to the misunderstanding, confusion or misuse of certain imprecise conceptualizations. In general, the effect was to impede progress in turning insight into behavior change.

I began to teach my students the technical changes I had myself initiated. Some of them were merely extensions of analytic technique. Others were based on the principles of psychoanalytic ego psychology and objects relations theory. But I did not hesitate to draw on the newer nonanalytic approaches such as group dynamics, humanistic experientialism, gestalt exercises or encounter tactics if they solved clinical problems. Since I am primarily a clinician, I felt I did not need to be a theoretical purist.

Let me indicate the kinds of errors I found to be most common among my supervisees:

1) They tended to misuse the intentionally open-ended analytic concepts, ego, id, and superego, by making vitalistic or anthropomorphic interpretations.
2) The concept of resistance had originated in the clinical context to explain the patient's periodic defection from the working alliance. Therapists were likely to regard it as a personal affront and give way to their narcissistic frustration, instead of analyzing the resistance straightforwardly. They had a tendency to fall into negative countertransference and either make disparaging interventions or compensate for their irritation by playing the role of the all-giving parent who is permissive even with resistance. In either case a great deal of time was wasted or treatment came to an impasse.
3) In attempting to explore the origins of transference behavior, therapists often became so caught up in historical material that they lost sight of the fact that in psychoanalytic treatment self-understanding is intended to serve only the purpose of replacing transference behavior with more spontaneous and realistic modes of interacting.
4) Other well intentioned but perhaps overeager therapists were so intent upon making precise interpretations that instead of waiting until transference interactions in the group were at an emotional peak they spoke too soon. They handed out insights too quickly. Such intellectual interpretations are, of course, not conducive to the growth of patient insight, much less to activating change in behavior.

CORRECTING THE TECHNICAL PROBLEMS

I felt there was some truth to the criticism that many analytic group therapists intellectualize the therapeutic process. They often put too much emphasis on the cognitive aspect of interpretations. Because I felt it was this common error, more than any other, that prevented self-awareness from being converted into normal behavior change, I decided that I would choose from among the whole array of technical changes I had made only those which helped to stimulate the intensity of the emotional experience of analytic group therapy. On the other hand, the encounterists had gone to the opposite extreme of ruling out thinking altogether, so I made sure that once an emotional shift had occurred, the therapist would endeavor to bring the members' thinking to bear on what had happened. This enabled them to articulate the change as the first step toward using the new behavior and eventually to structuralize it. Thus, group psychoanalytic practice would improve and Fenichel's (1954) principle that there should always be a reciprocal interaction between emotion and reason would be reinstated.

Examples of Technical Changes

The first change I made consisted simply of reformulating the basic role of free association, which was ill-suited to the group situation. I had found that asking for associations in the group situation tended to produce an excess of verbiage, much of which consisted of rationalizations and other intellectualizations which served only to cover up the underlying emotional dynamics. Therefore, I began by asking the group members to try to say whatever they might be inwardly experiencing as we all talked together. My intention was to encourage direct, open exchanges of feelings among them in order to create both a permissive climate and one that would be dynamically challenging.

My second technique carried this aim a bit further. I decided to interrupt individuals, or the group as a whole, whenever they showed an inclination to rationalize or obsess extensively. For instance, when the traditional attempt to deal with this kind of resistance failed to bring about change, I might say, "Please stop talking for a moment and try to get in touch with what is going on inside you." If necessary, I might facilitate the process by adding, "Do you notice any bodily tension?" and/or, "Any images or quick fringe thoughts?"

I was repeatedly surprised to find how rapidly most patients can change the level of their communications. Some members became quickly aware of quite primitive images. Others became aware of body tension first. I would ask them to concentrate on the uncomfortable spot and see what happened next. I might follow through, in that case, with, "What is your body trying to say?" One or two members, instead of answering the question directly, characteristically and sometimes defiantly produced symbolic material at this point and proceeded to associate to it. Whatever their decision, there regularly followed a flood of genuine, emotionally tinged associations. These then generated a livelier group interaction. Occasionally, the patients involved became very angry with me. In that case I did not pursue the point, nor did I need to, for the membership simply took over by reacting to what I had said, and proceeded to develop its theme.

I recall one young lady who became aware of her very taut chest and neck muscles after a moment of silence. Almost immediately she then recalled a very early experience, starting with an image of herself as a baby, crying, and pinned down in a crib, with her mother somehow pressing down on her, choking her. She became very anxious and fantasied that she was about to die.

In one group, Tom, who always tried to comply with whatever he thought was wanted of him and automatically agreed with any intervention I might make, tensed up as if in anger. He said, "I feel a frightful knot in my stomach." He thrashed about a bit and hesitantly admitted, that, as usual, he was being pulled in two opposite directions. "It hurts," he said, and began to get very upset, saying "Oh, oh, I feel like lashing out at someone," and then he almost cried as he said, "I can't—damn, damn, I'm stuck, I can't do it anymore!"

After a shocked silence, the others began to compare experiences. They wondered why they felt so helpless. Finally, someone in a working alliance said, "I think we are hanging on to helplessness for some reason." At that point, the most aggressive member became Tom's spokesman by lashing out verbally at me. He evoked a variety of transferential interactions. A couple of members put him down, while others admitted for the first time that they saw me as a controlling or demanding parent. They were taking their first step to overcome their helplessness. After several such experiences Tom and the others were able to express unacceptable feelings more freely and eventually also to modify the global infantile rage which had heretofore rendered them impotent. These were Tom's first steps toward intrapersonal reorganization. My having facilitated his moving to a less mechanized level of communication and the group experience which followed had helped him to modify his maternal superego and release emotion and energy. The most dramatic change occurs in obsessive patients whose pseudo-associations simply serve to isolate their emotions from their thinking.

It was not long before the group began to recognize that they need not be subjected to long boring recitals. They began to speak up instead of automatically becoming passive victims of such intellectualizing. To sum up, notable changes in behavior were produced by simply interrupting their automatic ways of binding their unacceptable feelings, body tensions, or fringe thoughts. New energy and emotions were released and processed.

The new technique worked well. The Latin derivation of emotion ("e movere") proved to be true. The group members were indeed moved to change their insight into new behavior.

What I had tried to do in initiating these techniques was to help the group members turn their insights into actual changes in their ways of behaving, especially with "significant others." For this purpose I borrowed from the nonanalytic, innovative techniques of the sixties which were trying to increase the emotional intensity of the treatment experience. I did not, however, work from outside-in, as they do by setting up situations which would force the change. Instead, I continued to work as usual from inside-out by stopping those dysfunctional interactions which seemed too rigid to allow for change, and by putting the patients on a different and more emotional associative track by suggesting that they get in touch with what they were experiencing inwardly at the moment. And, of course, I made sure that once they had experienced a shift of their feelings, they would be able to bring their thinking to bear on what had happened, so that they could internalize or structuralize the change. At the time, I thought of it analytically as bringing "id" impulses under control of "the ego."*

The Transition to a GST Orientation

For a while I employed these new techniques experimentally and somewhat tentatively. I did not mind having defied a couple of sacred cows by stopping the process and giving directions, but I did feel somewhat uncomfortable about deviating from the internal consistency of a method that had stood me in good stead for so long. One of the reasons I welcomed GST was that it provided theoretical backing for my own new techniques, and for the broad spectrum of current approaches on which I had drawn. For a short time, then, I used my new techniques more systematically, but I soon became convinced that a more orderly, coherent, and effective solution to the technical problems could be achieved by adopting the superordinate theoretical framework which GST provided. I believed, also, that the analytic method could be incorporated as the critical conceptual subsystem within the overarching GST system. No eclectic piecemeal solution could be as satisfactory.

ON INTEGRATING GST AND
PSYCHOANALYTIC THEORY IN PRACTICE

From the beginning, I had come to the conclusion that GST and psychoanalytic theory were harmonious in principle, while systems thinkers like von Bertalanffy, Haley, Watzlawick and others felt that the concepts were mutually exclusive. Closer examination showed that the information each of these theories had generated was complementary rather than contradictory. But I wondered whether or not there was a sound empirical basis for applying, "in tandem," a theory about systems in general and one that was specific to human personality systems. Over a period of about a year, I combined them experimentally in my three therapy groups. It became apparent that they cover sufficient common ground

---

*This is similar to the principle, in Jim's Chapter 13, that structural transformation is an opening process experienced as feeling, and that structural consolidation is a subsequent closing process based on cognitive functions.

in respect to goal, method, and the actual clinical events to promise a cohesive model. Both focus on the actual verbal exchanges and their nonverbal accompaniments. Both begin by talking with the members in terms of this manifest content, and both aim gradually to call attention to underlying structural events for the purpose of illuminating and elaborating the manifest content.

They differ sharply in their ways of viewing the exchanges and in their hypotheses about the underlying implications. Psychoanalysis provides additional information about the members' earlier familial experiences and the unconscious dynamics which led to their current dysfunction. GST provides additional information concerning their boundary structure and the effect which opening or closing boundaries has on their ability to maintain their identity or to change and grow. Taken together, they lead to broader vision and heightened group interaction. For this reason, the effort of trying to integrate them seemed to me to be worthwhile. But two such powerful theories could not simply be added together; it was necessary to reorganize the material and reintegrate it into a coherent new theory of group therapy.

My confidence in the venture was enormously increased because the clinical events had confirmed my hypothesis that what GST referred to as energy and information in systems in general was experienced by the group members as feeling and thinking (emotion and cognition; see Chapters 11, 13 and 14). Since they were concerned about the same phenomena, I saw it as a strong connecting link between the two approaches. Further evidence of a close connection between them came with the discovery that most of the dysfunctional modes of exchanging emotion and cognition which occurred could be clearly identified as transferential in character. And dysfunctional boundary closing could, in analytic terms, be seen as resistance.* The pertinent phenomena were the same; only the vantage points differed. I became increasingly certain that there was enough common ground at all levels to justify integrating them to form a more comprehensive framework which was also unifying in its effect.

The Therapist's Transition to the Dual Approach

I now had the choice of intervening either from the GST perspective to facilitate boundary closing/opening, or from an analytical perspective to help the members find out how they came by their dysfunctional ways of interacting and to experience for themselves that they no longer needed these self-defeating protective measures. At first I tended to give preference to the analytic interventions with which I was so familiar. However, I soon accommodated the new structural

---

*In Chapter 13, Jim describes the repetitive neurotic configuration as a linear feedback structure which showed up as resistance when the feedback was negatively oriented, and as crisis cycles which go nowhere when the feedback was positively oriented.

viewpoint. I had already discovered that, in analysis, structural interventions were more likely to lead to changed behavior than genetic ones. At any rate, it was not long before I was able to swing easily and intuitively from one to the other. Nor was it difficult to use my clinical judgment as to which was more likely to "ring the bell" for the patient. What he or she said could be depended on to give me the clues.

I was glad to find that the members quickly comprehended what the effect of opening and closing boundaries had on their modes of interacting. Some of them were, for example, tremendously relieved when they discovered that the boundaries between themselves and their mothers had always been much too open and they quickly saw that they were no longer helpless, and were able to close certain boundaries and increase their sense of separate identity. Once this had happened, they could cope with their mothers without either fighting or subjugating themselves.

Moreover, I was delighted to have a second way of dealing with the here and now which did not depend on a transference crisis. I recalled with pleasure that Freud had long ago pointed out that when the patient is dealing only with the past, it is time to bring in the present, and vice-versa.*

The Merging Streams of Psychoanalytic Therapy and GST

As I continued to work in this way, I was not surprised to find that a productive interplay between the two kinds of interventions took place regularly in the ongoing group therapeutic process. Let me use as an example a single interchange which took place during a preliminary phase of transformation.

Clare opened the group discussion saying, "I saw my mother yesterday and as usual she made me furious and we both ended in tears." Her flashing eyes and sharp gestures at the beginning gave way to a bowed head. Ben took up the theme. He said, "Gee, I admire your nerve, Clare, I am always so damn accommodating." His voice and eyes were alert, but his posture remained slumped.

Here we observe a small segment of interaction in which there is as yet very little mutual influence between the participants.** But it is apparent that their modes or patterns of interacting with their mothers were dysfunctional and would need to be transformed. Psychoanalytic and GST therapists would agree that the group therapist should remain silent and wait to hear what other members have to say so that he or she can assess how much influence for change the group as

---

*Jim sees this as a situation to handle with the principle of staying closed to closedness and open to openness. If the preoccupation with the past or present is closed, shift away. If it is open and moving, stick with it and support it.

**I reserve the term "transaction" for systems exchanges in which the participants show considerable mutual influences on each other.

such can exert on its members. At some point, however, the flow of the exchanges will slow down and the therapist's intervention will be needed in order to facilitate the group process. GST and analytic therapists will agree, also, that the intervention should start by addressing either the group or the individual participants of the interaction in their own language. The therapist should begin with the manifest content. The members will be experiencing it as thoughts, feelings, and actions, but many of these are not recognized by them. Therapists of all schools will begin by helping patients get in touch with a wider range of their responses. This is the first step to transformation.

The Therapist's Options in a GST Context

The therapist has several options in selecting his techniques. He may employ methods that depend upon the manifest verbal and nonverbal content and on his own perception of its underlying significance. According to GST he is open to a number of viewpoints in assessing the clinical events and is, therefore, not limited to a particular technique. He may choose to analyze transference and resistance, to use action or encounter techniques, or he may concentrate on opening or closing the relevant dysfunctional boundaries.

Let us say, for example, that in the case of Clare and Ben's exchange, the therapist simply waits for responses from other members. It may turn out that some of the members identify with them and others identify with the mothers. They may begin to express their own reactions on a common "emotional preoccupation" (Whitaker & Lieberman, 1967). As he listens, the therapist may find that they keep repeating themselves, that no feelings or perceptions change. No energy or information is crossing the tight boundary that has formed between the two subgroups. In Jim Durkin's terms, they are only summing, not systeming at all (see Chapter 13). If the therapist sees that as the salient feature of the interaction, he may address the group as a whole or their strongest spokesman, by stimulating enough emotion to break through the rigid subgroup boundary. Once this happens, there is likely to be a definite change in the nature of the interaction. The members will begin to be influenced by one another again (to system).

If the group members should begin to compare their early maternal experiences, the therapist will facilitate the process whenever they get stuck (closed boundary-resistance). On the other hand, Clare (or Ben) may develop a strong negative transferential exchange with another group member, such as Anne, who is an older woman clearly on the mother's side. The other group members may point out the distortions. If they don't, the therapist may proceed to analyze the part that each played in the transferential interaction. Their temporal boundary system will change and a transformation is likely to take place. They will restructure themselves and begin to react more spontaneously and realistically with each other. This change will, of course, influence all the members and the group as a whole.

Here we have some examples of the possible interplay between the two approaches. Each serves a somewhat different function, but both change the manifest content and lead to transformations. Often using one technique leads to clinical events which require a different technique. Both approaches foster movement toward the goal of remobilizing the normal system potentials of the group, at the intrapsychic and the interpersonal levels.

In the three successive clinical sessions which I have described in Chapter 14, the reader will find further examples of the way these two theoretical streams merge and supplement each other in the therapeutic process.

The Theoretical Foundation for Complementarity and Integration Between GST and Psychoanalytic Theory

1) Because psychoanalysis lays down a rather clearly and narrowly defined technique, the experienced therapist comes to feel comfortably in control of the process and its outcome. The danger lies in that it is easy to slip into the countertransferential illusion that he can change the patient. In the broader perspective of GST, all living processes, including group psychotherapy, are considered equifinal. This means that at any moment in time, any of its major systems, which are continually importing energy and information from one another and the environment, may change the clinical events. The therapist, whether or not he has initiated the change, has the task of facilitating the intake, processing, and transformation of the system. On the other hand, if he feels the new input will lead to dysfunctional closing of its boundaries (resistance), he may attempt to block it (see Chapter 11). Thus, he has an additional opportunity to counter a patient's tendency to repeat inappropriate behavior which was conditioned by the original family situation. Furthermore, the therapist who is open to these ecological sources of change will be open enough to scrap his own plan and respond to fortuitous events for the purpose of facilitating creative self-structuring.*

2) GST increases the analytic group therapist's ability to convert insight into changed behavior because it puts a premium on the process of changing systems. The group therapist focuses consistently on the flow of the exchanges of energy and information in the group interaction by facilitating opening or closing boundaries at the group, the interpersonal, or the intrapsychic levels. He evokes structural transformations in systems which in turn mobilize new

---

*Jim (Chapter 13) calls this "systeming" when member and leader are both open to each other and neither is following a plan. In such cases the directional flow may go either way in changing the leader or the member.

functional systems or modes of interacting. Dysfunctional transferential or defensive modes of interacting are step by step replaced by more spontaneous and realistic patterns of behavior. The therapist who is continuously focusing on the very area and events which generate change is unlikely to forget that self-awareness is only one means of achieving the goal of behavior change. He will no longer permit the members to avoid changing by merely talking about their new insights. To sum up—change constitutes the goal, the process, and the outcome of the GST model of group psychotherapy.

3) GST provides an additional source of energy to foster therapeutic change. Energy is the sine qua non of therapeutic change. Without it, no change in structure or behavior is possible. Libido theory provides us with a biological and psychological source of energy (in spite of the fact that it was expressed in 19th century instinct terms). I believe the more pertinent criticism of libido theory is its failure to take ecological sources into account. GST fills that gap with a thermodynamic theory of energy. It shows that normal living systems are capable of locally defying the Second Law of Thermodynamics, which states that complex organized phenomena (i.e., systems) are subject to entropy. Without extra energy in the form of work, they return to a random state. Living systems, on the other hand, are able by the very nature of their structures (such as their capacity to regulate the permeability of their own boundaries) to import and export energy in their exchanges with other systems and the environment. They are negentropic. The therapist, in his role as organizing subsystem (ego), is carrying out the boundarying function and is able to regulate the supply and distribution of energy. This added ecological source of energy is a potent contribution to his therapeutic armamentarium. W. Gruen and I. Kraft have discussed their investigation of this subject in their chapters.

GST extends the therapeutic influence in group psychotherapy into new areas. Traditional psychoanalysis, based primarily on the study of patients in treatment,* accounts very well for the numerous kinds and degrees of pathological behavior which we encounter in our therapy groups, but it fails to give us a systematic account of normal behavior and of the extraordinary capacity of human and social systems for spontaneity, growth, and creativity. GST gives us a strong new model of normal living systems which is based on extensive biological research and provides us with a more robust view of living systems. It gives a new prominence to their active, creative, and autonomous capacities and a new priority to the therapist's task of catalyzing these hitherto relatively neglected potentials.

4) Psychoanalysis is based on a homeostatic principle and provides techniques

---

*Psychoanalytic research in child development has helped to overcome this lack, but the tendency to regard their patients as "sick" rather than as potentially vigorous still continues.

for reducing tension in order to restore equilibrium. But GST has discovered that phenomenologically a certain amount of tension is an essential prerequisite for the creative functions of living systems. GST, therefore, takes the innovative position that these systems are heterostatic. Their normal dynamic equilibrium is accurately perceived to be a quasi-disequilibrium in which tension is always a factor. This contribution is particularly productive because it has enabled creative group therapists to formulate a powerful new technique which is able to overcome serious impasses in the therapeutic process (see the following section for examples).

Taken together these four comparisons of the two theories demonstrate their complementary nature and attest to a powerful theoretical foundation for integrating them in a new group therapy model.

TWO MORE NEW TECHNIQUES

The present section will be devoted to describing two new techniques creative group therapists have culled out of the principles of GST. They illustrate the way in which GST has been able to extend the territory of group therapy.

The New Growth Technique

Let me start with the growth technique which is the product of von Bertalanffy's new organismic model of living structure. It considers organic growth to be an essential capacity of the total organism. In the treatment of dysfunctional systems it is, in my opinion, to be distinguished from the relatively simpler process of transforming particular modes of interacting. It is used when most of the transformations have already taken place. It appears to provide an entirely new pattern of behavior, but really represents the reawakening of originally spontaneous impulses which have long been repressed. Once "the onion has been peeled to its core" and a genuine shift in the patient's "basic emotional position" (Kubie, 1950) has been facilitated, long repressed feelings, perceptions, or actions may surface. The GST therapist expects such signs of awakening creative potential and is ready to facilitate their development into organizing foci (see Chapter 11) for new growth in the total system.

Psychoanalytic ego psychology has moved in this direction by suggesting that the patient's ego strengths be underlined. But therapists like Edrita Fried (1980), who has applied it clinically, have been exceptional. GST has clarified the purpose of this tactic and provides specific information about how it can be accomplished. It may be useful to describe how I arrived at this kind of technique over a rather long period of gestation.

What Is the New Growth Technique?

The technique consists of keeping a sharp lookout for those seemingly accidental and very fleeting emotions, thoughts, or actions (i.e., system precursors) (see Chapter 11), which patients habitually deny or avoid by a process of selective inattention. Their unexpected occurrence generally goes unnoticed by the group because its interaction moves swiftly on. I decided to call attention to such incidents, even if I have to interrupt a patient or the whole group process. I ask the patient and his fellow members to take note of the unusual feeling, thought, or action, and stay with it, giving it time and space, until eventually he can "own it" and begin to give it conscious expression. The intent is to find the seed, to cultivate the soil, and to encourage the group to feed it—in short, to develop a new organizing focus.

Evolution of the Technique

I had long been trying to find a way of overcoming the apparent "repetition compulsion" which gripped the less mature group members. They seemed unable to initiate their own growth. I had also noticed that, in the unstructured group situation, these members were sometimes fortuitously stimulated to express spontaneous feelings, thoughts, or actions which they otherwise repressed or ignored. It occurred to me that here was another place to apply the tactic of stopping the content of the narrative in order to concentrate intensively on the unusual exchange event, which seemed at least momentarily to defy the repetition compulsion, and to expose a minimal sign of long ignored spontaneous behavior. But what triggered these ideas into a new technical configuration was Maruyama's (1963) example in "The Second Cybernetics," in which an accidental event was "kicked off," and then cultivated by positive feedback into developing a new, much more complex structure. I felt that by the law of isomorphies I could apply his idea on the level of personality organization. I translated the idea into the terms of the organismic model I used, as a dynamic nonlinear interaction.*

Examples

Let me give you two examples. The first is somewhat atypical, as you will see, but closely related. The story will show you why I give it in this order.

Jonathan was well liked by his group, except for the fact that he continually denigrated himself. They took him to task because he refused to acknowledge what they called his "good instincts." In spite of his inability to express positive

---

*Editor's Note. Maruyama and most others, including Laszlo (1973) and Miller (1978), call this positive feedback as opposed to negative. Actually, it is accommodative nonlinear feedback.

feelings, his strong latent emotionality got across to them by means of nonverbal communication. One day he seemed to be under great tension. He told them about the painful experience he was having with his unmarried daughter, who had become pregnant during an affair with "an undesirable married man." His actions had been admirable, yet he blamed himself, as usual, for his "rotten" behavior. He owned up to being old-fashioned, and voiced the fear that he had alienated her affections forever. In this case it was the group which first called attention to his unacknowledged behavior, and it was they who "stopped the process" to tell him he had been wonderful. How come he didn't know it? Several women said they wished he had been their father. I asked him if he had ever noticed that he regularly avoided giving himself credit for his loving actions. His breathless laugh indicated both "the assent of the unconscious" (Freud) and some dismay at having been found out. This combination of interrupting the content to focus on an unacknowledged bit of behavior was the beginning of fundamental new growth in Jonathan as a human system. This time the group found the seed of his lost spontaneity. I cultivated the soil, and they continued to fertilize it. They also provided the "nutrient bed" (see Chapter 11) in which it could grow.

In subsequent sessions the seed began to germinate. The very next session he told us, with a big grin, that his wife had given him a birthday party and that instead of being grouchy about it, he had fully participated and enjoyed every minute. Then he became sober, and in a voice that was shaking with feeling, he told us how much he really cared for her. He talked for the first time like someone who was entitled to love and to be loved. The change in his fundamental emotional position (Kubie, 1950) altered his self-concept. It registered inner growth that was to make a profound change in his personal organization and his future relationships. He restructured himself around this new and basic organizing focus and developed several new interrelated modes of transaction.

The next example is more typical of how this growth technique usually works. Judy, a pretty young woman of 28, was a member of the same group. She came for treatment because she had recently panicked and broken off her second engagement, and had not felt up to dating any man since. It gradually became evident that Judy lived in constant fear of being rejected. She said that she had never felt loved by her "crazy" mother and had been badly treated by her harsh, arrogant father. He "pounced" on her, she said, if she disagreed with him and whenever she asserted herself in any way.

The members liked her and listened to her empathically. But, before long, they became openly irritated with her long-windedness. They also told her that they were put off by the "whiny baby-voice" she used when she went into her "complaint number."

At first Judy responded to their criticism with sullen withdrawal and, when they questioned her, she would burst into tears and accuse them of shutting her out, "just like her mother always did." At that point they helped her see that it was her everlasting discontent that actually made them feel like picking on her. "As long as you complain, you'll be rejected," they said.

Judy went through this routine many times. She never seemed to learn, yet she told us she got along better with her mother these days and had started to go out with men again. Whenever she reverted to this pattern in the session, they would say, "Stop it, Judy, you are just doing your number on us again." She repeated her number again after she became engaged, when she got married, and when she became pregnant. Each time she allowed the group to rescue her from disaster. She would express gratitude and then forget all about it and revert to her preoccupation with grievances.

I began to think she was an incurable victim of the repetition compulsion and I determined to elicit something new by trying my new technique with her. The opportunity came in the very next session. The group members were engaged in a spirited discussion about their reactions to her pregnancy.

Jane, who had recently given birth, suddenly asked Judy in a caring voice: "Don't you ever feel how great it will be to have a tiny new being all your own? I was so thrilled." Taken unaware, Judy responded immediately and spontaneously. Her eyes glowed for a moment with joy and tenderness, such as she had never shown before. She said, "Oh, yes—of course! Only last week my husband and I were looking over the layette. We were so close!" With that the glow faded and Judy slipped automatically into the old pattern, saying, "He got very quiet and right away I felt a pang stab through me. I thought it would be the same old thing over again." The group mood changed too. Disappointment quickly replaced the anticipation and hope in their faces.

To keep still another round of fruitless repetition from drowning out the momentary spontaneity, I had to intervene quickly. I held up my hand and said, "Wait a minute. Hold everything! A moment ago I saw something new happening. When Jane asked her question, Judy suddenly looked radiant for a moment and you all seemed very responsive. Can you get back into that moment?" Judy said, "Oh yes!" The others looked interested. I went on, "Try to recapture that good feeling!" She was quiet a few seconds. Then her whole face softened again. She looked thoughtful and said, "Gee, I really know in my heart that I wasn't reading him right. I know he is probably as afraid of reaching out for something good between us as I am." She laughed, and went on, "By the way, my mother wasn't that bad either—I forgot to tell you that she actually offered to come over to help if I wanted her!" They all laughed in understanding. Jonathan spoke for them, saying, "You hate to give up that feeling of being deprived—just like me!—It takes one to know one." They all laughed and became a "work group" again.

Another member, David, who had steadfastly denied having a similar problem, and often scorned Judy for her self-pity, now asked her in a sincere manner, "Judy, do you know why you always have to get rid of good feelings? I'm asking because I'm the same way. I'm happy for a minute whenever anyone is good to me and then I immediately begin to find fault with them. It's awful. I don't like it, but I can't stop it.'' Judy said, ''Oh, I don't know—I think it's because I'm so afraid of being disappointed. It's happened a million times. As soon as I feel love for my husband or anyone, I always think, 'now everything's going to be perfect,' and at the first little thing, I plunge into despair and am sure he'll change and I'll be deprived all over again. Maybe you and I both just expect too much!'' David nodded. He seemed deeply impressed. The whole group joined in this new cycle of exchanges in an up-beat, problem-solving way.

What had happened? I believe that several factors came together at the right time. In the immediate situation, the spontaneous emotion (a kind of accidental event, kicked off by Jane's question) responded to our positive feedback by gaining momentum. It carried enough energy to open a last boundary which enabled her to process new information in the form of realistic perceptions, attitudes, and thoughts about a significant other. It was information which she had ignored many times before. In this instance, the new configuration was formed in the critical area of what Kubie (1950) calls the ''patient's central emotional position.'' It, therefore, had a profound effect on her personal organization. Clinical evidence that it also led to a new system of interacting followed.* Judy now took the lead in facilitating changes in David. Jonathan and the other members used the exchanges to work through related problems. Stopping the content narrative to focus (positive feedback) on a fortuitously expressed spontaneous emotion had acted as an organizing focus to develop a new behavioral configuration. Organic growth was achieved in this orally regressed patient.

Another New GST Technique

The second technique is based on the discovery that living systems are heterostatic and operate on a quasi-disequilibrium. Here again, GST supplements psychoanalytic theory and overcomes one of its limitations. Psychoanalysis has clung too long to a linear homeostatic principle and to tension-reducing techniques. GST therapists have accepted homeostasis and tension reduction as a constant source of a system's stability. They have, however, added a complementary heterostatic principle and new tension-increasing techniques.

The Prehistory of a New Technique

Group therapists have long been aware of situations in which the group interaction seems to reach a dead end—a static equilibrium. There seems to be no

---

*This is an example of Bill's process of thematic fluctuation in which the voicing of several different, but similar, themes suddenly acquires coherence and energy, and coalesces into a major theme which commands the whole group's attention (see Chapter 11).

life in the group. Nothing moves. The therapeutic process is at an impasse. In recent years, after the originally stringent caution about analyzing character defenses had relaxed, and group therapy experience had demonstrated that patients are not as vulnerable as had been thought, a number of confrontation techniques came into being. They emerged as intuitive responses, often the product of the therapist's frustration with a clinical emergency. They were, of course, subject to noxious countertransferential attitudes which only increased resistance, but on the whole they worked rather well, although no one knew why. They were by no means clearly conceptualized.

GST Fills the Need

GST provided a new rationale for such techniques and suggested a new technical principle for bringing these dying groups back to life. The discovery that systems operate on a quasi-disequilibrium, in which tensions play an important role, suggests that increasing tension is a viable technique for remobilizing systems which are approaching stasis. Group therapists who take this view will become sensitive to the condition of dynamic equilibrium (or quasi-disequilibrium) and will not hesitate to increase the tension in any system which seems to be losing its dynamic quality. They know that even one system or subsystem in this condition will tend to slow down the dynamic interaction of the total group. Continuing experience with GST seems to indicate that a new technical principle is emerging in which the complementary tension-reducing/tension-increasing techniques may be considered a critical variable in group therapy.

Forms of This Technique Which Emerged in the GST Task Force

Members of our Task Force have independently created an exciting array of techniques, all of which are based on this discovery. They may be characterized as deliberately creating disequilibrium by increasing tension in systems that are approaching stasis. For example, Jim Durkin reports (Chapter 13) that he "stays closed to closedness" by remaining silent or becoming playful, until the patient loses his static composure. I may unexpectedly use sarcasm, imitation, or direct confrontation to shake up a complacent patient or group. George Vassiliou (Chapter 12) frequently sets up a "therapeutic paradox" (Haley, 1963), which is similar to those used by family systems therapists. He was, I believe, the first to use the generic term "creating disequilibrium," which has the advantage of clearly reflecting its purpose of destructuring the whole defensive system or a mechanized mode of interacting, in order to create sufficient tension to release bound energy, which in turn may be used to develop a new dynamic equilibrium.

What these techniques have in common is sufficient emotional shock value to shatter the mechanized defensive system. The patient responds with strong, spontaneous anxiety and/or hostility. It is an integral part of the technique that the therapist refrain from responding in kind, that he listen empathically and "contain" their irrational outbursts. Once patients have realized that their worst imagined fears have not materialized, they begin to restructure themselves on a higher level of organization.

Two Examples of Creating Disequilibrium

Jules came into the group after many years of analysis, during which he had not resolved his compulsion to reenact his projective identification with the "bad mother" of infancy. His opening statement to me was that he was sure he would experience a good relationship with a woman because I was not "hostile." Yet after only a few very gentle interventions he began to complain that I was picking on him and preferred the other members.

In the group he was at first perceived as a warm person, but the women who responded to him soon reported that they were disappointed and angry with him, because he quickly became detached and seemed oblivious of their feelings. His reaction was to accuse them bitterly of being hostile. When he talked about his outside life, he often cried and portrayed himself as the innocent victim. In the group I was the most frequent target.

Over a period of two years there had been no apparent change in his behavior, yet he repeatedly gave lip service to treatment. At such times he seemed to be the spokesman for the group dilemma. The members unwittingly resonated with his conscious wish to change and his paradoxically deep-seated fear of giving up the defensive structure to which he had attached his sense of identity. In any discussion with him they would start by trying to show him how he provoked rejection, but he would disagree and become sullen. Then the interaction would lose its vitality.

I thought Jules' compulsive character kept him in a state of equilibrium. He was unaware of his own rage and could express it only after he had provoked rejection. Since he was the spokesman for the group, I decided to deliberately create disequilibrium in his personal organization, as soon as the opportunity arose. One day he came in a few minutes late. He looked stiff with rage, but totally unaware of his body language. He announced, "I'm disgusted with myself. I'm determined now to give up this terrible 'michugas'." The group seemed to take him at his word, but I recalled that he had several times told us he felt like a phony, so I felt the time was right. I looked at him steadily and said, "Bullshit, Jules, actions speak louder than words!" I blew his cover. After a stunned moment, he shot out of the room, muttering choice invectives, and slammed the door.

The group was shocked and its equilibrium was shattered too. They did not know whether he would return, and neither did I. They argued heatedly. Some of them said I was a bitch. Others said I was right on. I listened intently, saying nothing. They gradually became aware of their own ambivalence towards me and towards therapeutic change.

Jules called me for an individual hour, and I said I thought it would be better to come back and talk to us all. He agreed. He came early and as soon as the group assembled, he told them he had been ready to kill me! He had cried with rage but gradually developed a sneaking feeling that maybe I was right. He said he thought he had been holding on to an idealized image of himself, but recalled that he often did feel a phony, and maybe this was the time to change. Everybody, including myself, felt warmly toward him for his courage to face himself squarely. It was a turning point in his therapy, and began a new phase in the group as well. His communications became much more honest, and so did his outside relationships. Whenever he began to revert to his old pattern, under some outside stress, he was able to catch himself and stop crying and blaming others. He kept working well for about six months longer and was able to maintain the equifinal leap he had taken. He had a totally different look and manner about him. During this period, he began to help other members who suffered from a similar internalized bad mother image. His work also reflected his new assertiveness and changed self-image. He left at the end of the year with my blessing. Both the group and I were happy for him but sorry to see him leave.

Mary was a bright, charming and always ladylike young woman, who consistently held back her profound, infantile, impotent fury. In the group she participated and raged only when she ran into trouble in her relationships with men, but she always managed to restore her composure immediately afterward. This was not surprising since she usually kept a rigid control of her voice and manners as she talked. She could not seem to give up the myth that a long-term relationship with a caring man was not for her. One day she came in with what was evidently a very painful situation, but she talked about it with incredibly polite reasonableness. Nothing the members said to her had any effect. I decided to caricature her voice and manner in a slightly exaggerated way and mimicked her very controlled and understanding statements about a man who had been untrue to her. She completly lost her cool. She cried for a while. She admitted being hurt and very angry, first with me and with the man. She also realized that she was just as desperate at the thought of being trapped in the relationship. Really loving someone meant being totally swallowed up. The group reacted with empathy and affection.

These were two ways of creating disequilibrium which became turning points for the patients involved. They took some time to work through and there were occasional regressions, but it was evident that a radical reorganization of the basic character structure had begun after its static equilibrium was shattered in the confrontation with me.

When to Create Disequilibrium

Obviously, this powerful technique is not to be used in groups of patients whose personal structure is too fragile to withstand further tension. It is suitable in analytic groups which are presumably composed of patients with a fair degree of ego strength. Because it depends on shock value, it can be used only rarely and is best reserved for dealing with especially intransigent boundary structure, like that of obsessive-compulsives. Generally also, it is best reserved until late in treatment, after sufficient trust in the group and the therapist has been developed. Occasionally, it can serve to set the course of treatment, such as in the case of a patient whose fixed intention, from the start, was to change me rather than himself. It became apparent in his opening announcement that he was going to make me fall in love with him. At times, it may be the only way of dealing with the rigid character defenses of anally regressed patients. But its real value can be seen late in treatment when ordinary dysfunctional transferential exchanges have been transformed and the group members face a radical reorganization of their personal organization (character structure).

The very structure which has made it possible for them to cope with the exigencies of reality is very unwillingly given up (see Chapter 2). Frequently, patients have mistakenly attached their sense of identity to it. They struggle to avoid losing it. They have insight into their problems but they cannot bring themselves to change. They clutch. When a shocking interpretation is made, they become extremely anxious, and they use desperate ploys to avoid their dilemma. Usually, a spontaneous burst of global, infantile rage is released when the therapist intervenes. They may appear to become confused or disoriented. Sometimes they become ill. Their body expresses the message: "Father hold this cup for me," or "Stop, you bitch, you are killing me!" One of my patients developed vertigo whenever he got up from the couch during this phase. Another patient contracted a disease of the inner ear canal, but noticed that his attacks came on every time he attempted to get a divorce, even though he was living with another woman. Simultaneously, he would become impotent again. But he remembered an old tendency to say, "I can't, Mommy," and was able to acknowledge his real feeling. He laughed when he admitted his message was "I won't, I won't, and you can't change me!" Such an acknowledgment usually bodes well.

The therapist need not analyze the open resistance. Instead, he waits for the patient to realize that he has a choice and to act it out. Once he realizes that he can say no to a demand effectively, he begins to risk saying "yes" and to tolerate the resultant love and closeness. He is surprised when he finds that yielding gives him strength rather than enslavement. At such a point I once asked Fred to try to get in touch with what he was experiencing while he was hating the session, and to put it into simple words, like a child. He answered me with silence and a stiffened body posture. I laughed a little and said, "You found a good way of saying no. As you see, I don't have any power over you at all." He laughed too, and connected this incident with his recent lack of desire for sex and his inability to "get it up" with his fiancée. He came back smiling the next time saying, "I hate to admit it, but sex was great this week!"

The agony experienced while destructuring a basic defense system or a key part of it (as in Fred's case) is also difficult for the therapist. It requires a good deal of courage for the analytic therapist to take the risk of using a shock technique and then stand firmly but empathically by it. But it is of critical importance that he not retreat at this crucial crossroads when a radical reorganization of the personality system is within reach.

Some Caveats for the Group Therapist

Creating disequilibrium is a powerful technique. In untrained hands it could lead to disaster. The therapist should be sufficiently trained in pathology to assess the ego strength of each group member and to distinguish accurately between signs of a psychotic break and the desperate ploys of patients who want to be delivered from the agony of yielding to profound inner change.

The therapist's own personal organization must be strong enough to allow him to remain firm instead of retreating at this important crossroads, and to resist the countertransferential temptation to yield to the patient's neurotic pressure. At the same time, he must empathize with the patient's fear of radical reorganization of his personality system and make sure that morphostatic support is available to him during the crisis. That support may come from the group and/or from the therapist's nonverbal communications, which can signal his deep concern for the patient's ultimate welfare. I have found that it helps to communicate my knowledge that all human systems fear that they are in danger of losing their identity and that the aim of treatment is not to get rid of their defenses but to acquire choice over when to use them. Given this help I find that they can stay with their anxiety and ultimately achieve a higher level of organization and a firmer sense of identity and strength.

Of course, it must be remembered that not all patients can get this far in treatment, and that it is their autonomous decision whether to take action at this point or to opt for the status quo. Whatever the outcome, the group therapist must provide consistent careful attention during this phase.

Conclusions

1) GST, as such, does not provide us with a ready-made group therapy theory or an easy-made set of techniques. It does, however, provide group therapists with a new way of looking at the clinical events which generates new concepts,

hypotheses, and techniques that the therapist may apply to clarify the theory and increase the effectiveness of his practice.

2) Clinical testing confirmed my hypothesis that GST and psychoanalytic theory are compatible in principle and the information each generates is complementary rather than contradictory. For this reason it has proved possible to integrate analytic group therapy as a critical conceptual subsystem within a general systems theoretical framework.

3) GST does not replace the theory nor the technique of analytic group psychotherapy. Rather, it provides a new way of looking at the clinical events which has generated significant additional information concerning the organization and the operation of living systems. It supplements our present knowledge.

4) If we look at the group, its members, and their personal organization as three levels of living systems, we can incorporate this information to increase our therapeutic effectiveness in two major ways:

(a) The emphasis on the process of transforming living structure and the employment of GST's new ecological theory of energy makes it possible for analytic group therapists to achieve the goal of consistently converting insight into changed behavior.

(b) Viewing normal living structure as primarily active in influencing the environment and at the same time creatively able to restructure itself and thus establish its autonomy opens up new areas of dysfunctional human interaction to therapeutic influence.

Because GST puts a premium on changing the structure of systems and their modes of operation at the intrapsychic, the interpersonal, and the group levels, and also regards organic growth and the capacity for autonomous interactions with the environment as inherent characteristics of normal living structure, the group therapist becomes a coordinator in the world of action as well as a guide in the world of meaning.

5) Because GST provides a superordinate framework for group therapy, it is able to transcend certain divisive dichotomies, such as those about the role of emotion versus cognition, biological versus cultural factors, and intrapsychic versus interpersonal factors in group psychotherapy. It views them as complementary opposites (irreconcilable but inseparable). Thus, GST brings unifying tendencies into a presently fragmented field. By the same token it seems likely that it has the capacity to serve as an integrative theoretical framework.

6) Attempts have been made both within the psychoanalytic movement and by nonanalytic approaches to bring our treatment models up-to-date and to provide adequate services for the increasing number of narcissistic, borderline, and orally or anally regressed patients who ask for help today. Psychoanalytic ego psychology and object relations theory, Schaefer's development of an

action language, existentialism, TA's accent on patient responsibility, and the ability of gestalt, and encounter techniques to release emotion and energy for purposes of transformation have served the purpose up to a point. They provide important analytic information which should be incorporated. However, they consist of uncoordinated attempts and have produced more controversy than unity among group therapists. GST, on the other hand, provides a well ordered, internally consistent, comprehensive, and unifying framework.

Chapter 11

The Evolution of Emotional-Cognitive and System Precursor Theory

By William Gray, M.D.

Editor's Introduction. Bill Gray is a pioneer in the application of GST to psychiatry. In this chapter he chronicles the development of his work through several stages. He has called for a humanistic stance for GST as against a robot theory of man. He has stressed the role of feeling in organizing human systems and talked about the perversions of emotional life to which modern persons are subject. He has finally evolved "general system precursor theory," which focuses on the formation of living systems in humans rather than upon system maintenance. He feels that compensating emphasis on the prehistory and genesis of system configurations is necessary because of the current fascination of GST people with ongoing systems as they stand. This chapter goes into detail about the process of system formation and attempts to define the component terms in the process clearly.

The systems that Bill discusses are configurations of cognition and feeling that develop as "incidents" in a group therapy or other analogous or "metaphorical" interpersonal settings. The content issues of these systems in his clinical example have to do with the problems of court-referred delinquent offenders. Using GST as a tool, Bill analyzes the deep structure of the situation and develops concepts to account for how delinquent structures develop and how they are replaced through therapeutic interventions at the structural level.

In his explanation of his methods he suggests an isomorphism with the process of system formation within the biological cell wall. In a sense Bill's theory intervenes not in the "cytoplasm" of the delinquent pattern, that is, the motivation, retribution and other content issues, but moves directly into the "germplasm" of the delinquent structure involving the offender and his parents.

Another way of saying this is that Bill intervenes in the delinquent's family at the program level rather than the data level and essentially tries to modify inner instructions which, when embodied in behavior, bring the law down upon the child. While behavior therapists modify surface symptoms with learning techniques and psychodynamic therapists search for deep level insights so that awareness of neurotic patterns will lead to changed behavior, Bill in a sense attempts the process akin to genetic recombination which might be called system structure recombination. He directly attempts to modify or replace faulty delinquent behavior by harnessing the inherent process of system formation and fostering the appropriate conditions for rewiring system elements at the program level. His clinical examples are no less dramatic and human than those of content level workers, but they seem to get at the nucleus of the matter quite directly. This is the beginning of a basically new approach to psychotherapy, one for which we will await further validation.

My first venture into the field of becoming a general system theorist was my formulation of *humanistic general systems theory* (Gray, 1972). Collaborating with Ludwig von Bertalanffy, I undertook to explore and expand his very strong stand that GST must promote humanism. As he said, if the individual were to succumb to the Leviathan of organization, he would much rather see GST discarded (von Bertalanffy, 1967).

LvB's emphasis on the need for a humanistic general systems theory began with his criticism of stimulus-response psychology, which he felt led directly to a robot conception of man. It implied that nothing would happen except in response to some message or stimulus from outside the living system, while the living system's repertoire of activity would be limited to reactivity, or responsiveness. This was inimical to LvB's free spirit and scientifically untenable for him, for in his studies of embryology he (as well as others) had determined that spontaneous activity was the primary characteristic of living tissue and could be seen to occur continuously and without outside stimulation (von Bertalanffy, 1933, 1952).

The second stage of my evolution was in my formulation of *emotional-cognitive structural theory* (Gray, 1973, 1974, 1975), in which I proposed that the system precursors of creative thought and humanistic thought were emotions in modulated, precised, and nuanced* forms, which had the capacity for thematic formation. In this form they proceeded to organize scattered cognitions into what I called emotional-cognitive structures, which for me were the equivalent of human thought, productive thought, and creative thought.

In this theory I saw as the enemies of humanistic thought two misuses of emotion which frequently occur in therapy group members:

1) *Emotional drivenness,* in which the intensity of feelings pushes ideas into action and short-circuits what I consider the fundamentally nuanced themes. It leads to the evidences of inhumanity in man's behavior, such as occur from

---

Editor's Note. Modulating, nuancing and precising are operations through which raw global emotions are gradually transformed and organized by cognitions into much more subtle and differentiated forms.

what Freud called mob psychology. This kind of behavior is recognized as having caused perhaps more deaths of others than has actual violence.
2) *De-emotionalization* along obsessive and compulsive lines by precising and nuancing carried to such extremes that little emotion is left, resulting in the production of a pathologically sterilized form of thought.

In my opinion it is the spontaneous emotional life that carries the thread of humanity in our species. Thus, whether one is dealing with an emotionally driven zealot or with a de-emotionalized scientist who has lost the emotional meaning of the work that he has done, the result is all the same—a disregard for humanity in terms of caring and feeling.

I then developed *emotional-cognitive structuralism* as the therapeutic form which I hoped would bring balance into our treatment of emotions and cognitions, with the result that humanism would be both preserved and enhanced.

The third stage is what I now call *general system precursor theory*. It is a shift that I made from the study of emotions in a broad sense as the originators of human thought to a more specific study of the types of feelings that I thought had system potential and therefore called system precursors. I made this study in connection with a series of delinquent and offender acts that I was called upon to treat in my position as Director of a Court Clinic in the Commonwealth of Massachusetts (Gray, 1976a, 1976b, 1977a).

It is obvious in retrospect that it was simply a transfer of the idea of emotional-cognitive structuralism to a more specific form, which could be more easily related and applied if the emotional precursors that one spoke of were clearly defined and could be tied into specific system formations which, in the case of the population with which we worked and studied, were of criminal type.

General system precursor theory has worked out clinically and is being increasingly used by other agencies in our own area and by co-workers in Yugoslavia and Greece, in the training of probation officers in the Commonwealth of Massachusetts, in the training of counselors at Boston University and Harvard University, and in the treatment of delinquent and other court-supervised children at a large child care agency in New York.

BASIC DEFINITIONS

Now it is time to turn to the generically new definition of "system" that I formulated in the third stage in the evolution of my work, for it is here that I have made the break with the prevalent notion of permanent systems, and have proposed instead a definition of "system" that focuses on the process of system formation rather than on the effects of ongoing systems.

My new definition of "system" then is that a system is that which forms when two or more system precursors come together to form an organizing focus and establish appropriate mutual input-output links with one another. This new definition of system focuses its primary concentration on the prehistory of systems and the act of system formation and tends to neglect ongoing system effect and identity preservation. I recognize that both are necessary to complete GST, but until now, system formation has been neglected. For this reason I focus on it. System formation is, of course, essential for understanding how to apply GST to intensive group psychotherapy (Gray, 1977b).

What Is a System Precursor?

The relationship between the precursor and the formation of a new system can be compared to that between a seed and the full-grown flower. A good analogy is DNA as system precursor. Just as in the construction of a protein where a subunit of a receptor molecule interacts with DNA to form messenger RNA that serves as a template for the protein, the group provides a locus, a psychological field. In our terms, it is a relevant nurturing environment where system precursors can become activated and construct themselves into systems, and where former neurotic traits, perceptions, identities, methods of relating, or ways of acting that have become dysfunctional can be system blocked. The system precursors become the organizing focus, which in a relevant nurturing environment may produce new system formations.

What Is an Organizing Focus?

My definition of an organizing focus is that of a set of neighborhood relations of such a type that an array of system precursors, such as feelings, thoughts, and actions, which have self-organizing potential of time-limited duration, become linked together. To endure they must system form. It is important, however, to note that organizational foci arise spontaneously, and so system forming always remains possible when system precursors come together and mutually establish relationships which permit them to exist over time. Then system formation has occurred.

What Is a Theme?

Linked precursors or organizing foci then develop chains of emotions which form themes. They do not have linear causality, in the sense of a single effect, but are probabilistic. In this process the themes fluctuate. Since they are mutually interactive, previous system formations also influence the new precursors. In fact, precursors are also formed transitively by a process of transformation from former system formations. So there is reentry again, introducing nonlinearity. For example, if I have resolved some problem of hidden hostility with you, the new output reenters input and I can deal with a number of people I have not dealt with before, and with groups of people I could not deal with before. That is, the emotional energy has become free as the normalized system has been formed, and it becomes an emotional theme available to be used productively in a new system formation.

The process of thematic fluctuation (see LaViolette, 1977; Prigogine 1976) is characteristic of a double input open system.* Once a theme has emerged, discrepancies between what is received from each input tend to produce minor variations of the theme itself. Characteristically, the fluctuating state is not stable, and so one of the variations that compose the theme becomes subject to amplification. It is the same type of phenomenon that occurs in any form of tuning in. It is this amplified emotional nuance, then, that becomes the organizing force at that time and place.

What Is a Relevant Nurturing Environment?

Gradually I revised my formulations to give more equality in terms of organizing capacity to the relevant nurturing environment, for I believe that the organizing effort is not always unidirectional, but that it is possible also for relevant nurturing environments to organize system precursors in the same way that it is possible for cognitions to organize emotions. But I believe that in general the pathway of organization is from emotions to the organization of cognitions,** and from system precursors to the organization of relevant nurturing environments. To my mind this is necessary to preserve the tenets of humanistic GST, which insists on the primacy of spontaneous activity. Emotional cognitive structuralism insists on the primacy of emotions in modulated and nuanced forms as the preservers of human values.

The Boundarying Process

First the organizing focus forms a new system, but it is followed rather quickly by boundary formation. Thus, boundaries are essential to the continued functioning of the newly organized system.

---

*Editor's Note. A double input open system has inputs generated from inner emotional experience which interact with externally based cognitive perceptual experience. This model and the thematic fluctuation processes in which these two inputs generate self-organization are discussed more fully in Chapter 17.

**Editor's Note. While Bill feels that emotions organize fragmentary cognitions into a theme, I feel that emotional energy is organized by boundaries drawn in the process of cognition. Since we both assume that the two kinds of processes operate in complementary fashion, the discrepancy is not great. When Bill talks about emotions, he is speaking about the content of emotional themes. He sees these themes as the wellsprings of humanism. When I talk about emotions, I am more focused at the structural level of flowing energy. In either case cognition and emotion must operate together in the system formation process.

In the therapeutic group an extremely important function for the therapist is to provide the missing arrays of system precursors which the patient's global emotions can be helped to organize and then modulate. In the past this has been called clarification and interpretation, but if it is carried too far, needed attention will be diverted from the emotional organizing forces within the patient.

In order to change the inner structure of a system, its boundary must be penetrated. The boundary itself is an organizing force. Since boundary function is the presenting aspect of most disorders seen in therapy, the therapist's boundary function is of crucial importance.

It is considered that, as a system precursor moves toward system formation and new system formation takes place, boundary formation takes place immediately afterwards to consolidate and protect the integrity of the newly formed system. This view of boundaries is an essentially protective one and serves the purpose of protecting the organizing centers against inappropriate distortions that might otherwise be introduced into the organizing focus.*

Getting back to the example in the biological field, DNA is considered as a system precursor. Thus, DNA itself is restricted to being within the nuclear membrane, with the consequence that the act of system formation requires a transcription of the relevant part of the DNA chain into messenger RNA, which can leave the nuclear membrane and enter cytoplasm. If we utilize similar terminology to view group therapeutic situations, we would say that boundarying penetration brings about therapeutic change within the nuclear membrane of the group system and the individual systems.

This view, then, requires that nuclear membranes also be seen as permeable, but much less permeable than the cell wall itself (or boundary). Therapy, if directed at system precursors, is seen as inducing change by penetrating the nuclear membrane. It induces change in the patterns of organizing activity,** and is in contrast to ordinary feedback, which simply regulates intake and does not change the pattern of organizing activity.

There is also, however, another function of boundaries, boundary open/closed. It is a more active way and involves control through selective permeability. This relates to the open system nature of living systems and is regulatory for the admission or exclusion of matter/energy and information from the outside, as is

---

Editor's Note. When Bill talks about boundaries here he refers only to boundary closing. When I talk about boundarying in my chapters I define boundarying as both the opening and closing events. I see boundary opening as a transforming event where existing structures are dissolved only to be subsequently restructured by the drawing of boundaries. We both stress the importance of system formation or system transformation, but in different ways.

**Editor's Note.* What Bill's analogy between psychotherapy and biology is saying is this: Just as penetrating the nuclear structure rather than just the cytoplasm means that changes are made in the way the cell organizes itself rather than simply altering the product of this organizing activity, so system formation processes if set properly in motion will modify the organizing programs that generate behavior rather than simply modifying the behavior itself.

required in an open system, but has nothing to do with organizational closure. In this latter aspect boundaries are necessary to protect against disruption of organizational closures.

How System Precursor Theory Operates in a Therapy Group

The group as a whole, under the guidance of the therapist, forms a nutrient bed. However, its individual members are often challenging enough to facilitate change on their own as individuals as well. Thus, they share both the morphostatic and the morphogenic function of the therapist and the group as a whole.

In the beginning of a session there is a kind of idling process, in which the members produce multiple inputs which include an array of thought, feelings, and actions which have system precursor potential. They may be passed by, recur, and be passed by again, for unless connecting links are made they are short-lived. At some point, however, those members who resonate with a particular input will make connecting links with it, and amplify it until its potential as a system precursor is realized. Then it acts as an organizing focus for the group interaction. As the exchanges continue, there is considerable fluctuation because each member's input is similar to, but not identical with, the original one. For this reason, the members are able to exert mutual influence on one another. They are "systeming."* And the result is that an emotional theme develops and transformations begin to occur in some of the member's modes or systems of interacting. If, during this entire process, they reach an impasse (usually because some of their old dysfunctional modes of interacting interfere with progress), then the therapist intervenes to facilitate the opening of whatever dysfunctionally closed boundary has brought about the impasse. In this way he/she brings about new fluctuations. In other words, he may treat old systems of interacting like precursors when they occur in the group. However, he may decide to block a precursor, if he perceives it as negative, and help form new functional systems.

Once the theme is well established and transformations have taken place, the therapist waits to give the members time to reorder their internal dynamic interaction. Once a transformation to a new system has been formed, he makes an interpretation for the purpose of drawing a new boundary around the transformed or new system, in order to give it stability.

---

*Editor's Note. The process of thematic fluctuation described by Bill and the process of systeming I have described are very similar. It is a turbulent resonance process that leads to self-organization on a higher level. When the cognitive/emotional pattern of two (or more) group members interacting around a common concern is very similar but not identical, the superimposition of these patterns begins to fluctuate, that is, to generate intense energy and organization. Phenomenologically, the theme seems to capture intense interest, become exciting and focused and lead to compelling conclusions. Prigogine's work (1976) on self-organizing "dissipative structures" gets at the same principle of order through fluctuation.

It often happens that the members cling to an emotional theme beyond the point of natural closure because here too they tend to avoid change. If no new fluctuations appear, then the therapist intervenes to set the process going again in a new cycle of fluctuations.

The Function of the Therapist

The function of the therapist, then, is to facilitate the selection of the precursors which are to be amplified. Or he may facilitate their repair (transformation) by boundarying changes. If the precursors are the driven kind, he may decide to block them, to avoid wasting time in endless repetition. When an organizing focus has developed and the members are systeming, he merely observes the process. If it comes to a standstill, he facilitates boundary opening.

Summary

Recently it occurred to me that all of these previous theories fit into a broader classification of general system precursor theory, which has as its focus understanding of the prehistory of systems, consisting of system precursors and relevant nurturing environments. These two come together in the act of system formation. I think there is an advantage to dealing with problems while they are still in the system precursor state, instead of attempting to repair the dysfunctional systems which are already locked in.

I might have called the new theory general system formation theory, since this would have also emphasized that my interest is in the act of system formation, but I considered this somewhat less desirable since my interest is even more in studying the nature of defects in system precursors and relevant nurturing environments, with the hope of repairing them in an isolated state before the process of system formation takes place.

The value then, of these twin theories of *emotional-cognitive structuralism* and *general system precursor formation theory* is that they offer the group therapist a new way to view and to use GST concepts in understanding and practicing group therapy. They present a new way of viewing system precursors as open system formation processes and utilizing them in therapeutic interventions to guide the system formation stage. These twin theories are essentially a new way of viewing emotions as the organizers of the mind.

CLINICAL EXAMPLES

I will choose to use metaphorical or isomorphic equivalents of group therapy*

Editor's Note. Bill calls his clinical case examples "metaphorical groups" under the assumption that whether the patients seen are in group form, family form, or even nontherapeutic work group form, the same system-forming processes take place.

for my clinical examples because the nature of my work and activity brings me into more intimate and continuing contact with those groups known as the criminal justice system, various scientific societies, task force activities, collegial relationships with co-workers, and supervisory activities with various mental health professionals.

This set of clinical illustrations will be drawn from the metaphorical group therapy experience that I have had with those people who commit the crime of breaking and entering, their parents, and those mental health workers with whom I have talked about this theory and practice. The metaphorical group formation is enhanced because the system precursor chain or the organizing emotional theme is essentially similar for them all. Revisions occur both in the clients and in the mental health workers as a result of the group process. The system formations include myself as a special member of the group who is metaphorically equivalent to the group therapist. The whole group displays properties of a self-referential or self-reentering system, in that there is both organizational closure and reentry on higher levels. It fulfills the requirements of nonlinearity and circular causality that are essential in the concepts of living systems.

First Clinical Event

The first clinical example suggests guidelines for the group therapist in dealing with groups of people who have entered group therapy as a result of breaking and entering activity. It is drawn from two years of very successful treatment of a young man, now 17, who was initially heavily involved in breaking and entering activity. During the past year and a half therapy has been carried on with him and his father, who presented himself initially as a rather compulsive, highly successful professional man. His excessive rules and regulations had resulted in emotionally locking out his son. There has been equivalent marked change in the father in the course of this therapy. The particular incidents that I want to describe began approximately one year ago. There had already at that time been marked clinical improvement, but it did not have a solid base, for there was as yet insufficient autonomy of function, in that their acceptance of the twin theory concepts had not been thoroughly integrated, so that they were operating still with borrowed ''nurtenergy'' from me (see Chapter 4).

Underlying this block to system precursor repair (i.e., blocking differentiation of emotional organizing themes that could produce autonomy) was a heavily endowed competitiveness with me on the part of the young man. It was aided and abetted in more subtle ways by his father. The competitive theme was equivalent to that encountered in all therapeutic groups and carried the message or meaning of, ''Kill the father'' or ''Discredit the group leader and his ideas.'' There was, of course, the usual type of disregard of the effect that this would have on their own welfare.

At the same time, this oppositional trend serves the positive function of binding the various individuals into a group by means of shared opposition. It represents that stage in group process of passing from seeing the group leader as a messiah to anger that he is not, and finally to a beginning of wrestling with problems on their own. This is the essential base for the development of an autonomous group.

The three episodes I will discuss in regard to this father and son, in terms of the metaphorical group process, will be interpreted according to the twin theories and in terms of group process.

The case histories will be presented as poems, as this will make them more concise and give them a system theme, an emotional-cognitive structure theme, and a system precursor-system formation theme.

> Young Tom, young Tom
> Why do you break in so?
> It seems as if you do not know
> That if you break in
> You'll be locked in
> A dubious way to go about
> The living of your life.
> To go from lockout to lockin
> Will happen if you break in
> Sadly, sadly so.
>
> I know that both you and Dad
> Are voyagers at heart
> But he explores within the fences
> That society sets apart.
> While you act as if
> Any fence is something to tear apart.
> So he locks you out
> And you break in
> In ways that are against the law
> And with your smile and with your charm
> And with your interest that's so warm
> Truthful with self those voyager trails
> That will not end you up in jail
> Of course we all know the underlying theme
> That organizes your acts and dreams
> To lock Dad out as he's done to you
> Including more than quite a few

Of those who remind you of your Dad
Alas! Alack! That is quite sad.
So you heard I'd been invited to
Work at the detention center
That once held you
You sit and smile and say you know
I'll not be able to help them so
I might as well not try at all.
You know indeed that I will fall
In my attempts to do so.
You said it many times before
In the beginning of our joint work
You'd win, I'd fail
You'd end up in jail
And smile at my defeat
For if I try too hard to break in
To all you think and all you feel
Then I'm a break in artist, too
Just the same as you—
And for this you'll lock me out.

So I won't bring up the past today
For there is a better voyaging way
So I tell you, Tom and Dad,
The situation may not be so bad
If young Tom you will agree
To help me when I go to sea—
The break in artists now locked in
For they have committed the same sin
That you committed once before
And so of course they'll trust me more
If you will go along.

This was the incident. The organizing emotional themes centered around locking out all helpers, and anger that I had been called on to help these young people in serious trouble. Part of his personal experience with lockout had occurred when his parents were divorced when he was nine years old, and he had been left or had chosen to be the person who tried to help the emotionally disturbed mother regain some sense of balance. It had not worked out as well as he had hoped, nevertheless he took considerable pride in his effort and the partial success that it had. But the emotional theme contained other nuances, as revealed by the warmth of his smile as he ridiculed the invitation I had received. This smile was a nuance which represented new hope for an old and important wish of his cooperative work with older people, with older men, with his father, with me—a wish that had been blunted and frustrated in the past.

From a system precursor point of view, the feeling of again being locked out was certainly present and could again activate into criminal breaking and entering. But the other system precursors were also present, still feeble, but growing in strength, which represented a hope for cooperative action and for confirmation that he was not really being locked out. My simple remarks, about working in the detention center, then, acted as a source of thematic fluctuation that might lead to amplification of this more feeble nuance. These remarks also served at the time as a system-blocking element to the old antisocial precursor that said, "Break and enter if you feel locked out."

In terms of the metaphor with group process, my remark was representative of what other members of an ongoing group probably have told him, or would have interpreted as his real intention, to lose his feeling of being locked out by his prediction that I would certainly fail.

The same would be true about those group processes going on in society that are always present, whether we realize it or not, whenever a new idea or approach is broached—that is to say, whenever there is an aspect of distinctiveness, such as an in-group feeling, which in the course of time will lessen and will integrate with feelings that will bring unity with one's fellow human beings. There will, of course, be alternating periods of differentiation or distinction and integration.

The principles of thematic fluctuation and the amplification of organizing emotional nuances, which represent more favorable system precursor formation, become then a generalized phenomenon in members of such metaphorical groups. The mental health workers with whom I meet regularly in collegial seminars constitute such a group in which the twin theories are the center of focus.

What can the practicing group therapist learn from this single example of how the twin theories modify and shape the group therapist's response and his spontaneous reaction to the type of clinical situation which the example illustrates? Here is a young man whose future evolution depends upon whether or not modification of the organizing emotional theme can be developed. The question is whether the reentering cycles will stay on the same level and lead to repetitions of lockout precursors and proceed to actual breaking and entering, or whether modification of the system precursor of lockout will take place, so that a distinctive, more appropriate action will occur which is both less self-destructive and less antisocial.

The act of system formation itself should receive the primary focus of our attention, as should the probabilistic aspects of new, healthier system formations. That is the crucial issue. If the group therapist himself is aware of the organizing potential of the precursor, he or she will have an easier, more successful time with it, for it is easier to track what is going on and it increases his own potentials for spontaneity. It also tends to balance probabilistic and reactive components within the therapist. Thus, he will gain a real feeling for the value and beauty of following the emotional themes within himself. He will learn the vocabulary of such emotional themes and come to understand how they, like DNA transcribed into messenger RNA, are in very specific ways like system precursor organizers.

Second Clinical Event

I will turn now to another important incident in which the metaphorical group was faced with an issue that led to the reshaping of system precursors so that new system formation could take place. The question was whether reentry would continue on the same level without change or would be on new levels and thus promote growth. A turn of events (in line with a continuing evolutionary process that had led to the new system precursor possibilities) occurred when I received a call from a local television station asking me to do a program on the work we had been doing in our court clinic and the results we had been getting. The policy of the courts is not to be secretive about the work we do, so we receive such requests occasionally.

I told the television interviewer that I would check with our colleagues and with the clients. I had some hesitation about this in terms of confidentiality, and yet I felt that not being secretive was an important issue. My colleagues were enthusiastic, and so it was left in their hands to prepare for the videotaping, as I had to go out of town for a week. When I returned I found that the decision had been made to concentrate on three of our lock out and break in cases which had been successfully treated, and that these young men and their families had been enthusiastic when first contacted. This included Tom and his father. The colleagues, however, reported that the initial enthusiasm had been replaced by a change of heart and hesitation.

This is typical of "lock out and break in" youngsters, since they are very sensitive to invasion of privacy and have learned lockout defenses from their elders. They have internalized this, and tend to lock out other people quite quickly. We could have gone ahead to present another type of system precursor therapy, but by this time the reservations had spread to me, so I delayed the television presentation until some time in the future.

I would like to return now to what this turnabout meant in terms of the twin theories and how this might be dealt with psychotherapeutically. On one level the behavior was positive, in that it meant a disaffiliation on Tom's part with the kind of criminal behavior in which he was previously engaged. What seemed most important to me was the lack of balance between giving and taking that is also characteristic of this behavior. He was still not at the point where he would allow system precursors of a help-giving type to form within himself, so that changed behavior was still not easy for him. The system precursors had been blocked as part of a neurotic system formation that constituted his characterological problem. I assumed that this derived from his bad experience of being the only helper to his mother at a time when he was not really capable of giving such help and when he did not have adult support in his efforts.

But the situation was different and it was time for him to undo these system blocks which will impede his growth and development. This was the same theme as the first episode that I reported. He was again dubious about my ability to help youngsters in youth detention centers, and again I told him that it might work if he would help. In between the first and the second episode there had been a third episode of significance. On one occasion he had salvaged a rowboat, gotten it into shape, and found an old motor for it, only to have the motor fail on him, so that he had to row the boat back to shore. He wanted to give up. In terms of the twin theories, this represented absence of needed system precursors, and so I told him at that time that he would not be a real sailor unless he learned to fix small motors. He had reacted to this in a disgruntled and dubious manner but with evidence on his face that he understood the point. There seemed to be a glimmer of understanding that gave promise of his becoming autonomous, self-organizing, and self-monitoring. I therefore surmised that perhaps he would some day undertake this and tell me about it. At present he still felt he had to lock me out from his plans.

The system precursor/system-forming process was illustrated in a conversation with his father, who told me with great joy that Tom had signed up for a course in small motor repair. He also reported that Tom was enjoying school tremendously, had gotten all A's, whereas before he had been flunking. Now he plans to go to college and he has a desire to get to know those members of the family he had previously locked out totally. It is important to note here that it was a matter of some months between the beginning of the system-forming process and its coming into actualization.

The illustration is important theoretically, for in using the twin theories one cannot form systems for the other person and one must avoid pushing too hard. Thus, one must act as a catalyst and must be aware that the same process is going on within oneself.

I would like to return to the second incident and discuss the appropriate therapeutic action in regard to his unwillingness to appear on the television show. I consider the incident of the motor as an example of Walter Gruen's notion of "injecting energy" (Chapter 4). After my comment regarding the motor, however, it was necessary to wait, lest I interfere with Tom's own autonomy. It seemed to me at this point, in terms of theory, that it was time for me to unblock my own system precursors that wished to lock Tom out as he had locked me out.

And so I allowed my own feeling of indifference to surface to some degree by not calling back immediately when the father left a message about wanting an appointment. I would not have ignored a second or third call if it had been made, but figured they were working out the problem of why they had reversed themselves. Even before the call regarding the appointment, I had received a note from the father apologizing for not appearing on television, in view of how much they had gotten out of this approach and how they felt it ought to be shared with others. But I had not responded to this. This, again, was part of my unblocking my own system precursors to indifference. I had some faith that the emotional organizing process in myself was behaving appropriately and that this meant that the therapy was going well and that I simply had to wait.

Later, when the father did call, I talked to him on the phone and shared my feelings that they had locked us out by not coming for the television program. He stated that he had felt badly about it and had talked with Tom about it. I said that an opportunity to share and be helpful to others had been lost, but that the primary issue was the problem of balance between giving and taking in himself and in Tom. He understood the point and said he understood my withdrawal. We made an appointment to meet in a few weeks. They did come in and this was the session in which the tremendous improvement was reported. Tom had really blossomed, and the precursors for giving as well as taking had been now activated; he brought quahogs for my wife, a product of his own labor as a quahog raker, an occupation of which he was proud, for it afforded him a living at a time when jobs were hard to get. It represented a real sharing of himself with others. Tom and his father are now giving and taking with people and are enjoying life tremendously. In earlier days, school had not been enjoyable because he had been so sensitive to lockout by others and so he locked them out in response.

I will now end this example with a short poem to bring it into organizational closure:

A New Theme for Tom and Dad

Young Tom is past the middle
He has completed the salmon jump
No longer needs to struggle
In an eternal back and forth
Up and down, repeating always
What was there before
Repetitiously repeating
Chapter I of life
And meticulously avoiding
Turning to Chapter II.

You, too, Dad, have come to see
The flowingness of life
That dikes and dams can be overdone
And, leading in an equal way
To a prolonged prison stay
Also so with your son
But in another way.
Thus now lockout lockin
Are subtle rhythms
The ebb and flow of life
And so are lockout and breakin
And other improvisations on this theme.
The middle is passed
You give and take in rhythmic flow
Suddenly you know it's so
That life is possible and prudential—
The voyaging trip's a pleasant adventure
For yourselves and others.

No longer is paradox
The dreadful stumbling block it was before
So that with ECs[a] and SPs[b] and SFs[c] and SBs[d]
And reentry of course
You are on your way
For now you know as much as me and more.

Discussion of Second Incident

This example is important for the group therapist because it demonstrates the way in which my system precursor/system-forming theory applies the principles of GST and its perspectives on living systems to clinical practice. My interventions, "It would be better if you would help," "You will not be a sailor unless you learn to fix small motors," and my partial withdrawal and locking out response to the TV episode, are to be seen as emotional/cognitive and system precursor/system-forming techniques. They use a certain amount of system blocking in the hope that the patient's own neurotic system blocks will be open to a reentry process and will thus regain the patient's aliveness and his ability to

---

[a]Emotional Cognitive Structures
[b]System Precursors
[c]System Formations
[d]System Blocks

repair and reorganize himself. My intervention also aims to make available feelings, thoughts, and actions of needed system precursors which can then be turned into new system formations when the appropriate situation arises. Once this is done, I must wait for the patient to restructure himself while I explore my own experience and use it for therapeutic purposes.

The examples also illustrate that more recent advance in GST, which replaces Aristotelian two-valued logic with relational logic (Spenser Brown, 1967; von Foerster, 1976, 1977; Varela, 1975; J. Durkin, Chapter 2; Gray, Chapter 17). We deal with self-referential systems, in spite of the fact that their nonlinear state is impossible to reduce to categories. Any categorization catches only a particular shadow of an ongoing living process, fixes it in time, and thus in a sense ends its appropriateness. But since we have to rely solely on language communications, we must utilize categories with a full realization that they never fully describe what we mean. This is, I think, what Glenn Swogger means when he says that the group therapist must always be in "over his head" (Chapter 3). The paradox in this new logic can be transcended by the notions of complementarity and self-referential cycling, making it part of the model of living systems (Chapter 2).

According to Varela, the actual categories represent more or less accurate materializations in phenomenal form, of the underlying system structures. James Durkin expresses the same idea when he thinks of categories as embodiments of the living structure.

We are at present studying the whole question of how much the new logic will, in the future, be able to contribute to group therapy.* We hope to be able to write about it more specifically in the future.

At this point we may presume that the heart of Tom's and his father's work with us, or our work with them (for these again are self-reentering, self-referential statements) was done in concordance with this new general systems logic. From its point of view Tom and his father can be seen as attempting to categorize the world into Aristotelian logical forms and to believe the categorization they have made has some sort of eternal verity. So our guideline in the therapeutic work was to help them gradually shift their conception of what they were, what they are, and what they may become.

In their search for security they had used fixed terms which locked them in. They began to realize that if they opened up, change with reentry at higher levels is possible. A group therapy model that includes these elements in its very format provides a new way to avoid imprisonment in categories of one's own making.

---

*The new logic which has a central place for self-referential forms will not solve the problems of therapy, but it will provide ways of describing phenomena such as self-description and self-transformation (which are kinds of system formations) without paradox and contradictions.

Chapter 12

Outlining The Synallactic Collective Image Technique as Used within a Systemic-Dialectic Approach

By George Vassiliou, M.D. and Vasso Vassiliou, Ph.D.

Editor's Introduction. George and Vasso Vassilliou are with world's first general system theory psychotherapists. They have been autonomously generating, maintaining, evolving and dissolving living groups for decades. As with all living structures their specific methods have gone through metamorphoses in their equifinal development. In the present chapter they utilize S.C.I.T., the Synallactic Collective Image Technique, to help people change their own personal structures in a group setting. Patients are assigned to draw, paint, scribble, or otherwise render an image which reflects themselves. One of the contributions is chosen by the group and the work of the group for that session is a dialogue of sharing and differentiating the inner meaning of the work between the members.

The Vassilious and their current living system of psychotherapy exemplify living structure at its finest. Their methods might transform themselves, but, it seems to me, the work of the Vassilious will go on developing forever within the fecund context of GST!

AN INTRODUCTORY NOTE

The approach of systemic-dialectic intervention to human malfunctioning which has been developed and followed at the Athenian Institute of Anthropos has been described elsewhere (Vassiliou, G. & V., 1976), and it is based on conceptualizations that are becoming prevalent in the behavioral sciences (Ashby, 1956, 1960; Bertalanffy, 1968; Buckley, 1967; Gray, Duhl & Rizzo, 1969; Grinker, 1967; Miller, 1978; Spiegel, 1971; Sutherland, 1973).

The approach includes all modalities of therapeutic intervention. It does not dichotomize them in either/or categories—for instance, individual therapy or family therapy or group therapy or psychodrama or community therapy, clubs, etc. On the contrary, it actualizes all modalities, alternating or combining them in a systemic-dialectic way. Intervention starts usually with a diagnostic-exploratory family session. Only when this is technically impossible do we see couples or individuals. Families, couples or individuals are asked at the close of the diagnostic-exploratory session to write the following text, which is dictated to them:

Drs. V. responsibly inform me that I am in a position to undertake the effort which will enable me to overcome my present difficulties and problems. But they warn me that however "miserable" or "unhappy" I feel under these difficulties and problems, as soon as I will start experiencing the fact that I can really succeed in overcoming them, I will find a number of objective reasons for which I will be obliged to discontinue my effort.

With such a therapeutic double bind, modified in each personal case accordingly, we begin our therapeutic intervention, one form of which is the technique described presently, S.C.I.T.

The technique has been developed and followed in group therapy. We previously had termed the technique Transactional Group Image Technique. (Vassiliou, G., 1968). We have modified the term etymologically in order to avoid the confusion which exists currently around the term "transactional."

The term transaction has always been used by us as it has been defined by Dewey and Bentley and introduced into psychiatry by Grinker, Ruesch, Spiegel, Shakow, etc., meaning one entity in process, in mutual interpenetration, with another. This is expressed most accurately with the Greek noun *Synallage,* synallactic being its derivative adjective (Vassiliou, G. & V., 1974).

BASIC CONCEPTUALIZATION OF ANTHROPOS

Anthropos (in Greek, the human being) is conceptualized as a biopsychosocial system, the outcome of the transaction of processes, which can be grouped in the following general categories: biological, psychosocial, sociocultural and economicosocial. The psychosocial process is one and undivided, but presents intra- and interpersonal aspects depending upon the point from which the observer chooses to observe the developing phenomena. Channels of transaction are established and maintained among these processes. In this way, what is termed the organized complexity of the system increases. Its functioning is enhanced. When the channels of transaction are interfered with, a state of disorganized complexity prevails and malfunctioning is the result (see Chapter 4). Living structure can be embodied at any level; it is virtual behind the manifest.

The therapist is the original Catalytic-Regulatory (Ca-Re) System, but he is joined at different times by different members of the group, depending on their ever-changing cognitive-emotional integration. When a member is emotionally motivated to join the Ca-Re System, he still may lack the ability to structure cognitions which enable him to be an effective member of the Ca-Re System. Eventually, all members of the group join this system and work together with the therapist. (The more negative and resistant a member was, the greater the impact his joining actually has.)

The second Ca-Re System, the Collective Image, is auxilliary and methodological. It is conceptual and in flux. Its structuring is the first operational goal of the group. It emerges from the overlapping projections and associations of group members on a painting at each session. (By painting, in this presentation, we will mean all kinds of free artistic creation such as painting, drawing, doodling, etc.) Paintings are produced by the group members during their leisure time and brought to group sessions.

Members start their session by voting for the painting to be discussed. A majority of one vote wins. Watching carefully the attitude, the behavior, and the alliances formed during the voting (majority versus minority) provides invaluable insights about group processes. Preliminary indications emerge as to the direction the group transaction is likely to take. When placed in this context, it is particularly meaningful when a member will not paint. The number and the content of paintings, the variety of colors used, and the size can be revealing indices. The therapist can draw conclusions about the resistance of various members and their intentions concerning the session to follow.

The voted painting is fixed at an easel and members are invited to project associations, a title, feelings experienced when looking at it, and life experiences. The "painter" goes first. To the extent of the overlapping, two channels of communication are established among the members. One is direct and personal. The other is indirect and impersonal. Members each talk about the painting. When they say, "This makes me feel happy or awful," they may be conveying indirectly the way they feel about the "painter." The overlapping of projections comprises what is termed the "Collective Image." The communality of feelings and experiences which emerges is very supportive to all. In the context of this common theme, members are encouraged to probe more into the conflicts and the problems revealed. Of course, non-overlapping projections reveal individual variations of the common theme. The sequence of individual paintings indicates individual, intrapersonal developments. The sequence of Collective Images which are formed in a number of sessions reveals the alternation of the patterns of transaction which the members follow.

During the structuring of the Collective Image, a number of interrelational incidents develop. The use of them in order to understand the members involved is another operational goal of the S.C.I.T. technique. Both the Collective Image and the interrelational incidents are offered as operational goals with which the

Ca-Re System provides all the opportunities needed to catalyze-regulate various transactions under the circumstances.

Communality makes the group situation supportive. Members are discovering that they share similar difficulties. They are encouraged to develop ways of overcoming problems. They are mutually helped. At this point individual variations become instrumental because of the comparisons they permit and the alternative actions they reveal. Boundary structuring (see Chapter 2) at the group level offers a steady frame for reality-testing, for finding alternative solutions and novel ways of implementing them.

When using this approach, the important intrapersonal processes emerge with less anxiety and greater ease. It has been widely recognized that the content and the structure of paintings are as revealing as dreams. The important point is that in paintings the psychodynamics involved have been fixed and no "secondary elaboration" could alter them. Members who repainted their paintings in order to "cover up something revealing" have found to their astonishment that, despite their repainting, the latent elements were revealed again. That proved to be a "scary" but at the same time "comforting" experience to them.

The common group theme of discussion is illuminated in a number of ways by the individual variations. The variations, in turn, become more meaningful when they are examined in the context of the common theme, provided the focus will be alternated from member to member in the indicated way. Both common theme and individual variations are aspects which need to be interrelated with the "here and now" attitudes of members. By doing that, the Ca-Re System makes members aware of attitudes and behavior which causes them difficulties.

SOME EXAMPLES OF S.C.I.T. THAT DEMONSTRATE FOCUS ALTERNATION

Three young adults, 25-30 years old, whom we shall call Bill, John, and Demetri, had chosen for discussion, after much hesitation, Bill's painting, which was abstract. The lower half of it was painted with a rather dark blue color and the top half a very light blue. In the middle there was a black, abstract design, vaguely suggesting a sailboat.

Bill named it "sailing" and associated with it feelings of apprehension. "Now that I see it, I experience anxiety; the group situation in general makes me anxious. It feels like sailing on unknown waters to an unknown destination." He associated it with his first experiences in kindergarten. He experienced such apprehension any time he found himself in "unknown situations" and felt the same upon joining the group.

John named it "fishing" and associated with it the feelings he usually had upon expecting an uncertain outcome. He had such a feeling when he went fishing as a child with his father in deep waters. He recalled his wondering if he would be able to catch fish and the great disappointment he felt when he failed to do so.

Demetri named it "playing" and associated with it feelings of being carefree, like the feelings he had in childhood whenever he was playing with toy sailing boats in the pond of his neighborhood park.

Group members realized quickly that what they had in common at that time was their concern with "doing something" ("sailing," "fishing," "playing") which symbolically represented their participation in the group. John and Demetri suggested that Bill think about the similarity of his projections and recollections to the attitude that he usually displayed in the group. They thought of him as being apprehensive about participating in the group and anxious about the outcome of their discussions.

Bill became irritated and said that, to the contrary, John was giving him that feeling. Bill was feeling that John was always impatient to "catch something in the group"—"something," though, related to somebody else. John argued with Bill at length on this issue. The situation made all participants rather tense and the Ca-Re System (the therapist alone at the moment) attempted to decrease the tension by diverting the group's attention to the painting itself. After some remarks about the painting, Bill said rather aggressively that it was reminding him of a kindergarten, "childish" affair. His remark made Demetri defensive this time because, "Obviously, Bill is suggesting that my attitude in the group is childish." The Ca-Re System (therapist, Bill and John this time) associated events from Demetri's participation in the group. They attempted to assist Demetri to understand the immature aspect of his attitude. At that time Demetri, by becoming silent like a stubborn child, gave additional evidence of such "immature aspects."

The therapist kept tension and anxiety at an optimum level by again referring the group to the painting and the Collective Image ("doing something"). Group members started using the impersonal channel of communication and very gradually shifted to the personal. The Collective Image, "doing something" and the individual variations, which became obvious, gave them the opportunity to detect similarities which increased their cohesive movement towards the goal they had defined in the beginning. They felt it was a vaguely defined goal—"doing something" in the group. The individual variations contributed to their further understanding of their ineffective patterns of behavior which they had to overcome in order to develop more effective ways of coping. In this way, "work group" patterns emerged gradually and group members started realizing some of the differences between their varied expectations of the group: an expectation of "something" to be achieved causing so much anxiety as to be associated with kindergarten anxiety-producing experiences (Bill); an expectation of "something" associated with activities of an unknown, uncertain outcome in the presence of the authority figure (John); an expectation of a carefree, playful situation of dependence associated with childhood playing (Demetri).

They gradually realized that in the group they were repeating patterns characteristic of their overall way of acting in life. Following this realization, the Ca-Re System had tangible information at hand in order to stage effective confrontations. These confrontations were aimed at helping the member who was at the time resisting the realization of the malfunctional character of his behavior. These confrontations, based on concrete evidence, could hardly be avoided and at the same time they were collectively offered in an intrinsically supportive situation. Because of this, the member who was confronted was finding it less painful and more rewarding to accept his contradictory behavior. Acceptance under the circumstances meant always joining the collective, something which was strengthening both members and the group each time.

CLOSING THE SESSION

S.C.I.T. is particularly useful in providing the therapist with opportunities to methodically stage an encouraging, supportive closure of each session. The Collective Image and the group theme present a number of positive aspects. On the other hand, individual variations present a number of aspects which are used for strengthening the positive ones. Contrasting them with the negative aspects of individual variations of the group theme, the Ca-Re system allows for the collection of all the constructive elements that are included in the projections, associations, allegories, similies and interelational incidents. In the context of the sequence of group sessions, therapist and members are enabled to reach a synthesis meaningful for their progress.

For the closure of each session the positive aspects of the group theme and the individual variations are synthesized by the Ca-Re system. They become particularly meaningful, by being examined in the context of the developing sequence of collective images and themes of the sessions. The closure of each session is based on a similar synthesis, encouraging and strengthening the most positive aspects of the members. They reenter their everyday life encouraged to try novel approaches. While trying them in their everyday life, they are reassured by the fact that the group is always available to hear their positive or negative experiences and assist them to become more effective.

ANTHROPOS MALFUNCTIONING

What has been presented so far leads to the conclusion that the grouping process is fundamental for the functioning and growth of the human being. Upon joining the grouping process, all group members exchange information. Input is regulated through the boundarying process, an aspect of which is termed the "decider system." It functions on certain criterial attributes related to what is most operational for the maintenance and further differentiation (growth) of the system. It catalyzes and regulates throughput and output. Such a systeming development means functioning. This process, at times, reaches a plateau—a morphostasis—but the functioning system eventually opens up new morphogenetic directions.

Prolonged morphostasis could lead to the disruption of previously established channels of transaction. The previous organized complexity of the system is gradually replaced by a situation termed "disorganized complexity," manifested in terms of all the processes of the system Anthropos.

Boundary Structuring in Group Psychotherapy

In therapeutic groups we deal with malfunctioning people. They need a therapist who himself is a system spiraling as uneventfully as possible to levels of more organized complexity, maintaining the optimum equilibrium of openness in organization and organization in openness concerning the structuring of his own boundaries. In short, they need a therapist who will fulfill an important axiom—that is, it does not matter so much what the therapist does or says; what really matters is what he humanly is. Only such a therapist is capable of having an adequate grasp of the direction in which the group is moving, the development of its morphogenesis, and the directions which group members want to pursue and avoid. He can judge effectively the required positive and negative feedbacks, timing and content, which the group transaction requires. Such a therapist has the operational-for-living value orientation and so he is able to catalyze and regulate the self-leading processes of his group members and eventually help them to develop a creative, critical participation in life.

The therapist has to keep in mind that malfunctioning individuals do not necessarily comprise a malfunctioning group. The explanation of the above is simple and offered by the very fact that the group is a system. This means that from the moment that the group is formed, a process is initiated—group boundary-structuring. The group members (people with defective, nonoperational boundary-structuring) find possibilities to function subsystemically within the group boundaries. By giving direction and goals and by controlling and regulating strong emotions, the group situation provides a boundary-structuring on the group level. Thus, in this setting, group members with rigidified boundaries can increase their openness while the chaotic group members are provided with a structure in which they can function.

The assistance which the group as a setting offers, however, cannot proceed beyond this point without the active, direct intervention (optimal-to-therapy activity) of the therapist and those members of the group who are able to reach the emotional-cognitive integration required to join the group process constructively and become the Catalytic-Regulatory Systems.

The therapist operates on the assumption that whatever improves the functioning of one group member by enabling him to transact with the other members improves the functioning of the whole group; that is, it increases the organization of the suprasystem's complexity. This, in turn, increases the organized complexity of each individual member.

A fundamental aspect of the therapist's role is to keep intervening and contributing to the process of boundary-structuring, both at the individual and group level. Upon joining the group, members are giving him a mandate. They expect him to undertake a catalytic-regulatory role, counteract possible negative injunctions and enhance positive ones, and apply, as needed, negative or positive feedbacks. In order to fulfill this role successfully, the therapist has to follow the principle of optimal-to-therapy activity, becoming active or inactive, direct or indirect as it is indicated, in order to generate self-leading processes in the group members. With such processes reactivated, members will be able to join him, at different times, in his catalytic-regulatory function and thus become part of the Ca-Re System which he originally represents. Consequently, the leadership effectiveness of the therapist will be directly related to his ability to develop self-leading processes in the group members.

We will present our views on boundary-structuring by giving actual examples from group therapy.

ASPECTS OF BOUNDARY-STRUCTURING IN GROUP THERAPY

During group transaction, a group theme is formed in ways which vary according to the technique used by the therapist, which is in our case the Synallactic Collective Image Technique (Vassiliou, G., 1968, 1973; Vassiliou, G. & V., 1974; Vassiliou, V., 1975a, 1975b).

Upon the formation of the group theme, the boundaries of the group as a whole and of each one of its members enter into a process of structuring. A communality of problems to be solved emerges. To the extent that individual variations of the group theme also emerge, the therapist is provided with opportunities to illuminate the individual variations of the group theme by alternating from member to member, as indicated above. This "focus alternation" illuminates aspects of the group theme which have a personal meaning for each member.

For instance, the painting of Mary has been selected which she calls "My Grandmother's Basement." It actually depicts a rather unstructured, dark, and closed configuration. She explains that it was the basement of her paternal house, where her grandmother usually placed her for punishment when she misbehaved. Katerina, projecting next, entitles the painting "The Storage Room." She recalls warm feelings of security coming from her recollection of her grandparents' basement in which they used to store apples and dry fruits—very appealing items in her childhood which, as she said, she cherished during her visits to her grandparents. Dimitri gives to the painting the title "My Workshop." He associates it with the workshop he has organized in his own basement, where he spends a lot of leisure time fixing electronic musical equipment, something which is his hobby, as well as "self-training as a future electrical engineer." He associates it with feelings of accomplishment which he experiences at times when he successfully assembles a piece of equipment.

The common theme is a place of seclusion. However, for Mary it is a threatening issue implying punishment, associated probably with both negative feelings towards authority figures and guilt. For Katerina, it is a quite nurturant place of seclusion, triggering feelings of security, need fulfillment, and parental care. For Dimitri, it is again a place of seclusion, but one which helps him to focus on activities, both pleasurable and syntonic to his overall aims and goals in life.

When the therapist asked, at the proper moment, why something which reminded all of them of a place of seclusion proved to have such different individual variations, the group members entered into a transaction which illuminated for them a number of past experiences and here-and-now behavioral patterns. Mary, for example, was asked by the other group members the following: "In the group you also tend to perceive yourself as being excluded by us, as being secluded in a kind of basement for punishment, but don't you realize that by misinterpreting certain of our interventions in this way you make them a self-fulfilling prophecy?"

The therapist, by alternating focus from Mary to Katerina, then to Mary, then again to Katerina and as a next step to Dimitri, was able to lead the group members to realize that similar life situations can be interpreted individually and can lead, quite differently, to largely varying end results in actual life. In this way, all members are helped to achieve further boundary differentiation. As it is expected, this does not develop uneventfully. Group members have a tendency to avoid the elucidation of the ways which are disturbing to them, becoming, instead, entangled in vicious circles. Therefore, they will attempt to disrupt the process, distract the attention to secondary or unimportant issues and deprive the Ca-Re System of the opportunity to differentiate input and throughput and to introduce into the group task-oriented and problem-solving processes. In attempting this, they will try to increase either their closedness to the point of rigidity or their openness to the point of chaos.

Actually, during the above-mentioned session, when Mary was confronted by the other group members with her tendency to misinterpret their interventions, which were intended to help her perceive her negative feelings towards authority figures and her disproportionate guilt because of them, Mary became extremely obstinate. She refused outright to accept this point of view by telling them flatly,

"This is your interpretation." Then she crossed her arms and remained silent for a rather prolonged period of time. But then, Dimitri, smiling, remarked in a soft tone and in a good-hearted manner, "So, Mary, once again you have managed to seclude yourself in a punitive place which you don't actually deserve. Even if you had reasons to feel guilty towards your grandmother, don't you realize that right now you manufacture reasons to make yourself feel really guilty for what you do to us right now?"

This brief illustration indicates that focus alternation offers to the Ca-Re System (in this case, the therapist, Dimitri and Katerina) all the needed concrete means to proceed in an optimal structuring of individual and group boundaries.

The following examples illustrate two individuals whose boundaries are respectively organized with rigidity (too closed) and chaotically disorganized (too open).

Helen, a 23-year-old medical student, explains to her group that she relies on her father for decisive advice concerning the medical specialty she will eventually choose. The group confronts her with the fact that her father, being a merchant in a provincial town, cannot possibly have the necessary information concerning her personal scientific and human strengths which will determine for her a successful career. The multifaceted problems that a successful medical career in Greece currently present are necessarily outside his conceptual field. She resolutely insists that he is the only person whom she "trusts," "respects," and "holds in high esteem as an achiever." The members of the group point out to her that being a successful merchant does not make one an expert on her very special problems. Her father cannot have adequate objective criteria upon which to base professional guidance. Under the group pressure, though, she becomes increasingly insistent to the theme: "But he is the only person whom I trust, whom I respect, and whom I consider an achiever."

Thus, by rigidifying her boundaries, Helen blocks input (information) given by the other group members, who try to impress on her the painful realization that she is not working to develop personal aims and goals, personal value orientation, and the stamina to mobilize her personal resources. As long as Helen is operating on the assumption that "trusted nurturant authority" = "expert authority" (a legitimate assumption for the less complex traditional milieu where she was raised but "a stereotype" for her present sociocultural environment), the information provided by the group will threaten her and force her to resort more and more to stereotypical thinking. As part of Helen's boundaries, this attitude contributes to her "closedness" to new information. What she fears is twofold: On the one hand she is afraid that by turning to other sources of guidance she will betray her value system; on the other hand, if she rejects guidance of the authority figure, she will have to mobilize personal resources and set personal goals and use personal criteria—a thing which greatly threatens her because she is unprepared and untrained to do so.

Thus, to avoid both threats, she remains rigidly fixed to a line of thinking which is "parataxic" for her present environment. She associates her trust, respect, and esteem for her father's achievement with her need for professional guidance and life planning, Needless to say, by rigidifying her boundaries, Helen once again misses the opportunity for modification of her functioning towards more operational lines.

A chaotic disorganization of boundaries is exemplified by another 23-year-old member of the same group, whom we shall call John. During one period he is confronted by increasing parental demands for achievement as a mathematician and develops a momentary "dizzy spell" while driving with his father. This triggers an endless series of physical complaints and medical examinations. Parents and the malfunctioning son get involved in a mutual entanglement. None of them realizes that John has reached the limit in his efforts to fulfill unrealistic demands. This is due to the fact that up to that point John was moving within boundaries structured by external factors—his parents and the community. Now, having completed his professional degree, he finds himself on the threshold of a new stage. Life conditions force him to undertake a role which demands self-leading and the ability for self-directed boundary-structuring which he is not prepared to assume.

This becomes evident when group members, in their attempt to help John, offer all kinds of different explanations for his situation. John agrees with every one of them, irrespective of the contradictions involved. Then, when group members ask him about his personal aims and goals, John proves completely unable to answer coherently. His answers are so inconsistent and his handling of the group's questions is such that it causes laughter in the group.

At the point where group members start laughing, the therapist questions the group members about this reaction. After a prolonged silence, John asks hesitantly, "Is it because I say foolish things?" The therapist confronts him then with a therapeutic double bind: "But John, are you really a fool?" When he says, "I don't think so," the therapist says, "How come, then, without being a fool, you say foolish things tonight? Is it possible that the confrontation with reality forced you to the illogical conclusion that one and one does not make two but eleven? Don't you think that in this way you permit yourself to become a kind of cloud? But then, how do you expect us to reach a cloud? We want you in this room to be the real John with your real problems and not the medical escapades into the 'illnesses' you describe. After all, one year's medical examinations proved that you are in perfect physical condition."

John came to that group meeting puzzled and obviously unable to put some order into the chaotic condition of his boundaries. Under these circumstances, he remained unable to receive the input offered by the group members. The therapist first catalyzed the development of a self-evaluation attitude which initiated a minimum amount of self-leading. John was then helped by the therapist to process the information offered by the "laughing" which provided some criteria for evaluation and put some initial order to the chaos and some alternatives for action.

It should be noted that both Helen and John are moving within other-structured boundaries. However, when confronted with demands for self-direction, while both experience threat, Helen clings rigidly to her externally structured boundaries, objecting to and rejecting any alternative ideas, interpretation or view, while John "floats" and accepts indiscriminately all suggestions offered to him.

Helen and John illustrate that whenever either rigid closedness or indiscriminate openness prevails over functional organization, the result is that the group member fails to receive the offered input, process it adequately, and thus actualize therapy. In other words, the boundaries of these dysfunctional group members do not present the flexible opening/closing boundaries of a functioning member. In functioning normal groups, a member's participation in group transaction will be readily accepted and actualized when this member is structuring boundaries in a way that enables him to perform as a differentiated participant. In such cases, the group is able to proceed creatively. From clearly presented individual themes, a synthesis emerges during the group process, which, as a group theme, illuminates, enriches and complements, in turn, each one's individual variations.

Chapter 13

Outside/Inside/Opening/Closing: Instructions for Living Groups

By James E. Durkin, Ph.D.

Editor's Introduction. The present chapter shows how the author puts his GST model of autonomous living structure into practice. He translates certain structural concepts which characterize living systems, such as matter/energy and information, isomorphism, self-organization, self-reference, and complementarity, into clinical interventions. The purpose is to restore or enhance the autonomy of the group, its members, and their personal structures. Complementary boundary opening/closing, the basic operation by which autonomous living structures are able to organize and transform themselves, becomes the major therapeutic tool of the group therapist.

In the opening sessions, the therapist demonstrates the meaning of boundaries and boundarying by encouraging the members to step inside or outside of the rope which objectifies the boundary around the "lifespace" of the group. The leader acting as a model makes similar choices. They learn through this experience to become clear about where they want to be and to take responsibility for it.

In the middle phases of treatment, the therapist also focuses on their interpersonal boundaries. Experience shows that they, like the leader, possess an intuitive knowledge about their contact at the boundaries. They learn that when two or more members are open to each other, there is a free flow of energy between them that permits them to change and grow to a new level of personal organization. This is called systeming. If they remain closed to one another, their contact at the boundary maintains their identity and increases their stability. This is called summing. Both of these boundary contacts are constructive, and it is one of the leader's important functions to facilitate this alternating process. He does it either by engaging with them as a participant member or by providing information to close boundaries after a transformation has occurred. Faulty contact at the boundaries results from being open to closedness or closed to openness and leads to miscommunication and confusion. What requires the therapist's facilitative intervention is the general aim of staying open to openness and closed to closedness to provide a model for them. But a number of exceptions are described, such as false or masked openness intended to make an appeal to the leader in order to avoid change. If the therapist errs, he acknowledges it.

To summarize, at the group level the leader facilitates free movement inside or outside of the group boundary. At the structural level he catalyzes the processes of opening and closing, systeming or summing, and at the content level he intervenes to keep the communications clear. He operates as an example by engaging his own feeling autonomously in boundarying contacts with them, or as a conductor by stepping outside the group boundary to provide cognitive input.

Readers who are accustomed to working with the current group therapeutic approaches will be aware that Jim's interpretation of the GST view reflects his humanistic background. Others may find it illuminating to view the technique as tantamount to a structural form of dealing with resistance, which has the advantage of avoiding the complicated power struggle which is sometimes easily engendered by the analytic method (H.E.D.).

In the second chapter of this volume, I introduced the GST phenomenon of autonomous living structure, the paradigm of autonomy which provided the necessary framework for achieving an understanding of this phenomenon. I outlined the four foundational ideas that lie at the base of our intuition of autonomy. In the present chapter I would like to utilize these new ideas in one particular domain of living structure, that of groups and group members. I will try to build upon the GST premise that groups and group members are alive in the same sense that biological organisms are alive, that is, by virtue of the autonomous configurations and processes they exhibit. By seeing the embodiments of living structure in living groups and living group members, I will try to harness the insights into the structure of autonomy achieved by GST into a set of instructions which can guide group leaders and their members in the process of building, maintaining, evolving and, finally, dissolving the life of their own groups.

It is the basic hypothesis of this chapter that one of the main functions of human groups which become living groups by virtue of their achieving the structure of autonomy is to generate or restore the individual autonomy of their members. It is in this sense that living groups are inherently therapeutic. Because of this, measures that are taken to enhance the process of the group coming alive will also be measures which will foster therapeutic effects in its members. Groups of people who commit themselves to meet together to help each other change personal structures are usually called psychotherapy groups. The same helping processes often go on in groups that operate under other names. The configurations and processes identified by GST as the operations underlying the structure of autonomy will be adapted here into a set of methods with which group members and leaders can work within living groups to develop their autonomy.

The GST-based structural model of living groups presented here supplements the traditional psychodynamic models of group therapy by offering leaders and members some new options. The model also provides a more generalized frame-work for group therapy which offers a basis for choice between psychodynamic interpretations and structural actions. Helping people change their personal struc-tures is arduous work, particularly when they are heavily invested in their de-fensive systems. The GST-based model of living groups presented here can make some choices more simply and can bring a new set of therapeutic interventions within a systematic framework.

THE EXPANDED PERSPECTIVE OF THE LIVING STRUCTURE MODEL OF HUMAN GROUPS

In the second chapter of this book I introduced the concept of autonomous living structure and defined it as that self-organizing structure embodied in manifest content which underlies all life forms from cell to society. After arguing that viewing the phenomenon of living structure from the traditional objective paradigm of science led to paradox, I suggested that the broader perspective of a paradigm of autonomy was necessary as a framework within which to inves-tigate this important phenomenon. Finally, I reviewed four foundational ideas underlying our intuitions of autonomy. The first is that living structure must be dually defined in terms of its conplementary physical action structures and its informational knowledge structures. Second, living structure forms its own hier-archies through the interplay of action and knowledge. Third, living structure generates self-referential configurations which enable it to regulate itself and transform itself. Fourth, living structure operates through the basic act of bound-arying which is dually defined as opening/closing. Much of this chapter will center around boundarying in groups, group members and group leaders, for the key to understanding of the structure of autonomy and how to facilitate its emergence in groups is tied up in the boundarying operation.

Few working group leaders would object to the assertion that the goal of group psychotherapy should be to generate or restore the autonomy of its members. Many would espouse the same goal of autonomy for the group itself. But this unanimity of opinion probably covers a wide diversity of definitions of the idea of autonomy. Most current definitions of autonomy are focused on the content level in terms of a person's intrapsychic, interpersonal or social adjustment. The GST-based model presented here focuses on the structure of autonomy as well as its content by identifying a number of autonomous structural events that go on during the group process and by showing how they function to achieve autonomy. A dual perspective is required because every structural event is nec-essarily embodied in some particular content level context. What the model offers is the option of a second path, the path of engaging in a structure level action as an alternative to working at the level of content, which is often vul-nerable to ambiguity, manipulation and the insidious intrusion of value judgment. Often in the group process there are points where the content issues being dealt with fall into ambiguity or impasse. It is here where the leader or experienced member can effectively jump to the structure level and keep the action going without remaining enmeshed in the content. Very often such a detour will bypass the impasse so that it will appear, upon resuming the content path, to have taken care of itself. After that point has been reached, content level discussion and analysis are quite useful and appropriate for formulating an understanding of what went on in the structural action. One of the chief skills that must be learned by those who use this model is to sense these choice-points and to move back and forth easily between the structure and content levels.

Everyday language is rooted in the paradigm of objectivity, and yet it is an important part of the therapeutic process to formulate in verbal terms descriptions of the autonomous events that have occurred. Objective events are externally caused, but autonomous events cause themselves. Verbal descriptions of autonomous events such as "he transformed himself" can be stated grammatically, but, like all self-referential statements, are paradoxical in meaning. It is important for the group leader to reorient the language of objectivity to accommodate to the autonomous events that will be encountered in the group process. One important way to foster the use of language within the group that describes autonomous action is for the leader to take every opportunity to use self-referential forms to describe events which appear autonomous. This is a heuristic tactic of pasting words on top of events in hopes that they will take root. As this prescribed juxtaposition between autonomous action events and the words formulated to describe them proceeds, the descriptions and the actions will begin to clarify each other.

Finally, one of the most difficult readjustments that the group leader has to work with within the expanded living structure model of groups is redefining the leader's role in the light of operation of autonomous processes. The paradigm of objectivity is rooted in the idea of causality. From that perspective it seems natural for the leader to assume the responsibility for causing the group to get organized and for generating interventions toward or between group members that cause therapeutic change. Indeed, there are many events during the group process where the leader is the prime mover of action. But under the new assumption that the leader, each member and the group as a whole are each embodiments of autonomous living structure and each operating under isomorphic principles of self-organization, ideas about who causes what have to be modified. Each structure transforms itself, or, if it chooses, resists change. The only structure that the leader can change unilaterally is his or her own. The process of helping group members change, to which the leader is professionally committed, becomes a process under the living structure model where peers in autonomy throw themselves into interactions with uncertain outcomes. The leader knows more and has been through the group process many times before. The group members know that too and the leader knows that they know and respect it. But the ultimate fact is that autonomous structures regulate themselves and transform themselves whether they be leaders, members, or even living groups themselves. A more open attitude is necessary under these conditions, one in which the leader can give up control of the situation and defer to autonomous forces and just as readily pick up the reins of control again when that is indicated. The inert mechanistic world of objectivity sits there waiting for the leader's controlling efforts. The alive world of autonomy swirls actively and the leader must make autonomous choices whether to be outside it or inside it, open to it or closed to it.

I have here presented terms such as autonomy, autonomous processes and autonomous living structure without defining them objectively. And yet the general concept plays and will continue to play a central part in fulfilling the purpose in this chapter of providing guidelines for working with groups under this new model. One of the basic propositions in this chapter is that the phenomenon of autonomous living structure is a new kind of idea that requires a new conceptual framework or paradigm in order to understand it. Since our language comes out of the traditional paradigm, it is necessary to use old language in a new way. In this chapter I will take my own advice offered above and "paste on" words like "autonomous" wherever they seem to fit and hope that they will take root and generate their own deeper meaning, autonomously.

OUTSIDE/INSIDE: HELPING A GROUP TO BECOME ALIVE THROUGH BOUNDARYING

According to our model, one of the functions of a living group is to generate or restore autonomy in its individual members' personal structures. This means that one of the primary aims of the leader is to facilitate the processes by means of which the group becomes alive. There are other tasks such as handling fees and scheduling, but catalyzing autonomy in a group structure is a very different process. It is a paradoxical task for the leader who must operate outside the group as a guiding authority as well as operating inside and engaging in personal action as a member of the living group that the rules describe. The leader, when entering into this dual context of autonomy, must be prepared to move back and forth easily between these complementary positions. The boundarying procedures described in this section can help here.

Although catalyzing the development of life in a group can be done in many particular ways, I am going to describe the special procedures I have developed in the groups I have been working with lately. I prefer to work on a large mat and only use chairs during the preliminary orientation periods at the beginning of the session or series of sessions. At the beginning of a session the members are met with a "boundary" all folded up in the center of the mat. My particular physical boundary is made of braided foam rubber. When it is spread out, it forms a large ring 12 feet in diameter and about five inches thick. In my orientation I inform the members that I would like them to honor a simple rule about the boundary: *The group lifespace is located on the inside of the boundary and the rest of the world is located outside of the boundary circle.* I tell them that I expect them to make a personal commitment to this basic boundary rule and to honor it as best they can during the group sessions. Sometimes I even ask them to sign a prepared statement to that effect. At the same time I make clear my own personal commitment to the basic boundary rule and pledge as leader to do all I can to enhance the clarity of the boundary both through instructional interventions and by example in action.

There is only one more initial commitment that I request of each member before the group lifespace is opened up. This is more of a value orientation than a specific rule of conduct. It is the proposition that it is not of inherently higher therapeutic value to be inside the group than outside. Rather, what is of high value, and therefore to be encouraged and facilitated at every opportunity, is free, clean and clear movement from outside to inside and from inside to outside back and forth across the group boundary. I tell them that these are autonomous actions of free choice which I as leader will do my best to support and protect. If they feel too much pressure within the group, they should freely move out. If they are bored or repelled by what goes on within, they should simply move out. If they are outside and they become curious, emotionally involved or feel the desire of personal contact with the leader or members, they should step back over the boundary and rejoin the group space. I tell them, finally, that although they might not clearly comprehend why at this time, this free movement across the boundary is not only the best way for each member to embody his or her own personal autonomy, but it is also the best way to catalyze the process of the group itself becoming a living structure that can support the autonomy goals of each of us. When the group becomes alive through the members' exercise of their freedom, the members can develop enough trust in the group to begin to open and close their personal boundaries to each other within the group.

The goal of the initial orientation session is to make sure that all the members are aware of and at least verbally committed to the two basic boundary rules. It is also an opportunity for some preliminary description of the kinds of structures that are likely to develop as the group becomes alive. But, as time goes on, particularly in subsequent preliminary sessions, the leader should indicate that it is better to see what happens when the group space gets opened up. The members know too that it is time to stop talking about it and get into it. Usually, I make a little ritual of both opening and closing the boundary, with all members simultaneously lifting the braided ring over their heads. It clarifies the idea that we are all creating and dissolving our own group space autonomously.

Some Structural Consequences of the Boundary

The utilization of a large physical object with no other function except to serve as a group boundary sounds like a cute gimmick, but it is more than that. This physical embodiment of an interpersonal commitment functions as a powerful device for catalyzing this elusive property of autonomy in groups. On a practical basis it divides the room into an action space and an observation space so that members can withdraw from the action without revoking their commitment to the group. But there are several other consequences that seem to flow directly out of drawing this boundary distinction. Each of these consequences plays an important part in the development of autonomy for the group.

First of all, the boundary defines a clear-cut space where a new social system can develop and autonomously generate its own social rules and action dynamics. Because of the boundary, this system can diverge from and develop independently of the norms, rules and laws of the outside world. The process of differentiation between the two worlds must be gradual because people do not suddenly drop the values and conduct that they have held for years. But the constant reminder of the physical boundary and the frequent crossings of the members and leader constantly reinforce the widening separation between the two living structures. In here there is us, here, now. Outside, out in the world there are the demands made by "them" and issues such as "Will I make it?" and "How long is it going to take?" The leader's job is to continually enhance the emergence of the new world both in terms of verbal reflections about the process and in personal actions such as boundary crossings.

The second emergent process that arises out of the drawing of the boundary distinction has to do with the way that events that occur on the other side of the boundary begin to be experienced as the boundary solidifies. What are boundaries made of? They are made of information. The general function of a boundary, or one of them, is to transform actions into messages. When a member is in the group space, the real life events that occur on the outside acquire a symbolic status; they are evaluations that things out there are going well or badly, but not here-and-now actions that can take the group to a new place in the same way that events inside the group can. In the same fashion, the events inside the group are transformed into messages when the member is outside. The messages indicate that the therapeutic process is taking place, but they do not have the same aliveness as the daily events with which the person must cope.

When the group begins, there is inevitably a confusion between inside and outside, between the messages from the outside that members bring in as complaints and the actions on the inside which constitute work within the group process. The leader can help clarify this distinction by making verbal interventions pointing out that a member is sitting inside and living outside, by suggesting that a member move across the boundary into a part of the space that is more aligned with the member's true focus of consciousness. As an alternative, the leader can engage in boundary action as a structural confrontation of the member's inside/outside equivocation. The leader can cross the boundary in order to be on the same or opposite side of the member and change his or her mode of exchange from symbolic message contact if they are on opposite sides to direct personal action contact if they are on the same side. There is no particular content that will automatically convey the distinction between message contact and action contact. But a relationship that is "only words and symbols" is clearly distinct from a relationship coming out of the concrete physical-emotional person. This message-action option on the part of the leader can serve as a strong tool for helping members clarify whether they are in the here-and-now inside the group or out in their own outside a worlds away from the presence of the group and its emotional involvement. This distinction could not be brought home as strongly if the boundary distinction were not there.

OPENING/CLOSING: HOW TO SEE LIVING STRUCTURE AT THE LEVEL OF THE PERSON

Our usual mode of experience as we conduct daily interactions between ourselves and others is at the level of content. The process of exchanging content-coded messages by means of a common language is called communication. Because all members of a given culture have common training in the use of language, we are relatively successful in informing, instructing, questioning, sharing sentiments and many other functions through the medium of language communication. As we gain skill in communication, we learn to send and receive extremely subtle messages through several verbal and nonverbal channels at once.

But very often people who join psychotherapy groups to help themselves with their personal problems have as one of their symptoms the habit of abusing their immense language skills. Such misuse of language in the conduct of their lives is usually unintentional and they find themselves trapped in their own words. Major forms of language abuse are equivocality, which is shaky encoding, and ambiguity, which is shaky decoding of communication content. A group member can elude clear communication with the others in the group for a long time partly because all encoding and decoding operates within the person and cannot easily be externally checked. Another abuse of communication is the subtle intrusion of value judgment. A group member can relate facts with words that make him or her sound good or sound bad and, once again, this manipulation of words cannot be externally checked. Thus, at the level of content communication, the usual mode of group interactions, there are pitfalls inherent in the use of language that can impede therapeutic progress.

The living structure model of group psychotherapy offered here proposes an alternative channel of contact action between group members to supplement the content level of language communication. Structural contact action, as we shall call it, and language communication are complementary forms of the same interaction process between group members or between the leader and his members. Structural contact action has to be talked about in content language and language can only represent symptoms of a structural attitude. However, the leader has the option of moving through the interaction at one level or the other, often with different results. The indicators for choosing each option will be discussed later. We have all been familiar with the techniques of managing content communication since childhood, but developing a skill for using the structural contact action in our model requires that people develop a whole new image of other people with whom they interact. It is a much simpler image than the one defined by verbal meaning space with all its semantic curves and sub-tleties. In fact, it is an image which focuses on one basic distinction between "open" and "closed" configurations seen in the other person.

Perhaps an attempt to describe the living structure image of the person in verbal terms will show why such an utterly simple discrimination can be used as a therapeutically effective tool. The structural image of the person disregards all the particulars of the content, as the meaning model obviously cannot. We can "see" a personal structure by imagining a lifespace made up of a three-dimensional solid, life-sized. It is transparent because all the colors and textures are the content meanings that have been washed out. In fact, there are only two features of this large lifespace structure reminiscent of Kurt Lewin's (1951) lifespace representations. There are only complex configurations of sheets of boundary structures which contain the swirling energy of flow processes. The boundary membranes in this living structure are layered concentrically, but there are also many independently layered subsystems and clusters of subsystems within the overall lifespace. The life of the configuration is in the dynamic dialectical interplay between the constraining boundary membranes and the active turbulent energy of the flow processes which press the boundaries in every direction.

It is not necessary to analyze the architecture of this living structure image of the personal lifespace. The relative size and placement of the bounded seg-ments of the space are content details that are better dealt with at the content level. What is important is the single distinction between being open on the outside and being closed on the outside, where contact between living structures can occur. It must be emphasized that we are focusing on contact action events that occur at a given moment between living structures as group members. No person is all open or all closed all over the outer boundary. There are points of both openness and closedness distributed throughout. What counts is the joint nature of the contact. Contact events where the participants in the contact are either open or closed at the point of contact can come in four types—open to openness, closed to closedness, open to closedness, and closed to openness. The open to open contact will be called *systeming*. The closed to closed contact will be called *summing*. The mismatched categories are usually transient in nature and, with a few exceptions to be discussed below, represent faulty contact events.

Thus, we are led to a terribly simple catalogue of group contact action events at the structural level—summing, systeming and mismatch. Within this limited array, the leader or group member who elects to jump from the content level to the structural level has to do little else than make the single discrimination in order to operate.

It is assumed that everyone who has grown up as a human has the capability of distinguishing summing contact action from systeming. One of the jobs of the group leader is to help the members sharpen up this ability to discriminate, recollect it if it has been forgotten, and explore ingrained structures in group members where nondiscrimination or reversal has persisted too long. Another part of the leader's job is to encourage and assist the group members to utilize these distinctions in their interactions with other members. The goal of the group and of each of the group members is to establish or restore autonomy. Autonomy may be defined in terms of the structural level as the ability to engage in summing when conditions are appropriate and to engage in systeming when those are appropriate. At the structural level, the leader's main tool for helping others discriminate summing and systeming is his or her own personal structure as it engages in discriminative behavior with respect to these basic events.

SUMMING AND SYSTEMING CONFIGURATIONS BETWEEN GROUP MEMBERS

Summing is boundary contact action characterized by being closed to closedness. Closed does not mean rigid and unmoving, for these are living, growing boundaries that are constantly active and moving, as are the living structures they bound. In terms of our visual image, living boundaries are plastic and flexible. A directed action on the part of one person directed to the other could be visualized, as in Figure 1, as a long process extending out in one direction

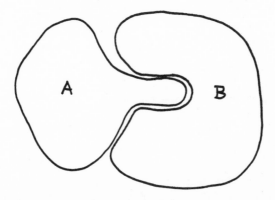

Figure 1. Summing: being closed to closedness

like an amoeba putting out a pseudopod for locomotion. Such an extension would occur, for example, when one member asked another a question. The reciprocal action of the other person, in our example giving an answer to the question, would be to invaginate his or her lifespace, as in the figure, in order to make a harbor to contain the question. The response to the question and the reception of the response by the original questioner would reverse the shape of the boundary contact. A full topological representation of the summing dialog with all its multiple levels and subtleties would require the rendering of many complex shapes. But in the end it boils down to a reciprocal assimilative interplay of active boundary contacts, which both remain separately controlled by factors within each participant and attempt to adapt to the activity of the other in a way which maintains their own structural integrity and equilibrium.

Being closed has a negative connotation at the level of content communication and being open has a good value. But at the level of boundary contact action there is no such value judgment, for both attitudes are functional and necessary for life. The closed attitude is simply an individuated attitude where the center of equilibrium is within each participant and the influence of the other is a real but external influence that must be interpreted. Verbal communication and other information exchanges between people are essential forms of the summing process. Boundaries are made of information and function to transform actions into messages. The receiver of a message always decodes it on his or her own terms rather than on the terms of the sender. Reciprocal summing represents two one-way streets. The action of one *deforms* the other's lifespace for the moment, but it doesn't break boundaries and transform the other's structural organization directly. It is possible, of course, that under the momentary deformation of a summing interaction, internal transformations separately controlled could be facilitated, but this is different from the mutually transforming systeming contact to be discussed below.

Summing can, and really should be, intelligent, creative, and refreshing. People's lifespaces are interesting places and always developing and changing. Boundary contact in which information about each other is reciprocally exchanged is a rewarding and interesting process, as is the process of transmitting environmental experiences between the persons so that each may learn more about the world indirectly through the other. But because summing is essentially assimilative, the process of interaction itself, as opposed to the information transmitted in the interaction, does not change the participants' structures. People summing aren't moved by each other. One good sign of unresolved emotional problems in group members is that they are defensively locked in summing configurations. They strongly need to defend their positions and cannot risk opening up to restructure them. In the group process their interactions appear as repetitive, even though the content might be highly, even compulsively, varied. If a leader can begin to sense this redundancy of structure beneath varied content, it suggests that ways must be found to develop open boundaried systeming contacts again.

Systeming is boundary contact action characterized by being open to openness. The reason for choosing this word must be made clear. Just as opening and closing are the two complementary aspects of the boundarying operation, so summing and systeming are the two complementary aspects of boundary contact action. LvB called his living configuration an open system when what he was actually describing was a structure that selectively opened *and* closed itself autonomously. It is common in GST models to use the term "system" as the configuration which would include both the weak interactions called summing here and the strong interactions called systeming here. In this context the term living structure and the activity of structuring are used as the superordinate terms which included both summing and systeming events.

LvB employed the term "dyanmic interaction" to describe the play of forces between a self-organizing active "open system" and its environment, whereby the open system pursued an equifinal path of development. Equifinal means that the path was not preplanned but opportunistic, using immediately available environmental pathways and utilizing natural laws of organization in a manner which found ways to restructure at higher levels of development. Systeming between group members is a similar flow process because, when organizing boundaries are opened up, planned purpose and control are left behind and each individual, within the limits of the openness the group permits, is left to flow along a spontaneous, creative, and unpredictable equifinal path.

It is paradoxical, at least in Western scientific terms, to think of letting go of control as a form of purposive control. In this model this capacity to open boundaries to each other and let the unstructured flow between individuals move spontaneously toward new structuring is just as essential for autonomy as the planned control achieved by drawing boundaries. In terms of our visual image, systeming would be seen in Figure 2, where as two members, or the leader and

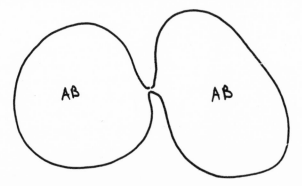

Figure 2. Systeming: being open to openness

a member, open their individual boundaries to each other. A common boundary, including the systeming pair as a new whole, distinguishes their mutual structure from other members' structures and from the environment. Our myths of objective existence compel us to think of our own lifespaces as unalterably separate, with only communication possible between us, but this model, which gives equal reality value to living structures at the psychological and group level as to biological structures embodied in protoplasm, admits the reality of temporary formation of systeming structures which are in every sense alive, arising from the opening of two or more persons to each other. It is the essence of the living process that actively organized living structures open and flow and merge into higher level structures and alternately close and differentiate back into separate structures. At the group level the process goes on constantly between pairs and subgroups; at times, the group as a whole operates as a unified living structure through the autonomous choices of each of the members to join this unity.

It is difficult to countenance this process of forming and unforming living structures from the perspective of the paradigm of objectivity. The objective view would see summing as biologically fixed individuals in cognitive exchange of information and see systeming as emotional exchange processes which effectively dissolve and reorient established cognitive attitudes. Our living structure model has no objection to that interpretation as far as it goes, because summing is basically experienced as cognitive or thinking activity at the content level and systeming is experienced as emotional interchange at the content level.

The basic function of cognition within the person is to stabilize and control the inner world in the face of disturbances of one form or another in the environment. The generation and maintenance of boundary structures within the person, between persons as in summing and between the person or group and the nonliving environment fulfill that stabilizing and consolidating function efficiently. The basic function of emotion within the person is to provide a pathway for destructuring and restructuring of personal organization. Emotional activity is traditionally seen as a dysfunctional reaction of an involuntary nature to frustration and stress. This shortsightedness is due in part to the bias in our views toward rationality. But perhaps what is experienced as emotional upheaval at the content level and is characterized as the controlled opening of boundaries at the structural level has a positive and unique function all its own in the personal economy. We experience feeling as moving through us, but maybe it is the other way around. Perhaps we move through feeling, that is, perhaps the feeling event is a personal destructuring event that permits our boundaries to dissolve so that we can accommodate ourselves to new realities and restructure ourselves on a new more adaptive basis.

The living structure model holds that we change in feeling as boundary structures autonomously dissolve themselves and consolidate ourselves by constructing a new organization through the cognitive process of building up boundaries.

These opening and closing processes experienced as feeling and thinking at the content level work together in the person to keep the balance between growth and stability, between morphogenesis and morphostasis. In the group process systeming and summing boundary contact actions are the vehicle by means of which this inherent dialectical interplay of autonomous boundarying is carried out. Autonomy can be achieved in the group by a process of gaining clear knowledge of the differences between the two and effective skills in putting each in action and developing the awareness of our autonomy in choosing one path or the other at a given moment.

LEADING LIVING GROUPS INTO SUMMING AND SYSTEMING

Leaders of living groups facilitate free movement inside and outside the group boundary at the group level, keep communication channels clear at the content level and catalyze the cyclic process of summing and systeming between group members at the structural level. Helping group members feel comfortable and gain skill in these modes of interaction is done through both the leader's instruction and through his or her example as an active autonomous personal structure.

Helping the group members gradually develop willingness and skill in engaging in summing and systeming interaction configurations with each other is one of the leader's most important tasks. It is assumed that we all have the ability to distinguish opening and closing, both within ourselves and in others. The job of the leader is to awaken and sharpen this clarity and to help group members trust their discrimination enough to risk it in action. Our ability to manipulate with language at the content level generates situations in the group process where openness is given the appearance of closedness and closedness is given the appearance of openness. It is in these situations where the leader may teach by engaging his or her own personal structure in boundary contact action in a way which distinguishes true from masked openness and closedness.

The guiding principle for the leader, and gradually for the members as they begin to risk summing and systeming with each other, is to be closed to the other's closedness until it opens and open to the other's openness until it closes. Tough choices frequently arise when the leader employs this principle. The leader is seen as a knowledgeable, compassionate authority, ready at all times to give aid and support to his or her group members. If the leader encounters a member he or she sees as closed, despite the presentation of a vulnerable and poignant appeal for help, following the principle means remaining closed and appearing cold and heartless to those members who have bought into the appeal, which usually includes the appealing member himself. But if one is open to closedness, a manipulation has been accepted and reinforced, thus digging the unaware manipulator deeper into his or her own repetitive trap. But if the leader steadfastly remains closed to closedness despite the social pressure, the manipulator, as well as the other group members, who at some level retain their clarity of discrimination, will trust the leader more for his or her insight and courage.

It is always possible for the leader to make a misjudgment in this situation and take a closed attitude to genuine openness. Fortunately, such mistakes at the boundary contact action level are usually much more productive than mistaken interpretations of meaning at the content level. In some cases a member whose truly open feeling flow has been met with closedness from the leader will move in reaction to an even deeper and more credible feeling, such as anger or pain at the rejection. One of the chief indicators of true open feeling is that it moves you to a new place rather than leaving you stuck in the same place ready for a repeat cycle. If this intensified situation occurs, it provides the leader with an occasion to examine why he or she failed to make the correct discrimination and gives the member a chance to restructure the original appeal on the basis of a deeper feeling than before. But if no error is made and the leader has been appropriately closed to closedness despite the seductive manipulation and the social pressure from the group, the same situation will repeat itself in other forms with that member and the true pattern will slowly emerge if the leader remains steadfast.

How does the leader or a member articulate the attitude of being closed to perceived closedness? A dull intransigent rejection of the member's appeal would simply stop the conversation at loggerheads and would not take into account that the member was really trying to move, albeit in a misguided and self-defeating way. In discussing summing above it was stated that it should be interesting, creative and exploratory. There are lively ways to keep summing alive and moving, while still keeping it clear that it is a closed to closedness situation. One strategy for doing this might be called psychological judo. The principle of judo is that when your opponent pushes, you pull him, and when your opponent pulls, you push him. This means you will be using his energy to achieve your ends. In summing, if both participants are bounded away from each other, it doesn't matter exactly what they say to each other for that will not open up the situation. However, it is advisable to be in the same "ballpark" so that you will be there when the summing situation suddenly opens up into systeming. Judo tactics would include airing your own personal complaints about how hard life is in response to your member's list of complaints. They would include pseudoserious elaborations of the member's complaints and a subtle mimicking of the defensive mask feelings accompanying those complaints. In general, the summing situation is defined as a situation that is going nowhere because of the closedness, but in the process the leader can explore the situation a little and have a little creative fun, all the time keeping in focus the basic closedness of the interaction.

But boundarying is basically a dialectical process. This means that in time every open boundary closes of itself and every closed boundary opens of itself.

It is true that many people, particularly those who seek help in groups, have generated self-regulated closed configurations in their personal structure in which they trap themselves. But even these people have brief moments where, if help is there, the slow process of restructuring a living balance between opening and closing can get started.

The group leader, no matter how involved he or she may be in maintaining the summing interaction, must be constantly on the alert for hints of opening on the part of members. The point of opening will seldom be up front at the central focus of the interaction. It will usually appear as a very minor event in an obscure corner of the situation. It might be ushered in by a chance remark, a lilt in the voice or an unintended movement. When such moments of openness appear and seem to have potential as a pathway for feeling transformation, the leader must shift from closedness to openness as well, to give systeming a chance to do its work.

There is personal risk and vulnerability for the leader in being open to openness. Just as there are social and professional pressures which militate against being closed to closedness, the assumption of an attitude of open to openness would be seen by many as too personally involved in the process to be therapeutically effective and professionally independent. But if our boundarying model is correct, the only way to touch openness is with openness. The model also assumes that beneath the level of content, where the helping leader and the help-needing group member are cast into very different roles, both people are living structures where the cyclic process of opening and closing and summing and systeming is a natural concomitant of autonomy. When the leader opens, he or she will let leader's feelings flow, not patient's feelings. The living structure model makes it possible, indeed desirable, to use a fuller range of the leader's own personal human response than does the traditional professional model of the skilled helper. It gives credit to both leader and member for the capability to be able to handle a much wider range of disequilibrium, both in summing and systeming, and still recover in a renewed and transformed state to resume functioning.

Managing systeming events is a subtle process. Systeming is a very unstructured process, a time of uncertainty where things could flow in several directions. One of the main tasks is precisely to maintain this open state so that this flow has a chance to find itself in spite of the leader's, the systeming members', and the rest of the group's defensive needs to bring things under individual control. One of the first things that must be done is to give the feeling flow time and space to establish itself and develop. Very often, when a boundary opens up in a person, conversation drops off. For those in the group who are not aware that a subtle flow process is just beginning, this seems like an empty place where they have an opportunity to get the group's attention. The leader must hold up traffic, indicating, vigorously if necessary, that although the words have stopped, the flow is still developing. Group members learn to trust this because of the eventual results of respecting pregnant silences.

Very often in summing interchanges between members or between member and leader, a statement will be dropped almost offhandedly that is full of potential open feeling flow. The leader can stop the conversation, even backtrack and ask the member to connect with someone, the leader or another member, and repeat the pregnant statement, focusing on the feeling expressed in it. This repetition, taken out of the conversational context, will often open up, focus, and amplify a flow of feeling through which people can system together. Both participants in systeming need not have the same feeling content, but if they are open to what flows between them, a transformation of structure will take place.

Just as we saw before that a false openness can mask an underlying closed attitude, the reverse can hold and a true capacity for flow through a feeling can be covered and held in check by a cut-off attitude or an obstinate position on a content issue. At this point it is time for the leader to take the risk of being open to apparent closedness. Often truculent anger will be sensed to be covering up a good deal of vulnerable pain. Often helpless, clinging pain will cover a healthy transforming rage. If the leader responds openly and directly, cutting right through the defensive context, the defense might hold and attack the leader's vulnerable open position. The leader's openness, whether in the form of an angry confrontation or a tender gesture of compassion, would be ridiculed or put down as wrong and inappropriate to the situation.

Then there is always the possibility of the mistake of being open to closedness. Closed attitudes tend to repeat, so that a leader can learn in time and such errors can be informative to both the opener and closer, but the process is often costly in embarrassment and trust in the eyes of the group, at least in the short run.

THERAPEUTIC SEQUENCES AND OPTIONS IN LIVING GROUPS

The model of living groups presented here enables the group leader to be quite active, to make creative use of his or her own autonomous living structure, and to be safely mistaken. As they learn the workings of the model, the group members can develop the same opportunities. The model distinguishes several spheres of action—the group boundary level, the content level of interaction, and the structural level of boundary contact action between members. At each level there are complementary paths where the leader or members can move back and forth as the situation indicates. At the group level, there is the option of moving inside or moving outside the boundary. At the interpersonal level, there is the option of working at the content level or working at the structural level. And once at the level of boundary contact action there is the option of summing or systeming.

The typical therapeutic process involves sequences where members, in interaction with the leader or other members, move through the levels of the model and move back and forth through the available options. The art of helping a working member through his or her therapeutic sequence depends upon the helper's ability to utilize his or her own personal structure creatively and to sense intuitively when to make moves between the options. But the process of negotiating this sequence is not based on intuition alone. At each step along the way, at each choice-point, there should be an evaluation of whether appropriate gains have been made up to the present point and whether a shift in focus is indicated or not. It might be that further work is needed, it might be that a shift in options or levels is needed, or it might be that a retreat in the sequence is indicated. The model provides a basis for a clinical experimental approach where choices are made not only by intuition but through a clinical evaluation of results. However, it is not an objective experiment because it is a situation in which both the leader and the member being helped are involved with their own personal structures and both are involved in the evaluation and choice of how to proceed.

A sequence is often initiated by a member from a position essentially outside the boundary. Complaints are voiced or reports are given about events in the outside world. Many times the story is told impersonally and addressed to the group as if they were outside authorities. It takes an autonomous event which might be called "becoming present" to bring the participants in the dialogue into personal connection and thus shift the focus into the here-and-now inside the group space. If sufficient energy and involvement are maintained, an engagement will take place, usually centered around a content level theme. As work is done at the content level, such as questioning, supporting, clarifying feelings or interpreting patterns, choice-points arise where option shifts or level shifts can be made to keep the sequence progressing or to let the sequence terminate in favor of another sequence with greater therapeutic potential arising from another member of the group.

When the group process has settled in with a theme at the content level, the leader has to keep aware of his or her choice between operating in an authority role as a group facilitator and helping professional and the option of shifting to the personal power role that would have to be assumed if the leader elected to initiate boundary contact action. There are many functions falling to the leader that are simply authority-based functions. The leader must define and defend the ground rules of the group. The leader, particularly in the early stages of group development, has to catalyze each member into risking self-disclosure, both of the facts and of the feelings behind them. The leader has to engender an attitude within the whole group of concerned inquiry, with a detective's eye for subtle self-defeating patterns. All of these authoritative interventions come out of the role of a concerned helping professional organizing and supporting the therapeutic work functions of the group. If the leader can engender a cooperative spirit of communicative clarity and curiosity, which includes a sharp eye for indirectness as well as empathic concern, he or she will have set up the proper working attitude of the group at the content level.

But there comes a time after the stories and complaints have been presented and the self-defeating patterns pointed out again and again that continued making sense out of the situation doesn't seem to make sense anymore. This is the time when a shift should be considered in the group process from the knowledge level of content to the action level of personal boundarying. At first it is only the leader who makes such interventions, but, as we have indicated earlier, the group members can sense the differences between open and closed and can learn in a relatively short time to use their own personal structures in boundary contact action. The leader can clarify his or her shifts from professional authority to personal power by shifting physically from outside to inside the group boundary, but, in general, the group has to learn gradually about the nature of this shift in levels from content to structure.

There are signs of a readiness to shift to summing and systeming within the working member as well. Emotional tension builds as content level work gradually becomes less and less productive. Awareness at some level gradually builds that well intentioned attempts at clear communication and disclosure are hitting up against a closed system which is at once subtle and unyielding. GST offers us some clues about the way these closed configurations work. They are, in general, linear feedback structures where linear means that boundaries are not broken. A fixed attitude has been built into the personal structure and any kind of interaction experience that pulls the person away from that set point generates a strong homeostatic response that blindly drives the person through anxiety, rationalization or other defensive behavior to reduce "error signals" that signify a departure from the set attitude. The difficulty is that the response is not a meaningful response to the attitude but a blind mechanized response to error in the system. Thus, constructive attempts to reach understanding of the underlying attitude are experienced as error and responded to just as blindly and automatically as the threats which originally engendered the closed system in the first place. The fixed attitude operating at the heart of this configuration could be embodied in any content. Typical of these might be inner injunctions like "Don't feel good," "Put people down who threaten you" and so on. This is a structural way of seeing the phenomenon of resistance.

There are variations on these closed linear defensive configurations. Transference phenomena can be seen in the same structural light. A fixed view of the leader or member is planted on top of the reality of the person, and any deviation from the requirements of that image is responded to vigorously as error. Positive feedback, where the error is amplified to the point of saturation, also comes into play. Here the group member repeatedly locks into situations which generate more and more anxiety, pain, anger or other mask emotion until the point of crisis is reached. Then the defensive system collapses, only to begin building itself up again. The experience is familiar in therapy of people who build up the same crises again and again to the frustration of those whose empathy they hold and who ride out these chronic crisis cycles with them.

Our model opens up an alternative to the content level approach of attempting to break through this closed system by discovering what motivated it to close. The alternative is for the leader to employ his or her own personal structure and power to meet closedness with closedness in a summing configuration. The decision to enter summing is often sudden and intuitive in its timing. Often a leader will "smell" that the content-defined situation is at impasse, even though everyone, including the closed person, is still trying. Sometimes the summing event comes as a jolt to the person who feels it as an affront to his or her sincerity. Other times the closed person is so wrapped up that summing continues and extends to elaborate lengths. A person in a group a few years ago was coming on very cooperative but essentially closed, so I put him through an increasingly elaborate series of "helping" exercises and it was 15 minutes before he saw that I was summing him and broke open into a much needed flow of anger.

If a leader is closed to closedness it does not really matter what he or she says or does with the member because direct influence is cut off by the boundaries between them. I use wit, irony, paradox, self-centeredness, but a different leader would do well to use whatever he has as a closed person. What is the therapeutic utility of being closed to closedness, as opposed to the traditional approach of standing outside and interpreting the meaning of the situation? First, it reflects the closedness of the person in lively action rather than sterile judgments. Second, it circumvents the necessity to explain *why* or prove that the person is closed. Third, it generates creative responses for which the system is not prepared and shakes it up, often in fun, rather than presenting the very responses the closed system was prepared to defend against. In a sense the non sequitur Koan of Zen is a closed to closedness summing technique.

One of the "laws" of boundarying is that it is a dialectical operation. Every closed boundary opens of itself and every open boundary closes of itself. Even the most ingrained linear feedback systems loosen up sooner or later. Actually, the autonomous act of summing will catalyze such loosening more rapidly than the goal-directed response of probing closedness analytically. Openness breaks through unexpectedly and in unpredictable forms. It often vanishes quickly so the leader must really be alert for a sudden shift to mutual openness and systeming. The cue will sometimes be little more than a break in voice quality or a subtle expressive movement. Whatever it is, the leader had better be there with openness to openness, and prepared for mutual transformation of personal structure.

Systeming is experienced as feeling exchange at the content level. "Suddenly we looked at each other and a rush of warmth arose between us." "The whole group fell into a meaningful silence that we all knew reflected our newfound understanding.'' ''She suddenly cut through the pain which had enveloped her for so long and angrily shouted that she didn't have to put up with that.'' Often the leader or a member more experienced in the autonomous action of opening boundaries will initiate the systeming event. A leader might erupt with an angry confrontation on the members' manipulation of their helplessness. The leader might sense, trust and reach out on the basis of a flow of loving concern to a member who has been massively defending against the need to be reached out to.

While systeming events can only be described in content terms to show their emotional impact, it must be stressed that systeming, like summing, operates at the structural level and must be utilized in the therapeutic process at that level. It is not that we feel love or anger within ourselves and therefore we open our boundaries to express it. It is rather that we open our boundaries and the mutual flow that is generated between us subsequently gets encoded in terms of such content experiences. Meaning is generated separately within each of us. The energy flow configurations that develop in systeming arise through mutual openness between us as a unitary pair system. The powerful function of systeming is to transform personal structures through mutual flow contact between individuals who trust for the moment in openness. Systeming is just as much a risk for the leader as it is for the member being led because the flow could go either in the direction of the member's needs or the leader's, or even in a way which is totally unexpected by both. It is an autonomous act to open up to destructuring flow and the subsequent development of restructuring on a new basis, but this capacity for metamorphosis has been a necessary part of living structure since it began. The summing/systeming process finds its expression in living groups in sequences such as those described.

Both summing and systeming types of boundary contact action generate strong experiences in both leader and members that often have absolutely no bearing on the more rational level of the content communication process that is typical of traditional group process. In many ways, the more eccentric the content of the summing, the more likely it is to shake up entrenched defensive structures and lead to systeming movement. The more emotionally intense the systeming is, the more thoroughgoing the restructuring process can be. In short, the addition of summing and systeming operations to the repertoire of group process adds some very powerful and very personal techniques for catalyzing and consolidating structural transformation.

But the option of calling up this additional power of the group process calls for safeguards against the countertherapeutic abuse of such power. Both summing and systeming recruit deep creative resources from leaders and members, resources that might very well arise from irrational or neurotic bases. If a leader is operating in the domain of outside authority, there is little chance of abuse since the guidelines of that authority are public and specific and preclude such "personalized" boundary contact action. But at the inside level of personal power the guidelines are not specific and the line between acting out neurotic problems under the guise of charismatic intervention and truly creative use of the age-old living structure which is the wellspring of creativity for all humans is sometimes hard to draw. Both summing and systeming interventions are far from foolproof. In fact, they should be "right on" no more than eighty or ninety percent of the time to utilize their full creative potential. Thus, the power of these strong interventions must be covered for with safety devices.

The group boundary option of moving out of the group without moving out of the room provides such a safety valve. If the action of moving out is institutionalized as a basic group ground rule, supported strongly and practiced often without recriminations, the leader will be more willing to risk stronger speculative and intuitive interventions and the members will have the courage to ride with such boundarying events for a while until boundary withdrawal seems absolutely necessary. Many workers in the group field are aware that the potential of group process as a powerful tool of personal change has been only partially tapped. But prudence dictates that vulnerable group members must be protected by a policy of conservatism in interventions. We have stressed that a group can come alive and develop power as a change agent if its members are free to engage in the autonomous actions of moving inside and outside of group boundaries. This option should be exercised several times in each session if the group is to stay alive. The leader can set the norms of how strong summing and systeming interventions should be to generate a level of intensity which results in some withdrawal. Naturally, interventions should not be arbitrarily manufactured as mere provocative maneuvers. It is, rather, a matter of slowly rising to the optimal level of this power, with the leader showing the way and supporting the members' efforts to calibrate the intensity of their boundarying action with each other. Summing and systeming action, tempered by support of boundary withdrawal, provides a group process which safely opens up the way to a much greater degree of utilization of personal and group embodiments of living structure and its not yet fully realized power to regulate itself and evolve itself progressively through autonomous action. If a living group dedicated to helping its members change their personal structures finds the balance of intensity and safety where they can experience one or two withdrawals per session and still be ready to come back and go at it again the next time, they will know that they are working together on their task to a degree that approaches full capacity.

Although there are often fast starts and early terminations, the sequence is quite clear. Once inside and engaged in personal discussion at the content level of exploration, entrenched positions and the thicket of "secret meanings" that come with fixed defensive configurations can be bypassed by shifting into direct boundary contact action which attends to the closed or open structure and sees right through the meanings generated by these structures. Summing actions can loosen up these closed structures without the need to decode them and liberate

structure transforming systeming processes. But when the mutual flow of systeming has come to an end and fragile new perspectives have been developed,
there is a need for consolidation of these structures so that they can be harnessed,
not just in the special trusting world of the group, but in the outside world where
the pressures are greater. It is at this point where a return to the content level
is called for. At this point it becomes a cooperative situation between helper and
helped rather than a conflict between a defender of an unhappy neurotic castle
and a therapeutic knight trying to scale the walls. After a systeming transformation, both are interested in solidifying and consolidating the new position.
Here the appropriate procedures are interpretation, support, reinforcement and
all the content-mediated mechanisms that came to impasse against entrenched
defenses but are now welcomed by both helper and helped. We are transformed
in feeling-flow-based systeming and the transformations are consolidated in cognitive boundary-building processes. Summing operations can also be used here
in a positive way to entrench the newly transformed individual's personal structure and toughen it up for dealing with the outside world.

A word must be said about the act of jumping within and between levels of
the model, from inside to outside and back, from content to structure and back
and from summing to systeming and back. These have been characterized both
in this chapter and in Chapter 2 as autonomous actions. The idea of autonomous
living structure is a difficult and deep one and I have tried hard to show some
of the ways it works in action in the context of living groups. Autonomous
actions are not prewired or environmentally shaped. They are the key operations
through which all living things generate, maintain, evolve and finally dissolve
themselves. I hope the contexts in which we have discussed autonomous actions
have helped to make clear how the introduction of this new idea is necessary
and useful to our understanding of living groups.

The sequence we have discussed in this section is embedded in a higher order
sequence that continues throughout the long-term course of therapeutic living
groups. As each member gains confidence and skill in the process of moving
autonomously from outside to inside to opening to closing and back, and watches
others do the same, they can begin to take stronger risks and permit more
fundamental restructuring operations to take place. The basic idea is that destructuring must precede restructuring. It is relatively easy to change one's
personal structure in little ways. But as the group process goes on, the changes
become more and more fundamental. Old structures are shed and the group
member begins to feel disoriented and naked without the trusty defenses. But
it is only when almost all of the defensive baggage has been sloughed away that
a fundamental turning around can be accomplished. The events, processes and
sequences outlined in this model provide a set of guidelines and concepts for
understanding and enacting this difficult but rewarding process of structural self-
transformation and the consequent emergence of a stronger personal autonomy.

Part IV

New Directions and
Applications for
General System
Theory Groups

Chapter 14

Three Clinical Sessions from a General System Theory Viewpoint

By Helen E. Durkin, Ph.D.

Editor's Introduction. This chapter includes clinical material which illustrates the GST framework broadening the analytic approach to group psychotherapy. Helen demonstrates her views of the levels of systems (group, individual and individual personality organization) with common structural features under the unifying conceptual umbrella of GST.

These examples make clear many GST concepts such as boundarying, the role of emotional and cognitive processes, destructuring and restructuring of organization, and energy exchanges. Throughout, Helen comments on the ongoing clinical experiences.

These three consecutive sessions form a kind of working unit in the total therapeutic process. They were taken from an open, eight-member group in the private practice of combined group and individual psychotherapy. Most of the members had been working together for about two and one-half years. I was unaware at the time that I would be recording the sessions for publication. I worked in my usual way, relegating all theoretical formulations to the background and concentrating on what was going on in the group transactions (i.e., on the empirical phenomena). I relied, as usual, on intuition, guided by training and experience, to produce associations which would enable me to intervene effectively. That way, I could be much more spontaneous within the limits of my role and function as a therapist.

The clinical material will illustrate the way in which employing a general systems supraframework broadens the base and widens the perspective of a core analytic approach to group therapy. Inasmuch as I view the therapy group, its individual members, and their personality organization as three levels of open active systems with common structural features, I have at my command a larger but unifying conceptual umbrella which eliminates certain counterproductive dichotomies, and provides a single overall technical principle which increases my options in selecting specific techniques.

Von Bertalanffy's new model of living structure has particular relevance for the group therapist because it provides vital new information about the isomorphic structural features of human and social systems which determine their mode of exchanging information and energy. I have found it practical to extend the application of this model to the member's personality subsystems.

Therapy groups are composed of members whose personality organization has lost its capacity in the course of ontogenetic experience (i.e., the earliest exchanges with more powerful parental systems) to regulate its own exchanges. The group therapist's essential task from a systems point of view is to remobilize the personality's normal system potential as described by von Bertalanffy. One practical way of implementing this goal is for the therapist to assume responsibility for monitoring the boundarying process, which has proved to be the primary source of change in normal systems. The new model of open systems will provide him with the norms and standards which he aims to achieve. It will serve as a guide for his therapeutic interventions.

The clinical sessions will provide some evidence that, if the group therapist systematically facilitates change in the permeability of dysfunctional boundaries at all three levels of system, they* will undergo progressive transformations which will be reflected in their modes of transacting. Once the suprasystem is functioning as a normal open system, it will serve the therapeutic goal by its influence on its component member systems. Reciprocally, once the therapist facilitates sufficient transformations in the members' personality organizations, the total group transactions will become more effective. The therapist and the group as a whole, then, are partners in the functioning therapeutic system. When any given target system achieves an optimal, though continually changing, proportion of open and closed boundaries, the member will be ready to regulate his or her own transactions. He or she is ready to leave the group.

PATTERNS OF TRANSACTING

We cannot employ the technical strategy of regulating boundary permeability without attending to what flows across the boundaries. According to GST, matter/energy and information cross permeable boundaries and are shut out by impermeable ones. These very general terms were intended to provide a common

---

*Group as suprasystem, individual member as target system, and member's personality as subsystem.

denominator for all living systems. For purposes of therapy, they must be translated into terms which indicate the special characteristics of human and social systems. Experience in individual and group psychotherapy has shown that energy and information in these systems take the form of emotional and cognitive processes. In individual development, they interact from the beginning to form the structural units of the personality and they are regularly reflected in the members' patterns of transacting with others. In groups these patterns of transacting convey energy and information across the interpersonal boundaries.

I am indebted to James Durkin (Chapter 13) and William Gray (Chapter 11), who built their general systems models of group therapy around the role of emotional and cognitive processes in treatment. My application of their findings will be illustrated in the three clinical sessions. I believe that these authors have provided the connecting link between the general and the special characteristics of systems and between the older approaches and the new GST models of group therapy. Their findings will facilitate the transition phase for those who wish to move into a general systems theoretical framework.

TRANSFORMATION

This GST concept refers to the process of reorganization which may occur in any living system (or in its supra- or subsystems) that has imported and processed energy and information in order to counteract its loss of organization from entropy. In the therapy group, transformations may occur in the group (therapeutic suprasystem), in the individual member (target system), or in the member's personality structure (the crucial subsystem). The change will be reflected in the intragroup transactions. On the whole it is a step-by-step process, but when it occurs in a key defensive subsystem it may result in a radical reorganization of the total personality. Each such transformation will affect all other systems and the group as a whole. Transformations in the group as a whole will effect changes in all the members. It has been suggested that therapy groups might well be called transformation groups (J. Durkin, 1976b).

CLINICAL EVIDENCE

The following illustrations are intended to show the way in which changing boundary permeability on any of the three levels will bring about transformations in the members' dysfunctional patterns of transacting, one by one, until they can establish a dynamic equilibrium and can begin to regulate their own exchanges again. The role of emotion and cognition in the operation of human and social systems will become evident. The clinical material will demonstrate also the way in which the new information about systems in general, and the psychoanalytic information about personality systems in particular, may be used to supplement each other in the therapeutic process.

Having ventilated a good deal of anger in the previous session, the group members were in good spirits. This session began with hesitant exchanges of positive feelings among the members. Appreciative and loving comments were expressed between several pairs, irrespective of gender. Their interpersonal boundaries seemed to be opening up and to give promise of further transformations. The therapist listened carefully and soon heard evidence that unwelcome sexual impulses, memories, and fantasies were creating tensions and interfering with the existing interaction. As the attempt at pairing became sexual, angry feelings began to dominate the interactions again.

For instance, Jack admitted that he had been fantasizing about taking Julie home after group some day and kissing her goodbye. Some interjected, "And making love to her?" Jack grimaced and said, "Well . . . fucking her." Jane, who had complimented him for his honesty, now said, "That word! It only means you are more hostile than loving! The hell with that." Julie, who had heretofore been consistently out of touch with her anger, now burst out, "You can fuck off, Jack—I don't need any more like you!" And with that she launched into the sexual problems she had with her husband. She had found herself cold to his advances for quite a while—yet, she said, she wanted to have sex—in fact, needed it, to relieve her constant state of tension. But she felt he always just grabbed at her to satisfy himself. "He never wants to sit down and talk with me—like we do here. He does anything to avoid it." In answer to some questions from the members, she elaborated, "He keeps criticizing me for everything—the way I run the house, treat the children, dress—and for everything." At that point I asked, "What about in bed?" She looked startled and angry but hung her head, bit her lip, blushed, and said, "Oh, you know I can't talk about that . . . it was hard enough to say this much, but mm, a . . . well . . . I did want to tell you I've never had an orgasm—isn't that awful?"

The members asked her to be specific, which she found very difficult. But they began to exchange their experiences with her and a great variety of sexual problems were revealed. Again, Jack was the most candid. He told about the girl he lived with, saying, "Well, you know how it is with Sylvia. How upset I am with her, but I can't ask her to leave . . . well, it's happened with a lot of girls. I make a play for them—never with the girls I admire—but pretty ones, and once I've 'had' them, I get bored and begin to fantasize that they are dirty and probably whores. Oh, I hate it all—but I can't stop it."

I said, "How about here, in the group?" Again, Jack took the lead. Now he added, "I have to confess I've had all those fantasies about Julie—and oh, oh (with a painful expression), she kept getting mixed up in my mind with my kid sister and the horrible escapades we had all the time." He slumped into his chair and looked more and more pained and depressed. But several other members picked up the thread and revealed their fantasies about one another. The interaction was very emotional and mutually influential. They were "systeming" (see Chapter 13).

Toward the end of the hour, Julie was looking angry, but before she could marshal her forces to speak, Margot, who had become increasingly tense and looked "uptight," spoke up loud and clear. In rising decibels she gave Jack a first-rate tongue-lashing, calling him, among worse epithets, a "sneaky, sleezy male chauvinist." She spoke with utter contempt and then turned to Julie and said, in a different voice, "You know, I have to apologize to you. I keep putting you down, but if your husband is like this—you're exonerated in my book. Get rid of him."

Comments on Preliminary Session I

1) The vicissitudes of the group structure in this and the following sessions show a definite relation between the degree of the group organization and the emergence of transformations, or at least their precursors, in the members. It becomes evident that in order to maximize the suprasystem's influence on its members, the group therapist must intervene to keep the group operating as a normal living system as defined by von Bertalanffy. Monitoring the intragroup boundaries is an effective tool for this purpose.

   In the beginning of the session it seemed as if the group might develop a sufficiently stable therapeutic system; however, after a few minutes it became apparent that its dynamic equilibrium could not be established just yet. Their positive feelings had led naturally to sexual feelings and fantasies. Their nonverbal communications and choice of words indicated that their exchanges were increasingly tinged with anxiety and hostility. They created enough palpable tension to prevent optimal movement. Their interpersonal boundaries became less permeable. They listened to one another, but were not about to be influenced any further.

2) At this point, the therapist had to decide whether or not to intervene, and if so, at what level. In the GST context the therapist has several options. An interpretation of the dysfunctional aspects of the interaction between the two group members might have brought about a transformation in their transactions and might have changed the total interaction. Similar results might be expected if the therapist indicated that the group was stuck for the moment in a fight/flight operation. Both were considered briefly, but it seemed best, since according to GST self-determined transformations are

more effective and durable, to allow more time to see if the group could transform itself.

3) I was very much influenced in this decision by my psychoanalytic knowledge of the special characteristics of human personality systems. This group was composed of members who had complained that they were unable to sustain enduring, intimate relationships with the opposite sex. In my clinical experience with them I had learned that, in their earliest loving exchanges with their parental systems, they had felt disappointed, hurt, frustrated, angry and helpless. They had experienced these exchanges as severe limitations on their autonomy, and in some cases as threats to their very existence as separate systems. The patterns they developed to cope with these were ineffectual. Over time the patterns had become mechanized so that the members repeated them automatically whenever they perceived a threat to their identity. Consequently, when they became old enough to be aware of sexual differences and to experience sexual impulses, their old fears were reactivated. To this was added oedipal guilt and fear of punishment. They resorted to their old patterns and were unable to develop new, spontaneous, and realistic sexual patterns of transacting. The group interaction seemed to me to be reflecting this dilemma. Apparently, it was the prospect of loving exchanges which triggered the closing of their boundaries.

4) It seemed to me that if they were given an uninterrupted chance to interact freely on this more primitive level of experience, they might well begin again to open up to one another and gradually restore a new group dynamic equilibrium which would foster change. It was a time for encouraging them to fully amplify their malfunctioning patterns until they became aware of just what they had been doing automatically and to experience how self-defeating their patterns were. Such realization was, I thought, a necessary precursor of change. I therefore listened with particular care to test my analytic hypotheses, and I determined to make no interventions except to give positive feedback or active transport to any new energy and information over momentarily sticky boundaries.

5) My expectations were realized up to a point. The members became involved in exchanging experiences. Their boundaries obviously became increasingly permeable. For instance, Jack "let it all hang out." Some of the others were more cautious, but they did begin to speak more freely. The product of their open interaction was a new dynamic equilibrium in the total group. A group transformation had occurred.

6) It led to several individual transformations. For instance, stimulated by Jack's attitude and supported energetically by the women, Julie was able to get in touch with her formerly repressed rage and to express it unequivocally. She also got in touch with her sexual impulses and fantasies. These were the necessary precursors of more complete transformations to come.

It was not until the following session that she and the others could begin to realize that the defenses which had once served to maintain their separate identity were presently interfering with their ability to accept the love and sexual satisfaction that they consciously wanted so much. For the present they were becoming more clearly aware of the patterns they had been using automatically and beginning reluctantly to sense the need to change.

7) As the group interaction became more dynamic, Margot's face and posture began to show signs of anxiety. I assumed that her fragile personality organization was being threatened by the group's exchanges of energy and information which signaled imminent change. Her own dysfunctional sexual patterns might easily be exposed unless she kept a tight rein on her boundaries. As usual, she summoned hostility to keep her boundary intact. There was enough residual fear of change in the others to make them quite willing to escape to this safer level. The interaction was converted into a dead-end fight in which they dented one another's boundaries, but did not penetrate them. This is an example of dysfunctionally closed boundaries, tantamount to "resistance."

8) The state of the group therapist's personal system is, of course, extremely important in influencing the group transactions. I did not pick up Margot's well-disguised purpose in verbally trouncing Jack, nor his passive masochistic response. Later in the week I realized that I had conveniently rationalized my reluctance to face the global rage which Margot might turn on me if I succeeded in breaking through her boundaries. Unconscious anxiety had closed my own boundaries for the moment. The realization prepared me to utilize the next opportunity to restore a more dynamic group structure. I suspected, rightly, that the group would move into an even tighter static equilibrium at the next session.

9) This section also serves as a reminder to the group therapist that individual systems can influence the structure of the group as well as vice versa.

10) This series of events provides clinical evidence that psychoanalytic information about the special characteristics of human personality system can be harmoniously integrated with the new information generated by general systems theory. They supplement one another.

SESSION II, SECTION A

Where the Action Was: Boundary Change and Transformations

Margot came in briskly and announced, "I'm feeling marvelous. I am so proud of the self-confident way I've acted all week. I took my first tennis lesson—you know, my mother was a great tennis player—and it's the first time I've dared to try it. I always felt so awkward compared to her." The members began to question her, but she did not respond. Instead, speaking volubly enough to shut them out and with great energy, she introduced the news about Billy Jean King's tennis victory over Bobby Riggs. She felt triumphant about it and used it to express her contempt for Bobby and for men in general.

Jack squirmed in his seat and the other men took it as a personal putdown. The group was almost instantly lined up, women versus men. Emotions ran high; the interchange was exciting (energy dissipation), but brought no changes in each other's opinions or feelings. Gradually it turned into a sociological debate with reasonable arguments on both sides. Then it rapidly became repetitive and signs of restlessness began. The boundaries between the two groups were all but impermeable. The group had reached a state of static equilibrium. Clearly an intervention was called for. I said, "I certainly agree with you about some of these sociological issues, but I believe you are using them to avoid your more deeply personal feelings and the experiences which brought you to this group and to this "battle of the sexes."

There was complete silence for a moment—the faces looked stunned. Margot, who had heretofore tended to idealize me and to blot out quickly any negative response to what I said, now burst out furiously: "Sociology—bullshit! You just don't give a damn. You pretend to be modern! You're just an old-fashioned Freudian—you are hostile as hell to women. I remember how mean you were to Elizabeth, a few months ago. You can't fool . . . Jesus, I don't think I can work with you anymore. I'm going to have to leave!"

The other group members looked anxiously at me and quickly away again. I set my discomfort aside and endeavored to stay as open and relaxed as possible. Apparently reassured, they began to express their reactions. Bob, who was a therapist, backed up Margot by pointing out firmly, with a pleased smile, "You are out of order. It was a bad mistake to interfere with our strong emotional interaction!" There were vigorous smiles and nods in the group. But Margot paid no attention. She had retired into deep silence. Her facial expression registered pain; her posture reflected depression. I felt for her but said nothing.

Comments on Session II, Section A

1) As Margot later told us, my silence during her attack on Jack last week had convinced her that I was on her side, so that now she felt betrayed (even a mistake can be useful). Her fantasy of "omnipotence through perfect union with the ideal mother" had been rekindled. Her euphoria served to counteract her growing fear that the open group exchanges would threaten the shaky self-protective patterns to which she had attached her uncertain identity. Her focus on the tennis match had served to disrupt the open exchanges and converted the interaction into a dead-end fight, i.e., a static equilibrium. She split the group in the same way she had split her internal images of the "good" and the "bad" mother, by completely closing the boundaries between

them. Her need to maintain her fragile stability diminished her capacity for growth at this point. Her intervention had the same effect on the group.

2) The intention of my comment was to stimulate the encapsulated "bound out" emotions of the group members, via their spokesman. The release of Margot's undiluted and uncontrollable rage simultaneously broke through her tight inner boundaries and those between the subgroups.

3) The incident gives clinical support to J. Durkin's hypothesis (Chapter 13) that spontaneous emotions, being formless and carrying high energy, have the capacity to penetrate boundaries. In this connection the distinction between Margot's uncontrollable outburst at me and her controlled purposeful attack on Jack in the preliminary session is significant. It warns the general systems therapist that emotions may also be used in the service of maintaining dysfunctional boundaries. They can sit like a dense fog on boundaries.

4) My intervention was a mild example of the technique of creating disequilibrium in a static situation. In order to release its morphogenetic potential, the therapist must take their morphostatic needs into account. In some cases the group provides this support. In the present instance I made a point of calling attention to the common group goals for this purpose and followed through by "containing" their defensive anxiety and rage. My silence was also experienced as "positive feedback."

Margot was completely disorganized for a while. The destructuring which took place when her key boundaries were broken through evoked strong hostility to disguise her fears of system destructuring. My empathic silence probably also had a morphostatic effect of helping her to maintain a sense of identity while facing system reorganization. Quiet acceptance also allows the patient time to decide whether or not to change the dysfunctional patterns which have been challenged. I had to await the outcome. Self-regulation and self-organization are systems capacities which must be respected.

5) The group was somewhat disorganized too, but only nonverbal signs of it were observable. There was stiffness in their postures and tension and anxiety in their faces. Only their eyes darted about with a frightened questioning expression. When they began to speak, their voices were weak and shaky. But they, too, seemed encouraged by my silence and began to express their hidden rebelliousness. Soon there developed a workable, dynamic equilibrium again where further transformations could be expected.

SESSION II, SECTION B: CONTINUED INTERACTION

Restructuring: The Transformation of the Group

Gradually the members began to recall associated experiences from their childhood. I continued to remain silent and serious because I felt that emotions would release bound energy so that precursors of transformations in their transacting patterns would begin to develop. Julie and Robert quickly seized the pause to talk animatedly in a kind of duet about their bitter childhood experiences with their mothers, whom they perceived as harsh and tyrannical. Julie proved the more aggressive. She spoke with great feeling about her fear and rage at her mother, citing some painful childhood experiences in which she had been helpless and ashamed while her mother betrayed her confidences in public. She had, of course, experienced me that way in the preliminary session, but dared not say so. Some members expressed sympathy for her, but Peter told her she had probably been a brat, "Just like you've often been in the group—and you probably deserved everything you got." Other members went into their own experiences and got roughly equivalent feedback. Presently, Julie turned to Peter and said, "You made me mad at first, Peter, but I have a hunch you aren't all wrong." Robert, whom Julie had out-talked, used that as one more example of how selfish and aggressive she had been in the group. Someone added, "What Julie wants, Julie gets!" Julie, instead of breaking into her usual tears, looked very thoughtful and nodded her head. These were first steps in transformation. There were similar exchanges among the others. Most members were participating actively. As they told their own experiences, they got feedback which repeatedly connected their problems at home with their patterns of communicating in the group.

Comments on Session II, Section B

1) Julie led the restructuring process. She had not responded to Margot's sudden bid for alliance last week. She may have been encouraged by what she saw as the downfall of Margot, who formerly had consistently depreciated her as a weak woman. Now she angrily released considerable bound energy. She also began to make connections between her present rebelliousness and her early family experiences. The others followed suit and got in touch with their own rebellious feelings. They exchanged experiences and discovered common feelings of fear and anger at being controlled. Obviously their interpersonal boundaries were wide open. The newly acknowledged feelings and thoughts constituted the first step in the process of transforming the mechanized patterns of transaction they had been using. For example, Julie's unprecedented acceptance of Peter's criticism and her ability to acknowledge her bratty way of asserting herself registered change. So did her ability to respond without resorting to tears and blame. These were but two among the many transformations in process.

2) The transformation of the group suprasystem was apparent in their alert postures, the slowed tempo, and lowered decibels, as well as in the changed content of the communications. It is not the volume but the spontaneity and intensity of the emotional exchanges that indicate the likelihood of mutual

influence among the members. The group had been restructured and could be expected to continue facilitating transformations in the members.

SESSION II, SECTION C: CONTINUED INTERACTION

Completed Restructuring: Unfinished Business, The Reentry of Margot

Margot was still in a funk and I knew this breach had to be healed. I would have intervened if the group were not functioning so effectively. Elizabeth, who had not been as deeply engaged in the last go-around, spoke up first. Very gently and with considerable empathy, for silence was one of her own dysfunctional patterns, she expressed her concern and asked Margot to "come back," because "we need you in." Others agreed.

Now in an entirely different, low shaky voice, Margot admitted, "I have been wanting to get back in, but I also feel like running. In fact, I feel like getting out of here, right now, but I know from experience that I can get more out of sticking it out." At least two members told her how much they valued her presence and her many wise contributions. There were nods and smiles all around. Margot said faintly, "Gee, thanks—I wanted to talk, but every time I started I just felt like blowing my fuse again." Then, sitting up and shifting her tone of voice to a normal one for her, she said, "I've been wondering why the feelings I have toward my father are the same ones some of you have toward your mothers."

Comments on Session II, Section C

1) The group's action expressed the members' joint rebellion against me as an authority figure as much as it did their empathy for Margot. They were working on their own now except for occasional angry remarks to me which kept the channels of communications between us open.
2) Margot's responses revealed the continuing struggle in herself, but the members' positive feedback seemed to have helped her open her boundaries again and take the risk of change. Her transformation was apparent in her willingness to take the lead in continuing the exploration of their attitudes toward parental and current control by authorities.

SESSION II, SECTION D: CONTINUED INTERACTION

Continued Transformations Resulting from Exchanges of Energy and Information

In turn, they asked Margot some specific questions. She said, "That tennis match sure got me going. You know my mother was a brilliant tennis player. She expected me to be too, but she laughed at me for being clumsy instead of helping me and, of course, I didn't make it.'' In a crescendo of feeling, she added, ''Not that she would give me success if she were alive. In fact, she rarely did. She pretended to be loving, but she never really heard what I was trying to tell her.'' Margot began to cry, and as they expressed sympathy, she told us that her mother had taken drugs from time to time—and that made her a different person—a slob. Margot added that she also used to think that her mother was having affairs with a number of men who came to the house.

Someone reminded her how she had hated her father alternately for his weakness toward her mother and for his aggressiveness toward herself. She did not answer, but Bob went on to say, ''You know, that's exactly how I felt about my mother as well as my sister. They were submissive to my father and aggressive toward me.'' He gave some specific incidents. Peter nodded vigorously and said in a small voice, ''It's like you were talking about me and my father—a great big roaring lion, who was meek as a lamb with my bossy, bossy mother. He never backed me up.'' Margot nodded but looked very puzzled.

There was increasing evidence, in this lively interaction which ensued upon Margot's reentry, that most members were acquiring new energy and information and processing it. They seemed to be sensing the connection between their early fears of losing identity and their present modes of interaction. When they had gone as far as they could, I articulated the connection for them by saying something like, ''You seem to be as afraid and angry about losing your independence nowadays, as when you were little and helpless. It doesn't matter whether it's to a woman or a man.''

There were a variety of reactions, but the tendency to express their anger more openly to me was general and the connections with the past were more frequently referred to. For instance, Robert came in quickly. He looked directly at me and said firmly, ''That's exactly why I got so mad at you before when you shut us off. It was like being ordered to come in from play and being marched to bed when I was a kid.'' Others joined in the chorus. Finally, Jane added, ''I didn't mind that, but I was upset when you hurt Margot's feelings. I felt like crying.'' And she became teary again. But Margot herself looked at me a bit sheepishly and said, ''Gee, I hate to admit it but I'm glad you did that. I feel better now that I know I yelled at you mercilessly and yet no one got killed. You didn't even collapse and cry like my mother always did.''

Comments on Session II, Section D

1) Margot's renewed participation in the group showed that, however slowly and painfully, she *had* undergone a shift in her personality organization. She had opened the inner barrier to thoughts and feelings which had long been

ruled out. The transformation was reflected in her group participation. Chiefly, she gave vent to some of her infantile rage to the mother of her childhood. She also got in touch with her heretofore "bounded out" striving for love and the hurt feelings she had hidden from herself. The process of healing the split that had disturbed so many of her adult relationships was begun. She no longer felt compelled to idealize me, nor to provoke Jack with her excessive contempt. She said that she "felt more equal" on the outside too. Her sense of identity became much firmer.

2) Her difficult transformation illustrates the necessity of balancing morphogenetic interventions with morphostatic support. In this case, my quiet acceptance of her anger and the group's strong positive feedback served to reduce her fear of changing.

3) The transformation in Margot added impetus to the other group members. They seemed astonished but relieved at her changed attitude toward me. They closed ranks and brought the group to a higher level of organization. A great deal of energy and information was now being exchanged in their emotional/cognitive transactions. There was a continued open recognition of their rebelliousness toward their parents and they seemed to have an increasing sense of its connection with what had been going on in the group. For this reason they were able to respond readily when I made the connection for them. Robert's answer was a case in point. They were now able to express anger to me directly.

4) The intention of my intervention was to provide information, which, if processed, would allow them, now that their emotions were released, to close the temporal boundaries between their present and past experiences. Old fears of losing their separate identity and autonomy were decreasingly reactivated in their relations with the opposite sex. Their defensive aggressiveness became less necessary. With adequate working-through, it could be anticipated that the released energy could then be utilized in developing new appropriate patterns of transacting in love and sexual relationships on an oedipal level.

SESSION III. INTERACTION

Margot arrived at the next session in a more realistic mood, neither euphoric, depressed, nor in a rage. She was able to look right at me. She said, "I feel more like myself today." She then looked at Jack and said, "You know, Jack, I owe you an apology—I have to admit I don't like your attitude toward women—I hope you can change it—but that was no reason for exploding at you and saying all those rotten things. You are not at all that bad. In fact, I suddenly realize I like you in some ways. I really did take out on you all the contempt I have for my father . . . and . . . yes, and my mother. I don't know which you remind me of more—but I don't like myself for it. I should be fair to you." Jack still slumped down in his chair, said weakly, "Oh, don't apologize, I liked you for it." Margot threw up her hands and with modified, realistic anger said, "Oh, for heaven's sake, Jack—cut that out. You can't really mean it—can't you be honest with yourself and with us for once?" The group chorused their agreement. Later in the hour, Margot was able to talk again about her deep disappointment in what she had experienced as her mother's abandonment. She admitted that it was exactly how she had felt when I proved not to be on her side against Jack the week before. The group explorations continued until the end of the hour. They were "systeming" again.

Comments on Session III

1) Margot's transformation was confirmed by her more realistic and spontaneous comments to both Jack and to me. My uncertainty about the change disappeared when she remained firm in her attitude that he must change in his sexual attitudes toward women. Her more realistic inner images of self and others were again reflected in her transactions.

2) Jack was not yet able to give up his dysfunctional pattern of transacting with the women he chose. He still covered up his fear with subjugation and hostility and then denigrated himself. However, some undigested sign of change was revealed in that he began to be attracted both in the group and outside by stronger, more mature women.

Chapter 15

Experiencing/Leading/ Learning/Observing in the Group Psychotherapy Community Structure

By James E. Durkin Ph.D.

Editor's Introduction. In this chapter I have shifted the GST focus one step up the hierarchy to what I call the group psychotherapy community structure, the level of the hierarchy of living structure that has the group therapy process as a component subcommunity. A boundarying diagnosis is made of traditional group therapy community structures which indicates that they tend to be too strong on the weak or summing interactions and too weak on the strong or systeming interaction modes. A design for a group psychotherapy community is proposed which realigns weak/strong interactions between the experiencing, leading, learning, and observing subcommunities. Such a realignment should generate a more vital balance between summing and systeming processes between people cast in these different roles.

One of the unique features of this design is that all the members of the community observe and systematically analyze the tapes of their own and others' group process as an integral part of their commitment to their community. A device called a "radiance filter" helps to reduce the volume of observer processing by picking out significant episodes in the group process on a structural, as opposed to a content, basis that is relatively free of personal value judgments of the observers. The effect of the observation component will be to "horizontalize" role behaviors and informalize the usually restricted conversations between people in different roles. Such procedures, though unorthodox, should serve to revitalize the group therapy community and their subcommunities, and restore or enhance members' autonomy.

THE DISTINCTION BETWEEN STRONG AND WEAK BOUNDARYING PROCESSES IN THE GROUP THERAPY COMMUNITY

The GST investigator has the option of selecting which level of the hierarchy of living structure is to be focused upon as long as the level chosen is clearly specified. In most of the other chapters of *Living Groups* the target living structure has been the group therapy process, that is, the process of human exchange that goes on in the room during the session. In this chapter I would like to focus upon the level of living structure that contains the group therapy process within it as a substructure. I will call this level of living structure the group psychotherapy community structure.

The group psychotherapy community as a whole structure can be divided into four distinct subcommunities: 1) the *experiencing* subcommunity composed of clients who have agreed to meet together to help each other change their personal structures; 2) the *leading* subcommunity composed of group therapists and co-therapists who employ their theoretical and clinical skills to catalyze and regulate the group psychotherapy process; 3) the *training* subcommunity composed of students of group therapy who are developing their skills and understanding in order to become group therapists; and 4) the *observing* subcommunity composed of (a) supervisors who, on behalf of the institution sponsoring the group therapy process, and (b) researchers who, on behalf of the profession and the public, monitor the process of group psychotherapy.

In Chapter 2 of *Living Groups* I presented a model of the structure of autonomy in living systems in which I asserted that the autonomy exhibited by living forms from cell to society was achieved through the boundarying operation. The boundarying operation was defined as the dialectical play of the event pair opening/closing in a complementarity relationship. The autonomous events of opening one's own boundaries/closing one's own boundaries were seen to be events which caused themselves. Although opening/closing might be responsible to external events, they were not, according to the model, directly caused by such events. The complementarity relationship was described as one in which opening/closing were inseparable but irreconcilable and one in which neither can be deduced from nor reduced to the other. Because there are no deeper level concepts in terms of which to further define opening/closing, they are considered as primitive undefined terms within this conceptual framework. The paradigmatic implications of admitting into the domain of scientific investigation and clinical application events that stood in the complementarity relationships and caused themselves to occur were discussed in the above-mentioned chapter and will only be dealt with implicitly here.

The event pair constituting the boundarying operation is given different names in different contexts within this model. Opening/closing is a boundarying event pair occurring within an individual living structure. Systeming/summing is a boundarying event pair occurring between living structures at the same level when they open to each other's openness/close to each other's closedness respectively. Moving inside/moving outside is a boundarying event pair occurring between living structures at different levels, such as between a group and its individual members. In this discussion of the relations between the subcommunities of the group psychotherapy community structure, I would like to introduce the terms weak interactions/strong interactions to designate the boundarying event pair appropriate to this level of inquiry. The basic thesis of this chapter is that the traditional group psychotherapy community structure tends to be out of balance because of a preponderance of weak interaction processes over the strong kind. After a brief review of the strong/weak balance typical of such communities today, I will set forth a design for an alternative way of structuring the group psychotherapy community structure which should generate a better boundarying balance. Several of the features of this design will seem quite unorthodox. But if it is indeed true that current group therapy communities are out of boundarying balance, such a realignment as the one suggested, or perhaps some other design, should improve the effectiveness of group therapy in performing its prime function of restoring or enhancing the autonomy of the group members who seek help for themselves through this therapeutic modality.

What are the common distinguishing marks that strong/weak interactions and the other boundarying complementarities exhibit? In the first place, boundarying events are structural level events and as such can only be directly observed when they are manifested at the phenomenal level of content experience. Because boundaries are made up of information, closing events are experienced at the human content level as cognitive processing or, in general, thinking. Dissolving boundaries, on the other hand, is experienced at the human content level as emotional flow. Being open to another's openness, systeming, is experienced as an emotional encounter, while being closed to closedness, summing, is experienced as cognitive exchange. We use cognitions to draw distinctions, make definitions, make decisions, and levy value judgments, all boundary-drawing processes. We use feelings to dissolve distinctions so that we, or the contents of our interactions with each other, can flow together in oneness.

Boundarying processes are adaptive; they help us generate, maintain, evolve and, ultimately, dissolve our own personal structures within their environments. The process of adaptation has traditionally been viewed as the interplay of two complementary subprocesses, assimilation and accommodation. Assimilation of environmental influences involves retaining one's own structure by transforming outside influences to suit our internal picture, while accommodation involves transforming one's own internal picture in order to suit outside influences. Weak or summing interactions are assimilative in that, while the assimilating system allows external influences to temporarily deform it, it defends against basic structural transformations. Strong or systeming interactions are accommodative in that structures are transformed through the mutual contact. In Chapter 13, I described how summing and systeming, weak and strong interactions, respectively, lay at the basis of the therapeutic change process and defined the stance of the therapist. Group members transform their personal structures in feeling systems and consolidate those transformations in thinking sums. In order to catalyze this process, the group leader follows the strategy of becoming closed to closedness until it opens and becoming open to openness until it closes.

These differentiating characteristics of the boundarying complementarities provide a background for differentiating strong and weak interactions at the specific level of the group therapy community structure. In the weak interaction mode, the subcommunity boundaries are closed to each other. Because of this, the interaction between members from different subcommunities is pretty much limited to the role behaviors appropriate to their respective positions within the subcommunities. In strong interaction mode, on the other hand, the subcommunity boundaries dissolve themselves, with the result that personal boundarying which leads to systeming between individuals and the mutual structural transformation it brings become possible. The constraining forces of the norms of each subcommunity, while they minimize disorder, preserve status hierarchies and serve to minimize affective interchange and the mutual transformation of structures that such flow brings in its wake. The flow of strong interaction dehierarchicalizes status and informalizes communication so that roles are often reversed, spontaneous processes are equifinally generated, and mutual restructuring of community issues emerges. As an example, when members of the therapist community and the patient community interact in weak mode, strong homeostatic forces induced by their respective roles keep the interchange going according to norms and expectations. But if the therapist and the patient become stuck for an hour in the elevator of the building, unforseeable redefinitions of the relationships could ensue.

Intervening boundaries transform actions into messages. Thus, in a weak interaction mode communication is formalized and denotative, while in a strong interaction mode communication is infused with affective energy and becomes more connotative. Message exchange is an assimilative process because the receiver of a message is always able to decode it in terms not necessarily intended by the sender. This reciprocally corrective process assures that each subcommunity is not overly disturbed by influence from the others. Informal feeling-based connotative language, on the other hand, is both cause and effect of the dissolving of subcommunity boundary structures, an opening process that generates new processes and relational structures among the community substructures.

Boundarying theory at the community structure level or at any other level of living structure prescribes neither openness nor closedness as an end in itself. It prescribes autonomy, which is the self-caused freedom to fluctuate between opening and closing. Autonomy is limited by system constraints which prevent this dialectical movement. The contrasts cited above showing the difference between strong and weak interactions modes operating within the group psychotherapy community structure do not imply that opening is good and closing is bad. Without the organizing functions of roles, and consistent explicit communication, there could be no growth, no feeling in these all-too-human enterprises. But with primarily role-dictated behavior and dictionary-dictated conversation permitted, the subcommunities of the group therapy community structure would "look good" on their own isolated terms but wouldn't grow, wouldn't be alive.

Let us look at some examples of the addiction of our typical group therapy community to weak interaction processes and suggest some possibilities for realignment. Patients don't work with supervisors. In fact, supervisors seldom even observe patients firsthand; rather, they usually deal only with the therapist-supervisee's reports about his or her patients. Naturally, the role hierarchy prohibits patient-supervisor interaction, but with the appropriate flexibility of context a patient could easily communicate a great deal of information about the therapist that could be of immense help in the task of performing the goals of the supervisory relationship. A leader cannot be a *bona fide* research observer. The canons of objectivity which guide contemporary scientific investigation preclude scientific observers observing themselves as subjects of scientific scrutiny. While self-confrontation is considered therapeutic for patients and on rare supervisory occasions is used to help train therapists, it would be unthinkable as a method of collecting serious scientific data.

As a final example of the effects of the predominance of weak interaction mode in the group therapy community structure, consider the dilemma of the trainee who learns to lead by participating in groups alongside group members who come for help. For the patients he is a therapist and for the therapist he is a patient. The trainee is constrained by his equivocal role in the process to close off to the nontrainee members because he is expected not to appear "sick," but at the same time he is considered to be a second-class therapist by leader and member alike. Clearly his ability to both give and receive therapeutic help is limited by his role position within his community substructure. If the rigidity of these subcommunity role positions were liberated by the emergence of strong interactions, the trainee could fluctuate more autonomously between being a whole-hearted patient and being a whole-hearted therapist.

The evolution of this weak interaction-dominated design of the traditional group therapy community was not planned in advance so as to conform to some theory of the optimal therapeutic process. The best explanation for the phenomenon is probably that a series of personal, professional, and sociological accidents got frozen into place and subsequently sealed there by theoretical and policy statements that merely justified what had already taken place. Boundarying theory would suggest that if weak (or strong) interactions completely dominated in any living structure, autonomy would suffer and the structure's life would not be long for this world. If this is the case, how can it be explained that group therapy communities all over the world seem to be far from languishing? This calls for a clarification and elaboration of the criticism upon which this chapter is based. The theory and policies of practice which have come to define the structure and function of the group therapy community are not consistent with the actual practice. What actually goes on in the room during the session and in the training or supervisory sessions is frequently quite at variance with the prescriptions found in books, articles and training manuals. It is more than coincidence that the unexpected breakthroughs dissolving impasses in therapy training supervision or research of group process occur when role behaviors are relinquished or reversed, when the participants "throw away the book," or when an "irrelevant" event causes the participants to open up their boundaries to each other and radically restructure the definition of the situation defined by established policy or theory. It is not the living reality that fails the living theory in our communities; it is, rather, the prescribed theory that fails the living reality.

One can only conclude on the basis of the more-than-chance appearance of these critical opening incidents that the living reality of the various substructures of the group therapy community has evolved as well as it has as much in spite of weak interaction-dominated theory and practice as because of it. This is the fundamental basis for the proposal in this chapter for a design for a group therapy community which realigns the proportion of strong and weak interactions processes in the direction of a more vital balance both between each interacting pair of subcommunities, and between the interacting members of them. If we alter our policies to accommodate to the realities of our actual practices, they can serve as a more potent organizing and guiding influence.

A PROPOSAL FOR A GROUP THERAPY COMMUNITY STRUCTURE WITH REALIGNED INTERACTIONS BETWEEN THE EXPERIENCING, LEADING, TRAINING, AND OBSERVING SUBSYSTEMS

In this outline for the design of a group psychotherapy community structure which is realigned for a more vital balance between weak and strong interactions, I would like to spell out the major features of the community structure in a way which will be flexible enough to accommodate to a variety of different sets of local constraints imposed by the supersystem within which the community might be implemented. This design could be realized alternatively within a clinic, medical school, an academic department, a clinical psychology or social work program, or a traditional or nontraditional service agency. Specific procedures could be adjusted accordingly. The description will be general and practical, as any proposal generated without a specific institutional context in mind would have to be. The exception to this level of generality will be the description of the technique by means of which videotapes of the group's sessions will be reduced to "radiant episodes" at a rate which will keep observation functions current week by week with the other community functions. More detailed focus will be given to this phase of the structure's activities because of the unfamiliarity of the procedure as well as its technical nature.

The major part of the project should run its course in a single year, although there should probably be about a year of preparation and a year of wrap-up afterwards as well. Only the main year will be fully staffed and salaried. The group psychotherapy community structure I envisage will consist of 18 primary participants and three back-up staff. All 18 will be joint members of the experiencing, leading, training, and observing subcommunities. There will be three individuals designated as leaders, presumably of markedly different "schools" of psychotherapy, but the other 15 participants will share the co-leading function on a rotating basis. The technical back-up force will consist of one full-time cameraman/videotape technician and two part-time observation specialists who will also serve various administrative and clerical functions. One leader, the project director, will serve full-time on the project while the two other leaders will serve one or two days a week. The participants who will be selected from the client community, the paraprofessional community, and the community of interns and residents will serve one full day and one evening per week during the year.

The activities of the community will alternate between experiencing, leading, training, and observing the group therapy process. The central event, of course, is the session experience. Although there are 18 primary members of the community, sessions will consist of only six of them at a time—one leader, one co-leader designated for that session, and four members. Each leader will lead one session a week, each member will experience a session once a week, and each member will be designated as co-leader about every five weeks. The membership of each six-person session will not be constant however, but rather systematically rotated so that over the long haul all possible pairs and triplets of community members will attend the same session together with equal frequency. In general, this means that every member will be in a session with every other member and every other pair of members in a triplet about every third session. Holding group psychotherapy sessions with nonuniform membership in each succeeding session is unorthodox, to be sure, but such a procedure is necessary for the operation of the "radiance filter" for videotape reduction to be discussed in detail below. The rotation system can be rationalized therapeutically by conceiving it as an 18-person group in which it takes a little longer to get to know all the members than one in which everyone physically meets every session. Actually, if videotape observation is included as a meeting event, each of the 18 community members will see each other at least one two-hour session a week and one-third of them for eight hours a week. Thus, every member will witness every session one way or the other.

In the weekly routine each member will experience one group session, do a live observation of the second group, and do a more extended videotape observation of the third group. The portions of the time that are not taken up by these primary tasks will be devoted to individual supervisory sessions, observation training, quality control sessions, and presentation of videotape documentaries, which focus on themselves, other members, or group phenomena that occur in or out of the sessions produced by any of the members of the community.

It is clear that the main innovation in this realigned group psychotherapy community system is the opening up the formerly closed (weak interaction mode) boundaries of the community subsystems to each other. The most obvious addition is the task of systematically observing the group process, on line and on videotape. This means that the experiencing, leading, learning and observing subcommunities suddenly have a new task, or, more properly, a strongly modified task, other than what goes on in the room during the session. Although at first glance it would seem that the second task merely creates a second set of four roles for each of the four subcommunities, the effect of this innovation is not of moving merely to a second order system, but the more fundamental transformation of moving to a second degree system in which the relationship between the roles of each subsystem is fundamentally altered as it is opened into strong interaction mode. It will not be a matter of first performing in the experiencing role and then moving across a boundary to role two, the observing role, for the new reality will be the shifting back and forth across roles and dealing with the creative disruption that such fluctuation will inflict on each of the formerly neatly defined roles.

Earlier on in this discussion we reviewed the two basic effects of a predominance of weak interaction mode on the group psychotherapy community system's subsystem interactions. In brief, it was asserted that in the weak mode role behavior was homeostatically controlled and conversation was formalized and explicit. With the infusion of strong interaction processes into the community, roles should become "horizontalized." Traditionally, the group leader has a higher status role than the patient. As a result, the leader is condemned to being right. When a patient violates his or her role assignment by questioning the question put by the leader rather than answering it as is expected of patients, homeostatic forces of the system quash this untoward incident by defining the point as inadmissible, interpreting it as transference material, or condemning it as acting-out. The arbiter of such issues is, of course, the therapist, although it is *de rigeur* for therapists to modestly deny this prerequisite of ultimate authority when confronted with the issue.

But when we add the new dimension of the community's task of sitting down every week and making sense about what "those people" on the videotape are doing, members of the community usually assigned the high status roles should soon discover to their surprise that the rules of the game have changed. The structure of the situation has been transformed by the inclusion of a new participant, the taped material from the sessions. In the live sessions, decisions about what happened are made, often by changing the subject or the level of the conversation, by dint of the authority of the leader. But when leadership and membership are sitting side by side in front of a tape that can be replayed as many times as necessary, they find themselves to be co-equal peers who both must defer to the tape as the final authority. To win issues by resort to special knowledge or by punctuation events becomes much more difficult than it is for leaders during the session. Alger (1969) has noted this effect.

The quality of conversation is also changed by the introduction of strong interactions. In the human species, many of the goals of its members are achieved and many of the problems of its members worked through in conversation. Conversation abounds in the typical group therapy session. Questions are put and answers are given. Opinions are solicited, expressed, and countered. Suggestions and demands are made and decisions articulated. When weak interactions dominate and relationships are bounded by role demands, the content of conversations is explicit and denotative. When strong interactions are opened up in the community, the opportunity emerges for "I-Thou" conversations where mutual openness, liberating the flow and uncertainty, leads to restructuring of problems and unexpected resolutions of situations. The complexity of the situation generated by the process of flipping back and forth between the sessions and the observation of the sessions should result in conversations of an emotional and connotative nature.

Special mention must be made about the training benefits of this realigned group therapy community structure. It has been suggested that psychotherapy trainees suffer the fate of all students, namely that they are expected to demonstrate learning without showing ignorance. This dilemma is exacerbated when what it is they are expected to learn is how to be just like the wise and perfect person who is their trainer-model. Questioning the question, as students must do to gain autonomy, is so easily taken as a threat by leader-trainers because it appears to question their adequacy and authority as well as their knowledge. The horizontalizing of the training process brought about by the suggested design will liberate the trainees to learn and grow in many ways. Because there are three different group modalities going on rather than only one supreme method, comparisons can be made and their relative effectiveness questioned and tested without blame. Trainees can now check things out with fellow experiencers, leaders, and observers in the observation task in a way they could not do exclusively in session. If the norm is set for open dialogue rather than authoritative edict, experiencers, leaders, trainees, supervisors and researchers will all benefit.

PROBLEMS OF SELF-OBSERVATION AND THE FUNCTION OF THE "RADIANCE FILTER"

The observing subcommunity is usually bounded away securely from the experiencing and leading subcommunities in the traditional weak interaction-dominated group psychotherapy community structure. This tends to be true in the supervising, research and training functions of the observing subcommunity. The currently orthodox paradigm of objectivity, which has defined scientific investigation for the past few centuries, holds to this fundamental canon: The subjective properties of the observer shall not enter into the description of the observed. That is basically what objectivity means to a working scientist committed to maximizing objectivity at all costs. This objective attitude carries over into the group therapy community in the leading subcommunity where many therapists feel that the uncovering of transference reactions is the *sine qua non* of psychotherapeutic practice. In a transference reaction the subjective properties of the patient are attributed by that patient to the therapist.

The need for a clean separation between the knower and the known, between the observer and the observed, is integral to practice of psychotherapy process research as it is currently constituted under the paradigm of objectivity. Those who conduct such research typically try to steer quite clear of the experiencers and leaders as *persons,* transform records of these subjects' behavior to objective data as early on in the research process as possible and try never to make contact with the generators of those data subsequently. The aim of this research subcommunity is to employ analytical techniques to discover "what is really going on" in the sessions so that the professional community of fellow process observers will be enlightened and stimulated toward further research effort. It is clear that this objective model of psychotherapy process research is in a state of very weak interaction with the experiencing, leading, and learning communities.

Most members of the research community would be of the opinion that "serious research" is impossible with patients, trainees, and leaders processing their own process. They would assume that if the process is generated out of one's own subjective life experience, it would not be possible subsequently to assume an objective research attitude about the data as a serious researcher must. Feedback confrontations are perhaps therapeutic tools, but they are incompatible with the goals of objective research. It is little wonder that when researchers invade the session with their cameras and clipboards, the patients and leaders distrust what is going on. The distrust is probably justified on the basis that there is very little direct connection between what the researchers are after and what will directly benefit this particular experiencing subcommunity. But it is perfectly possible for an autonomous research community to establish other goals for itself than the enlightenment of the research reading/writing profession. In this community design the primary goal of the research process is the autonomous goal of clarifying the theory and improving the practice of its own community!

The self-observation of the tapes and the in-session self-observation form two complementary components of the proposed group psychotherapy community structure. The goal of the observation component is to develop a theory of the community's group experience by assembling a network of critical incidents from the tapes into a working model of their own group process. The complementary goal of the group process is to develop a working theory of self-observation which will stand the members in good stead out in the world, including their real world observation task. The problem of self-reference is devastating to the paradigm of objectivity, but it is the crucial point of growth of the paradigm of autonomy. In the boundarying model of autonomy I presented in Chapter 2, I interpreted opening/closing in terms of the complementarity action structure/language structure. The complementary experiencing/observing process proposed for this community can be seen in these boundarying terms as an observation task whose goal is to encode the action structure of the experiencing process into a language structure which articulates a theory of that process. In complementary fashion, the experiencing task could be seen as one whose goal is to embody the theory of groups autonomously formulated by the members in the work of the observation process into an action structure which operates during the sessions. Only a vital balance of strong interaction/weak interaction structure can make this yin/yang system of experiencing and observing a practical ongoing reality.

Under conditions of a better alignment between strong and weak interactions, the self-observation process, rather than being a bothersome accommodation to essentially foreign research demands, becomes the vital turning point generating autonomy for the community and its members. The traditional weak interaction-dominated group therapy community is limited by its one-way exclusively vertical status system. Because the therapist is always "wise and perfect" and the patient is always "getting better," the therapeutic conversation is often condemned to explicit cyclicity, and the "you pay, I cure" status quo proceeds interminably or until, by fiat, the patient and doctor announce a cure. The new dimension added by this way of achieving strong interactions means that role restrictions are opened up. Suddenly the doctor and the patient are sitting side by side on a common task outside the session, a task which either party has equal power to impede or facilitate. It might be a restructuring revelation for the therapist to see how the patient works on the job, or for the patient to see the doctor racking his or her brains. One of the big problems of therapy is that there is no practical means except by potentially biased self-report to evaluate how the patient (or therapist) is doing in the outside world, even though the patient is actually going to the therapy for the specific purpose of doing better there. The task of observing accomplished this. The observation task that they share should be a natural therapeutic working alliance between them.

But the autonomy for the community as a whole and for the members of its subcommunities does not exist exclusively in the observing process, no more than it does in the experiencing process. The locus of autonomy is in the boundarying. The goal of therapy lies precisely in the jumping back and forth between the language structure task of codifying a theory of change and the action structure task of working through to an embodiment of that change in personal structure in the sessions. Only by having a distinction or boundary between the inside task and outside task, a boundary which at the right moment of transformation needs to be dissolved, can the deep-seated autonomy process that operates in every patient, every group, and every living structure be restored and enhanced within the community.

But what about the specifics of the observation task? What are the means by which the observational goal of constructing a theory of their own group is to be implemented? The goal of the experiencing function—to utilize the group process to change one's own personal structure—the goal of the training function—to utilize experiences with the group process to develop one's own leading skills—are all goals whose end products are essentially invisible because such skills reside within the heads of the members of the subcommunities who aspire to these goals. The observing function's goal, as defined above, is fundamentally different, for the aim of the observing process is, through research activity, to produce a physical tape document in language structure that will codify the guiding theory which guides the flow of action in the experiencing subcommunity. As a language structure, the end product of the observing function must be explicit and out in the open. It is not the goal of observing to make better or more scientific observers out of the observing teams, nor is it to publish articles. It is the more applied goal of making the therapy process more effective in helping experiencers change their personal structures. Thus, the observing process must deal with explicit pictures, numbers or words, both in their process and in their final product contribution to the community.

Historically there have been two different approaches to the systematic observation of the kind of complex interaction process that goes on in the room during the sessions, the scaling approach and the scoring approach. The scaling approach proceeds by 1) exposing the scaler to the stream of behavior; 2) having the scaler integrate the meaning of what went on in that stream inside his or her head; and 3) having the scaler read out on a number of rating scales the degree of a judged quality estimated to inhere in the scaler's perception of interaction process. The scoring approach proceeds by 1) exposing the scorer to the stream of behavior; 2) having the scorer isolate the designated units of interaction; 3) having the scorer assign each isolated unit to one of a number of categories on one of a number of category sets. In each case the final product is usually a data matrix of persons × events × categories or scale scores which can be compared or contrasted according to certain theoretical predictions or hypotheses. Although the scaling approach is procedurally less cumbersome because it exploits the natural power of the human mind to integrate and evaluate perceptual experience in step 2) of the scaling process, while in the scoring process the definitions, combinations, and tagging procedures of the units and categories have to be worked out painstakingly in the open, we will adopt the scoring approach in this project. The main reason is that scoring is reversible and scaling is not. One can go back to the raw tapes to retrieve a particular unit or a sample or a particular sequence of episodes, to check on the reliability of the scaling, or to check back to verify an hypothesis that has been subsequently developed. In scaling you have the numbers but no way of coordinating particular events on tape with particular scaling judgments emanating from the scaler's head.

If the project runs for 40 or so weeks and three two-hour sessions are run each week, the total amount of experiencing process will run to 240 hours. Since the analysis time to raw tape time ratio can run up to 100 hours of analysis for each hour of tape, the problem of keeping feedback current with the ongoing weekly experiencing sessions is obviously critical. The key to the effective observation of such high volumes of interaction process is in deciding what data to *disregard*. As maximum volume can be disregarded with a minimum of loss of meaning, the problem becomes tractable.

While the naturally occurring unit of individual behavior is the utterance, the naturally occurring unit of group interaction process is the episode. An episode consists of a set of utterances by two, three or more group members which is united by a common structure, function, process, or content. A practical method of unitizing episodes has been devised and a measure of the reliability of such unitization decisions has been worked out (J.E. Durkin, 1960). A model of the flow of unit episodes which accounts for abortive or fragmentary episodes, overlapping episodes and hierarchically structured sets of episodes has been developed (J.E. Durkin, 1960). In practice, a well-formed episode usually lasts for between 20 seconds and four minutes and anywhere from 20 to 50 well-formed episodes can be dug out of a one-and-a-half to two-hour session. Summing all the relevant figures, we come up with a library of about 5000 episodes. This constitutes the pool of raw data for the group psychotherapy community structure.

But the job of processing episodes every week, each lasting, say, two minutes on the average, is too much volume for the community to handle. Further data reduction and elimination are necessary. One filtering device will be to restrict consideration to well-formed episodes involving only three individuals, one of whom must be either the leader or the co-leader designated for that session. These leader-member-member episodes will be called LMM episodes for short. What is the rationale for such a restriction? First, a record of a therapeutic process needs a leader and a patient for individual therapy and a leader and at least two members for group therapy. Other than that it is simply that choices must be made and sacrifices countenanced to make the system a practical one. Besides, in a strongly interacting community, everybody knows everything, with the result that both experiencers and observers will be fully aware of the LMM filter and gear their decisions accordingly.

My guess is that well-formed LMM episodes will amount to about 1600 over a year, 40 over a week, and about a dozen over a session. But still further filtering is necessary if episodes are to be not only prepared but also fed back meaningfully into the experiencing, leading, and training functions. However, all seasoned experiencers, leaders, learners and observers of the group therapy process are well aware that all episodes are not uniformly eventful; nor are they equally contributory to the goals of therapy. To tell the truth, most episodes are rather redundant, while a few represent a truly significant change in the state of affairs of one or more group members. If a good deal of the episode units of the process must be simply disregarded because of the time limitations of working up episodes for feedback to the group members involved, not to mention the time it takes to consider such episodes, then it would be good strategy to select as rich a vein of episodes as possible. Let us name an episode in which a significant transformation in the group process has taken place, a "radiant episode." The problem then becomes to develop a "radiance filter," and presumably one with a "control knob" so that the volume of radiant episodes can be increased in accordance with time and observer efficiency conditions that might vary from week to week.

But, of course, the big problem with the radiance filter concept is that each radiance filterer will filter out a different kind of radiance depending upon his or her personal or theoretical involvement in the process being filtered. What would be desirable is a filter that would filter radiance on a structural level rather than the content level that is so susceptible to idiosyncratic interpretation. Fortunately, an application of boundarying theory provides us with just such a structural radiance filter. It will be recalled from the summary of the complementary manifestations of opening/closing in different contexts that two interpersonal processes, systeming/summing, were distinguished, interpreted for the content level of human interaction as feeling/thinking, respectively, distinguished as to their adaptive functions of accommodation/assimilation, respectively, and identified as embodied in matter-energy/encoded in information, respectively. In Chapter 13 the therapeutic dynamic that we transform ourselves in feeling systems and consolidate the transformations in thinking sums says in essence how boundarying processes operate in the therapeutic process. It suggests that summing functions are homeostatic and keep members convergent on an equilibrium state defined by their general personality dispositions, neurotically acquired or otherwise. Systeming functions, however, are structure-transforming processes and represent the organic destructuring and subsequent restructuring of personal structures that catalyze the desired movement in therapy. In terms of this model, it would be desirable for a radiance filter to select such systeming events while passing over summing events.

It was mentioned in Chapter 2 that summing and systeming themselves summed together, that is, the two processes were linearly related and operated together in a mixture like salt and pepper rather than in a compound like sodium and chloride in salt. There is a statistical model and procedure which can and

has been adapted (J.E. Durkin, 1970) to separate out the salt of summing from the pepper of systeming in an empirical way. The several studies conducted which used this methodology have in general supported the assertions of boundarying theory. The method is called a subjects by subject factorial design in the analysis of variance (S × S ANOVA). Rather than using levels of a given treatment, the S × S ANOVA design systematically rotates the membership of groups, as we have done in our rotation scheme described above, in order to disentangle the variance attributable to convergent personality variance stemming from individual group members from divergent "encounter variance" which emerges out of mutual systeming interaction of groups or subgroups as autonomous wholes. It is an empirical method of determining quantitatively the degree to which a whole system is greater or lesser than the sum of the contributions of the members making up the parts of that system. In experimental work (J.E. Durkin, 1970) it has been shown that experimental situations predisposing and persons predisposed to accommodative restructuring through mutual openness generate a greater proportion of systeming variance than those who are disposed only to assimilative structure-maintaining processes. It can be inferred from the logic of this S × S model, together with the support of these empirical findings, that radiant episodes, episodes of transformation in the group, are structurally equivalent to systeming variance and can be picked up by means of this method.*
Thus, there is an operational radiance filter available for our task.

To give an example of the radiance filter, let us assume that the homeostatically consistent part of each group member's interaction performance is averaged over all the partners in interaction that they have interacted with in the history of the community. This average score on some descriptive measures could function as a baseline for the convergent individual personality disposition effect on each of the members of a given LMM episode. To be specific, let us hypothesize that the emotional intensity, scored on a one to nine rating scale, has been calculated over all the episodes to date in which each of three participants in a given LMM participated. Let us assume that all three have achieved a low emotional intensity "batting average," say 2-2-2 for the three of them. If the next episode in which this combination of three members generates is scored "5," this rating would be radiantly high because it exceeds their usual baseline levels. On the other hand, if the emotional batting averages of the three participants averaged 8-8-8, then the same score of "5" would be radiantly low because it fell below their homeostatically guided individual dispositional expectations. This somewhat simplified example should give an idea of how radiance can be picked up independently of subjective bias as to what radiance is in each context.

It must be made clear that a variety of different kinds of scoring category systems can be utilized by the radiance filter. But no matter what the code is,

---

*The equivalent method of multiple regression is probably more practical to use in this project.

the radiance filter will "light up" when three individuals who habitually behave in one way all of a sudden begin to diverge from that path because they are restructuring themselves. The radiance filter can be adjusted to pull out a greater or lesser proportion of all well-formed units. As a practical matter, there are times when an observing team cannot handle a large volume, as when they are learning a new coding system or when they are going through an emotional struggle in their group and acting it out in the observation task. At this point the community's workload can be lightened by reducing the volume of radiant episodes chunked out by the filter.

Probably the most unique characteristic feature of the radiance filter is that it is a structure-based measure rather than a content-based measure. Because of this it can be said that episodes of significance are selected without the intervention of human value judgments. To be sure, the original coding decisions such as the one in the example of coding the level of emotional intensity are based on human judgment and its attendant error, but the crucial step of computing radiance based on structural continuities and discontinuities in these measures is in a real sense "untouched by human hands and minds." With the radiance filter the nonlinear feedback loop between experiencing and observing can be closed, as tightly or as loosely as necessary, on a session-by-session basis. If the observing can help the community develop a theory, and therefore a guide to action, of where the group sessions and its members are going, detect when they are beginning to lose it, and identify what new events and influences are emerging in the group process, then the opening up of strong interactions based on this trusty data can facilitate the development of a robust autonomy both within and between community subsystems.

SUMMARY AND CONCLUSION

Ian Alger (1969), in a pioneering article on the use of videotape feedback in psychotherapy, summarizes his experiences in the following way:

One of the most interesting consequences of the videotape playback technique is the encouragement of a more democratic and equalitarian therapeutic relationship. When both therapist and patient have equal access to the objective data of the therapy session, the traditional roles are challenged. The more mutual task of observing data and attempting to understand the interactions, as emotional reactions are now recalled during playback in relation to the incidents under review, promotes the development of a true research project. In this, the emphasis falls not only on the suffering of the patient, and the skill of the therapist, but also on the televised, and now so evident, humanness of them both (p. 430).

These words, spoken over a decade ago, say very much what this chapter is trying to say. GST is a theory of life, a theory of the structure of autonomy through boundarying. The community that has grown up around the group therapy session is, or can become, alive in the same literal sense that the group and its members can become alive. If the diagnosis of the group psychotherapy community structure postulated in this chapter is true, then explorations have to be made which develop a community structure with more room for strong interactions and the destructuring-restructuring encounters that they generate. The closing of role boundaries, and the conservative codification of role-determined conversation patterns is essential to the life of the therapeutic process, but the complementary opening of boundaries leads to equally essential life functions. I have argued that any living group or community will equifinally hit upon ways of generating, maintaining, evolving and dissolving its own autonomy, but that the traditional structure of present-day therapeutic communities and the prescribed policies and practices that seal such structures in place simply do not preach what they practice. A way of organizing stronger interactions is needed. The project proposed in these pages is one such exploratory attempt. There may be many other ways of realigning the group therapy community structure, but many facets of the boundarying theory of the structure of living autonomy are brought together in this particular design. Central to the idea, of course, is the inclusion of a research observation-oriented component of the community in strong interaction with the experiencing and other components. The radiance filter, described in a simplified manner above, should go a long way toward making the time requirements of productive systematic observation a practical matter.

Naturally there will be a host of practical problems that will arise during the planning and execution of such a project. Many in the field who are entrenched in the traditional ways will find objections galore to this new departure. For example, can this structure survive and thrive with relatively disturbed patients? If you break the whole structure into its component subcommunities, each traditional subcommunity will probably claim staunchly: "Why that's not the way we do (experiencing)(leading)(learning)(observing)!" Perhaps that is a testament to the organic cohesion of this design, for the parts, then, would be completely integral to the whole. To those who would object to the unorthodoxy of this group psychotherapy community structure, autonomous living structure says: "Grow in your own way with your own design, for life that doesn't grow dies."

Chapter 16

Learning General System Theory through an Experiential Workshop

By Donald T. Brown, M.D.

Editor's Introduction. Articulating a complete and consistent account of GST is one thing, but making working clinicians curious about GST comfortably familiar with the concepts and applications of GST is quite another. This is exactly what Don Brown has taken as his task over the past few years and this chapter is a report of his efforts. He points out correctly that the mission of the GST committee is to explore the ways in which GST can clarify the theory *and* improve the practice of group therapy, *but* no single spokesperson has been able to accomplish both parts of this mandate. In his experiential workshop on GST, Don seems to be finding a way to do just that.

Don is in the lead on the implicit second stage of the GST committee's task—to get people to actually internalize and use GST in their clinical work. You might even call Don's workshop a GST consciousness-raising workshop, for, after all, we gain autonomy by learning about the autonomy which GST offers us.

Don's methods are experiential. He generates involvement, draws on prior knowledge, and taps in on people's personal learning objectives. These educational methods are in perfect harmony with the nature of GST as a self-conscious way of life. The syllabus of one of his typical workshops is clearly self-conscious, for it specifies not only the content (column one) and the instructional purpose (column two) but also the living events that occur within the hierarchical system of workshop participants. This kind of workshop plan reveals both the subject and object of the workshop: to generate a living system that learns about itself in the process of living!

One of the problems that has faced the members of the GST committee is that we never seem to get around to coming up with clinical examples, a procedure that is *de rigeur* for all clinical reporting. At first we thought is was just a matter of time—after we really got the concepts down pat, the examples would simply fall into our hands. But we have done that and the clinical examples are still a problem. When we do generate them we are not quite sure whether we are simply pasting on new labels. But Don has somehow cracked that problem. What he does is to enable the people to *live* their clinical examples. In terms of the complementary concepts of action structure and language structure spelled out in the foundations chapter, living structure needs to fluctuate back and forth between them if it is to become alive and autonomous. What Don has done is to provide a format where this is just what happens. As an example, the experience of moving from a three-person system to a six-person system and then to a twelve-person system lets people experience the action impact of systemness. It does not make rational sense for the people in the six-person group whom you felt so negative about when they intruded on the sanctity of your triad to give you such a positive feeling when in the next level of grouping our holy six are subsequently intruded upon by those horrible other six. It is this juxtaposition between language structure and action structure and the jolting fluctuations between the one and the other that makes the experience a living one as well as a learning one. Don has not gone beyond an all-day format, but my guess is that if the group were allowed to live and grow together, the clinical examples, unforgettable ones, would soon appear.

Soon after its creation, the Task Force on General System Theory of the American Group Psychotherapy Association agreed that general system theory could serve as a unifying principle within which group therapists of widely different theoretical persuasions could communicate and that an understanding of systems concepts could have practical implications in conducting therapeutic groups. Our task, then, was to make the theory familiar and comfortable to the Association's members, most of whom are primarily oriented toward clinical work in private practice or agency settings. Papers by individual task force members helped to clarify their specific areas of interest, interpretations and applications, but for a time there was no single voice to state the basic theory and relate it to the members' concerns. Our presentations, at first, tended to provoke the reaction that we were introducing "new words for the same old ideas," which were no more useful than the existing set of theoretical formulations.

It was in response to this situation that I developed a small workshop format in which the experience of the individual participants as they became a working group could be used to illustrate some fundamental general systems concepts and thus set the scene for discussions of their own clinical experiences in a new frame of reference. This workshop has now been presented more than half a dozen times in different settings and, to judge from participants' evaluations, has achieved its purpose. In this paper, I will review the factors involved in designing the workshop, describe the process, and discuss some experiences in applying this approach to learning general system theory.

THE DESIGN DECISIONS

The instructional challenge was as follows: "How can one convey some or all of general system theory to group psychotherapists so that they will both understand and be able to apply their understanding to their clinical work?'' Some first order constraints grew out of the structure of the annual conference of AGPA, the major forum for Task Force presentations. Workshops could last either two and a half or five hours. Group size could be either small (25) or large (up to 100). The setting would be a barren room with uncomfortable chairs but with flexibility in seating arrangement and some audiovisual capabilities.

A second set of considerations was related to the potential participants. Experience indicated that they would differ widely in discipline, background, work setting and experience, but that the specific composition of the group could not be determined in advance. Moreover, individual understanding of general system theory might range from complete unfamiliarity to considerable sophistication. In some instances, participants might consider themselves to be "using systems" in their work, but their ideas of systems theory might be quite out of line with the basic framework developed by the Task Force.

The material to be taught also influenced the potential workshop design. In its purest form, general system theory is highly abstract and this high level of generality must be maintained if the material is not to be seen as one more theoretical framework in conflict with those already internalized by participants. On the other hand, the principles, once grasped, make sense in everyday, commonsense terms. Moreover, the training workshop is a system with all the properties thereof, and the training process can be used as an example of a system in operation.

A final group of factors grow out of my bias, as a teacher and consultant, toward the use of the andragogical principles of Malcom Knowles*. He holds that adults learn best from experiences which are involving, which draw on their own prior knowledge, and which are seen as relevant to their personal learning objectives. The atmosphere of the AGPA conference favors this kind of learning. There is a tradition of the use of experiential designs and participants expect to share in a teaching/learning process.

After considering all these dimensions, the instructional intent was stated as follows: "Given no more than 25 participants with at least two years' experience in group psychotherapy, to conduct a two and a half hour workshop in which the early stages of development of the group will be organized so as to provide participants with cognitive and experiential exposure to selected GST concepts and to allow them to make associations to their personal clinical experiences."

The concepts selected for presentation were:

1) General system theory as a set of general principles applicable to all systems, including therapeutic groups.

The Modern Practice of Adult Education: Andragogy vs Pedagogy, 1970.

2) The concept of system hierarchies and the possibility of shifts in frame of reference between hierarchical levels (the holon phenomenon).
3) Isomorphy of system functions between hierarchical levels.
4) System boundaries: their nature, importance and management.
5) Flowing balance (*Fliessgleichgewicht*), autonomy, growth and equifinality.
6) Positive and negative feedback cycles.

Once these decisions were made, it was possible to evolve a detailed plan for the workshop.

THE WORKSHOP

Time	Activity	Instructional Purpose	System Effects
9:30 a.m.	Leader introduces self and briefly describes workshop plan: to experience, discuss and look at applications.	Set general expectations; reduce anxiety; establish learning climate.	External boundaries defined by leader; role as boundary manager accepted.
9:40	Individual self-appraisal and commitment: each person silently reviews what he or she knows about GST and writes a personal learning objective for the workshop, e.g., "By the end of this workshop I will be able to see how GST relates to my work with abusing parents."	Focus on needs of participants; prepare for next exercise; set base for evaluation of individual learning.	Individual, as system, autonomously sets boundary level of openness/closedness to information.
9:45	First stage of group formation: triads are created by a "counting off" process and asked to share data on what each knows and doesn't know about GST. Each person formulates a question, e.g., "I would like to know how feedback loops work.", which the triad has not answered satisfactorily.	Limit information and initial anxiety to personally manageable level; create bonds in small group; begin to define small group roles.	Through information exchange, small group defines member roles and boundary. Often an "expert" emerges.

Time	Activity	Instructional Purpose	System Effects
10:00	Second stage of group formation: two triads are combined and get acquainted by discussing their unanswered questions. They attempt to compile what is not known and of general interest to the group of six.	Increase information available; focus on what is not known to set stage for input to be provided.	Triad becomes subsystem of group of six; boundaries must open and new boundary form around larger group. Often some rivalry/conflict within group appears.
10:15	Cognitive input: short lecture by leader on "Universal Properties of Living Systems."* No questions or discussion allowed.	Provide reference point for clarifying misconceptions and redefining individual needs; surface conflict with leader.	Leader's function as "expert subsystem" is defined; total system quality begins to emerge; negative feedback cycle between subsystems and leader regarding questioning and discussion; individuals (subsystems) open boundaries to new information.
10:30	Process cognitive input: groups of six review lecture and identify unanswered questions. Workshop leader instructs group to agree on a single question of common interest and presses groups to achieve consensus within time boundaries.	Rework knowledge base; test for understanding; experience coming to consensus; questions selected set stage for final discussion.	Group of six as system must integrate new information in its subsystems. Process of arriving at consensus strengthens group's external boundaries and clarifies internal functions. Groups often have difficulty with consensus task.

*See Appendix A.

Time	Activity	Instructional Purpose	System Effects
10:45	Coffee break: leader reacts informally with participants, reinforcing their learnings, correcting misconceptions, and answering individuals' questions.	Reduce tension; allow further interchange of information.	Leader (subsystem) interacting with individuals (sub-subsystems) provides positive feedback for specific behaviors within group of six (subsystem) and modifies leader's role in total workshop group (system). Small groups tend to stick together during break, leading to increased awareness of intergroup boundaries.
10:55	Processing of remaining questions: individuals from one group of six pair with individuals from another. Each pair discusses the consensus questions of their two groups. (Examples of group questions are given below.)	Learn by asking a question and explaining it if necessary. Test level of personal knowledge.	Subsystem boundaries opened to information from outside.
11:10	Sharing data from consultations: groups of six reassemble and share information gained in cross-group pairs.	Second review of knowledge gained individually and collectively.	Subsystem integrates input gained during open stage; boundaries close again.
11:25	Examining process: return to original triads and discuss what happened in the morning. Workshop leader suggests that they use systems terms in stating their observations, e.g., "As we interacted, we defined boundaries for our small group."	Begin linkage of knowledge with experience.	Further reinforcement of subsystem functioning by internal feedback cycles. Individuals are simultaneously within and outside the group (referential process).

Time	Activity	Instructional Purpose	System Effects
11:40	General discussion: individuals and subgroup spokespersons share their ideas on process of workshop. Leader provides connections to concepts. Examples from clinical practice of participants introduced.	Complete linkage with here-and-now events in the workshop and past experience.	Awareness of relationship of small groups and leader in workshop as total system. Individuals (sub-subsystems) now can see the multiple, isomorphically-functioning levels in the present setting and relate this awareness to experiences elsewhere.
11:55	Evaluation of learning: individuals review their written personal learning objectives, appraise and write down their level of achievement, and rate the usefulness of learning.	Cementing of learning through review and consideration of application; evaluation of the workshop.	Dissolution of subsystem and total system boundaries; individuals become separate systems, changed by experience.
12:00	Termination: leader states his sense of group accomplishment, asks for and processes feedback, e.g., "I had a sense this morning that most of you were becoming comfortable with GST concepts. How does that fit with your perceptions?"	Closure	Leader and individuals interact in feedback cycle (usually positive or deviation-reinforcing re new behavior).

EXPERIENCES IN CONDUCTING THE WORKSHOP

The example described in detail above is a synthesis of the timing and sequencing used in several presentations of the workshop. Certain events have occurred repeatedly and have been the focus of profitable discussion. Among these are:

1) The emergence of one member of the original triad as an "expert" and the need for the two "experts" to negotiate role definitions when the two triads merge and the sextet needs to reach consensus. The isomorphy between the process in the triad and that in the group of six is easily seen by all.

2) Participants become exquisitely aware of boundaries at the point when the

two original triads are merged into a sextet. Each triad is initially a self-contained system and its boundaries must open before the sextet can work as a whole system. Even then the triad remains a subsystem. In later discussion, this experience serves as an example of the forces which establish, maintain and dissolve boundaries and allows exploration of specific techniques of boundary management.

3) When the leader finishes the mini-lecture, individual participants usually ask questions. The leader does not respond to these directly but suggests that they be discussed in the groups. Later this interaction is used as an example of a negative (deviation-reducing) feedback cycle which maintains the stability of the original groups rather than allowing more general interaction. This example sets the stage for clarification of the common confusion between the popular usage of the terms "positive feedback" and "negative feedback" and the specific meanings of these terms in general system theory.

The kinds of group consensus questions chosen give a sense of the level of understanding achieved by the participants. In one workshop the list was as follows:

1) What is the practical application of GST for an individual trying to make sense of interrelated systems to which he belongs?
2) With reference to a family, how does one use GST in identifying problems and determining interventions?
3) How can this theory be used to help people approach their individual problems?
4) What level within a suprasystem do I look at to solve a particular problem?
5) What is the difference in how you would go about changing a living system versus a non-living one?
6) How do you define the boundaries of a system in order to intervene to solve a problem?

This set of questions clearly maps out the primary concern of the participants, i.e., applicability of GST to individual change efforts. It also indicates a beginning appreciation of the concept that the therapist has many options for action designed to produce change at a particular level in a hierarchy. (The subsystem can be changed by a suprasystem intervention and vice versa.) Further, there is growing awareness of the interactive nature of the intervention process: The therapist does not act on the client but is in interaction with the client, as both are parts of a system.

In the workshop which generated these questions, the workshop group went on to discuss specific examples of these general concerns. The evaluations of the workshop were uniformly high and indicated that most of the participants felt that they could make practical use of the concepts presented.

Variations have included: 1) The elimination of the pairing exercise in favor of a second stage of merging the groups of six into a total workshop group—This allowed a second experience in boundary expansion and reintegration; however, the dynamics of the larger group were so complex that it was more difficult to see the isomorphy with the earlier experience. 2) Extension of the workshop duration to a full day and introducing mechanisms to allow sharing of clinical experiences and their analysis in general systems terms—Because the workshop participants have been so heterogeneous in level of experience, work setting and theoretical persuasion, this design did not achieve its intended purpose. It seemed as if each individual had to reinterpret the material presented in his/her personal frame of reference and that this process took precedence over the use of the general systems frame. As a result, the discussions remained at a level similar to that seen in multidisciplinary case conferences. One experiment in which the leader modeled the translation process seemed to bypass this dynamic, but it, in turn, intensified the reliance on the leader as the sole source of expertise. Perhaps the direct application of general system theory to clinical incidents must be deferred to a second stage in the educational process. The internal experience of the Task Force would indicate that the concepts must be fairly well accepted before such a process can occur.

Ultimately, the work of the General System Theory Task Force should validate the aphorism "There is nothing so practical as a good theory." This training design begins that process. Obviously, a single short workshop is not going to change the long-established beliefs and practices of participant group therapists. What this approach does do, however, is to introduce the concepts in the context of a here-and-now experience and allow a beginning consideration of what applications might be developed. The workshop serves as a living analogue of the change process in therapeutic groups. Individuals have allowed new knowledge to cross their boundaries and have been changed thereby. The next steps in the validation must be to develop further educational experiences which will allow participants to test for themselves the utility of general system theory both as a framework for productive discussion of divergent theories and as a base for clinical interventions.

Appendix
PROPERTIES OF LIVING SYSTEMS

1) A system is an organization of parts in dynamic interaction. The properties of the system consist of more than the aggregate of the properties of the individual parts and interactions; the organized whole is more than the sum of its parts.
2) Every system is part of a *suprasystem* which itself displays all the qualities of a system. Suprasystems, in turn, are parts of a next level order—"supra-suprasystem," and so forth ad infinitum.
3) Similarly, the parts of a system are themselves *subsystems* which display system

properties. Subsystems have parts, "sub-subsystems," and so forth.
4) It is possible to view any organization of parts as an entity (system), as a suprasystem to its component parts, or as a subsystem of a larger organization. Such viewing, sequential or simultaneous, does not create conflict since all views are equally "real." This is known as the *holon phenomenon.*
5) Similar properties and/or functions are observable in all systems, hence in subsystems and suprasystems. This similarity is known as *isomorphy.*
6) The limits of a system comprise its *boundary.* Interactions with other systems take place across the boundary. Boundary transactions consist of the input or output of energy and/or information. The nature of the boundary, its state of openness or closedness (permeability), defines the possible transactions.
7) Random transactions across a boundary will eventually result in a state of *entropy* (randomness, non-differentiation, non-organization).
8) In *living systems* the opening/closing of the boundary is *autonomously* controlled. This continuous opening/closing process, called *boundarying,* distinguishes living systems from non-living systems.
9) Because of their property of autonomous boundarying, living systems can maintain a state of *negentropy.* They regulate input and output to maintain stability and to move toward increasingly complex organization, e.g., to grow; differentiate functions; develop specialized subsystems.
10) The processes of maintaining stability (morphostasis) and differentiating/ growing/changing (morphogenesis) occur simultaneously and continuously in all living systems. The interaction of these processes is a *flowing equilibrium (Fliessgleichgewicht),* which appears as a *steady state* (the recognizable wholeness of the system, its *gestalt).*
11) As systems develop and grow, specialized structures (subsystems) are differentiated to deal with the autonomous processes of boundarying and the maintainance of the steady state of stability and change. Such structures often operate through *feedback* principles.
12) In a *feedback mechanism,* a transaction across a boundary initiates a return transaction (message) which affects the continuation of the original transaction.
   a) In *negative feedback,* the returned message acts to cancel the original transaction (limit deviations) and thus maintain stability. Too much negative feedback can lead to maladaptive limitations.
   b) In *positive feedback,* the returned message acts to reinforce the original transaction (amplify deviations) and thus create change. Too much positive feedback can lead to maladaptive excesses.
13) The path of differentiation and growth in any given system will be affected by both external factors and internal autonomous operations. It will, however, tend toward an *equifinal state* which is characteristic of its class and limited by its inherent possibilities.
14) Over time, systems display states of relative overall stability (*morphostatic*) and relative overall growth (*heterogenetic*). Shifts between these states may occur suddenly. Within a heterogenetic state there may be a relatively sudden development to a higher level of organization. Such *equifinal jumps* may result from the accumulation of a critical level of negentropy (an excess of available energy) or may be stimulated by an interchange of energy with another system through an especially open boundary.

Chapter 17

System-forming Aspects of General System Theory, Group Forming and Group Functioning

By William Gray, M.D.

Editor's Introduction. Bill Gray has been involved at the heart of GST for many years. He was a personal friend and protege of LvB and for a long time has contributed to the theoretical and scientific development centered around the Society for General Systems Research.

This chapter is a theoretical tour de force presenting some of the conceptual underpinnings of his basic goal of studying system formations rather than just standing systems. He presents detailed explanations of several profound and basic ideas which lie at the foundations of system-forming in particular and GST in general. He then tries to draw the connection between them and relate them to stages in therapy group development.

Included in this list of systems ideas is 1) anamorphosis, the inherent negentropic buildup of living structure which offers an alternative to the mutation with selection synthetic theory of evolution; 2) autopoiesis, which provides a structural model of an autonomous life-sustaining system; 3) Prigogine's principle of dissipative structures which suggests a model of how nonequilibrium structures generate themselves; 4) some recent neurological findings concerning the relation between higher and lower brain centers which support his formulations in emotional cognitive structure theory; 5) some work of LaViolette which supports the notion of the intimate interplay of emotions and cognitions in the buildup of system formations; and 6) some new work of Beck demonstrating structural sequences of development in therapy groups.

Gray attempts to relate all these fundamental new ideas to the basic process of system formation presented in Chapter 11 and recapitulated in this one. Gray's model of system formation, with its bonding of fragmentary system precursors when supported by a relevant nurturing environment and energized and organized into a fully functioning system through the equifinal process of thematic fluctuation, is clearly related to the general autopoiesis model in the abstract and the very kind of exploration and improvisation going on in the therapy room that suddenly coalesces into a productive episode.

This chapter is not easy reading because of the concentration of profound and somewhat abstract theoretical constructions. But the reader must realize that many of these ideas are as new and speculative as they are profound and that they have yet to be worked through theoretically and given a wide range of applications. Thus, an approach of merely getting the sense of the ideas and finding how they relate to Bill's methods might be more appropriate than trying to sweat through each detail of each idea until full detailed comprehension is reached. This section of the book is on future trends. The details of clinical use of system formation theory are spelled out in Bill's Chapter 11. This chapter should be read as a looser, more speculative attempt to bring order into the process of system formation which Bill has pioneered.

General system theory (GST) deals with the world of living structures, whether these be biological or psychocultural. Group psychotherapy also deals with living structures and is itself an evolving, evolutionary living system—thus the interest of group psychotherapists in GST. One might hope that understanding what a system is would be enough, but it is not. Again a quotation from von Bertalanffy:

Every machine—the most complicated servomechanisms and electronic brains of modern technology included—consists of lasting components: transistors, wires, circuits and the like. Exactly this, however, does not apply to the living organism which is a prototype of the Heraclitean *panta rhei,* maintaining itself in a continuous flow and change of components. The structures controlling the processes within the system itself are at the same time maintained and destroyed, amalgamated and regenerated, decomposed and recomposed. Modern scientific research has shown that this "dying and becoming" in an organism is taking place at an unsuspected speed (von Bertalanffy, 1975, p. 119).

Thus systems are always forming and unforming, and so the study of system-forming is simply an essential part of the general system theory. It is an unfortunate but historical fact that the study of the prehistory of systems has been neglected in the field of GST, apparently because the notion of "system" was a new and exciting entity. To a degree this appears also to have been true in group psychotherapy, where more attention has been paid to group process than to how it is that a group forms.

From the beginning von Bertalanffy was critical of the neglect of the study of organizing forces, and expressed this most clearly in his disagreement with the total acceptance of neo-Darwinism, or the "synthetic theory of evolution." What he disliked was the "nothing but" claim of synthetic theory that evolution was essentially accidental in nature, with selection, acting by way of differential reproduction, being the directive agent in evolution.

Selection *presupposes* self maintenance, adaptability, reproduction, etc., of the living system. These, therefore, cannot be the *effect* of selection. This is the oft-discussed circularity of the selectionist argument. Proto-organisms would arise in the primeval slime, and from them organisms would evolve by chance mutation and subsequent selection. But in order to do so, they must already *have* the essential attributes of life. . . . If we are unwilling to accept preformation, we cannot assume that all human genes were present in the primeval amoeba and that evolution consisted merely in genetic loss or deletion. Such a notion would be more fantastic than that of the seventeenth century preformationists who assumed that all future humans were preformed in Eve's ovary. Little is known, however, about the origin of new genes, with the exception of rare cases of duplication which might make genes available for new functions. This seems a rather poor mechanism for the great sweep of evolution (von Bertalanffy, 1968b, p. 71).

Von Bertalanffy's answers were that there were principles of self-organization at various levels, which had an emergent quality requiring formulation at each particular stage and at each level. But in their expression there are what von Bertalanffy refers to as "technological constraints;" that is, only certain pathways appear to open at each level, expressed as parallelism at the genetic, developmental, and organizational levels. Thus, some new system formations are compatible with ongoing viability, and others are not. It is this type of variety with constraint that accounts for the close similarities, or isomorphisms—the formal correspondences between widely differing systems—that are at the base of von Bertalanffy's formulation of GST. Thus, also, the basic characteristic of living systems is their magnificent order within an enormous number of elements and processes. The characteristics of life do not lie in the specificity of individual processes but in the fact that they follow a certain pattern which guarantees the maintenance, restoration, or reproduction of the system. Thus, the basis for living structures is invariance, but with the emergence of new properties it not only preserves invariance, but may enhance it.

For a therapy group to emerge as a self-organizing living system, an invariant developmental process must be present, although the particular structure can be expected to be unique. This is described with exquisite clarity by Beck (1974).

AUTOPOIESIS AS THE BASIS OF LIVING SYSTEMS

The basic objection of von Bertalanffy to the synthetic theory of evolution was its reliance on "accident," with selection acting by way of differential reproduction as the directive agent in evolution. The telling point is that selection presupposes self-maintenance, adaptability, and reproduction of the living system, and as such cannot be the effect of selection. This has been answered in the work of Varela, Maturana, and Uribe (1974) in their formulation of autopoiesis as the fundamental organization of living systems.

Notwithstanding their diversity, all living systems must share a common organization which we implicity recognize by calling them "living." At present there is no formulation of this organization, mainly because the great developments of molecular, genetic and

evolutionary notions in contemporary biology have led to overemphasis of isolated components, e.g., to consider reproduction as a necessary feature of the living organization and, hence, not to ask about the organization which makes a living system a whole, autonomous unity that is alive regardless of whether it reproduces or not. As a result, processes that are history dependent (evolution, ontogenesis) and history independent (individual organization) have been confused in the attempt to provide a single mechanistic explanation for phenomena which, although related, are fundamentally distinct. . . .
We assert that reproduction and evolution are not constitutive features of the living organization and that the properties of a unity cannot be accounted for only through accounting for the properties of its components. In contrast, we claim that the living organization can only be characterized unambiguously by specifying the network of interactions of components which constitute a living system as a whole, that is, as a "unity." We also claim that all biological phenomenology, including reproduction and evolution, is secondary to the establishment of this unitary organization. Thus, instead of asking, "What are the necessary properties of the components that make a living system possible?" we ask "What is the necessary and sufficient organization for a given system to be a living unity?" In other words, instead of asking what makes a living system reproduce, we ask what is the organization reproduced when a living system gives origin to another living unity? (pp. 187-8).

The autopoietic organization "is defined as a unity by a network of productions of components which 1) participate recursively in the same network of productions of components which produced these components, and 2) realize the network of productions as a unity in the space in which the components exist. Consider, for example, the case of a cell: it is a network of chemical reactions which produce molecules such that 1) through their interactions generate and participate recursively in the same network of reactions which produced them, and 2) realize the cell as a material unity. Thus the cell as a physical unity, topographically and operationally separable from the background, remains as such only insofar as this organization is continuously realized under permanent turnover of matter, regardless of its changes in form and specificity of its constitutive chemical reactions."

The biological evidence available today clearly shows that living systems belong to the class of autopoietic systems. To prove that the autopoietic organization is the living organization, it is then sufficient to show, on the other hand, that an autopoietic system is a living system. This has been done by showing that for a system to have the phenomenology of a living system it suffices that its organization be autopoietic.
Presently, however, it should be noticed that in this characterization, reproduction does not enter as a requisite feature of the living organization. In fact, for reproduction to take place there must be a unity to be reproduced: the establishment of the unity is logically and operationally antecedent to its reproduction. In living systems the organization reproduced is the autopoietic organization, and reproduction takes place in the process of autopoiesis; that is, the new unity arises in the realization of the autopoiesis of the old one. Reproduction in a living system is a process of *division* which consists, in principle, of a process of fragmentation of an autopoietic unity with distributed autopoiesis such that the cleavage separates fragments that carry the same autopoietic network of production of components that defined the original unity. Yet, although self-reproduction is not a

requisite feature of the living organization, its occurrence in living systems as we know them is a necessary condition for the generation of a historical network of successively generated, not necessarily identical, autopoietic unities, that is, for evolution (Varela et al., 1974, pp. 188-9).

Thus in the autopoietic concept, when reproduction is introduced, the pathway is open for increase in complexity and organizational richness, that is, the negentropic and anamorphic features that are so prominent in evolutionary process.

ANAMORPHOSIS AS THE BASIS FOR EVOLUTION AND CHANGE IN LIVING SYSTEMS

An ascent, or "anamorphosis" in evolution . . . a general progression of evolution towards higher organization, comparable to a similar trend in individual development, is a phenomenological fact and a matter of the paleontological record. This transition toward higher organization is not an expression of a subjective value judgment, nor connected with vitalism; it is a statement of fact, describable at any length in anatomical, physiological, behavioral, or psychological terms. . . . The conventional theory of evolution considers adaptation and evolution under the same terms of reference, both to be explained by random mutation, selective advantage, and differential reproduction. However, in my opinion, there is no scintilla of scientific proof that evolution, in the sense of progression from less to more complicated organisms, had anything to do with better adaptation, selective advantage, or production of more numerous offspring (von Bertalanffy, 1968b, pp. 66-7).

Bertalanffy's answer to this problem was that

. . . there are principles of "self-organization" at various levels which require no genetic control. Immanent laws run through the gamut of biological organization. But then, these obviously are not the outcome of random mutations *cum* selection, nor is evolution completely outer-directed (von Bertalanffy, 1968b, p. 69).

Thermodynamic considerations introduce another dimension into the problem of evolution. Any organismic system is both thermodynamically open and information-carrying. If one of these features is lacking, we cannot speak of a "living" system. . . . Considered thermodynamically, the problem of neo-Darwinism is the production of order by random events. Order and local decrease in entropy can, of course, take place if "organizing forces" are present. For instance, a crystal can be formed in a solution due to the action of lattice forces. But in the absence of such forces, information can only be converted into noise, but not vice versa. . . . We may expect further insights from a future synthesis of irreversible thermodynamics, information theory, and the laws of supermolecular organization (von Bertalanffy, 1968b, p. 73).

Bertalanffy's theory of open systems was the beginning of thermodynamic explanation of anamorphosis. Thus,

Another seemingly vitalistic characteristic of life is its apparent violation of the second law of thermodynamics, which states that physical processes must tend toward increasing probability, toward increasing entropy. Living systems, in spite of continuous metabolic reactions, maintain themselves in a state of fantastic improbability. In embryonic development as well as in evolution negentropic processes result in increasingly higher order and organization. The contrast becomes explainable, however, if we realize that organizations are open systems. For here the physical and chemical reactions are not limited to those which increase entropy; we now have to reckon also with a transport of entropy. By introducing matter, the system is supplied with free energy or negative entropy. For this reason the maintenance of an improbable state, the transition to higher organization and the decrease of entropy become thermodynamically possible and permitted in open systems (von Bertalanffy, 1975, p. 120).

But as Bertalanffy well knew, an understanding of living systems requires an understanding of the origin of life, that is, an understanding of organizing forces in the non-living realm that could produce anamorphic structures, and which through their enhancement could lead to a series of transitional forms and eventuate finally in living systems themselves.

PRIGOGINE'S PRINCIPLE OF ORDER THROUGH FLUCTUATION AS THE BASIC ANAMORPHOSIS FORMING PROCESS

The 1977 Nobel Prize in Chemistry was awarded to Ilya Prigogine for his discovery that in certain systems, such as self-catalytic chemical reactions, perturbations that get far enough away from thermal equilibrium will no longer subside, but will continue to grow, eventually reaching new stable configurations far from equilibrium. Further, they have the property of being able to maintain themselves against thermal disruption by a continuous throughput of matter and energy, which carry off internally generated entropy to the outside. Because of this ability to dissipate entropy, Prigogine gave them the name of "dissipative structures."

What is fundamental is that such dissipative structures are not limited to living systems, and thus serve as the self-organizing forces out of which living systems later evolve. Thus, as Prigogine explained in an interview, his own work can be traced from the example of the vortexes and convection currents that develop in a fluid being unevenly heated.

Vortexes are highly correlated motions. Here is an example where the theorem of minimum entropy production for near equilibrium systems, as I proposed in 1945, is not valid. On the contrary, nonequilibrium differences of temperature create molecular order. This is the prototype of a dissipative structure. I reasoned that if this is possible in hydrodynamics, why wouldn't it be possible in chemistry generally? So I came to the idea of dissipative structure in chemistry that would exist at some distance from equilibrium. What I went on to prove is that the condition necessary so that new structures may appear is some kind of catalytic or cross-catalytic step. Since then many reactions of this type have been discovered experimentally in biological and other systems. It is clear that we are dealing here with structures that exist in states that are far from equilibrium. This is what is so interesting, because life processes work under nonequilibrium conditions. And we see now that in the form of dissipative structures the same is true of many ordinary physical chemical reactions, and so we begin to see the origins of resins, chemical associations, and life itself (Prigogine, 1977, p. 4).

Because the system-forming process of order through fluctuation is the fundamental source of increased complexity, it would seem justified to refer to this process as leading to anamorphic structures, and therefore to rename what Prigogine "dubbed" "dissipative structures" as anamorphic structures. Anamorphosis is *the* critically important function, although, of course, it depends on the capacity of such structures to dissipate entropy, but goes beyond this.

AUTOPOIESIS AND ANAMORPHOSIS AS THE BASIC SELF-ORGANIZING PROCESSES

Both autopoiesis and anamorphosis have been demonstrated to be the organizing forces that would have to be present for living systems to have emerged. Prigogine has demonstrated the frequent formation of anamorphic structures in the non-living realm, while Varela and Maturana have done the same for autopoietic systems. Thus, Varela, Maturana, and Uribe (1974) summarize the autopoietic process as follows:

A. There are mechanistic systems that are defined as unities by a particular organization which we call autopoietic. These systems are different from any other mechanistic system in that the product of their operation as systems thus defined is necessarily always the system itself. If the network of processes that constitutes the autopoietic system is disrupted, the system disintegrates.

B. The phenomenology of an autopoietic system is the phenomenology of autonomy: all changes of state (internal relations) in the system that take place without disintegration are changes in autopoiesis which perpetuate autopoiesis.

C. An autopoietic system arises spontaneously from the interaction of otherwise independent elements when these interactions constitute a spatially contiguous network of productions which manifests itself as a unity in the space of its elements.

D. The properties of the components of an autopoietic system *do not* determine its properties as a unity. The properties of an autopoietic system (as is the case for every system) are determined by the constitution of this unity, and are, in fact, the properties of the *network* created by, and creating, its components. Therefore, to ascribe a determinant value to any component or to any of its properties because they seem to be "essential" is a semantic artifice. In other words, all the components, and the components' properties, as well as the circumstances which permit their productive interactions, are necessary when they participate in the realization of an autopoietic network, and none is determinant of the constitution of the network or of its properties as a unity (Varela et al., 1974, pp. 192-4).

THE RELATIONSHIP BETWEEN ANAMORPHOSIS AND AUTOPOIESIS

It is important to note that the condition of autopoiesis is itself the result of an anamorphic process, that is, a system-forming process, but one which would have no meaning if autopoiesis did not ensue. Thus a dualistic interpretation between "forming" and "ongoingness" is recommended. The central feature of autopoiesis is autonomy, but the interaction of anamorphosis and autopoiesis is featured by additional capacity for the development of allopoietic systems, that is, systems such as artifactual productions, as classified by Kenneth Boulding (1977) as being of material, organizational, and personal types. Interestingly, artifactual systems, which begin in an allopoietic, or "other produced" fashion, tend, as they become more complex, to become autopoietic, an experience that is easily verifiable in group therapy. In this way social systems, economic systems, ideological systems, etc. tend to become autonomous and create "situational logics" that we as individuals must then deal with. To the degree that they serve as organizing forces in our own system-forming processes, both individuals and groups have an allopoietic side. Concepts, then, such as allopoiesis, anamorphosis, autopoiesis, and situational logic, are names to describe "organizational laws at all levels," a search for which has been strongly recommended by von Bertalanffy (1975, pp. 144-5).

GENERAL SYSTEM PRECURSOR FORMATION THEORY

This is an original theory begun in 1956 that addresses itself to the question of how it is that systems form, an expression of my own interest in origins, and which turned out to be an attempt to redress the imbalance in general system theory of overfocused attention to the study of ongoing systems and neglect of their origins. In regard to the latter point the opinions of James E. Durkin and Jerzy A. Wojciechowski are critical. Durkin states, in a report entitled, "Bill Gray's Mysteries Revealed!":

Definitions: Synchronic—an ahistorical orientation which looks at a structure as a contemporary interplay of forces at a given moment in time. Diachronic (dialectical-chronometer) is a developmental approach which focuses upon structures changing through time. GST people and structuralists tend to get stuck in a synchronic orientation, but Bill Gray properly insists upon equal time for the diachronic orientation. His model focuses on the system-forming/system-blocking event, and properly so because of our neglect of this process (1978a).

Wojciechowski, a Canadian philosopher, who has developed the field of the Ecology of Knowledge, stated in a personal communication (1979),

I am very pleased to tell you that your paper, "General System Formation Precursor Theory" is absolutely first rate. It impressed me greatly for two reasons. First, because of its truly creative approach to the treatment of criminal patients and the very revealing use of systems theory with apparently such good results. Your work proves the usefulness of the systems approach in yet another area. The second reason why your work has impressed me is of a more technically philosophical nature. In your very perspicacious criticism of Standard Systems Theory, you have rediscovered the Aristotelian analysis of change. Contrary to Platonic idealism, which underlies Systems Theory, Aristotle accepted change as an aspect of reality which has to be analyzed and understood if we want to understand the world we live in, because change is the basic mode of being of the material realm. His explanation expounded in his "Physics", is based on the theory of matter and form, i.e., on the idea that whatever changes is essentially and necessarily composed of two contrary yet complementary principles: passive-matter and active-form. Neither of them is capable of separate existence, at least in the material world. Change is then seen as the actualization of a potency.

It is the enhancement of capacity to deal with diachronic processes and change that underlies the value of general system precursor formation theory in therapeutic settings. It has proven to be particularly valuable in the treatment of juvenile delinquents and offenders against the law, where rapid development of an internalized awareness of the system-forming process and its precursors is essential, for system formations of criminal type are also autopoietic, so recidivism will tend to occur unless system precursors are modified so that a new and noncriminal autopoietic system emerges.

The important elements in the use of general system precursor formation theory in therapy are the following concepts:

1) *System precursors.* This is the name we give to entities which have the capacity for forming an ongoing system when two or more are brought together in a relational sense. The world is full of system precursors, ranging from simple ones, such as a candle and oxygen, which can "system form" into a candle flame if an organizing event is present, in this case a method of achieving ignition temperature. A man and a woman are necessary precursors for that system formation called marriage, and individual people are the system precursors to the formation of a psychotherapy group. In the case of criminal activity we have found that, in the crime of "breaking and entering," feeling locked out is a necessary, although not sufficient, system precursor, while a sensitivity to the detection of evil and a conviction that evil must be fought are always to be found as system precursors to the crime of assault and battery. One might say that it is better not to introduce yet another term, and simply say that all these events are the result of system activity, but then one would have to postulate ongoing system activity, even in the case of events that occur infrequently, as well as for enormous numbers of events, burdening then the notion of system with a degree of complexity that would make it meaningless. It appears to me much better to assume, and there is much evidence for it, that what might otherwise be called inactive systems are really systems in the precursor state. Thus it is better to think of system activation in terms of system formation, for this appears to be closer to the actuality of what goes on. Although there is some system "ongoingness," the great majority of potential systems are in the switched-off state, that is, they have reverted to a system precursor form.

2) *System Formation*. This is the name we give to the anamorphic process that results in the production of an ongoing system, i.e., the act of system formation.

3) *System Block*. This is the name that we have chosen for processes that either prevent system formation or return an ongoing system to a precursor state.

4) *System Precursor Activation*. The opposite of (3). Usually accomplished by an organizing force, a catalytic agent, or an initiator.

5) *System-forming Space*. A protective space of relational, rather than geometric type, around organizing forces and system precursors that provides the necessary degree of isolation for system-forming to take place.

EMOTIONAL-COGNITIVE STRUCTURALISM AND ITS NEUROLOGICAL SUBSTRATE

This is also an original theory that had its beginning in 1956, an expression of my own interest in the value of feelings and intuitions, in the way in which meaningful events and knowledge are stored in memory, in the enhancement of more civilized or human behavior, in the way in which significant events and learning are coded for storage in memory, and in what I felt was a necessary role in the origin of thought that would explain the otherwise mysterious fact that each person has tens of thousands of discrete feeling tones, or emotional nuances, and which has been increasingly corroborated by recent neurological research.

Starting with the notion of emotional nuances as the coding device for memory and knowledge, usually considered a property of cognitive systems, it became obvious that coding must be a reflection of previous organizing activity, and so the notion that thinking was an emotional-cognitive operation was born, and with it the idea of renaming thoughts as "emotional cognitive structures" to indicate the pathway of their formation, and to indicate their relationship to GST, that is, thoughts are to be considered as system formations between emotions and cognitions. Thus, for me thoughts became open systems, that is, enduring patterns of emotional cognitive flow, and isomorphic with what Bertalanffy had shown to be the case for all other aspects of living systems.

For this concept of emotional-cognitive structuralism to be true, however, would require extensive fiber tract connections between the limbic system, or emotional brain, and the neocortex, or cognitive brain, evidence for which was lacking at that time. Improvement of methodology of study of fiber tract connections within the brain has led to the interesting result that there are very extensive fiber tract connections between the two, and even to the discovery that all impulses entering the cortex or leaving it are routed through the limbic system and other subcortical structures. These findings are extensively reported on by Paul A. LaViolette in his paper on, "The Neurophysiology of Thought and Perception" (1978). The basic evidence of neurophysiological type supporting the origin of thought in organizing flows of recursive or self-entering type between a living system and other subcortical structures and the cerebral cortex are discoveries by Pribram (1969) and associates that specific neurophysiological wave forms are correlated with specific mental events, the wave forms then representing a coding of mental experience. There is clear evidence that neural sense receptors operate by coding and recoding their stimulus information. This evidence amounts to a rejection of the previously held idea that learning is based on association by fiber tracts in the cerebral cortex, for meaning appears now clearly to lie in the associational relationship between wave forms.

Thus information becomes portable, accounting for the holographic characteristics of brain function, where the whole visual image may be reconstructed from just a portion of the wave pattern, suffering only in reduced clarity. Further evidence in the work of Pribram and associates (1967) that speaks against the origin of learning through direct association through cortical fiber tracts is the evidence that simple disconnection of intracortical pathways has no effect on learning and recognition abilities, while the cutting of the neural pathways connecting the cortex with subcortical structures produces learning and recognition difficulties as severe as destruction of the neuronal parts of the cerebral cortex. Thus Pribram supports the notion that the entire cerebral cortex is connected to the subcortical region through both incoming and outcoming fibers, with a subcortical region including the limbic system, the basal ganglia, the hypothalamus, the thalamus, and the reticular formation. For this reason regions thought to be purely motor or purely sensory have been found to be mixed, a condition necessary for thought to be based on self-referential cycling between coded forms of thought and action, as well as feeling and cognition.

Creative thought formation involves the frontal lobe of the neocortex in interaction with subcortical structures in the limbic system, and since it is this area of the brain that is involved with context dependent thinking and behavior, its function is critical in carrying out context sensitive social interaction so characteristic of human beings. Thus Pribram (1961) notes that surgical interference with the limbic system or the frontal pole of the brain impairs context sensitive discrimination. Further, the organism's ability to use tokens or symbols, which are at the heart of context dependency, previously thought to be so dependent on the frontal cortex, appears now to be derived from interaction between feelings and cortex. Constructing sets of contexts depends on a memory mechanism that embodies self-referral or self-referencing, and suggests that closed loop connectivities of the limbic system make them likely candidates for establishing context dependency.

The anatomic investigations of Dobzhansky (1970) indicate that the great difference between the human brain and that of primates has two features—a larger forebrain and a greater degree of connectivity of the frontal lobe with the limbic region. LaViolette (1979) suggests that it is probably the evolutionary development of the frontal-limbic system, both in size and integration, which is responsible for man's intelligence and his greater degree of caring. He further suggests that evidence points to the fact that association between sense modalities and various brain functions does not occur in the cerebrum, but in the subcortical regions. Thus, contrary to popular belief, the importance of the cerebral region is not to integrate the diverse mental experiences, but to separate them, to give them breathing room not possible in the lower brain centers. The subcortex may be thought of as the marketplace where emotional nuances cross paths and influence one another.

The importance of these concepts is portrayed in a similarly beautiful fashion by LaViolette in his paper, "Thoughts About Thoughts About Thoughts" (1977). Commenting on "Thought: Essence or Substance," he states:

Part of the confusion in the past regarding the relation of thought and symbolism arose due to the vagueness with which thought was defined. Philosophers as far back as ancient Greece have regarded thought as insubstantial as belonging to the world of ideas. With the advent of Gray's emotional-cognitive structure theory, and with the distinction between conscious and subconscious process offered by the emotional-perceptive cycle theory, a new perspective may now be gained. Thoughts become just as "concrete" as atoms, tornadoes, or biological organisms: they become viewed as stabilized patterns of flow. By pinning thoughts down in this "concrete" fashion, we can now begin to deal with the world of the psyche just as effectively as we have dealt with the phenomenal world. In so doing, we should not negate the possibility that there is a noumenal world, a world of ideas having essense, but no substance. Emotional-cognitive structures may be regarded as materializations of these imminent noumenal possibilities into physical reality (pp. 22-4).

Given then that emotional-cognitive structures are an accurate portrayal of the way in which the mind works, its implications are that continuing human growth and development are crucially dependent upon a process of differentiation of global emotions into an increasing array of modulated emotional nuances, for it is the clear and differentiated characteristics of emotional nuances that permit their increasing capacity to organize arrays of cognitions into sets of emotional cognitive autopoietic systems, which are themselves then subject to the anamorphic process. Emotionally driven thoughts or emotionally empty thoughts do not have such organizing qualities, and their presence is indicative of system blocks in the normative process. It is essential that "thoughts," or emotional-cognitive structures, have continuing components of emotional and cognitive type for developments to move in the direction of greater ability to think and greater ability to care. The key, then, is that emotions and cognitions must system form with each other, a point strongly emphasized also by James E. Durkin (1976b), although from a different perspective.

THE EMOTIONAL PERCEPTIVE CYCLE THEORY OF PAUL LAVIOLETTE

This was developed by LaViolette as a result of his own work on self-organizing systems, together with my work on emotional-cognitive structuralism, the work of Ilya Prigogine (1976) on order through fluctuation, and the work of Ludwig von Bertalanffy (1968b) on open systems and symbolism. At the foundation of his theory is the supposition that emotions and perceptions (the precursor to cognition) are mutually interrelated in a circularly causal process. Thus the typical psychophysical organism functions as a double input open system, as illustrated in Figure 1.

The mental behavior of a typical psychophysical organism is primarily active, rather than reactive. That is, emotion arises spontaneously or autonomously from within the organism, A to E, and is expressed as exploratory or testing behavior in its environment, E to B. But there is also input from the environment, from the outside world, O to P, and such perceptions elicit emotional nuances, P to E, and the overall function then produces either activity, A to E to B, or reactivity, O to P to E to B. But circularly functioning consists of self-recurring sets of system formations in which emotions organize perceptions and perceptions organize emotions. That is, one can perceive how one feels, and one has feelings about what one perceives, including, of course, feelings about one's perceptions about what one feels, and perceptions of feelings about perceptions, etc. Out of this self-recursive process then emerge higher levels of awareness, creative thought, and caringness. But, as emotions differentiate into nuances, the need

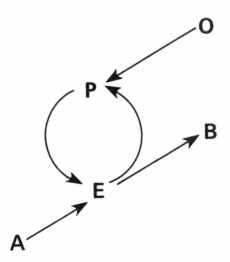

Figure 1. Diagram of a Double Input Open System of Emotional-Perceptive Cycle

for coherence results in emotional theme formation, recognizable as more enduring feeling tones. However, in such an emotional theme formation, different nuances are constantly surfacing, becoming momentarily more emphatic in the theme, a state, then, of thematic fluctuation. The *emotional perceptive cycle theory* outlined is what is known as a double input open system, and the work of Ilya Prigogine (1976) has shown that such systems are the key feature in self-organization, for they promote the anamorphic, system-forming process that Prigogine has signified as "order through fluctuation."

Order through fluctuation occurs because such double input open systems tend in time to selectively amplify a component emotional nuance which suddenly then becomes the predominant organizing theme and thus drives the theme to a new state of order. When this happens the emotional theme spontaneously changes its emotional state from being a highly complex pattern of emotional nuances to being a relatively simple characterization. It is this spontaneous self-simplifying process which constitutes the emergence of a new emotional cognitive structure, a new creative thought, and so what is ordinarily thought of as a "symbol" is now seen as a new emotional cognitive structure that brings about a new level of coherence and understanding, usually exemplified by the "Aha!" reaction. The process can be steered, but not forced, and its result can be approximated, but never known for sure in advance, and thus is stochastic rather than deterministic. So the concretion of thought is in effect a set to superset transition.

The process is recursive in that the new organizing emotional-cognitive structure becomes then a member of a new and more complex emotional theme, and the process repeats itself. LaViolette suggests that what are called peak experiences are the alignment of a number of emotional themes into a megatheme, which as a new autopoietic system maintains itself for some time, as does a new emotional-cognitive structure, but as anamorphosis continues its time duration is limited.

Emotional perceptive cycle theory sheds light on the relation of the conscious to the subconscious, with subconsciousness being related to subliminal processes of emotional nuance association and theme formation. Such system formations are feelings about feelings, whereas consciousness is born when system formation becomes emotional cognitive. The process is bottom-up, one of emergence, one of self-organization.

TOWARDS AN UNDERSTANDING OF DEVELOPMENTAL STAGES

That growth and development occur not only by accretion, but by definitely recognizable stages is beyond dispute in all developing, living structures, and thus a fundamental element in understanding group therapy is the capacity to understand the rather invariant steps of developmental stages that indicate that group process is going on, as outlined in the work of Ariadne Beck (1974). In terms of emotional cognitive structuralism, the reason for this phenomenon is that the emotional cognitive structuring process produces areas of local coherence which, as they increase in number, assume a degree of complexity such that their coherence-forming function runs into the problem of competing coherences. This is only resolvable in systems with growing complexity if the nature of the coherence-producing patterning becomes itself subject to a revision of its basic form; that is, competing coherences are only resolvable by a shift in the pattern of what is considered to constitute coherence. These are comparable to the paradigm shifts that are so clearly evident in the evolution of knowledge itself. Each such shift in coherence definition represents that new set of system formations known as stages in development, each of which will remain autopoietic for a while, until the demands for coherence become answerable only in terms of a new anamorphic advance in the level of ordering.

AN EMOTIONAL-COGNITIVE AND SYSTEM PRECURSOR/SYSTEM-FORMING VIEW OF GROUP PSYCHOTHERAPY

This view will be applied to the findings of Ariadne Beck on phases in the development of structure in therapy and encounter groups. That capacity for group therapy is dependent upon structure-forming capacity is clearly indicated in Beck's statement:

Therefore, at any particular time, the individual's ability to make use of the persons available in his environment to create functional relationships in which the process of development can proceed is a critical factor. . . . In more general terms, then, there are skills involved in understanding oneself, one's internal processes, needs, and experiences in such a way as to represent these in awareness with a fair degree of accuracy; there are other skills involved in the understanding of other individuals, for themselves; still other skills in the recognition of relevant dimensions in the relationship between self and other; and still other skills involved in the recognition of relevant group processes and patterns and one's own part in these. As I see it, then, the adequacy of the communication skills and the presence or absence of conflict in the individual in relationship to these levels are the primary determining factors in whether or not the person is able to develop the kinds of relationships that lead to growth for him. In certain instances individual work is necessary to help cope with the conflicts or the development of basic communication skills. Many clients, as well as persons not seeking therapy, can, however, profit from the use of growthful or therapeutic groups to work on these issues. Because the outcome for any individual is determined by the relationship he has to his social environment, group therapy allows the client and the therapist the unique opportunity to work directly with the problems the client has in relating to others in mutually facilitative ways (1974, pp. 425-6).

The capacity for group therapy depends crucially on the capacity of a client to understand and accept the basic system-forming nature of group therapy, and to accept that he himself has system-forming capacity, and that the nature of the systems he forms are dependent on the precursors. This is equivalent to our own approach in stressing system-forming and system precursors in the therapy of delinquents and offenders against the law. The requirements, however, that the process be basically self-organizational limits the degree to which the therapist can be didactic or constructive, for if one overdoes this, then, as the work of Lieberman, Yalom and Miles (1973) has demonstrated, the therapist is system-forming for his clients, creating allopoietic systems, rather than encouraging autopoiesis with its central feature of autonomy and self-organizing anamorphosis. But the system-forming aspect must be accepted or group therapy will fail, and the system precursors that serve as organizing forces for system formations must be experientially recognized and understood. Further, since in human function such precursors are feeling states, clients and therapists must be willing to accept the feelings that emerge as central to the way they organize their lives and relationships, and to allow such feeling tones to system form into emotional cognitive structures that expand and stabilize their understanding in a way equivalent to that described by James Durkin (1976b) in his systeming and summing approach to feelings and cognition.

This is also equivalent to Ariadne Beck's (1974) statement that,

The therapist-leader believes that problems and conflicts can be clarified and solved via a process of self-understanding, and the development of an empathic understanding of others. The primary mode of response of the therapist is therefore one that elicits a good deal of self-reflection from the client, and of checking perceptions with each other between clients (p. 428).

The necessity for continuing emotional cognitive structuring by the therapist is recognized in Beck's statement that, "The therapist recognizes the significance of maintaining as high a degree as possible of clarity about his own views, feelings, and reactions when he is in the therapeutic relationship" (1974, p. 429). Beck also recognizes the necessity for the therapist to understand the problem of maintaining clarity and its signification of coherence as the group process develops, and therefore the basis upon which developmental stages emerge, which represent resolution by paradigm shifts, or emotional-cognitive structuring about sets of emotional cognitive structures. Thus she states,

There is too much going on at one time, in terms of the simultaneous behaviors of the various members, their interactions with each other and the therapist's own reactions, for him to be able to sort out all that is important on the spot. You might say that the nervous system becomes overloaded. This is not a matter of inadequacy of the therapist (although for an inexperienced therapist this is an added problem) but a practical reality of complex situations. Under these conditions it becomes extremely important for the therapist to be aware of, and accepting of, his own limits. The degree of his willingness to know this and to communicate about it to the group, even though it may elicit disappointment or anxiety from them, is a significant dimension in his effectiveness as a leader (1974, p. 429).

Beck's statement that, to develop a complex theory dealing with various sources of influence, the invariant developmental process that holds all the variables together requires identification, is an extremely clear statement that group process is a system-forming process, and if this is not evident, no group exists. Her statement of the equal requirement that differentiation and cohesion within developmental phases be observable is again a recognition of the system-forming character of group development at all times, and is isomorphic with the requirement of emotional-cognitive structuralism that growth and development are dependent upon continuing differentiation of global emotions into more precise emotional nuances and their integration into coherent emotional themes.

SYSTEM-FORMING EMOTIONAL-COGNITIVE STRUCTURE VIEW OF BECK'S PHASES IN THE DEVELOPMENT OF GROUP STRUCTURE

Phase Number and Description	*System-Forming and Emotional-Cognitive Structuring Comments*
I. Making a Contract: The Agreement to Work on Becoming a Functional Group (cf. Beck, this volume)	The initial stage of necessary awareness of system precursor, system formation loopings. Without willingness to block inappropriate system precursors and modify them so that system formations compatible with group development can occur, group formation is impossible. Similar to our initial stage of dealing with those who commit the crime of breaking and entering. As we do, Beck also demonstrates how she would deal with personal exploration in the group, and will do so in a primarily spontaneous fashion, so as to insure self-organization rather than allopoietic organization. Two roles emerge and serve as organizing forces for the system formation at this stage. These are the designated leader, who provides basic skill at interpersonal processes, and the emotional leader, who supportively functions as a manager of the group's emotional life, thus combining an organizing focus and nutrient bed function.
Transitional Space	When members have established a sense of identity and a sense of similarity, a discernible degree of cohesion is experienced which, however, is rather shortly thereafter unable to maintain itself, as complexity grows, and so the group must anamorphically now go through a phase shift and a new paradigm for system-forming, with preservation of autopoietic autonomy for both group and individual.

II.	Establishment of a Group Identity and Direction	Beck's comment that scapegoating is the necessary organizing force for Phase II is confirmed in our own experience, where acceptance of understanding of faulty precursors and the need for their revision is now followed by a scapegoating of the therapist. That is, our clients now lock us out, although interestingly and necessarily with continuing understanding and acceptance of the system precursor/system-forming relationship, for the role reversal of scapegoating is implicit acceptance of the system-forming process. If the scapegoat is locked out, group development stops. Competition has "won out" in zero sum fashion (really no one wins without someone else losing), and the phasic transition from competitive to cooperative modes does not occur.
	Transitional Point	When the precursors that underlie the polarities of competition become sufficiently revised so that a new level of cohesion is reached, their function as organizing forces for the achievement of further cohesion disappears and signifies the need for an anamorphic process to provide a new organizing force capable of system-forming new levels of autonomy with coherence, as complexity grows.
III.	The Exploration of Individuals in the Group	The organizing force is recognition that the individuals in the group, with their differences and their unique problems, are the system precursors out of which autonomous group formation can now take place. Now exchange of information of a personal kind and experimentation with various modes of communication become the organizing forces, and personal growth begins to occur, with the emotional leader serving as an organizing focus for this. It is essential that everyone participate in some meaningful way, as a system precursor. Now the formation of a system-forming space is necessary, in which necessary caring about each individual can occur with safety. System formation has now achieved an emotional cognitive form.
	Transitional Point	When the system-forming process goes beyond modulation and differentiation of global feelings into emotional nuances, newfound capacity for emotional-cognitive structuring rapidly increases complexity so that emotional differentiation can no longer in itself produce coherence.
IV.	The Establishment of Intimacy	The organizing force here for the new stage is the challenge to the newly found emotional cognitive structuring capacity to deal in a new and more differentiated way with the global emotions that now arise as intimacy develops. That is, sexuality becomes a problem, as the intense wish for and fear of the dependency of intimacy develop. An essential organizing force in this phase is visible changes in the behavior

of the designated leader, a shift to participation so that he can be perceived by the members as a more complex person and not just an authority figure. Usually this new system formation is carried out between designated leader and emotional leader.

Transitional Phase   With the achievement of warmth and attraction they lose their capacity as organizing forces for futher system formations, for they induce marked increasing complexity.

V.   The Exploration of   The initial organizing forces are feelings of vulnerability.
     Mutuality   Will caring turn into being used, with unreasonable demands for support and loyalty now being made? There is an emotionally driven force to demonstrate good will that emerges and must, through an anamorphic process, turn into the achievement of good will through emotional organization of cognitions. Again global feelings arise and should be differentiated before emotional cognitive structuring can resume. The organizing force for this system-forming phase is the *defiant* member, a person who has not developed external mutual relationships, and so now expresses intense feelings of rejection by the group and demands for a great deal of self-protectiveness. Both the autopoietic existence of the group and its capacity for further anamorphosis become now dependent on the capacity for emotional-cognitive structuring to bring awareness of the need now to let go of dependency on the authority figure and the ability of the other members of the group to develop understanding of the critical role of the defiant member in group formation. The personal conflict of the defiant member helps the group to remain sensitively aware of the dangers of conformity, based on seeking fulfillment of dependency needs. Phase V can only be successfully completed by the group finding ways to cope with issues regarding dependency and frustration in a way that establishes some reasonable expectation for all.

Transitional Point   This is achieved when the group realizes that a special contract is needed for the defiant member, a necessary system formation that implies acceptance of the uniqueness of each individual so that autonomous individuality, which implies specialness, can coexist with autonomous group formation, also implying specialness. When this is achieved the defiant member can no longer function as an organizing force.

VI. The Achievement   The new organizing force centers around the recognition
     of Autonomy   that new system-forming processes to increase flexibility
     Through   and promote greater fluidity regarding role function must
     Reorganization of occur if the new levels of complexity that have emerged are
     the Group's   now to be dealt with. Now there are fewer personal controls
     Structure   operating, with the result that more complex and subtle
                       interactions occur, with a period of intense differentiation
                       of large numbers of new emotional nuances that serve to
                       code and thus make for ease of understanding the general
                       state of everyone else in the group. With this a new auto-
                       poietic level is reached in which some of the responsibilities
                       for initiation and control of group formation and function
                       shift from therapist to group members. There is now an
                       overt assertion that the potential for leadership and for play-
                       ing an organizing role that has existed in the membership
                       is now functional. This is the basic new organization and
                       marks the birth of the group as an autonomous, self-organ-
                       izing unit. The emotional leader emerges as a central or-
                       ganizing force in this phase, but he/she, like the designated
                       leader, must be prepared for the development of similar
                       capacities by each group member.

     Transitional Point   This is marked by the achievement of separateness from the
                       designated leader as authority or guardian and the achieve-
                       ment of a sense of self-direction. With this achievement a
                       new organizing force must be found.

VII. Self-Confrontation   Therapy must now undergo a new type of system formation
     and the   so that it shifts to the capacity for autonomous self devel-
     Achievement of   opment. As in Stage III it is featured by intensive differ-
     Interdependence   entiation as each individual begins to look at him/herself
                       and the issues that brought him/her to therapy. A massive
                       increase in variety of emotional nuances must result through
                       differentiation, so that their variety begins to match the
                       previously hidden profound complexity of each individual.
                       Here the group must function as a nutrient bed for a sense
                       of sharing the experience of struggle with oneself that is
                       involved in personal change. The system-forming process
                       both at group and individual levels must lead to a sense of
                       involvement in each person's personal battle with his limits
                       and fears. System-forming, emotional-cognitive loopings
                       have become massively more self-referential, and so aware-
                       ness of each person's growing edge and trajectories for
                       personal development must occur, in addition to the capacity
                       to find new concrete pathways for such growth. What has
                       been previously considered as transitions between phases
                       become now part of the phase itself. So this phase is char-
                       acterized by sudden increases in capacity for self-disclosure.
                       Capacity for system-forming, unforming, and reforming has
                       now become autonomous and fluid, and capacity for the

awareness of possibility for both group and individual has been achieved. The group reorganizes its perceptions of the scapegoat and he becomes a participating member and begins a somewhat belated change towards autonomy. The emotional leader integrates his experience and becomes aware of a new image of his potential in doing elsewhere what he has done in the group.

Transition Point

With the achievement of the capacity for creative and intensive work in the setting of the group, further system-forming activity localized to group formation loses its capacity for further organization.

VIII. Independence, the Transfer of Learning

The organizing force is now awareness that similar system-forming capacities will be needed for the formation of close relationships outside the group. Thus attempts to extrapolate the meaning of their experience in the group for their relationship elsewhere become prominent. The organizing focus then is reversal, for independence and the seeking of problem-solving help, and support for the transfer of new learning to outside life. Again global feelings arise, but the new variety that has developed in the group and the variety-increasing capacity that both they and the group have developed now permit levels of differentiation of old global feelings not previously possible. The scapegoat emerges as having particular capacity for such transfer of learning, while the emotional leader who has had a profound and exciting experience in the group has some difficulty in making the transition. He also has more to transfer, for more profound changes have occurred within him than in others.

Transition Point

The achievement of a sense of independence from the group signifies a readiness to cope with separation, and to cope with unfinished business.

IX. Termination of Group and Separation from Significant Persons

The organizing force here is awareness of the need for new system-forming and emotional-cognitive structuring to occur that can deal with separation from important persons. This requires a capacity for maintaining openness to one's own feelings and to others, that is, the capacity for autonomous emotional-cognitive structuring, in which feelings are no longer of the driven variety, nor are they dealt with by repression or denial. Resolving unfinished business includes dealing with frustrations not attended to earlier, a process again of awareness of somewhat global feelings and the capacity to allow for their modulation and differentiation. When the group can maintain an atmosphere of openness and honesty regarding their experience in this phase, they achieve what in some ways is the ultimate or prototype of cohesive experiences, a deep sense of togetherness, even as they part. *They have achieved then the fundamental point of emotional-cognitive structuralism, which is that for creative, progressive, and humanistic development to continue, both emotion and cognition must remain as continuing elements in the flow pattern that constitutes thought. Emotional-cognitive organization has been achieved.*

EMOTIONAL-COGNITIVE STRUCTURAL VIEW OF THE FUNCTION OF THE GROUP THERAPIST

It is probably true that any real learning from others, or teaching of others, can only occur by a sharing of the pathway of system-forming developments that ensues from the formation of that knowledge. But this is only possible when the system-forming path is conveyed both emotionally and cognitively, as well as emotional cognitively. So the group therapist's function can be seen as resulting from the development of this capacity within themselves, added to by their awareness that teaching is a myth. What they must understand is that learning is only possible if it is self-organizing, so the role of the teacher, then, is to share experience and understanding in such a way so that what he/she says will become organizing foci for a self-organizing process in the other.

The final caveat is that one must express what one feels to be true, but must also be willing to explain it as clearly as possible, and to be aware of discrepancies, and this can only be achieved when emotional patterns match with cognitions, and this, then, is the formation of an emotional-cognitive structure. But truth and knowledge are always partial, and so the search is a continuing one that proceeds by the anamorphic formation of autopoietic systems representing developmental stages which again undergo anamorphosis. Thus we see the wisdom of Socrates in understanding that the wise man is aware always of what he does not know.

Chapter 18

Developmental Characteristics of the System-forming Process

Ariadne P. Beck, M.A.

Editor's Introduction. Andy Beck joined the GST Committee in 1977, but her work with groups and group psychotherapy had been going on for a decade before that. It was a great mutual discovery that she had been a GST person all along! Andy's chapter is basically an interim report on one of the most thoroughgoing empirically based research projects in the psychotherapy group field. At the point of writing this chapter for *Living Groups* she and her colleagues have collected transcripts of scores of group sessions and have begun to formulate and test an integrated set of hypotheses about the way groups grow on the basis of their results. Because her assertions about group system-forming and transforming are empirically based, she is ahead of many of us who are still in the theoretical and clinical stages of our explorations. But what she has to say is equifinally congruent with what we have to say.

In her chapter she begins with a sweeping survey of all the sources of variation in the behavior of ongoing groups such as therapy groups. She then focuses on one of these sources, group structure, which she defines as the skeleton of group life out of which group level issues, group leadership roles, and group norms form. She then enumerates a set of propositions about group development which postulates a series of stages that a living group structure passes through in sequence. Groups grow not in a continuous gradual ascent, but rather in discrete phases which must each be completed to the satisfaction of the members if the next one is to be engaged. The phases each have characteristic transition points, usually an emerging focus on group level issues, and each phase has characteristic leader roles which arise to cope with the issues that appear.

In the course of this work Andy has discovered two new kinds of leaders! Group theory has for years recognized the task leader and the social-emotional leader, but Andy threatens to revolutionize the field by adding a scapegoat leader and a defiant leader to this roster. The four leaders each arise at different times and in different combinations to meet the demands of the different group phases.

Although Andy has adopted a number of GST terms for her chapter, her work matured before she learned about these terms from the Committee. It would be useful to ask, then, in just what way Andy's research program is a GST program. In the first place, she is a structuralist in the Piagetian and GST sense. She focuses on the structural activities below the surface contents that become embodied in a variety of particular ways in each group. Secondly, she considers the hierarchicalization process essential to system transformation, suggesting that when a new phase is ready there is a shift from group to individual level issues and back. Thirdly, she is concerned with boundarying operations. Although she doesn't employ the term "boundarying" explicitly in her chapter, she talks a good deal about opening and closing, flowing and defining. For example, one of the most salient characteristics of the scapegoat leader is that he/she is willing to be open and, in doing so, opens the group up to change.

All in all, Andy's work provides specific operations, sequences, and roles by means of which we may understand the structure of autonomy in living groups. Specifically, her work dovetails with that of Bill Gray on system-forming, since her phases are essentially a sequence of system reformations, and with that of Roy MacKenzie, who is concerned with the concept of role as a basis for understanding group process. Andy's work points the way to the next phase of the work of the GST Committee. With *Living Groups* we have articulated the theory and described in clinical case studies how GST can improve the practice and clarify the theory of group psychotherapy. Our next job is to tease out in empirical detail, as Andy has, the specific connection between system level events in the group and the psychotherapeutic process and progress which are the group's goal.

The focus of this chapter is on the developmental characteristics of the structure underlying the system-forming process (Gray, Chapter 11) in psychotherapy groups. The group level living structure, which emerges over time, gives order, organization and identity to a group, and acts as the underlying framework or skeleton of the total group process.

The thesis here is that the evolution of group structure is characterized by a dialectical interactional process, which leads to integration of the members of a group with respect to specific, group level issues. The issues differ from one phase to another, but are similar across groups for any particular phase. The phases emerge in an invariant sequence over time. This patterned, orderly evolution of group structure is only one of the major sources of influence which both facilitate and constrain the actual behavior of the members of a group. The attempt here is to identify the major sources of influence, which, taken together, would provide an adequate basis for formulating a model of group process having predictive value, if the dimensions from each source could be adequately specified for particular groups and the interactions between the dimensions were known. Needless to say, these conditions have not been met at this time. However, it is important to state that all six of these influential sources would have to be taken into consideration in making anything like a complete statement about group process. Following is a brief description of the major sources of influence on a group's process. They are offered as a context for the subject matter of this chapter, in an effort to clarify the fact that what is discussed here does not account for all of group behavior, simply one of the six sources—the development of structure.

MAJOR SOURCES OF INFLUENCE ON GROUP PROCESS

(a) *The environment or context within which the group and its members exist.* The entire system (group) is immersed in an environment which impinges on the group process in two primary ways: The physical-interpersonal setting in which it meets defines certain limitations, codes of behavior or criteria for participation. In addition, the entire complex of factors of each member's life outside the group determines his state upon entering and reentering the group and may influence the group in a variety of ways, but primarily through the perceptual sieve of the member himself.

(b) *The purpose for which the group comes together, as this is elaborated into a system of goals over the lifetime of the group.* This includes the intents, images and motivations of each member regarding the group, prior to its formation; the interaction of these intents, images and motivations as the members assess each other and the potential for meeting their own personal goals given the composition of the group; and, finally, the process of stating, restating and integrating the individual goals into a set of group goals that all can accept. These group goals evolve and are articulated further as the group progresses through each phase of development.

(c) *The specific work to be done or the content aspect of the group's task.* It is assumed here that subject matter has its own organizational component and, therefore, influence on the group's process. Included in this dimension would also be the knowledge that the members possess regarding the task of the group, the resources required to accomplish the task, and their availability, as well as the degree to which the group as a whole plus its resources can adequately provide all the necessary components required to complete the task.

(d) *The personalities and skills of the members.* The personality, for the purposes of group behavior, would include the developmental stage of the individual and therefore the salient issues for him at the particular time of his participation, the competence and sophistication of each person with respect to the goals and activities of the group (particularly as these are perceived by other participants), and the "readiness" or "neediness" of the individual to use the group to achieve or facilitate his own personal growth and goals.

(e) *The qualitative aspects of group life and the methods for facilitating or hindering them in the developmental context.* Included here are style of leadership, style of members in group participation, accuracy and inclusiveness of communication, the way members feel about each other, the amount and quality of conflict generated in differentiation of roles, the way in which work is done (in a therapy group, for example, the depth of emotional issues that are dealt with, and the adequacy of the resolution that is achieved), the comfort and meaningfulness of the group's norms for its members, the skill or ease with which the group progresses through its formative stages. Qualitative issues determine how one feels about the group, how one's experience takes shape.

(f) *The living structure of the group and the developmental sequence through which it evolves.* Structure can be observed in the emergence, reification, and final distribution of group leadership roles; in the group level issues that the members address in each phase; in the creation of group norms that guide behavior and in the group level identity which is formed and which gives a characteristic coherence to the group's process. The term structure is used here in the same sense in which it has been used in social psychological studies of small groups. The structure is akin to the skeleton, whereas the qualitative dimension is akin to the outward appearance of the body, the texture of the flesh, the color, the tone of voice, the "feel."

The qualitative dimension has a reciprocal relationship with developing group structure, both causing it and being caused by it, and both are strongly influenced by the group goals, member personalities, the context in which the group operates, and of course the content of their task together. Each of the six sources of influence are seen as being in process and interaction with each other. The output of any group in terms of productivity and effectiveness and the outcome of the group experience for any member are determined by the interaction of all the sources of input. Moreover, these dimensions interact in lawful ways, characteristic of all living systems. The many processes, inputs and outputs of a group that have been described by other researchers are understood here as having a variety of meanings, a variety of consequences and impacts on the group as a system depending on when they occur in its developmental history. A complete theoretical model of group process would develop each of these sources of influence and the dynamic interactions among them—clearly a task for future efforts. The present chapter continues this author's efforts to explicate the development of group structure (Beck, 1974) by formulating a set of propositions which might lead to empirical verification.

SOME GENERAL PROPOSITIONS FOR A THEORY OF THE DEVELOPMENT OF GROUP LIVING STRUCTURE

The initial thesis of the theory being developed here is that *there is a discernible developmental process, which is consistent across groups,* and which describes the way a collection of individuals structures itself into a relatively stable organization that we call a group (for the purposes of this statement group refers to small groups of up to ten members). Consistent with this proposition is the belief that the other five sources of influence take on greater meaning when they are seen in the context of this developmental sequence. The interaction of the inputs from the six sources of influence determines the rate at which a group progresses through the phases of development, the effectiveness of what is accomplished at each phase and the usefulness of the experience to each member. This interaction also determines whether or not a group is successful in organizing itself at all, for there is the possibility of failure or detour in this enterprise as in all others in which living systems participate. Following are some general propositions for a theory about the developmental process through which a group's living structure emerges and evolves.

Proposition 1

There is a discernible developmental process which characterizes the evolution of living structure in a small group. Further, an invariant sequence of phases can be observed in the development of a living structure which has the capacity to function adequately for the members as individuals and for the members as a group with a goal.

Proposition 2

This developmental pattern can be described in terms of phases, each of which deals with a unique set of group level issues. The group level issues are the same across groups, emerge because the functional needs in the creation of group living structure are the same across groups and are invariant in the sequence of their initial appearance in the group's life, i.e., the initial appearance of a later phase does not precede that of an earlier one, even though the earlier phase can be repeated. Although each group deals with a unique set of content topics, the major group level issues remain the same across groups, and are basically determined by the functional needs of the membership in each phase vis-à-vis the building of a relationship known as a group. The concept of developmental phasing is used here in the same sense as Piaget (1951) uses it to describe the development of thought in the child, that is, each phase is in some sense dependent upon the previous phase.

Group level issues can be described at a number of levels of abstraction, depending on the purpose of the description. Later in the chapter they will be described at a level that is useful to the clinician conducting a group. At this point in the presentation of propositions a more abstract level of description may serve a useful purpose. The term "group level" refers to issues or problems which are particularly relevant to the group as a whole at a particular time in its development. This does not mean that every member takes the issue or set of issues seriously or feels a need to contribute overtly to processing them. It does mean that all members are affected by the adequacy with which the issues are dealt at that time in the group's life and it means that the continued development of the group's living structure is determined by the addressing and resolving of these issues to the satisfaction of all participants. The group deals with the following major themes in the following sequence:

1) Creating a contract to become a group: This requires the settlement of membership composition because the group members will not make a "contract" until they know who all the participants will be. Members assess each other and estimate their own ability to cope with the other members. Some people will leave at this point if they feel too uncomfortable to be able to work with the others present.

2) Survival: personal influences and survival in particular group/ the resolution fo competitive needs/ determining a group identity: This is the actual testing of the assessments made in 1) above. Major group organizational issues are worked out such as leadership selection, establishment of important norms, defining group goals, the management of negative emotion, the resolution of competitive needs, and the definition of a group identity. None of these are handled for all time but they must be initiated at a level that engages the entire group in such a way that they can proceed in a cooperative manner beyond this point.

3) Disclosure of individual identity/ defining individual goals to be pursued in the group/ establishing a work style: The individuation process proceeds on a more personal disclosing level. In a therapy group this period introduces the therapeutic methods for dealing with personal change and growth. Each member is seen more clearly for himself.

4) Exploration of intimacy and closeness: Members identify problems in intimate relations outside of group, then explore the intimacy issues within the group. In a positive outcome a bond is formed on the basis of positive factors and feelings.

5) Establishment of mutuality and equality: Members explore the implications of the positive bond formed in 4). Particularly, they explore dependency and independency issues as these will be handled in the close relationships between members.

6) Autonomy of members from formal leader/therapist: Members move forward on the basis of their commitment to each other—this constitutes a major shift from the fact that they entered the group to get what they needed from the therapist. Formal leader(s) is incorporated into the group as a person.

7) Self-confrontation in the context of interdependence: Members address their

own issues with the explicit help and support of other members. Level of self-disclosure, quality of work, and level of personal responsibility are at the highest levels in group's life.

8) Pursuit of independence: Members deal with the transfer of learning from the group and relationships in the group to the rest of their life.

9) Coping with separation and termination: Members deal with the need to acknowledge their significance to each other and the pain this creates in dealing with termination.

All of these are seen as group level as well as individually relevant issues. These issues become a vehicle for the development of the group structure and for the individuation of each member. For example, in dealing with the task of survival in the competitive context, each member is pushing for the kind of resolution which will make him or her comfortable in the group. During this process he begins to identify his own needs, issues and limits. During the same period leadership selection is an important group process. Out of the struggle that occurs in this period, a differentiation of roles takes place and a number of the group's norms become defined. These are two important aspects in the formation of group structure. Further, each member's issues with competition become clearer and some of the conditions that each need met in order to be helped become defined.

Proposition 3

Any particular group may or may not complete all the phases. The complete set of identified phases of development appear in their invariant sequence only 1) when a group is able to complete the group level work in each phase successfully; 2) when a group has sufficient time to meet in order to complete its development; 3) when the membership remains unchanged; and 4) when the formal leader does not prevent the progress of the group either out of personal needs or because of a commitment to an authoritarian style of leadership. This developmental framework allows the meaningful integration of the variable influences in a particular group from its purposes and goals, the personalities involved, the qualitative dimension, the environment and the task. It also allows us to understand and describe the processes of groups which fail to develop; those which develop to a certain point in the phase sequence and become stuck; those which develop to a certain point in the sequence and remain actively involved in the development of the skills which are characteristic of that phase; or those which develop in an aberrant fashion. The developmental process of the group which completes all the phases becomes the norm against which we can compare and understand a wide range of variations in group process. There are many factors which may terminate or hinder the evolution of a group through all the phases. For example, the entrance of new members after the group's development has begun usually requires beginning again and retracing those phases already completed. In a well established group this process may be accomplished much more rapidly than it was accomplished originally or may even be done in almost "symbolic" terms, but the recycling will occur in all groups, and the length of time it takes will be determined by all the other sources of influence as well. When groups are unable to resolve group level issues, they may attempt to redo the phase they are in, in some new way, or by the use of a different substantive content issue as the vehicle.

Proposition 4

When a group does successfully traverse all of the group level problems in developing a living structure there are several outcomes that can be expected:

(a) a more aware and effective group, i.e., one that knows its needs, capabilities, and limits as a group fairly clearly and is therefore functional, able to do work in an efficient way.

(b) a more aware and effective individual, i.e., one who knows more than before about his own needs, strengths, and limits and one who is able to coordinate his efforts effectively with the other people in this group.

(c) the achievement of work on the substantive tasks for which the group gathered in the first place.

(d) a comfortable termination, which seems natural and appropriate to all involved. Typically, in groups that do not reach phase nine, members experience some degree of discomfort in terminating; the level of discomfort differs depending on which phase they were in when they had to stop, or when the membership was changed.

Proposition 5

Each phase of group development is characterized by a dialectical process of differentiation of the members and integration of the members with respect to the group level issues. In the integration process some aspect of group living structure evolves. In the differentiation process some aspect of the individual person's own structure evolves.

Any particular phase of group development includes interactions which deal with group level issues and interactions which deal with intrapersonal or interpersonal problems related to the growth of each member and to the evolution of each person as a system in his own right. The interactions dealing with group level issues (which are one aspect of the structure) can be adequately described as taking place via a dialectical process. That is, communication regarding group level issues involves different members posing their views from opposing, diverging or simply differing positions, or from differing levels of abstraction, or with differing emotional intents. The "posing" is usually done verbally in face-to-face groups, but some aspects of an issue may not be expressed verbally at all; instead, they may be communicated via nonverbal dimensions. In larger encounter-type groups an entire issue may be dealt with nonverbally through movement or other gestural dimensions. As the group dialogues the issues or set of interrelated issues, integration or systeming* dissipates (at least experientially) and individuation or summing increases. This natural and essential process creates the vehicle by which each group member defines himself and emerges more clearly to the group and to himself. In a therapy group these opportunities may be used for fairly elaborate self-expression or exploration, which might contribute to the individual member's own integrative process while at the group level maintaining an individuation process.

Once the full range of viewpoints or reactions has been expressed, the group is faced with the problem of finding a solution to the group level issues. Sometimes, two or more members may engage in a discussion aimed at convincing one another of their viewpoints, and one or the other may succeed. However, the more disparate the views, the greater the necessity to find a higher level of abstraction from which to view the problem and the solution. This offers the possibility of a solution that can encompass a broad range of viewpoints, allowing everyone to remain in the group with some degree of comfort. As a solution is articulated and explored, we find integration or systeming increasing and differentiation, individuation or summing decreasing. In this integration an aspect of group structure has been built in the group, in the sense that a subset of group level problems has been solved, and an aspect of group level identity has been defined.

Proposition 6

Certain leadership functions emerge naturally from the characteristics of the dialectical process itself. In each phase of the developmental process, several members are more active than the others, more challenged or threatened by the particular issues of that phase. These members tend to be the ones who explicate and develop the group level issues of that phase. In addition, the polar positions on either end of the range of responses made by members to group level issues are taken by two of four persons who share this function over the course of the group's history. Their articulate expression of their positions contributes to the clarification of the issue(s) and usually clearly defines the end points of the range to be encompassed by a solution. They also contribute heavily to or lead the

---

*See Chapter 2. Beck equates individuation with summing and integration with systeming, but it must be made clear that this is only from the perspective of the individual level. Summing and systeming are general inter-individual contact processes that can occur at all levels of living structure.

group in seeking and finding a solution. This is the operational sense in which they are leaders. (There are several other dimensions to their leadership which will be defined in the next proposition.) In a successfully functioning group, the leaders tend to work together with a commitment to the progress of the group. This is true even in phases where the overt communication is competitive or sometimes even angry. This commitment on the part of the leadership is probably essential to the successful resolution of group level problems. Of all the phases, the second phase tends to be especially problematic to groups because of the competitive interaction that characterizes the phase, generating some question in everyone's mind about commitment to the group and to its task.

Proposition 7

Although each member takes an active role in one or another phase, and may express leadership-like influence in a particular phase of group development, there are four persons who each fulfill unique ongoing leadership functions throughout the group's life. These functions appear to be characteristics of the system, i.e., the group, and not of the particular personalities performing them. If a member who has been performing one of these ongoing functions leaves, the group reorganizes and another person takes up the role. In groups of up to ten persons there is usually only one member that takes up the kind of role we are discussing. In larger groups and under unusual circumstances in small groups, there will be more than one person in the role. The behaviors which characterize each role are, of course, not the unique domain of the member who holds the role. MacKenzie (1978, Chapter 6) has suggested that the term role position be used and all members thought of as contributing in varying degrees to the functions involved. However, for the purpose of this model, the term leadership role is reserved for those persons who perform certain ongoing functions throughout the group's life and who take turns facilitating the clarification and resolution of group level issues, thereby regularly contributing to the emerging structure. Two other authors in this volume have also recently contributed to the formulation of the four leadership roles in terms of their significance in both defining and then opening and closing boundaries for the group as a system (Brown, 1979; J. E. Durkin, 1978a, 1979). This formulation adds greater depth to the conceptualization of the group process by which structure is generated. The reader is reminded here that we are discussing the development of autonomous living structure and not trying to account for all aspects of group life in this chapter. The concept of boundarying is here being used in the sense that J. E. Durkin has discussed it:

Autonomous living structure is alive because it is autonomous. . . .
What is new about the GST (general system theory) view is that it provides us with a structural view of the autonomy process instead of a content view as is traditional. . . .

The new idea from GST is that the process by means of which autonomy in living structures is achieved (or not achieved) is a boundarying process. . . . In boundarying a person, group or community defines its own structure by drawing its own boundaries. In complementary fashion it transforms its own structure by selectively opening its boundaries (J. E. Durkin, 1979, p. 2-3).

Following is a summary description of each of the four roles. It is a composite picture made up of the contributions of Beck (1974; Beck & Keil, 1967), Brown (1979), J. E. Durkin (1978a, 1979), MacKenzie (1978, Chapter 6), Dugo (Dugo & Beck, 1977), Peters (Beck & Peters, 1979) and Lewis (1979). The latter three are working currently on empirical measures of the developmental phases and on a sociometric questionnaire for identifying leaders. For each of the four leaders, there is a description of the boundaries with which they deal, and the ongoing functions they perform. The four roles are: Task Leader, Emotional Leader, Scapegoat, Defiant Leader.

A. TASK LEADER

1) Boundaries dealt with by Task Leader

(a) Is usually the convener of the group. In a therapy group, may also have selected the members who were to participate in the particular group.
(b) Manages the cognitive boundaries relating to the limits of the task to be done in the group.
(c) Monitors the boundary between the group itself and the setting in which it meets, including dealing with any suprastructure in that setting which might impinge on the group.
(d) Monitors the boundaries between members vis-à-vis extreme or high stress behavior, whether aggressive, psychotic or sexual.
(e) Has the primary influence on the opening of intrapsychic boundaries, especially in early phases.
(f) Monitors the boundaries between individual or group fantasies or projections and "reality."

2) Ongoing leadership and group maintenance functions of Task Leader

(a) Guide to the task of the group; facilitates member's self-exploration.
(b) Provides support and is available to all members of the group as individuals.
(c) Facilitates members' interpersonal interaction.
(d) Style characteristics of Task Leader strongly influence:
   i) the openness and ease with which norms are defined
   ii) the clarification of goals and sub-goals for group and for individuals
   iii) the style of communication in the group

iv) the level of participation of members

v) the depth of emotional issues addressed

(e) Participates in defining certain norms and certain goals.

(f) Accurately perceives and verbally represents what goes on in the group, at a group level and on individual member levels.

B. EMOTIONAL LEADER

1) Boundaries dealt with by Emotional Leader

(a) Monitors the opening of intrapsychic boundaries of fellow members.

(b) Models the opening of intrapsychic boundaries, boundaries between self and the rest of the group, and boundaries between self and the world outside of the group.

(c) Monitors the boundary between members and therapists in the group.

(d) Monitors the boundaries between members vis-à-vis intimacy issues.

(e) Because of the nature of his involvement he contributes heavily to structuring the internal life of the group.

2) Ongoing leadership and group maintenance functions of Emotional Leader

(a) Is interested in and focuses on emotional issues. Expresses concern for others and involvement in the group. Is well liked by others and serves as a positive focus.

(b) Is eager for support from others and ready to make use of it for personal growth. Is open to being affected.

(c) Models the change process. In a therapy group, the Emotional Leader usually enters ready for a developmental change; he or she is most ready to engage in task of the group. Works hard on accurately perceiving and representing his own reality to himself and to others (i.e., is self-aware and assertive).

Works hard on accurately perceiving and representing verbally what goes on in the group. May act as spokesman for the group when this is needed.

C. SCAPEGOAT

1) Boundaries dealt with by Scapegoat

(a) Monitors group level phase boundaries, usually from a stance of needing them to be clarified as they come to resolution, and from a stance of impatience regarding starting new phases.

(b) Monitors and tests the boundary between what members are willing to say explicitly and what members wish to communicate implicitly, nonverbally or symbolically.

(c) Makes self available in a vulnerable way, facilitating the group in opening various interpersonal boundaries. Monitors level of cohesiveness in the group.

(d) Group uses Scapegoat to define certain identity boundaries of the group as a system; Scapegoat monitors inclusiveness issues.

2) Ongoing leadership and group maintenance functions of Scapegoat

(a) Is generally oriented to working on clarifying his perception and the representation of his own reality to other members.

(b) Is perceived by other members as significantly different or deviant on some important dimension or criterion for membership. (It must be emphasized, however, that the content focused upon by the group may be a real issue or may be a projective fantasy on their part.)

(c) Is generally one step behind the group in understanding nonverbal messages—often asking for these messages to be made more explicit.

(d) In early phases of group may be object of negative or hostile feelings in context of discussions of normative issues and leadership selection. (In contrast to the Emotional Leader who is self-aware and assertive, the Scapegoat appears to be assertive but not self-aware.)

(e) In contrast to the way group perceives the Scapegoat, he is actually open, willing to be self-disclosing, and willing to engage in the give and take of the structure-forming process.

(f) Makes a strong contribution to resolving group level issues and a strong commitment to participation in the group, is strong enough to withstand negative perceptions of himself or herself.

(g) In later phases, the Scapegoat is integrated into group with greater openness; members perceptions of him usually change markedly, in a more positive direction.

D. DEFIANT LEADER

1) Boundaries dealt with by Defiant Leader

(a) Monitors the boundary between being an "autonomous individual" and participating as a "group member." Leads group's attention to issues of dependence/independence.

(b) Monitors the pull to cohesiveness and tends to pull self back from intense involvement. Facilitates the group to define self boundaries more clearly, to prevent loss of self in togetherness.

(c) Monitors trust issues. Group uses Defiant Leader to define space for individual differences and for individual/unique solutions to personal problems.

2) Ongoing leadership and maintenance functions of Defiant Leader

(a) The term defiant comes from this leader's emotional stance in the group, particularly in relation to dependency on the Task Leader and in relation to cohesiveness in the group.
(b) Expresses ambivalence regarding participation in the group from the start. Is likely to miss sessions, requiring others to then summarize, integrate and define the significance of what was accomplished.
(c) Is oriented toward helping others in the group and to representing verbally what is going on in the group. In some ways shares with Task Leader a somewhat participant/observer objectivity in the form of responses made to others.
(d) In contrast to (c) is usually not able to engage in very much self-disclosing or to work on own perceptions or representations of own experience in the group context.

The specific way in which the four leaders participate in the nine phases of development is not at this time known in detail. Those characteristics of the leadership process wait on future research, some of which is being conducted by the persons already referenced earlier in the chapter, and some of which cannot be done until adequate methods have been devised for the empirical identification of phase boundaries.

This chapter has presented a set of propositions regarding the development of group living structure, which is considered a critical aspect of the system-forming process. This has been an attempt to state the theory in rather formal terms. Although a case example of a group progressing through all nine phases would undoubtedly be illuminating at this point, that will also have to wait for future publication. It might be of some help to the clinician, however, to present a more detailed outline of the nine phases of development here (a more narrative description of the phases and the leaders appears in Beck, 1974). Table 1 summarizes the following items for each phase:

(a) the group level issues being dealt with in each phase;
(b) the questions raised for the individual member by his participation in each phase;
(c) the significant emergent leadership functions in each phase (some of these functions continue into other phases—only new leadership functions are identified for each phase).

TABLE 1

Phases in the Development of Group Living Structure

Phase Name	Group Level Issues	Individual Level Issues	Important Leadership Roles
1. Making a contract: the agreement to work on becoming a functional group	1. identification of each member (at least minimally) 2. clarification of group level and individual goals: initial attempt. 3. identification of limits or expectations (beginning of norm-creating process) 4. settlement of membership	1. can I survive or live in this group 2. can I accept or tolerate the others 3. can this group accept me	Task leader convener of group; task guide; in therapy group, communication expert Emotional leader manager of group's emotional process: spokesman; most change-ready member, model
2. Establishment of a group identity and direction	1. clarification of goals and subgoals 2. clarification of limits of operation 3. establishing mutually acceptable norms re: leadership style of communication competition 4. role differentiation 5. stereotypic relating	1. who are we as a collectivity 2. what are we here to do 3. how do we go about doing it 4. how do I fit in 5. what do I need 6. what do they want	Task leader influencing norms re: inclusion of all members Scapegoat object of attack; crystallizes issues of norms, goals, and leadership competition; becomes vehicle for group's clarification Emotional Leader integratively presenting view of group in positive terms
3. The exploration of a group identity and direction	1. recognitition of individuals and exploration of their issues 2. development of effective communication skills for work 3. establishment of cooperative interaction mode 4. establishing equality	1. who am I 2. what do I want to get done here 3. what do I need 4. who are each of the others	Emotional leader experiences significant change in this period Task leader facilitator re: group's experiments on effective communication

TABLE 1 *(continued)*

Phase Name	Group Level Issues	Individual Level Issues	Important Leadership Roles
4. The establishment of intimacy	1. coping with sexuality in personal relationships 2. expression of tenderness, and closeness in group 3. space for play and fantasy in group	1. sexuality as a problem in any relationship generally 2. dealing with my sexual responses to others in the group 3. finding ways to express tenderness and closeness 4. can I trust: will I be trusted	Task leader becomes more participative and expressive: shift from authority to person Emotional leader expansive, warm, giving
5. The exploration of mutuality	1. working out how dependency needs will be handled in the peer relationships 2. working out how hostility and frustration will be handled 3. closeness raises anxiety re: space and separateness 4. a new commitment to members	1. will I be used by group: or submerged in group 2. will my needs be met or ignored 3. will they make reasonable demands; can I meet them	Defiant leader peaks anxiety re: dependency needs; can't let go of TL to make commitment to group; bargains for a "special" contract Task leader challenged by DL; supporting movement to new commitment of members to each other
6. The achievement of autonomy through reorganization of the group's structure	1. reorganization of leadership structure 2. establishing group on basis of commitment to peers 3. self-directedness of group 4. incorporation of task leader as member	1. where do I want to take this experience 2. how do I feel about the other members, the therapists, as persons	Emotional leader emerges in a stronger role taking over initiation functions and support of members from TL Task leader withdraws some from initiation and support functions; enters as a member

TABLE 1 *(continued)*

Phase Name	Group Level Issues	Individual Level Issues	Important Leadership Roles
7. Self-confrontation and the achievement of interdependence	1. intensive work on individual issues 2. group shares with and supports each member 3. development of fluid role relations	1. can I face my own difficult issues 2. how can I help others	Group members generally assert themselves as needed; all are more self-disclosing and expressive Emotional leader continues to perform important support function to other members
8. Independence, the transfer of learning	1. review issues dealt with in group 2. extrapolate what they learned 3. rehearse development of relationships outside of group	1. can I do elsewhere what I've done here 2. what happened here that's different or new 3. what can I take with me	Scapegoat articulate processor re: transfer of learning Emotional leader experiences anxiety re: transfer of learning
9. Termination of group and separation from significant persons	1. completion of unfinished business 2. sharing of meaning of the experience	1. can I let people know how much I care 2. and, then feel OK being away from them 3. can I let people know how they affected me generally	Task Leader and Emotional Leader model process of sharing meaning

Epilogue: The Process
of Changing Paradigms

By James E. Durkin, Ph.D.

In this volume we have seen a number of explorations of the ways in which GST can clarify the theory and improve the practice of group psychotherapy. In Section I the need for a marriage between GST and the group psychotherapy field was clearly established. As Helen pointed out, the field was fragmented because on the one hand, the social context within which group psychotherapy was performed had changed, and on the other hand, in disorderly response to these changes, a host of new theories and techniques had proliferated. As I tried to show in the foundations chapter, GST is at the center of a paradigm shift in world intellectual and scientific circles. The shift centers around issues such as complexity, complementarity and autonomy, the systematic treatment of which could supply the field of group psychotherapy with a new foundation for growth and integration.

Section II includes explorations which focused on phenomena such as energy, information, role, catalytic regulation, and so on, which are important parts of the GST focus and applies them to theoretical and practical problems in group psychotherapy. The chapters in Section III take a more comprehensive view by exploring how GST could function as a basis for complete group therapy modalities. Some of the authors apply GST principles to traditional modalities such as TA; others demonstrate that a new synthesis, which utilizes the different strengths of GST and traditional psychoanalytic methods, can and should be achieved. Finally Bill Gray, the Vassilious, and I outline our own evolving methods of group therapy, methods which are largely based on GST foundations.

In Section IV the focus of concern is broadened even further as the authors examine GST applications to group psychotherapy training, research, and education, as well as reviewing the place of GST in the larger social and scientific context within which the field is embedded.

Looking at all these explorations, how can we assess the impact of GST on group psychotherapy in the present and, more importantly, in the future? What unity can be perceived beneath the diversity of the theoretical ideas and clinical data presented here? In the Introduction I reported that, in our committee's efforts to define GST for ourselves, we were surprised and, at first, disappointed to discover that GST meant many different things to many different people. It took us a while to begin to see that this uncertainty was the result neither of our obtuseness nor of the inability of GST writers to communicate unequivocally, but rather was due to an intrinsic and necessary uncertainty in GST itself. We began to understand that if GST could be defined as a unity at all, it would have to be understood as a living, changing conceptual unity that reflected the living changing unities of the communities of scientists that articulated their theories of GST. In a real sense, our committee's task was not to define what GST was, but to define what we wanted it to be for us. In short, GST had to be a reflection of our own consciousness.

In the Introduction I articulated not one but two models of GST. Model I focused on a population of objects called systems and fitted well within the traditional paradigm of objectivity. Model II focused on a dynamic process called living structure which, because it autonomously caused itself, required the assumptions of a new scientific paradigm which we called the paradigm of autonomy. Both of these models are integrations of common understandings arising over the course of our committee's work together, rather than officially proclaimed and documented manifestos. Nevertheless, the two models are distinct and represent modes of thinking that actually go on among members of our group. The reader who has reached this point will see that there is some of both models in every chapter.

The objective model and the autonomous model of GST differ mainly on the issue of self-reference. In the objective model, the GST theorist and the GST theory-making process are positioned offstage outside the theory itself. In the autonomy model, the GST theorist and the GST theory-making process are on stage and embedded within the model itself. The theorist dwells self-referentially within the theory. A parallel state of affairs holds, perhaps, with the position of the group therapist in the group setting. Living structure has the basic function of describing itself, of making theories about itself. That achievement and the achievement of self-transformation are the two basic functions of autonomy. The paradigm of objectivity simply does not have the capacity to handle such self-referential assertions. Such statements as "autonomy causes itself" are considered not "well formed statements" and are deemed inadmissible within the paradigm of objectivity.

Thus our explorations have brought us to a dilemma. In trying to articulate for ourselves and for our readers what GST is we have come to a choice of one model which is couched in familiar objective terms but which lacks completeness because self-reference is circumvented. The alternative is a model which is more complete because it utilizes self-reference, but appears inconsistent and paradoxical because it doesn't fit within the orthodox paradigm of objectivity. I don't think that any of us is in a position to make final judgment of one model over the other. Both have their strengths and weaknesses. What I propose as a resolution of the situation in this epilogue is to leave it up to the reader's autonomy. In reviewing these studies and in considering whether to adopt all or some of the theory and technique discussed in these pages, let the reader fluctuate back and forth between the two models just as we have done. But since the process of moving back and forth between paradigms is probably a new one for most readers, let us spend a little time in this epilogue, looking at the process of changing paradigms.

But isn't asking readers to change paradigms asking too much? We who wrote these chapters and you who read them came to this task with pretty much the same expectations. We wanted to find ways in which to clarify the theory and improve the practice of group psychotherapy and naively assumed that GST offered a new theory of group therapy which we could examine, with some resistance, of course, for possible adoption. We discovered that GST was not a theory of therapy that told us what to do or think about groups, but a generalized metatheory about organized complexity. Then we discovered that GST was not a unified conceptual framework that we could digest and evaluate, but rather a reflection of our own living structures that could be articulated differently for different individuals and groups of scientists. And now we are asked to move into the *terra incognita* of changing paradigms where we must leave behind our familiar ways of thinking and understanding. We must proceed cautiously.

If the process of changing paradigms is isomorphic across various levels of living structure, we might gain understanding about the course of the process of paradigm change at all levels by studying a few of them. First, let us look at the process of paradigm change during the history of Western science over the past five hundred years. Gradual progress in understanding and controlling the world of nature is punctuated by several scientific revolutions. Each of these "catastrophes" (Thom, 1975) resulted in a radical redefinition of humanity's place in the world. The Copernican catastrophe enabled us to relinquish the mythical belief that the earth was the controlling center of the universe. The Darwinian catastrophe enabled us to relinquish the mythical belief that *homo sapiens* was the controlling center of life on the earth. The Freudian catastrophe enabled us to relinquish the mythical belief that our conscious minds were the controlling centers of the totality of our affects, cognitions and behaviors. The scenario for each of these radical redefinitions of collective consciousness is the same. In each we held a model of the world, or some aspect of it, which erroneously placed ourselves at the controlling center.

What was the effect of the discrepancy between our model of the structure of the world before our paradigm shift and the way the structure of the world really was? Pre-Copernican, pre-Darwinian, or pre-Freudian science did not suffer immeasurably. In fact, we were quite complacent in our blindness. The main symptom was a lack of growth. In terms of boundarying language, it could be said that a summing process was going on with man's erroneous model ineffectively attempting to influence the world. It wasn't until we opened ourselves to the data which really showed us the way the world was that we were really able to develop effective ways of transacting with the world. But this opening process did not come easily to us. Such catastrophes were usually characterized by upheaval, struggle and dissent. Once they had run their course, however, another period of complacency ensued where the new establishment entrenched itself against the next catastrophe.

In a remarkable series of clinical demonstrations, the Swiss psychologist Jean Piaget has documented a process in the cognitive development of children that he calls *decentering*. His process of decentering could well apply to the description above of the development of Western scientific self-consciousness, to change in psychotherapy, and, in general, to what I have called changing paradigms. Piaget's studies provide an independent line of evidence about the structure of autonomy and its manifestation in the boundarying operation. Particularly relevant is his description of the process of *reversibility,* which corresponds to the elusive opening component of boundarying. It is probably no coincidence that Piaget generalized from his work with cognitive structure to the doctrine of structuralism which, as I pointed out in the foundations chapter, is one of the participants, along with GST, in the development of the paradigm of autonomy.

Piaget's decentering process is made manifest in his demonstrations of the achievement of conservation in children. Conservation is the ability to perceive invariance in an attribute of an object in the face of variation in the phenomenal values of that attribute. Conservation of volume in liquids, for example, is demonstrated by pouring a given amount of liquid back and forth between a tall thin vessel and a short flat vessel, thus causing variations in the value of the attribute volume. The child is asked in which vessel there is more liquid. The child who has yet to achieve conservation of volume will state that there is more liquid in the tall vessel, while the child who has achieved it will state that it is the same volume no matter what vessel the liquid is in. In achieving conservation, the child is able to transcend immediate sense data and respond to underlying invariance. Released from the bondage of the senses, the child achieves self-consciousness and autonomy.

By observing the fine details of the process of achieving conservation, Piaget was able to discern an event which he called the experience of *reversibility*. In the conservation of volume demonstration described above, the child apparently lets the boundary between the experience of the two values of the attribute, tall shape, flat shape, dissolve so that the two representations fluctuate back and forth tall/flat/tall/flat, etc. Prigogine (1976) speaks about the same kind of creative fluctuation process. As the once distinct internal representations flow together, an experience of the complementarity of the two values is generated. In turn, this destructuring of experience seems to engender an experience of synthesis at a higher level of awareness, the level where tall and flat are experienced as two phenomenal appearances of an underlying unity, the same volume of liquid poured into different shapes.

Piaget has catalogued an ordered sequence of these basic shifts of cognitive development in the growing child. There is evidence of isomorphy in the process with cognitive boundaries structuring, destructuring, and then restructuring at a higher level as a result of this fluctuation process. More and more subtle and complex domains are cognitively integrated through this process. Some have suggested that there are such paradigm shifts or catastrophes all through the life span. It is possible that they follow the same order-fluctuation/order-boundarying sequence. For example, an adolescent involved in a love relationship might achieve "conservation of love" by experiencing the "good times" and the "hard times" inevitable in such affairs in a fluctuation state and finally begin to comprehend that love is inherently the complementary combination of the two. A few of us are able to achieve a conservation of our own life and death.

Personality change in psychotherapy is explained quite rationally in *post hoc* case history reports, but the actual process of replacing one personal paradigm with another is not easily portrayed in discursive terms. There are long stretches of utter chaos where the therapist and client have neither a firm grasp of the content of what is happening between them nor a commitment of the ground rule structure of whatever it is that is happening. The informational boundaries that once organized the therapeutic relationship have all but dissolved and nothing but sheer habit seems to keep the sessions going. There seems no way forward and no way back. These periods are not recordable, mainly because they are not recordable except as chaos, but if the boundarying idea is correct, they are not periods of randomness but periods of undirected creative flow. These periods of indeterminacy often terminate quite suddenly with the crystallization of a breakthrough to new structuring, but it is uncertain whether the reasons for the new level of awareness are the cause or the effect of the breakthrough. When the transition is complete the old construction of the client's reality is now as unthinkable to the new one as the new one would have been to the old one before the new one was generated. And the process of transition is unthinkable for both. There is no perspective on reality in paradigm-changing, for the paradigm is the perspective.

We have examined the process of changing paradigms at three levels of living structure under the GST hypothesis that the self-organizing processes behind these vastly different experiences are isomorphic both to each other and to the problem we face of moving back and forth between GST Model I and GST Model II and its self-referential problem of self-reference. Piaget showed us how decentering and the autonomy it generates are manifested in the conservation achievement process and how the fluctuation of the reversibility experience is an essential step in the event sequence. In the more generalized boundarying terms of our GST model of the structure of autonomy, opening events of destructuring and closing events of restructuring are in an essential complementarity of structure together.

We are in a position not unlike the Piagetian child trying to decide which vessel has more liquid when we try to decide whether the objective or the autonomous model of GST is preferable as a basis for clarifying the theory and improving the practice of group psychotherapy. Can we achieve conservation on GST as the child-achieved conservation of volume? The boundary between the two models seems clear-cut—one is incomplete without self-reference and the other is inconsistent precisely because it includes self-reference. But let us open up the boundary between the models. We are inside of one model and outside of the other, subjective to one and objective to the other. We, as GST theory-makers, if we take our two models seriously, are forced to fluctuate between the two models because each model implies the other. If we look at systems as objects we reflect upon ourselves as subjects who are also systems. If we dwell within living structure as subjects and as part of it describe its self-referential nature, we objectify this existence through the description. There is an inherent experience of reversibility, for the two models are complementary, inseparable but irreconcilable. What conserves amidst this fluctuation? And how do we decenter ourselves as theorists from this vicious circle of description and involvement? What conserves amidst this fluctuation of subjectivity and objectivity is our autonomy as theory-makers. Whether we formulate theories of ourselves from the outside or from the inside we are still making theories of ourselves and thereby defining ourselves. In relinquishing the myth that we can define the truth of our own structures as we for so long have tried to do, and turning our attention to the processes of theory-making in which we engage, we have achieved a measure of decentering and a more effective autonomy with which to conduct our living structures.

Glossary of Living
Structure Terms

By James E. Durkin, Ph.D.

INTRODUCTION

This glossary is an alphabetical summary of the basic concepts developed by the various chapter authors in this volume. I have entitled this listing a living structure glossary rather than a general system theory glossary because a GST community such as our committee has a right to shape its definition of the boundaries of GST within a range of possible ways. In the Introduction to this book I distinguished between the system-object model of GST that we developed earlier on in our work as a committee and the autonomy model which came later and even now is in the process of development. The terms listed are for the most part terms that are part of the autonomy model. However, some of the terms are system-object terms. An attempt has been made, where possible, to show the connection between the two models.

Adaptation: Assimilation/Accommodation. The process whereby living structure adjusts to new environmental situations by assimilating or accommodating. Assimilating is a process of changing the environment to suit the individual's terms while accommodating is a process of changing the individual to suit the environment's terms.

Action Structure/Language Structure. Complementary aspects of living structure where action structure is embodied as matter/energy organized in time and space and language structure is encoded in information in meaning space, defined by boundary structure.

Active Transport. The process whereby the ''open system'' maintains a balance of matter/energy just off equilibrium so that it is empowered to perform the work of self-organization. LvB calls this process *Fliessgleichgewicht.*

Anamorphic. The morphogenetic or structure transforming process of building up one's own complexity of organization and differentiation. A negentropic process.

Anthropos. From the Greek meaning Man or Humanity, but interpreted more broadly as man and his higher organizations and hence equivalent to the general idea of living structure.

Autonomy. Functionally the ability to achieve wholeness, self-regulation and progressive self-transformation. Structurally the ability to open and close one's own boundaries.

Boundarying. The complementary processes whereby living structure opens/closes its own boundaries. At the content level what boundarying opens or closes to is diverse, but at the structural level opening/closing is isomorphic to all living structures. Opening leads to structural transformation and growth. Closing leads to structural consolidation and protection.

Collective Image. (Vassiliou) The overlapping projection of inner images embodied in a group sessions, usually in the form of a work of visual art.

Complementarity. A structure in which a pair of processes coexist as inseparable but irreconcilable events. Complementarity is experienced phenomenally as an oscillation between the pairs of the duality without apparent cause. Helpful in understanding the interplay of content/structure, assimilation/accommodation, law/rule, summing/systeming, manifest/virtual, closing/opening.

Content Level/Structure Level. Content level descriptions of living structure focus on their adaptive embodiments in particular environments and the evaluation of these achievements in symbolic terms. Structural level descriptions delineate the working configurations of parts and processes as they operate together to make the whole living structure.

Cybernetics. The science of communication and control in animals and machines. Relies on information processes and feedback control configurations rather than the metabolic dynamic interactions of open systems. Adopted as a metatheoretical basis of many family therapy perspectives.

Destructuring/Restructuring. The processes whereby living structure transforms its own structure through complementary opening to permit flow through boundaries and closing to permit the buildup of organizational boundary structures.

Dialectic. An orientation which sees change as the baseline of existence rather than stability and which assumes that any structure or state will transform to its complementary state without external cause. Under these assumptions it is persistence that requires explanation and not change.

Emergent. A process whereby structural configurations embody themselves spontaneously from the dyamic interplay of parts that are open to each other. Emergents are other than the sum of their parts, as when a group emerges from the interactions of its members.

Embodying. The process whereby a virtual structure engages in an adaptive struggle within a particular environment and is thereby made manifest at the content level. Embodying is complementary to encoding.

Emotional-Cognitive Structure. The process whereby systems are formed through the pairing of two or more system precursors operating within a relevant nurturing environment going through thematic fluctuation. During the process raw global emotions are nuanced and precised and combined with cognitions in a mutually organizing process to form emotional/cognitive structures.

Encoding/Decoding. The process whereby private messages are transformed into public signals in physical time and space (encoding) and back into private messages (decoding). The success of such information communication depends upon a common code book, a minimum of equivocation (shaky encoding), a minimum of ambiguity (shaky decoding) and a minimum of noise (shaky signal).

Entropy. The process whereby all matter/energy in the universe gradually but inexorably becomes degraded into less organized states. Living structure achieves local negentropy by borrowing and degrading environmental matter/energy to sustain itself and develop itself against the entropic tide.

Equifinality. The open-boundaried adaptive process whereby living structure achieves morphogenesis. The outcome of equifinal processes cannot be predicted from initial conditions, nor can its specific path of progress. Rather, it depends on the moment-to-moment opportunities available in the immediate environment. Equifinal processes generate emergent structures when living structures are systeming, that is, open to each other's openness.

Exchange: Interaction/Transaction, Summing/Systeming, Cognitive/Emotional. The general term for the process whereby living structures make contact and interact with each other either in closed or open configurations.

Fliessgleichgewicht (Steady State Control). LvB's regulation through flowing equilibrium process by means of which the energy for active self-organization is generated by the active transport of matter/energy into and out of the boundaries of living structure.

Flow. The process that boundaries bound and stabilize. Living structure is constructed of boundaries containing flow alternating with flow energy mobilizing boundaries. Flow and boundaries are complementary because boundaries would collapse without flow to mobilize them and flow would dissipate without boundaries to organize them.

Group. One level of embodiment of living structure that emerges when a set of individual living structures generates a rule which defines themselves as a unitary entity and provides constraints which gives each member freedom to express their autonomy.

Hierarchy. A structure where complex part operations are balanced against simplified whole operations at the next higher level. Living structure is hierarchically arrayed with each structure composed of substructures at a lower level and, at the same time, composing one of the parts of a superstructure at the next higher level. The GST researcher is expected to orient the reader as to where in this hierarchy the central focus of investigation lies. That is, the relevant "system" subsystems and supersystems must be specified.

Homeostatic/Heterostatic. Homeostasis is a function of living structure in which it maintains physiological, psychological or other structural equilibrium in the face of external disturbance. Heterostasis is a complementary function in living structure in which it transforms its physiological, psychological or other structural state in the direction of greater adaptiveness. The concepts of morphostasis and morphogenesis are parallel concepts articulated more in structural than functional terms. At all levels, living structure maintains a homeostatic/heterostatic balance.

Information-Generating. Living structure has the capacity for drawing boundaries to increase its own complexity. This process of increasing complexity can be evaluated as one of generating information. In human systems the function of information-generating is accomplished by the cognitive processes by making distinctions, formulating definitions, and other boundary-closing activities. Information-generating activities of living structure operate in complementarity to energy flow activities (q.v.) The function of information-generating is the autonomous self-consolidation of structure.

Insiding/Outsiding. Primitive complementary component events of the boundarying operation describing boundary contact action between individuals at different hierarchical levels. For example, an individual group member and his/her group engage in inside/outside boundarying operations. When living structure engages in autonomous self-hierarchicalization, it pulls/pushes its parts inside/outside its boundaries to transform parts into wholes or wholes into parts.

Isomorphy. An identity of structure lying beneath a diversity of content in the comparison between individual living structures. One of the basic propositions of GST is that all forms of living structure from cell to society order themselves according to the same self-organizing principles and processes. The differences that appear in the particular forms are the result of equifinal (q.v.) processes of encoding or embodiment by means of which individuals struggle for existence within a particular historical environment.

Language Structure. Living structure describes itself. It encodes a formulation describing its own structure in some sort of symbolic form, or language in the most general sense. This can range from the genetic code in which cells describe themselves to the constitutions or bylaws by means of which communities or corporations describe themselves.

Linear/Nonlinear Feedback Configurations. Feedback configurations have circular causal structures where part of the output of the configuration is returned as an input to the same configuration. Such configurations are hierarchically arrayed with a self-description encoded in language structure at one level and an action structure embodied at another level. In linear feedback configurations the language structure which encodes an ideal self-description of the system remains consistent despite disturbances imposed upon it by its action structure. For example, a neurotic who is locked into a linear feedback system blindly pursues his neurotic ideal despite cycle after cycle of unrewarding experience. In nonlinear configurations the action structure opens the boundaries of the guiding language structure ideal so that goals are changed in a way that is more in line with experience. The neurotic whose guiding language structure self-description can be opened up by action experience moves into a nonlinear feedback configuration and thereby is able to modify his guiding ideals.

Living Structure. Self-organizing, i.e., autonomous, configurations of parts and processes which are embodied and encoded in the full range of life forms from cell to society. The subject of investigation for GST.

Matter/Energy. Living structure has the capacity for dissolving boundaries to decrease its own complexity. This process of reducing complexity can be interpreted as one of generating flow of matter/energy. In the human system the function of energy flow is accomplished by the emotional processes of transforming structures, expanding definitions and other boundary-opening processes. Informational activities of living structure operate in complementarity to energy flow activities. The function of matter/energy flow is the autonomous self-transformation of structure. Although we cognitively encode emotional experiences as moving through us, it is more likely that it is we who move through feeling. For example, when we open ourselves to love, we transform ourselves into a new unified structure with our loved one.

Metatheory. GST has sometimes been called a metatheory because it does not deal directly with a particular set of natural phenomena in the same way that biology, psychology or sociology does, but rather is couched at some higher order level of inquiry where isomorphisms are drawn between biological, psychological and sociological phenomena. But in the strict sense of the term a metatheory is a theory about theories and theory-making, and that is not exactly the thrust of GST. A metatheory is a second order theory, a theory about theories, but GST is a theory about a second order phenomenon. We have called this second order phenomenon "living structure," where living structure refers to the isomorphic self-organizing principles and processes together with their particular embodiments at all levels of the hierarchy from cell to society.

Morphostatic/Morphogenetic. The parallel of homeostatic/heterostatic. The latter complementarity is couched in functional terms, suggesting the result, while the former are couched in structural terms, suggesting the configuration of parts and processes that work together to produce the stability/change in the living structure. Morphostatic structures preserve function while morphogenetic structures transform function.

Negative/Positive Feedback. A hierarchical self-referential configuration that can be either linear and therefore assimilative and structure-preserving or non-linear (q.v.) and structure-transforming. Negatively oriented feedback configurations utilize the error signal to force the action of the system back to the ideal or set point. Positive feedback configurations utilize the error signal to augment the deviation from the set point. Since positive feedback rapidly drives the action of the system to the limits of its functioning and beyond, such a configuration is usually characterized by oscillation where the system cycles through disintegration and reintegration. Neurotic cycles of crisis and exhaustion are positive linear feedback configurations because they don't transform themselves as a result of their experience.

Negentropy. Inherent self-organizing activity of living structure moving actively to counter the force of entropy, the inherent tendency to descend from organized to unorganized states. At the human level the cognitive creation of structure is activity that is negentropic, but the creative dissolving of boundaries in the service of self-transformation must also be seen as an act of autonomy and therefore not as entropic. The extension of the domain of information to negative values measured in "tibs" (see Chapter 2) is an attempt to resolve the ideas of entropy/negentropy with boundary closing/opening.

Nurtenergy. Specific psychic energy operating in therapy groups hypothesized by Gruen (Chapter 4); combines aspects of the nurturant group environment with energy transformation.

Opening/Closing. The primitive complementarities making up the boundarying operation. Any formal system can and must rely on certain primitive undefined terms within that system. For this reason the pair opening/closing will not be defined in terms of any deeper level concepts within this system.

Organizing Focus. An array of system precursors (q.v.) defined by Gray (Chapter 11) such as fragmentary feelings, thoughts and actions which have self-organizing potential when involved in the process of thematic fluctuation (q.v.) to become linked together. This is part of the general process of system-forming, the central focus of Gray's work in Chapter 11.

Precursor Theory. Gray's theory (Chapter 11) focuses on the process of system formation rather than system maintenence. This theory states that a system forms when two or more system precursors (q.v.) come together to form an organizing focus (q.v.) and establish appropriate input/output links with one another.

Reciprocal/Mutual. Summing processes are reciprocal while systeming processes are mutual. In reciprocal summing the boundaries of the summing participants are retained and only transiently deformed, while in mutual systeming the participants open their boundaries and, through a hierarchical leap, transform themselves into a higher or lower order "system." Reciprocal summing is two one-way streets and mutual systeming is one two-way street.

Restructuring/Destructuring. Complementary components of autonomous change in psychotherapy or other processes. Destructuring involves the elementary operation of opening boundaries, while restructuring involves the creation of boundaries.

Self-Referential. A configuration of living structure whereby it reenters its own boundaries so that it is both subject and object, both cause and effect of itself. Living structure describes itself and transforms itself through self-referential configurations. Such configurations appear paradoxical in classical objective logic. How can a self-description include the describing process within the description? How can self-transformation be controlled if the same structure that controls the transformation is the very structure that is being transformed?

Self-Description/Self-Transformation. Living structure defines itself by closing an informational boundary around itself. It transforms itself by opening its boundaries to flow. Both can involve hierarchical jumps. By opening their boundaries to each other a set of group members can transform themselves into a unitary therapy group. In complementary fashion the group unit describes itself at the new hierarchical level as a group.

Steady State. *(Fliessgleichgewicht).* A stationary or time-independent state of living structure where, through balancing of inputs and outputs of matter/energy through its boundaries, it maintains its own negentropic state of activity and growth. Steady state is not an equilibrium state, but one maintained just off equilibrium so that the natural tendency toward equilibrium can be harnessed for the work of self-organization and growth.

Structure. A configuration of parts and interconnecting processes organized to achieve a particular goal or function in their environment. Living structure is composed of action structures and language structures operating in complementarity.

System, Subsystem, Supersystem. The central foci of the GST model based on the paradigm of objectivity. They are objects which have the properties of 1) hierarchy, 2) isomorphy of underlying structure, 3) self-regulation and self-transformation functions, and 4) matter/energy and information processing achieved through the selective opening and closing of their boundaries. Every system except the lowest is made up of subsystems. Every system except the highest acts as a subsystem within a higher supersystem.

Systeming/Summing. The complementary events making up the boundarying operation which is the central focus of the GST model based on the paradigm of autonomy. Systeming occurs when living structures open their boundaries to each other. Summing occurs when living structures make contact with each other across closed boundaries. At the level of groups and group members, systeming is interpreted as emotional flow exchange and summing is interpreted as cognitive exchange.

System-Forming, System-Blocking. In Gray's system-forming theory (Chapter 11), the process of forming an ongoing group through the linking together of system precursors. System-blocking is a therapeutic intervention designed to prevent this process of system formation. The process is accomplished through the phenomenon of thematic fluctuation (q.v.).

Swirl. In Kraft's theory (Chapter 5) a flowing of emotional energy during the group psychotherapy process which is felt and detected but not identified and articulated by group members. Swirling enhances transactions and therapeutic movement. Isomorphic to systeming and perhaps to nurtenergy flow.

Synallage. In the Vassilious' theory, (Chapter 12), the process of one entity in mutual interpenetration with another. In their Synallactic Collective Image Technique (S.C.I.T.), this interpenetration is facilitated by common focus on a contributed product such as a painting.

Thematic Fluctuation. In Gray's theory (Chapter 11) the voicing of several different but quite similar themes functioning as system precursors which rather suddenly acquire coherence and energy and coalesce into a major theme. The phenomenon is much like a Moire resonance effect where similar patterns seem to generate apparent movement energy when they overlap. Prigogine (1976) described similar effects in his work with dissipative structures.

Transaction/Interaction. Parallels of systeming/summing in Grinker's theory (1967). In transactions participants show mutual influence on each other, while in interactions there is much more restricted influence.

Wholing. Living structure generates, maintains, evolves and dissolves its own wholeness. Autonomy is the capacity for boundarying in which boundaries are opened and closed to become part and whole members of the hierarchy of living structure.

Bibliography

Alger, I. Therapeutic use of videotape playback. *Journal of Nervous and Mental Discorders,* 1969, 148:4, 430-436.

Angyal, A. *Neurosis and Treatment—A Holistic View.* New York: Viking Press, 1973.

Anthony, J. E. Comparison between individual and group psychotherapy. In: H. I. Kaplan and B. J. Sadock (Eds.), *Comprehensive Group Psychotherapy.* New York: Williams and Wilkins, 1971.

Ashby, W. R. *Introduction to Cybernetics.* New York: Wiley, 1956.

Ashby, W. R. *Design for a Brain.* New York: Wiley, 1960.

Azima, F. J. *Effects manifested in ego functioning.* Paper presented at the 84th Annual Convention of the American Psychological Association. Washington, 1976.

Bales, R. F. *Interaction Process Analysis: A Method for the Study of Small Groups.* Cambridge, Massachusetts: Addison-Wesley, 1950.

Bales, R. F. Task roles and social roles in problem-solving groups. In: E. E. Maccoby, T. M. Newcomb, and E. L. Hartley (Eds.), *Readings in Social Psychology.* New York: Holt, Rinehart and Winston, 1958.

Bandura, A. *Principles of Behavior Modification.* New York: Holt, Rinehart and Winston, 1969.

Bateson, G. and Ruesch, J. *Communication: The Social Matrix of Society.* New York: Norton, 1951.

Beck, A. P. Phases in the development of structure in therapy and encounter groups. In: D. A. Wexler and L. N. Rice (Eds.), *Innovations in Client-Centered Therapy.* New York: Wiley, 1974.

Beck, A. P. and Keil, A. V. Observations on the development of client-centered, time-limited therapy groups. *Counseling Center Discussion Papers,* Chicago: University of Chicago Library, 13 (5), 1967.

Beck, A. P. and Peters, L. *The research evidence for distributed leadership in therapy groups.* Paper presented at the American Group Psychotherapy Association. New York, 1979.

Bennis, W. and Shephard, H. A theory of group development. *Human Relations,* 1956, 9:415-437.

Bentley, A. F. Kennetic inquiry. *Science,* 1950, 112:775-783.

Bergler, E. *The Basic Neurosis.* New York: Grune and Stratton, 1949.

Berne, E. *Transactional Analysis in Psychotherapy.* New York: Grove Press, 1961.

Berne, E. *The Structure and Dynamics of Organizations and Groups.* New York: Grove Press, 1963.

Berne, E. *Principles of Group Treatment.* England: Oxford University Press, 1966.

Berne, E. *What Do You Say After You Say Hello?* New York: Grove Press, 1972.

von Bertalanffy, L. *Modern Theories of Development: An Introduction to Theoretical Biology.* Oxford: Clarendon Press, 1933. Torchbook Edition, New York: Harper, 1961.

von Bertalanffy, L. The theory of open systems in physics and biology. *Science,* 1950, III, 23-29.

von Bertalanffy, L. *Problems of Life: An Evaluation of Modern Biological Thought.* New York: Wiley, 1952.

von Bertalanffy, L. General system theory. In: A. Rapoport (Ed.), *General Systems Yearbook,* 1956, 1:110.

von Bertalanffy, L. General system theory and psychiatry. In: S. Arieti (Ed.), *American Handbook of Psychiatry,* Vol. III:705-721. New York: Basic Books, 1966.

von Bertalanffy, L. *Robots, Men and Minds.* New York: Braziller, 1967.

von Bertalanffy, L. *General System Theory: Foundations, Development, Applications.* New York: Braziller, 1968.

von Bertalanffy, L. Chance or law. In: A. Koestler and J. R. Smythies (Eds.), *Beyond Reductionism.* London: Hutchinson, 1968b.

von Bertalanffy, L. An overview. In: W. Gray, F. Duhl and N. Rizzo (Eds.), *General Systems Theory and Psychiatry.* Boston: Little, Brown, 1969.

von Bertalanffy, L. *Perspectives on General System Theory,* Edited by Edgar Taschdjian. New York: Braziller, 1975.

Bion, W. R. Group dynamics: A review. *International Journal of Psychoanalysis,* 1952, 33:235-247.

Bion, W. R. *Experience in Groups.* New York: Basic Books. 1959.

Bion, W. R. *Experiences in Groups: And Other Papers.* New York: Basic Books, 1961.

Blood, R. *The Family.* New York: The Free Press, 1972.

Bohr, N. On the quantum theory of radiation and the structure of the atom. *Philosophical Magazine,* Vol. 30, 1915.

Boulding, K. E. The universe as a general system. Fourth Annual Ludwig von Bertalanffy Memorial Lecture. In: J. D. White (Ed.), *The General Systems Paradigm: Science of Change and Change of Science.* Proceedings of the Annual North American Meeting, Society for General Systems Research, 1977.

Braaten, L. J. Developmental phases of encounter groups and related intensive groups—A critical review of models and a new proposal. *Interpersonal Development,* 1974, 5:112-129.

Brown, D. Personal communication, 1979.

Buckley, W. *Sociology and Modern Systems Theory.* Englewood Cliffs, N. J.: Prentice-Hall, 1967.

Buckley, W. *Modern Systems Research for the Behavioral Scientist.* Chicago: Aldine, 1968.

Capra, F. *The Tao of Physics.* California: University of California Press, 1975.

Cozby, P. Self-disclosure: A literature review. *Psychological Bulletin,* 1973, 79:73-91.

Descartes, R. *The Philosophical Works of Descartes.* Edited by E. Haldane and G. Ross. New York: Dover Press, 1955.

Dewey, J. The reflex arc concept in psychology. *The Psychological Review,* 1896, 3:357-370. Reprinted in H. S. Thayer (Ed.), *Pragmatism: The Classic Writings.* New York: New American Library, 1970.

Dobzhansky, T. *Mankind Evolving.* New York: Bantam Books, 1970.

Dolgoff, T. Small groups and organizations. In: A. Rapoport (Ed.), *General Systems Yearbook,* 20, 1975.

Dugo, J. M. and Beck, A. P. *A leader's guide to dealing with hostility and intimacy in small group process.* Paper presented at the Illinois Group Psychotherapy Society, Chicago, 1977.

Durkin, H. Toward a common basis for group dynamics. *International Journal of Group Psychotherapy,* 1957, 7:7, 115-130.

Durkin, H. *The Group in Depth.* New York: International Universities Press, 1964.

Durkin, H. Transference in group therapy revisited. *International Journal of Group Psychotherapy,* 1971, 21:3.

Durkin, H. Group therapy and general system theory. In: C. J. Sager and H. Singer Kaplan (Eds.), *Progress in Group and Family Therapy.* New York: Brunner/Mazel, 1972.

Durkin, H. *The role of the therapist in a systems model.* Unpublished working paper for GST Task

Force, American Group Psychotherapy Association, 1974.

Durkin, H. *Think session of the GST Task Force.* 1975 Report on 1974 Aspen Conference to AGPA Board.

Durkin, J. E. *A programmable tape recorder to aid in the analysis of verbal interaction behavior.* Proposal submitted to National Science Foundation, 1960.

Durkin, J. E. Encountering: What low Machiavellians do. In: R. Christie and F. Geis (Eds.) *Studies in Machiavellianism.* New York: Academic Press, 1970.

Durkin, J. E. *Group systems therapy: The structure of thinking and feeling.* Paper presented at AGPA Conference in Boston, 1976a.

Durkin, J. E. *We are transformed in feeling systems and the transformations are consolidated in thinking sums.* Paper presented at the Annual North American Meeting, Society for General Systems Research, Boston, Massachusetts, 1976b.

Durkin, J. E. Personal communication, 1976c.

Durkin, J. E. *Bill Gray's Mysteries Revealed!* Unpublished, 1977.

Durkin, J. E. Report to General System Theory Task Force of the American Group Psychotherapy Association, 1978a.

Durkin, J. E. Personal communication, 1978b.

Durkin, J. E. *Boundarying processes in the formation of therapy groups.* Paper presented at the American Group Psychotherapy Association Conference, New York, 1979.

Durkin, J. E. *We are responsible for the paradigm of autonomy.* Paper presented at the American Psychological Association Meeting, Montreal, 1980a.

Durkin, J. E. *Boundarying: The structure of autonomy.* Seventh Annual Ludwig von Bertalanffy Memorial Address to the Society for General Systems Research, San Francisco, 1980b.

Erikson, E. H. *Childhood and Society, Revised Edition.* New York: Norton, 1964.

Ezriel, H. A psychoanalytic approach to group treatment. *British Journal of Medical Psychology,* 1950, 23:50-74.

Ezriel, H. Notes on psychoanalytic group therapy: II. Interpretation and research. *Psychiatry,* 1952, 15: 119-126.

Ezriel, H. The role of transference in psychoanalysis and other approaches. *Acta Therapeutica,* Zurich, 1959.

Fenichel, O. *Collected Papers of Otto Fenichel, II.* New York: Norton, 1954.

Fichte, J. *Critique of All Revelation.* Germany: Jena University Press, 1972.

Fiedler, R. E. *A Theory of Leadership Effectiveness.* New York: McGraw-Hill, 1967.

Fisher, A. *Small Group Decision Making: Communication and the Group Process.* New York: McGraw-Hill, 1974.

von Foerster, H. An epistemology for living things. In: K. Wilson (Ed.), *Collected Works of the Biological Computer Laboratory.* Urbana, Illinois: Illinois Blueprint Corporation, 1976.

von Foerster, H. *Second order concepts, or an elliptic parable of circular causality.* Presidential Address, 1977 Annual North American Meeting, Society for General Systems Research, 1977.

von Foerster, H. and Howe, H. Introductory comments to Frissisco Varela's calculus for self-reference. *Int. J. General Systems,* 1975, 2:1-3.

Foulkes, S. H. *Introduction of Group Analysis.* New York: Grune and Stratton, 1949.

Foulkes, S. H. *Group Analytic Psychotherapy.* New York: International Universities Press, 1964.

Foulkes, S. H. The application of group concepts to the treatment of the individual in the group. In: B. Stokvis (Ed.), *Topical Problems in Group Psychotherapy.* New York: Karger, 1960.

Frank, J. D. *Persuasion and Healing.* Baltimore, MD: John Hopkins University Press, 1973.

Freud, S. The future prospects of psychoanalytic therapy. In: *The Standard Edition of the Complete Psychological Works of Sigmund Freud.* Vol. 11:144. London: Hogarth Press, 1957.

Freud, S. Recommendations to physicians practicing psychoanalysis. In: *The Standard Edition of the Complete Psychological Works of Sigmund Freud.* Vol. 12:111. London: Hogarth Press, 1958.

Fried, E. *The Courage to Change: From Insight to Self-Innovation.* New York: Brunner/Mazel, 1980.

Fromm, E. *The Art of Loving.* New York: Harper and Row, 1956.

Ganzarain, R. *Transference and exorcism of the internalized bad mother in group analytic psychotherapy.* Presented at the 34th Annual Conference of the AGPA, San Francisco, February 4, 1977.

Gödel, K. Über Formal Unscheidbare Satze der Principia Mathematiks und Verwandter Systeme. *Monatschifte für Mathematik und Physik,* 1931, 38:173-198.

Goffman, E. *Presentation of Self in Everyday Life.* New York: Doubleday, 1959.

Goffman, E. *Asylums: Essays on the Social Situation of Mental Patients and Other Inmates.* New York: Doubleday, 1961.

Gray, W. Bertalanffian principles as a basis for humanistic psychiatry. In: E. Lazzlo (Ed.), *The Relevance of General Systems Theory.* New York: Braziller, 1972.

Gray, W. Emotional cognitive structures—A general systems theory of personality. In: A. Rapoport, *General Systems Yearbook,* 18:167-174, 1973.

Gray, W. Current issues in general systems theory and psychiatry. *General Systems Yearbook,* 19:97-100, 1974.

Gray, W. Emotional cognitive structure theory and the development of a general systems psychotherapy. *General Systems Yearbook,* 20:95-102, 1975.

Gray, W. *The system precursor, system forming approach in general systems theory.* Paper presented at VIth World Congress of Social Psychiatry, Opatija, Yugoslavia, 1976a.

Gray, W. *Lock out and break in: A system precursor view of crime.* Paper presented at VIth World Congress of Social Psychiatry, Opatija, Yugoslavia, 1976b.

Gray, W. A System of psychotherapy built on the concepts of organizing foci, relevant nurturing environments, and emotional cognitive integration. In: *General Systems Theorizing: An Assessment and Prospects for the Future.* Proceedings of the Annual North American Meeting. Washington: Society for General Systems Research, 1976c.

Gray, W. Epistemological implications of man as an emotional cognitive being. *General Systems Yearbook,* 21: 177-178, 1976d.

Gray, W. General systems theory in psychotherapy. *International Journal Offender Therapy and Comparative Criminology,* 20:107-116, 1976e.

Gray, W. *System formation/system precursors.* Paper presented at Sixth International Congress of Group Psychotherapy, Philadelphia, 1977a.

Gray, W. *General System Precursor Formation Theory.* Cambridge, Massachusetts: Aristocrat Press, 1977b.

Gray, W. *The role of emotional cognitive structuralism in an evolving general systems theory of group psychotherapy.* Paper presented at Annual Meeting of the American Group Psychotherapy Association, San Francisco, California, 1977c.

Gray, W. System specifics in "break-in": A therapeutic approach. *International Journal Offender Therapy and Comparative Criminology,* 21:31-40, 1977d.

Gray, W. System specifics in offender therapy. *International Journal Offender Therapy and Comparative Criminology,* 1978, 22:56-67.

Gray, W., Duhl, F., and Rizzo, N. (Eds.) *General Systems Theory and Psychiatry.* Boston: Little, Brown, 1969.

Greenson, R. *The Technique and Practice of Psychoanalysis.* New York: International Universities Press, 1961.

Grinker, R. R., Sr. *Toward a Unified Theory of Human Behavior.* New York: Basic Books, 1967.

Grinker, R. R., Sr. *Psychosomatic Concepts.* New York: Aronson, 1973.

Gruen, W. The stages in the development of a therapy group: Tell-tale symptoms and their origin in the dynamic group forces. *Group,* 1:10-25, 1977a.

Gruen, W. The encouragement and reinforcement of coping strength as a therapeutic goal and strategy in group therapy. In: L. R. Wolberg and M. L. Aronson (Eds.), *Group Therapy.* New York: Stratton Intercontinental Medical Book Corporation, 1977b.

Gruen, W. The transformation and generation of energy in group therapy as a negentropic system: Implication for the therapist. *Small Group Behavior,* 1978, 10:23-39.

Günther, G. Cybernetic ontology and transjunctional operations. In: Yovitz, M. C., Jacobi, and Goldstein (Eds.), *Self Organizing Systems.* Washington, D. C.: Spartan Books, 1962.

Guntrip, H. British schools of psychoanalysis: The object-relations theory of W. R. O. Fairbairn. In: S. Arieti (Ed), *American Handbook of Psychiatry.* New York: Basic Books, 1966.

Guntrip, H. *Schizoid Phenomena, Object Relations and the Self.* New York: International Universities Press, 1969.

Guntrip, H. *Psychoanalytic Theory, Therapy, and the Self.* New York: Basic Books, 1971.

Haley, J. *Strategies of Psychotherapy.* New York: Grune and Stratton, 1963.

Hall, A. and Fagen, R. Definition of system. *General Systems*, 1956, 1, 18-29. Louisville: Society for General Systems Research.

Hare, A. *Handbook of Small Group Research* (2nd Ed.). New York: The Free Press, 1976.

Hartman, H. *Essays on Ego Psychology*. New York: International Universities Press, 1964.

Hegel, G. *Science of Logic*. New York: Macmillan, 1929.

Heimann, P. On counter-transference. *International Journal of Psychoanalysis*, 1950, 31:81-84.

Heisenberg, W. *Physics and Philosophy*. New York: Harper Torchbooks, 1958.

Hill, W. F. and Gruner, L. A study of development in open and closed groups. *Small Group Behavior*, 1973, 4:355-381.

Hofstadter, D. *Gödel, Escher and Bach*. New York: Basic Books, 1979.

Holloway, W. *What About Working Through?* Medina, Ohio: Midwest Institute for Human Understanding, 1973.

Horwitz, L. *Projective identification in dyads and groups*. Paper presented at the Topeka Psychoanalytic Society, October, 1978.

Jaynes, J. *The Origin of Consciousness and the Breakdown of the Bicameral Mind*. Boston: Houghton Mifflin, 1976.

Kant, I. *Critique of Pure Reason*. New York: Macmillan, 1965.

Kaplan, S. R. and Roman, M. Phases of development in an adult therapy group. *International Journal of Group Psychotherapy*, 1963, 13:10-26.

Kaplan, H. I. and Sadock, B. J. (Eds.) *Comprehensive Group Psychotherapy*. Baltimore: Williams and Wilkins, 1971.

Kernberg, O. A systems approach to priority setting of interventions in groups. *International Journal of Group Psychotherapy*, 1975, 25:251-275.

Kernberg, O. Notes on countertransference. *Journal of the American Psychoanalytic Association*, 1965, 13:38-56.

Knowles, M. *The Modern Practice of Adult Education: Andragogy vs. Pedagogy*. New York: Association Press, 1970.

Kosok, M. The systematization of dialectical logic for the study of development and change. *Human Development*, 1976, 19:325-350.

Kubie, L. S. *Practical and Theoretical Aspects of Psychoanalysis*. New York: International Universities Press, 1950.

Kuhn, T. *The Structure of Scientific Revolutions* (2nd Ed.). Chicago: University of Chicago Press, 1970.

Lakin, M. and Dobbs, W. H. A study in group process. *International Journal of Group Psychotherapy*, 1962, 12:64-74.

Laszlo, E. *Introduction to Systems Philosophy*. New York: Harper Torchbooks, 1973.

LaViolette, P. A. *Thoughts about thoughts about thoughts*. Paper presented at 6th International Congress of Group Psychotherapy, Philadelphia, 1977.

LaViolette, P. A. *The neurophysiology of thought and perception*. Unpublished manuscript, 1978.

LaViolette, P. A. Thoughts about thoughts about thoughts: The emotional-perceptive cycle theory. *Man-Environment Systems*, 1979, 9:15-47.

Lennard, H. L. and Bernstein, A. *The Anatomy of Psychotherapy: Systems of Communication and Expectation*. New York: Columbia University Press, 1960.

Lennard, H. L. and Bernstein, A. *Patterns in Human Interaction*. San Francisco: Jossey-Bass, 1969.

Levinson, E. General systems theory: Model or muddle? *Contemporary Psychoanalysis*, 1978, 14:1.

Levinson, E. *The Fallacy of Understanding*. New York: Basic Books, 1972.

Lévi-Strauss, C. *Structural Anthropology*. New York: Basic Books, 1963.

Lewin, K. *Field Theory and Social Science*. New York: Harper and Row, 1951.

Lewis, C. Personal communication. 1979.

Lieberman, M. A., Yalom, I. D. and Miles, M. D. *Encounter Groups: First Facts*. New York: Basic Books, 1973.

MacKay, D. M. *Information, Mechanism and Meaning*. Cambridge, Massachusetts: M. I. T. Press, 1969.

MacKenzie, K. R. *Measurement of group climate: Preliminary experience with a new instrument*. Paper presented at the Annual Conference of the Society of Psychotherapy Research, Toronto, Canada, 1978.

Maruyama, M. The second cybernetics. *American Scientist*, 1963, 51:2:164.

Martin, E. A. and Hill, W. F. Toward a theory of group development: Six phases of therapy group development. *International Journal of Group Psychotherapy*, 1957, 7:20-30.

Maslow, A. *Motivation and Personality*. New York: Harper and Row, 1954.

Mead, G. H. *Mind, Self and Society*. Chicago: University of Chicago Press, 1934.

Meador, B. D. Individual process in a basic encounter group. *Journal of Counseling Psychology*, 1971, 18:70-76.

Meichenbaum, D. *Cognitive-Behavior Modification*. New York: Plenum Press, 1977.

Mendell, D. Leader as model. In: Z. Liff (Ed.), *The Leader in the Group*, New York: Aronson 1975, pp. 165-172.

Menninger, K. *The Vital Balance*. New York: Viking Press, 1963.

Mesarovic, M. Foundations for a general systems theory. In: M. Mesarovic (Ed.), *Views on General Systems Theory*. New York: Wiley, 1964.

Miller, J. G. *Living Systems*. New York: McGraw-Hill, 1978.

Mintz, E. Group therapy techniques and encounter techniques, comparison and rationale. *American Journal of Psychotherapy*, 1975, 25:1, 104-111.

Mischel, W. *Personality and Assessment*. New York: Wiley, 1968.

Monod, J. *Chance and Necessity*. New York: Knopf, 1971.

Moos, R. *Evaluating Treatment Environments: A Social Ecological Approach*. New York: Wiley, 1974.

Moos, R. and Humphrey, B. *Group environment scale, technical report*. Social Ecology Laboratory, Department of Psychiatry, Stanford University, Palo Alto, California, 1973.

Murray, H. A. *Exploration in Personality*. New York: Oxford, 1938.

Nye, F. and Bernardo, F. *The Family: Its Structure and Interaction*. New York: Macmillan, 1973.

Ornstein, R. E. *The Psychology of Consciousness*. New York: Viking Press, 1972.

Palan, J., Leitner, L., Drasgow, F., and Drasgo, J. Further improvement following therapy. *Group Psychotherapy and Psychodrama*, 1974, 27:42-47.

Pattee, H. *Hierarchy Theory*. New York: Braziller, 1973.

Pattee, H. The need for complementarity in social systems theory. In: A. Rapaport (Ed), *General Systems Yearbook*, 1976, 146-150.

Pattee, H. The complementarity principle in biological and social structures. *Journal of Social and Biological Structures*, 1978, 1:191-200.

Peck, H. B., Roman, M., Kaplan, S. R., and Bauman, G. An approach to the study of the small group in a psychiatric day hospital. *International Journal of Group Psychotherapy*, 1965, 15:207-219.

Piaget, J. *Play, Dreams and Imitation in Childhood*. New York: Norton, 1951.

Piaget, J. *The Construction of Reality in the Child*. New York: Basic Books, 1959.

Piaget, J. *Structuralism*. New York: Harper Torchbooks, 1970.

Polanyi, M. *Personal Knowledge*. Chicago: University of Chicago Press, 1958.

Poole, R. *Deep Subjectivity*. New York: Harper Torchbooks, 1974.

Pribram, K. A further experimental analysis of the behavioral deficit that follows injury to the primate frontal cortex. *Experimental Neurology*, 1961, 3: 432-466.

Pribram, K. The neurophysiology of remembering. *Scientific American*, 1969, 58:73-86.

Pribram, K. *Languages of the Brain*. Englewood Cliffs, N. J.: Prentice-Hall, 1971.

Pribram, K. Spinelli, D. and Kamback, M. Electrocortical correlates of stimulus, response and reinforcement. *Science*, 1967, 157:94-96.

Prigogine, I. Order through fluctuation: Self-organization and social systems. In: E. Jantsch and C. Waddington (Eds.), *Evolution and Consciousness: Human Systems in Transition*. New York: Addison-Wesley, 1976.

Prigogine, I. Nobel Prize to Belgian for thermodynamics. *Chemical and Engineering News*, October 17, 1977, p. 4.

Racher, H. *Transference and Countertransference*. London: Hogarth Press, 1968.

Rioch, M. The work of Wilfried Bion on groups. *Psychiatry*, 1970, 33:56-66.

Rogers, C. R. *Client-Centered Therapy: Its Current Practices, Implications, and Theory*. Boston: Houghton Mifflin, 1951.

Rogers, C. R. *On Encounter Groups*. New York: Basic Books, 1961.

Rosen, R. *Dynamical System Theory in Biology*. New York: Wiley, 1970.

Ruesch, J. *Therapeutic Communication.* New York: Norton, 1964.

Ruesch, J. and Bateson, G. *Communication: The Common Matrix of Psychiatry.* New York: Norton, 1951.

Russell, B. and Whitehead, A. *Principia Mathematica.* Cambridge, MA: University of Cambridge Press, 1908.

Schaefer, R. *A New Language for Psychotherapy.* New Haven and London: Yale University Press, 1976.

Scheflen, A. E. Behavioral programs in human communication. In: W. Gray, F. J. Duhl, and N. D. Rizzo (Eds.), *General Systems Theory and Psychiatry.* Boston: Little, Brown, 1969.

Scheflen, A. E. *Human Territories: How We Behave in Space and Time.* Englewood Cliffs, N.J.: Prentice-Hall, 1976.

Scheidlinger, S. Group process in group psychotherapy. I and II. *American Journal of Psychotherapy,* 1964, 14, 104-120 and 346-365.

Schelling, F. W. J. von. *The Unconditioned in Human Knowledge.* Translated with commentary by Fritz Mardi. Lewisburg, Pa.: Bucknell University Press, 1980.

Schroder, H. M. Conceptual complexity and personality organization. In: H. M. Schroder and P. Svedfeld (Eds.), *Personality Theory and Information Processing.* New York: Ronald Press, 1973.

Schrödinger, E. *What is Life and Mind and Matter.* New York: Cambridge University Press, 1967.

Schutz, W. C. *FIRO.* New York: Holt, Rinehart and Winston, 1958.

Shands, H. C. Psychoanalysis and the twentieth century revolution in communication. In: J. Marmor (Ed.), *Modern Psychoanalysis.* New York: Basic Books, 1968.

Shawchuck, N. *The process of merging two seminaries.* Dissertation, Northwestern University, Evanston, Illinois, 1974.

Slavson, S. R. Common sources of error and confusion. *International Journal of Group Psychotherapy,* 1953, 3:3-28.

Spenser Brown, G. *Laws of Form.* New York: Julian, 1972.

Spiegel, J. *Transactions.* New York: Science House, 1971.

Steiner, C. *Scripts People Live.* New York: Grove Press, 1974.

Stock, D. and Thelen, H. *Emotional Dynamics in Group Culture.* New York: New York University Press, 1958.

Stone, L. *The Psychoanalytic Situation.* New York: International Universities Press, 1961.

Sutherland, J. W. *A General Systems Philosophy for the Social Sciences.* New York: Braziller, 1973.

Thom, R. *Structural Stability and Morphogenesis.* New York: Benjamin, 1975.

Thelen, H. *Dynamics of Groups at Work.* Chicago: University of Chicago Press, 1954.

Thompson, C. W. N. and Rath, G. The administrative experiment: A special case of field testing or evaluations. *Journal of Educational Data Processing,* 1972, 9:5, 1-28.

Ticho, E. A. Donald W. Winnicott, Martin Buber and the theory of personal relationships. *Psychiatry,* 1974, 37:240-253.

Truax, C. B. and Wargo, D. G. Psychotherapeutic encounters that change behavior: For better or for worse. *American Journal of Psychotherapy,* 1966, 20:499-520.

Tuckman, B. W. Developmental sequence in small groups. *Psychological Bulletin,* 1965, 63:384-399.

Ulschak, F. Contracting: A process for defining tasks and relationships. *1978 Handbook for Group Facilitators.* La Jolla, California: University Associates, 1978.

Varela, F. Calculus for self-reference. *International Journal General Systems Theory,* 1975, 2: 5-24.

Varela, F. Not one, not two. *The Co-Evolution Quarterly,* Fall, 1976, 62-67.

Varela, F. The arithmetic of closure, *Journal of Cybernetics,* 1978, 8, 53-78.

Varela, F., Maturana, H. and Uribe, R. Autopoiesis: The organization of living systems, its characterization and a model. *Biosystems,* 1974, 5: 187-196.

Vassiliou, G. An introduction to transactional group image therapy. In: B. F. Riess (Ed.), *New Directions in Mental Health.* New York: Grune and Stratton, 1968.

Vassiliou, G. Introducing operational goals in group therapy. In: S. Arieti (Ed.), *World Biennial of Psychiatry and Psychotherapy.* New York: Basic Books, 1973.

Vassiliou, G. and Vassiliou, V. On the synallactic aspects of the grouping process. In: L. R. Wolberg and M. L. Aronson (Eds.), *Group Therapy*. New York: Stratton Intercontinental, 1974.

Vassiliou, G. and Vassiliou, V. Introducing disequilibrium in group therapy. In: L. R. Wolberg and M. L. Aronson (Eds.), *Group Therapy*. New York: Stratton Intercontinental, 1976.

Vassiliou, V. Introduction of the symposium catalyzing-regulating processes. In: A. Uchtenhagen, R. Battegay and A. Friedmann (Eds.), *Group Therapy and Social Environment*. Bern: Hans Huber, 1975a.

Vassiliou, V. On methodological procedures enhancing the catalytic-regulatory role of the therapist. In: A. Uchtenhagen, R. Battegay and A. Friedmann (Eds.), *Group Therapy and Social Environment*. Bern: Hans Huber, 1975b.

Waddington, C. *Toward Theoretical Biology*. Chicago: Aldine, 1970.

Wald, H. *An Introduction to Dialectical Logic*. Amsterdam: B. R. Grüner B. V., 1975.

Watts, A. W. The individual as man/world. *Psychedelic Review* 1963, 1:55-65. Reprinted in: P. Shepard and D. McKinley (Eds.), *The Subversive Science: Essays Toward an Ecology of Man*. Boston: Houghton Mifflin, 1969.

Watzlawick, P., Beavin, J. H., and Jackson, D. D. *Pragmatics of Human Communication*. New York: Norton, 1967.

Weiner, N. *Cybernetics*. New York: Wiley, 1948.

Whitaker, D. and Lieberman, M. *Psychotherapy Through the Group Process*. New York: Atherton Press, 1967.

Whyte, L. L. *The Universe of Experience*. New York: Harper Torchbooks, 1977.

Whyte, L. L., Wilson, A. and Wilson, D. *Hierarchical Structures*. New York: American Elsevier, 1969.

Winnicott, D. W. *The Maturational Processes and the Facilitating Environment*. New York: International Universities Press, 1965.

Wolf, A. and Schwartz, E. K. Psychoanalysis in groups: The mystique of group dynamics. In: B. Stokvis (Eds.), *Topical Problems in Group Psychotherapy*, New York: Karger, 1960.

Wolf, A. and Schwartz, E. K. Psychoanalysis in Groups. In: H. I. Kaplan and B. J. Sadock (Eds.), *Comprehensive Group Psychotherapy*. Baltimore: Williams and Wilkins, 1971.

Wojciechowski, J. A. The ecology of knowledge. In: N. H. Steneck (Ed.), *Science and Society: Past, Present, and Future*. Ann Arbor, MI: The University of Michigan Press, 1975.

Wojciechoski, J. A. *Knowledge as a source of problems: Can man survive the development of knowledge?* Paper presented at Congress of the International Society for Research on Civilization Diseases and Environment, Kirchberg, Luxembourg, 1976.

Wojciechowski, J. A. *Knowledge and the contemporary predicament*. Paper presented at General System Theory Symposium, VII World Congress of Social Psychiatry, Lisbon, Portugal, 1978.

Wojciechowski, J. A. Personal communication, 1979.

Yalom, I. D. *The Theory and Practice of Group Psychotherapy* (2nd Ed.), New York: Basic Books, 1975.

Zadeh, L. A. A fuzzy algorithmic approach to the definition of complex or imprecise concepts. *Int. J. Man-Machine Studies*, 1976, 8: 249-291.

Name Index

Alger, Ian, 275, 282, 349*n.*
Angyal, A., 80, 349*n.*
Aristotle, 172, 177, 215, 302
Ashby, W. Ross, 50, 216, 349*n.*
Azima, F. J., 89, 349*n.*

Bales, R. F., 88, 114, 159*n.*, 349*n.*
Bandura, A., 90, 349*n.*
Bateson, G., 8, 349*n.*
Bauman, G., 159, 160, 354*n.*
Beavin, J. H., 8, 356*n.*
Beck, Adriadne P., xxi, xxiv-xxv, 120, 124, 296, 308-32, 324*n.*, 326, 329, 349*n.*, 350*n.*
Bennis, W., 159*n.*, 349*n.*
Bentley, A. F., 217, 350*n.*
Bernardo, F., 123, 354*n.*
Berne, Eric, 121, 147, 149, 159, 160, 349*n.*-50*n.*
Bertalanffy, Ludwig von, xv, 5, 8, 9*n.*, 10, 12, 16, 17*n.*, 24, 27, 28, 36, 38, 49, 51, 81, 86, 170, 181, 187, 200, 216, 239, 254, 257, 294, 295, 296, 298, 299, 301, 303, 306, 340, 342, 350*n.*

Bion, W. R., 68, 70, 159*n.*, 160, 350*n.*
Blood, R., 123, 350*n.*
Bohr, Niels, 42, 350*n.*
Boulding, Kenneth E., 301, 350*n.*
Braaten, L. J., 85, 350*n.*
Brown, Donald T., xxiv, 55, 56, 284-93, 325, 326, 350*n.*
Buckley, W., 216, 350*n.*

Capra, F., 27, 350*n.*
Cozby, P., 120, 350*n.*

Descartes, R., 33, 43, 350*n.*
Dewey, J., 217, 350*n.*
Dobzhansky, T., 304, 350*n.*
Dugo, J. M., 120, 124, 326, 350*n.*
Duhl, F., 114, 216, 352*n.*
Durkin, Helen, xi, xiii, xviii, xxii, xxiii, 5-23, 11, 159, 162, 172-99, 253-66, 350*n.*-51*n.*
Durkin, James E., 15, 20, 24-59, 26, 29, 92, 184, 192, 215, 228-50, 255, 261, 267-83, 301, 305, 309, 325, 326, 333-47, 350*n.*, 351*n.*

Subject Index